How Our Hearts Were Stöllen

A Partial History of St. Louis Bakeries

HOW OUR HEARTS WERE STÖLLEN

A Partial History of St. Louis Bakeries

ISBN: 978-1-66788-201-7

Dedication

To Our Loving God
For Creating Bakery Goods!

To Borrow From A Famous Ben Franklin quote,
"BAKERY GOODS are proof that
GOD loves us and wants us to be happy!"

Let us give thanks to all BAKERS around the world,
but especially to the BAKERS OF ST. LOUIS,
who have given us so much joy and pleasure through their hard
work, creativity, and service in creating their bakery goods!

How Our Hearts Were Stöllen

A Partial History of St. Louis Bakeries

Rich Gaynor

Contents

ACKNOWLEDGEMENTS AND THANK YOUS

To David and Myndi McArthur and to Randy McArthur For Their Early Encouragement and For Their On-Loan Gift of 50 Years of Bulletins From The St. Louis Master Bakers Association.

To Joyce Schwarz For Preserving <u>All</u> of the St. Louis Bakers monthly Bulletins From 50 Years, From 1950 to 2000, that she organized in Binders and Sequenced by Months and Years.

To Rita Winkeler Andres and Mary Kay Ellerbrock Turner Of the Ellerbrock Family For Their Early Encouragement In The "Bakery Book Project."

To Connie Wolf Of The Wolf Bakery Family For Her Early Encouragement In The "Bakery Book Project."

To Tom Kavanaugh For His Early and Ongoing Encouragement.

To the 25 Bakers and 1 Baker Supplier of the "In-Person Interviews."

To Amanda Doyle, A Published Author of Multiple Local Interest Pieces For Her Encouragement and Advice As An Already Published Author.

To Ann Parise Hannan for Her Technical Help and Support.

To All of Our Friends and Family Who Frequently Reminded Me That They Were Waiting Patiently For This Book To Be Published.

To Our Son, Jerome, and our Two Daughters, Jenny and Katy for All of Their Gifts of Technical, Computer, and Design Expertise.

To My Wife, Sue, Who Generously Gave Me The Time and Space To Work On This Book For Over 10 Years.

FOREWORD

My career has been dedicated to making the best pastries and baked goods, in both taste and appearance. This pursuit has sent me all over the world—Paris, Tokyo, Las Vegas, New York City. While training and working with many other distinguished chefs in some of the biggest and most prestigious food hubs in the world, my dream was to open my own pastry shop. When it was time for that dream to become a reality, there was no better place for me than St. Louis, not far from my family and hometown in Farmington, Missouri.

I love being a part of the diverse food culture here, with such supportive chefs and loyal patrons. Many of us enjoy giving back to our community, and it is truly amazing seeing how much everyone cares about this city and its people.

Rich Gaynor has the same love I have for this city and its rich and diverse culinary history. He not only focuses on the celebrated bakers and bakeries of St. Louis, but on the city itself—the book is an important record of how the St. Louis food scene, in particular the bakeries, has grown and changed over the years: loving the traditional, but embracing the new, welcoming chefs of all backgrounds and heritage. I enjoy being a part of the St. Louis culinary culture and am honored to be included in this book alongside so many other remarkable people.

Nathaniel Reid
World-Class Pastry Chef
And Owner of Nathaniel Reid Bakery in St. Louis

PREFACE

O *ur story is a love story.*

For a long time the neighborhoods of St. Louis were enticed and wooed by the delicious attentions of the independent bakeries of St. Louis. This unique courtship spanned over a hundred years and is still continuing in a few locations. It was a love affair remembered by almost everyone who lived in St. Louis between the late 1800's and most of the 1900's. These attentive suitors tickled the fancy as well as the palette with great infatuation from their admirers. Of course, this love affair was particular to each person and each of us had a special affection for our own favorite bakery. That is what this story is all about. It is an effort to give a picture of these solicitous and enchanting lovers, the independent bakers of St. Louis!

I had been waiting for the right day and moment to break into those three big boxes of archive material sitting in our living room for nearly two years. I had received them as a gift on loan from one of the great old bakeries of St. Louis, the McArthur Bakery. The extraordinary story of the research for this book came first with the gift of these bulletins from David McArthur and his wife Myndi. I had been quietly praying for some kind of miracle find that would break the real story of St. Louis Bakeries during the last hundred years, and it came as sweetly as the danish rolls in one of the McArthur's display cases! For several years I had been visiting the McArthur Bakery on the special day of Christmas Eve.

A couple of months later, I stopped by on a non-Christmas Eve day to see if I could talk to David. He was busy, as bakers almost always are, but I was told that he would give me a call to arrange a meeting. With the phone call came a meeting time, and after an hour long visit I was given the three big boxes filled with fifty years of bulletins from the Bakers Association of Greater St. Louis. Not only were these bulletins made available to me they were already organized by some angel unknown to me at the time, someone who had a sense of their importance for a time in the future when they would eventually be discovered. In a later interview I learned that these historic treasures were assembled and protected by a thoughtful woman named Joyce Schwarz.

Two things gradually occurred to me after I received this precious gift — one, the daunting task that lay before me when I gazed upon the enormous amount of material contained in those boxes and two, my wife's words to me about this project when she said, "You know you'd better start writing this book because there are a lot of people who know about it and are counting on reading it."

So, I finally decided it was time to stop putting this off as a potential book, and begin making it into a real one. Besides the enlightening research that I enjoyed from all of the bulletins, the twenty-five plus interviews with active and retired bakers also contributed to this living history of St. Louis bakeries. In those interviews several things made this work not feel like work at all, but rather a joy for me. The bakers' pride in every case shined through in their willingness to talk about their bakery and its history. Their effervescent enthusiasm allowed me to share in *their* love for their own bakeries, their love for their fellow bakers, and their devotion to their craft.

I also experienced a consistent response whenever I would talk with friends and colleagues about my hope of writing this book. Without any exaggeration the responses were always positive, excited, and almost giddy. People would immediately start talking about their favorite bakery when they were growing up, their favorite treat from that bakery, and what it meant to them that bakeries were so present in their lives. Their buoyant responses were unmistakable because their eyes would get wider, their voices would become more animated, and one could see them longing for that crunchy peanut roll or that perfectly glazed donut from their youth! Because of all of these heart-warming perks it has been a great privilege to work on this tribute to the bakeries of St. Louis and the bakers whose hard work and artistry filled us with those delicious gifts that we enjoyed!

A DISCLAIMER

I would make no claim for *perfect* accuracy in the historical facts contained in this book. The reflections in Part I of the Autobiographical Introduction are my own.

The information contained in Part II of the "Bakers Bulletins" section, was taken directly from the bulletins of the St. Louis Master Bakers Association, and was quoted directly from those bulletins.

The information contained in Part III from the "In-Person Interviews" section was transcribed directly from the tape-recordings of those interviews, except in one case.

The additional information contained in the Appendix was taken from reputable sources and unedited in any way.

Of course, I am completely aware that errors in memory for all of us are always available. However, all of the bakers interviewed seemed of *very sound mind*!

Our story is a love story.

For a long time the neighborhoods of St. Louis were enticed and wooed

by the delicious attentions of the independent bakeries of St. Louis.

That is what this story is all about.

It is an effort to give a picture of these solicitous and enchanting lovers,

the independent bakeries of St. Louis!

PART 1

An Autobiographical Introduction

I t had been several Waffle House breakfasts since we had discussed the idea with any seriousness, even though there wasn't anything but fun whenever the topic came up. My friend Ed and I have laughed for years, and fantasized, about writing a book that revealed our not-at-all secret mistress! Yes, and one that we even "shared!" We had to finally admit it — we were both openly in love with the same heart-breaking, beautiful, and tantalizing temptation of our hearts — a love that always satisfied, never disappointed, and never teased. Well, maybe sometimes disappointed, though we never lost our longings because of it. We both had an ongoing love affair with the donut!

Ever since we'd been friends we had joked about not only how much we loved donuts, but actually any bakery goods that could tempt us from any direction. It was as if our street finder had the locations "Saved" for all of the important places in St. Louis, but that included only one category in its Favorites memory, and that was the Bakeries of St. Louis.

Of course, in our more realistic moments we realized that we had to share our secret love with others and that this mistress had stolen not only our hearts but the hearts of people in every part of the world. Yes, the love of carefully made bakery treats is something that seems to have always had an enchanting effect on people, but in this book we will be talking particularly about the bakeries and the bakers of St. Louis.

This is a book dedicated to the hard work and creative devotion of those baker artisans who are busy in the early hours of every morning as unseen servants for us all. It is an <u>every</u> morning schedule that they keep, and we'll be talking with some of them later to find out what this "job" really takes, this "job" that wasn't a job, but rather a labor of love.

CHAPTER 1

HOW IT ALL BEGAN
"A LOVE AT FIRST BITE"

I will have to start out by describing how this love affair began for me.

The story is a simple one, but also a pretty interesting one. At an early age I was led down the road of bakery flirting by my very serious, but very sweet-toothed German grandfather. My family and I were blessed to share our lives in a multi-generational home with my two maternal grandparents. From the very beginning of my story bakery goods were directly connected with going to Mass on early mornings with my grandpa. He would attend Mass, and I would serve, sometimes as early as six o'clock in the morning.

So, the routine was this. After Mass on most mornings we would simply move grandpa's car about a half block west on Meramec Street from the front of St. Anthony of Padua Church to the front of the St. Louis Pastry Shop near the corner of Virginia and Meramec. We would get out of the car, look briefly in the window, and proceed inside to order the cravings of our hearts. I think my grandpa saw himself as some sort of heroic patriarch who would set off each morning, pray for the clan, and then bring home the treats he had foraged from the forest of earthly delights. He would bring home his selections in snow white boxes tied with string as if they were cherished Christmas presents that he had wrapped himself for the family he loved.

After arriving back home he would walk into the kitchen, and his family would glow with anticipation at what surprising choices he had made for them on this particular morning. Since he and my grandmother were decidedly German he would always make sure that the treats were plentiful so that there could be enough leftovers for the three o'clock coffee klatch, a ritual that was seldom missed. So, my early experiences told me that, "Life is good!" and that we must celebrate it at least twice a day with coffee and cakes. Coffee? Oh, yes! At an early age? Ah, yes!

I can remember being raised partly by my German grandmother who I think actually "lived" in our kitchen. She was, of course, our own master baker. One day after watching her revel in her mid-morning third, fourth, or fifth cup of coffee, I can remember begging her for me to take a taste. So, at the age of five my grandmother carefully prepared my first cup of coffee that was more cream and sugar than anything else. And so, I credit my grandparents most of all with the corruption of my youth, at least in the habits of coffee and cakes!

Later in life, when I could figure some things out, I recognized my grandfather's wisdom because he had planted in my heart such a nourishing connection between the sweet bread of Eucharist and the delicious breads of life! Very wise was he indeed, for he had created in me a direct taste for "breaking bread" with the Christian community and then breaking open those snow-white boxes of bakery goods with my own family. Yep, both kinds of bread seemed to get inside of me! I guess there is something about genetic memories, or more pointedly, taste bud memories!

As my grandfather began to age my adventures each morning began to grow more perilous as we risked our lives to bring home the daily fare for the family. His driving began to be an adventure all its own as his judgment and perception both began to fade. Though slight in frame he was a self-assured man on the inside, very certain of his ways and very proud. On some mornings he was starting to drive more and more down the middle of South St. Louis's narrow streets. When we would barely miss colliding with an oncoming car the driver would sometimes honk his horn out of fear and the impending danger. In response to this aggressive gesture my grandfather would invariably honk his horn back at the fellow and would shout out the window, "What the Halifax is the matter with you?!" I would just chuckle quietly to myself.

As his driving worsened, I began to get a bit more fearful. But, the big event I remember best was the morning we moved the car that half block from the front of church to the front of the St. Louis Pastry Shop. We briefly looked over the variety in the bakery window, entered the bakery, made our selections for the day, and then got back into the car. In those days grandpa's 1950 Buick had not even the thought of safety features of any kind, and on this particular morning none having to do with what gear you were in when first restarting your car.

As fate would have it, my grandpa had forgotten that he'd left the car parked in reverse. Who knows why this was so, except that he probably had tried to position the car in the perfect spot before he had turned off the engine. What was most funny was that there were no other cars parked along this particular curb because of the early morning hour. And then, the inevitable happened. On this eventful morning he had also decided to pound the accelerator to the floor as he was starting the car. In a flash our 1950 Buick shot straight backwards nearly a hundred feet before he'd grasped what had happened. Fortunately, there were no cars parked anywhere behind us, and so no harm was done.

It was on that day that I learned how instinctively my foot could go through the floorboard as it tried to slam on the imaginary brake on my side of the car. I think that was also the day when my parents began to wean my grandfather from behind the wheel. I believe that experience unconsciously helped me remember forever how much I loved those mornings, with my wise grandfather who introduced me to the love of bakery goods!

My Grandmother In The Kitchen

How it all began? The living and breathing kitchen wench of my childhood wasn't an imaginary source of inspiration, but in reality the kitchen goddess that really turned my heart towards the miracles of sugar, flour, and butter. She was my German grandmother, a Schneiderhahn by marriage and an Abel by birth. She still lives in my memory in the same form as I had when I was three or four years old. She was a living and breathing caricature of everything German, elderly, and female. She was the family's matriarch, as "large" a figure physically as well as metaphysically as my driving-impaired grandfather who was the family's patriarch. In those days she seemed to float around her kitchen like a slow-moving, amorphous creature, but secretly a smart and gastronomical genius. She had that quality that great cooks do of appearing to just "throw things together," always within the perfect range of edible sweetness and always with a mystifying balance between a dash of flare and an instinctively measured care. She, my grandfather, and my family lived together in this unexpected jewel of a South St. Louis house, a home that had been in the Schneiderhahn family from the early 1900's.

So, it was from these early times as a child that I can remember running and rummaging around in this large, hearth-like kitchen with this equally oversized grandmother as my earliest surrogate mother. She was my earliest image of many things, but somehow her person and her baking seemed to merge in my experience as a single big cream puff! My grandmother became the things she baked, and the things she baked contained the puffy, soft sweetness of my grandmother.

One of several vivid memories I had of her were the pockets of over-sized non-muscle tissue that swayed and swung from beneath her upper arms. I would sometimes imagine playing with my miniature cowboy figures pretending that they were relaxing on that soft ledge of tissue, lounging there after a hard day's work as if they were on a front porch swing.

In describing this distinctive physical quality to our youngest daughter it occurred to me that maybe this was where all of that flour, sugar, and especially butter had been stored from all those endless personal "samples" from her count-less days of baking. She was a cream puff in many ways!

In the retelling of another story to our daughter I remembered the answers I gave to her very pointed question, "What were the best things she baked?" she asked. I had to stop and think, but the answers soon came quickly and clear. One of her very best baked goods was a special but very ordinary Christmas cookie that was our family's favor- ite. It was in all its simplicity the best "Butter Cookie" I had ever tasted. As far as I can remember, all there was to it was butter, flour, sugar, salt, some pure vanilla, an egg yolk, and lots more butter!

In thinking about my experi- ences with her on her Christmas baking days, I remembered she made me feel like I was a baker too,

even though I was only five. To my surprise on one of those days, I was given the important job of "smushing" the butter cookie balls onto the cookie sheets into perfectly round circles. Because of the "smushing" they had just enough of a fili- greed edge to make even the texture of the eating as tantalizing as the taste. The tradition of Christmas baking has continued into the present with grandma Po-Po now teaching her grandchild.

But, I could make no mistake about this process, because the quality control of my grandmother would come into play. I was the apprentice and she was the master. And so, she taught me the technique of "smushing" the butter cookie balls with the bottom of one of the family's gold-edged wine glasses. There was one additional touch. The bottom of the glass was covered with a snow-white linen napkin so that it would leave an embossed pattern on the face of the cookie. Why she trusted me with one of these priceless wine glasses as my baker's tool was a complete mystery to me, but she did.

As I thought back on this perplexing risk on her part, I realized that she was teaching me two important German lessons — one, you must always use the right tool for the job, and two, you must always take great care of your tools. So, I can

distinctly remember her caution that I should press down hard enough to "smush" the cookie dough, but not so hard as to break the delicate stem of the glass.

But, I think there was one more deeply felt reason for her selection of a precious antique wine glass for me to use as my cookie-making tool. I think she was actually infusing all of her family memories into her cookies from this particular glass, a glass that had been used during countless family dinners.

And so, each of those cookies was not just a delicious Christmas treat. It was also a sacred vessel filled with an abundance of cherished memories. So, those were the days of Christmas baking by the master and the apprentice, who worked by her side and followed at her heels.

But, "What else were her specialties," asked my daughter. Again, I had to stop and think, but within a few moments a flood of memories came to me, and these from an even earlier age. In those days, when mothers and grandmothers would still insist that their children take a nap, I can remember waking up to a smell that was hard to put into words. This might have had something to do with the fact that I didn't yet *have* many words, especially ones that could describe the sweet smells coming from the kitchen. But on this particular day, I recorded one smell that would stay with me forever. This was the distinctive aroma of "Hungarian Butter Horns" as they were coming out of the oven. There is a theory that one's sense of smell is a strong link to memories. So, to this day I think I can spot a butter horn from far away!

I could also tell that this day must be a Saturday! At an early age I knew that Saturday was "Baking Day," but I also knew that on Saturday afternoons my grandpa would be in his patriarchal chair in the living room pretending to listen to classical music. In fact, he was actually sleeping, and we were all required to be quiet during this time.

After being shushed repeatedly by my mother I can remember asking her why one person in the house could control what every other person in the house could do for an eternal two hours on a Saturday afternoon, the day of the week that I thought was made just for fun!

Apparently, I had forgotten that he was the patriarch. But, I did find one redeeming way to survive the classical music as I ran around the house and became the orchestra's conductor, especially during the fast and loud parts of those endless symphonies.

The story of my grandmother in the kitchen would not be complete without a description of the day the stove exploded! My grandmother's stove was an old gas one that had the problem of losing the flame on the pilot light as old stoves frequently did. And so, like any resourceful person of the times she would mold a scrap of newspaper into a small torch, light it, and then turn on the gas waiting for that familiar "whoosh" that would eventually suck the flame from the little torch into the burners of the oven. On this one morning, as I was playing with the pots and pans, I noticed that my grandmother was having trouble and that the time of an eventual lighting of the stove seemed to get longer and be repeated too many times.

Finally, too much of the gas had accumulated, and my grandmother's curious head had gotten too far into the opening of the oven. All of a sudden the "whoosh" of the ignition turned into a muffled "bam!" My grandmother was basically alright, yet definitely shaken. However, her eyebrows and bangs on her forehead somehow looked a little bit shorter!

So what does this experience have to do with baking? I suppose like any other dramatic experience in life I have always felt that these times serve as exclamation points that engrave these memories into our minds forever. They seem to help us remember that these were important times, and so our life experiences shout a "bam" to help us remember.

My Father In The Kitchen

So, these were the early experiences that began to form my taste buds or rather corrupt them as my natural foods father would often say. He had a theory that if a child's early flavor experiences were formed toward fruits and vegetables, they would naturally prefer these over the worldly temptations of sugar and other villains. Poor soul! I felt he was fighting a crusade like Don Quixote's, tilting at windmills in a sugar driven culture.

Later as an adult I noticed that main line grocery stores were putting in salad bars, and then to his surprise I'm sure, full sections of organic produce! My more centrist mother would often lament that she had to enforce all of the rules of this super healthy diet as the gatekeeper cook when she hadn't really been formed in them herself.

Ironically, this pure foods pioneer had been propelled in this direction with a religious fervor because of an early dietary experience! He had grown up in northern Ontario but had left home in his twenties to take a job in a Toronto bakery. He told us later that the smells of all of the fresh breads in the morning were so intoxicating that he may have eaten more of them than he sold. This over-indulgence in the sweet doughs of his reckless youth led to an extreme case of skin rash that he called eczema, apparently so severe a case that it led him to seek medical help for a cure. As fate would have it, he came upon a natural foods diet book written by a man named Dr. McCracken. We would often joke later, and beyond my father's hearing, that his real name had been Dr. McCrackpot and at other times Dr. McQuacken.

But, little did we know that his pure foods diet would serve us well as we moved through life with generally good health and consistent vitality. Perhaps it was because of his grandfatherly teaching or through the genetic memory of their bodies, our own children would eventually give good examples to their generation with very disciplined lifestyles of health and nutrition.

The most dramatic example of my father's influence would take form in his great grandchild, the daughter of our son. Apparently, our son had been listening so well to his grandfather that he passed the pure foods experience on to his own child, our granddaughter. For the first three years of her life she did not even know the tastes of chocolate, sugar, or for sure soda pop!

Old Maurice's theory seemed to prove true with high results. To this day at the age of twelve she seems to have a taste for almost all natural foods and a preference in that direction. Of course, our son has recently loosened the reins a bit with not infrequent and guiltless trips to a local soft serve drive-in named Ted Drewes, a famous one for people who know St. Louis.

But, there was one vestige and vice that was too strong in my dad, and that was his love of bakery goods. He himself had been a master baker, particularly of pies. As a young boy at the age of twelve he left home and walked to his first job, *thirty miles across a frozen lake.* Of course he did! There he would spend the entire winter at a lumber camp where the stories and the men he would describe were at least as tall as Paul Bunyan's. Perhaps because of his small frame and early age he was given the job of baking pies all day long for the tired and hungry men who did the actual work of logging. However, I remember one fact from his stories that did widen my skeptical eye. The pie makers would have to bake at least one half to one whole pie per lumberjack for each and every day.

So, this time of pie-baking for my father gave him some valuable experience, and our family reaped the benefits of his early "practice." He had some magical process that I could never really understand. All I can remember is this. At some point he would use ice water in the preparation of the dough. I would stand there looking up and over the edge of the table trying to notice what he was doing, but I am still unsure about how he put everything together. I can only recall that somehow this technique added a wonderful flakiness to the dough that was like no other that I ever had.

So, this was another of the early experiences that made me a set-up for my love affair with sweets. In addition to the perfect crusts of my father our double city lot was home to two prolific cherry trees, and not the ordinary kind. These cherries were Montmorency — the coveted sour cherries grown for the best of preserves and award-winning pies. As I matured into boyhood I was the natural candidate to be the cherry tree climber. After the rest of my family had harvested the abundant cherries on the lower branches, and after even the mid-range heights had been gleaned by the cherry thirsty birds in our yard, I was given the job of climbing to the highest limbs of these productive trees.

It was my mission to save the last cherries from the waiting birds who hoped we would overlook some of the higher branches. My task was to see that their wait was in vain, though secretly I would intentionally "miss" some of the last cherries that could have been picked. After this great harvesting of the cherries came the arduous and what seemed to be endless work of "cherry pitting."

I can still remember that "cherry pitting" was a family affair. Since no one was without sin, we all seemed destined to do this penance as a sacrifice for the coming fruits of paradise in the midst of the next winter — cherry preserves and cherry pies! We would all sit around the big kitchen table and alternate our complaining with spurts of serious pitting.

As much as my dad was in charge of pie-baking my grandmother was in charge of preserves. After simmering down the cherries with cup-for-cup amounts of sugar, she would ladle the cooled syrup and whole cherries into mason jars and then seal them with wax for cold winter mornings of toast and butter. What bottles of <u>Dandelion Wine</u> were to the author Ray Bradbury, cherry preserves were to our family. Those jars of red nectar would remind us of our past summer's fun and help us to look forward to the warmer days of the coming spring.

My Mother In The Kitchen

But where was my mom in the middle of all of this baking and preserving? She too was a good cook, but I think she probably knew she couldn't compete for playing time in the kitchen with her mother. After all, it was my grandparent's house and my grandmother's kitchen. As I thought back on my mother's cooking her dishes tended to be more basic and everyday. I think she knew that there could be no contest with my grandmother.

But I think she also knew that she couldn't compete with my father either. He definitely had the credentials, with his early pie-baking experiences and a semi-professional resume as a chef. He had started in Canadian lumber camps, moved on to five-star resorts, and then had many jobs on the restaurant circuit of the 1920's in St. Louis. Besides all of this, my mother had to contend with the intimidating restraints of my father's natural foods diet.

So, I can remember my mom tried to "keep things simple," and so our meals seemed predictably safe and rather unvarying. Tomato soup, tuna salad, chicken salad, and week-end waffles were some of our daily fare. But, when it came to family holiday celebrations or my parent's turn for their dinner club, things definitely took a turn upward. There seemed to be a dramatic cranking up of the dial towards much greater preparations and a more exotic menu!

However, there was one exception, and it was the pinnacle of my mom's cooking. It was a remarkable delicacy that pushed the envelope in the family for baked goods. It was my mom's Angel Pie! It was every bit angelic, and lived up to its name with what I can only describe as rare flavor blends combined with delicious textures. I have never tasted anything like it before or since. Who had invented this treat?!

This was a taste experience that has stayed with me to this day. Optimistically, I had promised my wife for years that I would bake an Angel Pie for the holidays, but I was not able to live up to that promise. I can only explain this contradiction between my baking aspirations and my lack of completion in this way. Perhaps it was from a fear of pressure to perform or from some feelings that I was not worthy to even try to achieve something that only my mother could perfect!

Eventually, I managed to find several recipes on the internet and became driven to recreate this dessert. So, with these available to me I made an attempt to walk among the angels. However, I was not very successful! I had failed miserably at the delicate job of creating a good crunch quality to the meringue. But, here is a description of this wonderful dessert. Imagine that your teeth and tongue are in slow motion as they bite down gently on a top layer of sweet whipped cream that has been generously sprinkled with baked egg white crumbles. As your teeth pass through this top layer of whipped cream they push through to a two inch layer of clear lemon filling. As your bite moves further down you finally hit the bottom crust of a quarter inch of pre-baked egg whites. Your teeth, mouth, and tongue then realize that this amazing dessert has been fully chilled for at least three hours.

The impact of this last dimension is really beyond description because the chill factor seems to pull all of these flavors and textures together into one explosive experience!

I thought of one more way of describing how distinctive this dessert really is. I truly believe that it should be in the ethereal company of the finest desserts in the world! Because I am a pretty inexperienced and underexposed "foodie," I have only recently even tasted Crème Brule.

How embarrassing, but my first experience with this delicacy was one in which I pretty much "lost control." I had been treated by one of my favorite students with a sample from Tony's, St. Louis's most famous restaurant. In the middle of a busy school day she asked me if I had tasted it yet. With some embarrassment I had to admit that it was still in the teachers' refrigerator from the day before. Since she was a very exuberant student, she insisted that I had to try it at that very moment. And so, I buckled under the pressure, but told myself that I had only enough time to take a small taste. Impossible! I quickly licked the bowl clean and was even late for a class!

Needless to say, I believe Angel Pie deserves to be listed among a small number of other world-class desserts, along with such items as Crème Brule, Baked

Alaska, and Baklava. My final thought on this for the reader is to just <u>try</u> making my mother's Angel Pie. And then after you make it, after it is well-chilled, after you take it out of the fridge, and after you pull out your largest serving spoon, invite no one else but yourself!

"I Wish I could eat a big spoon of that Angel Pie, but my Mama says for now I can only have a delicious spoonful of avocados and carrots!"

CHAPTER 2

FLIRTING WITH
FROSTED FLOOZIES!

Most people probably know that as a boy moves through the lower grades and into middle school he starts to notice the more glitzy and showy sources of attraction in his life. And, this would include the allures of the bakery gender! And so, this part of the story revolves around those treats that one could best describe as "cheap imitations" of those true loves that began in those early bakeries!

So, the St. Louis Pastry Shop was a hard act to follow, but eventually I had strayed and moved on to sample some of life's other sweet experiences. There were some smaller bakeries in the neighborhood with their own specialties, and that's what South St. Louis looked like. In those days people would say, "You never have to worry about surviving without the essential necessities on the streets of St. Louis."

Indeed, there were always the four central sources of life at every intersection — a gas station, a tavern, a confectionary, and a bakery. If your life broke down in any one of those four areas, no need to worry. You could walk a block in any direction and your need would be filled. As a kid I felt that two of these sources of life were critical, and the other two were not as much.

"Confectionaries" for me were actually candy stores, but in reality they were a type of convenience store, only in postage stamp size. A person could get anything from a box of cereal to a flashlight in these stores, but their original purpose as a candy store was the only thing that mattered to me. Fortunately, as a providential gift from God there was one that was placed like an oasis smack in the middle of my five block walk to school.

I can remember that as I got older my tastes in its confections seemed to change with the years. In the lower grades my buddies and I would buy the fun packs of baseball cards. The slabs of bubble gum that came with the cards were actually just a fringe benefit. The baseball cards were our real interest. "Who'd you get? Oh, I've got him already." "Whew—I'll trade you right away for him!" And then, after getting the one treasured card of our favorite player we would soon "lose" him in a fierce and painful game of flip cards at recess on that same day.

As we entered those parent-dreaded middle school years our tastes again began to change when we surveyed the penny candy at the confectionary. At that time we had been growing into that new music called "rock and roll." So, when the Elvis miniature licorice "records" came in we were truly amazed. Somehow these bite-sized mini-records were made out of narrow strips of black licorice that had been rolled into little disks. What was even more fascinating was that they had a tiny record label stuck to the middle with one of Elvis's songs printed small, but readable on each one. I can remember that I was totally captivated that they could look so much like a real record even though they were only the size of a quarter. I can still see myself buying "Heartbreak Hotel" and "Love Me Tender" as these small records and biting into that music in miniature.

But what does all of this have to do with bakery goods? Well, to understand our newfound fascination with store-bought bakery goods, one has to understand that we now had our own real money tucked away, usually in the form of quarters, pressed safely into the coin pockets of our jeans. But, penny candy wasn't the only treat sold at those confectionaries. We were also enticed by the Hostess who lived at those stores and who would tempt us toward *Flirtations with Frosted Floozies!*

And, who can forget biting into their first "Twinkie?" The sugar cream surprise inside was worth every penny of their over-priced cost at the corner confectionary. The next pre-packaged discoveries were the chocolate, white-drizzle-topped cupcakes. And then came the Swiss Cake Rolls, the coconut covered Sno-Balls, that a health food person once said took three days for you to digest! And finally, the chocolate Ding Dongs with that slightly crusted but resilient icing! "Whew!" The temptations were numerous and great, but deep down I knew that these were just passing fancies and that these *floozies* would give their attentions to another hundred thousand patrons each and every day. At this time my dad was still baking his cherry pies and making his simple cherry syrup for ice cream. So, my eyes and heart were not completely blinded by the lure of processed treats.

Besides that, I still had the daily reminders from my dad that those packages and their lists of ingredients were filled with artificial chemicals and preservatives. Those warnings alone were enough to keep me from sliding down the slippery slope of too many trysts with *Miss Hostess*.

Oh yes, I almost forgot about my times spent with *Miss Dolly*. That would be *Miss Dolly Madison*, of course! Surprisingly, my own dad introduced me to her! I think he secretly had a thing for her too. And since she was not one of those expensive dates he seemed to be willing to forego his scruples for the sake of economy. Because he was a grocer I think he even got a special deal from the delivery man at the end of the day.

Chocolate Milk And Donuts

There was one other grade school encounter that was deliciously etched into my memory, and one that was even given approval by the St. Anthony school that I attended. I can still remember sitting in the wooden pews at old St. Anthony's church waiting to go to communion so that we could fulfill our "First Friday of the Month" commitment. Going to communion on "First Fridays" was a devotion that was meant to please God and maybe even give us some time off in purgatory.

But, all I could think about was the *chocolate milk and donuts* that would be waiting for us in our classrooms back at school. As we walked back the two blocks from church to our school we didn't even notice the red buds and yellow flowers that were at the height of their blooms because we were too busy dreaming about the *chocolate milk and donuts* that we had ordered from the day before!

The icy cold milk would have been delivered from the Ozark Dairy on Minnesota Avenue and the glazed donuts from the St. Louis Pastry Shop on Meramec Street. For me chocolate milk was a rare treat option that I seldom had a choice about with my own family, but it was even more special when we drank it at our desks because it was so cold! However, the glazed donuts were the highlight because they not only had the perfect amount of boiled grease in them, they also had a crunchable glaze on them that I had never experienced before! So, the sensational flavors, textures, and cold chocolatey liquid that came together in my mouth were unlike anything that I could remember! As a result, those delicious experiences on those long ago "First Fridays" would cement my love of bakery goods to my love for the Eucharist forever!

CHAPTER 3

"YEAST FOR THE DOUGH"
THE BEGINNINGS OF
THE BAKERY BOOK PROJECT &
A CHRISTMAS MIRACLE

"St. Louis — the largest small town in America!" That's what a lot of people have called St. Louis, and this seems to be a description that fits. All kinds of transplant people from around the country have seemed to echo this moniker as well. Professional athletes and other out-of-towners new to the area are often heard to say that St. Louis has some qualities that you just don't find in other large cities. There seems to be a genuine friendliness, stimulating cultural offerings, free seats at the Muny Opera, free admission to the Zoo, and a helpful attitude towards strangers. I can confidently say that these positive traits were also a part of the independent bakers of St. Louis.

These qualities were present in their personal networks of relationships that I found in their larger *bakery family — a family of families*! During most of the 1900's there was a distinctively gracious feeling among the bakers who would often share their recipes and supplies, and even their lives.

I discovered this family feeling early in my search for the history of St. Louis baking when I first began my interviews with the twenty-five bakers who will give life to this book. I would like to thank all of them who shared with me not only their time, but also their pride in what they had achieved.

But, I would like to highlight my earliest of these interviews with David and Myndi McArthur who gave not only their time but also their enthusiasm for this

"Bakery Book Project," and on the busiest bakery morning of the year. I can only describe this encounter as a true Christmas miracle!

Over the years my family has come to know that I have an odd ritual of venturing out into the hubbub of shopping craziness on Christmas Eve mornings. I always have a game plan for the day with very particular goals. I have a list and a mental route that makes this nothing but fun! On these days I never have expectations that I will complete my list, so I try not to be in a hurry.

Surprisingly, I have always found this to be an uplifting experience, one in which people have been unexpectedly cordial and kind to one another, and to myself. For me there has always been something magical and grace-filled about Christmas Eve mornings.

On this particular morning I found myself with not just the usual excitement in the middle of my stomach, but the wonder of a fresh snowfall that was still falling! It was a special kind of snow. It was different, the way it was floating down in huge flakes, the way it was already sitting gracefully on trees, the way it had that ideal water content that made it perfect for snowballs, snowmen, and sledding. *Yep, we were having a white Christmas!*

But, I was a man on a mission, whereto I wasn't sure, except for the first stop! The McArthur Bakery would set the tone for this delicious adventure! My wife and I had just recently discovered this as a new bakery for us, and we were still in that honeymoon stage of trying lots of things at this new store. However, we had especially fallen for a particular treat. It was their perfectly made, caramel-topped, cinnamon-laced donuts! The edge on the top of the donut and the ring around the outside had an ideal crunch to it, and the quality of the caramel was amazing!

Anyway, on this particular morning I had gone in, made my selections, and was checking out when at the last moment I decided to try one more time to see if this bakery still had a connection to one of my former students. I had recently learned that one of our Notre Dame High School graduates had married and become part of the McArthur Bakery family. So, I asked if Myndi Bearden McArthur was still involved with the bakery. The young man who had just finished ringing me out immediately responded that her brother, Jay, was standing right next to him. Jay and I quickly renewed our acquaintance that had been dormant for thirty years.

And then, he immediately moved on to the next connection and asked me if I wanted to say "Hi" to his sister who I had taught as many years before.

This particular set of connections was about to prove that at least South St. Louis still had that small-town feeling that had also been so present among the St. Louis bakers. Later, my conclusion from my research was that there seemed to be an overflow of this close-knit quality into the St. Louis bakery community — I discovered that they were a *family of families*.

The brother and sister who were now standing in front of me had been two of our own children's playmates at their home, where their mother had been one of our own daycare sitters. A small world it was indeed.

And so, after making this reconnection with Myndi and after explaining briefly about my hopes to write a partial history of St. Louis baking, Myndi quickly asked if I would like to meet her husband, David MacArthur, one of the sons of the bakery's founder. My response was of course, "Yes," but with a quick qualification.

At this time on a Christmas Eve morning there were at least ten to fifteen workers behind the counter and about forty customers on my side of the counter. I quickly responded that I would love to meet her husband, but that I had no expectations that he would be able to talk with me at that time. But, Myndi's response was as accommodating as her brother's had been as she blurted out, "Oh, don't worry, I'll get him!" After a very short time, her husband came out of the kitchen, and after I tried to make the same disclaimer about how busy they were and how I didn't want to bother him at that time, his response was just as gracious. "Oh, don't worry," he said, "things are slowing down now, and I'm on kind of a break!" As I looked around the store I thought to myself, "Wow — 'on kind of a break!' This is an example of bakery grace and a clear sign of a well-run store!"

Little did I know that I would be in the middle of an even bigger Christmas miracle! David was as friendly and engaging as Myndi! Talking to him, and more listening than talking, was an indulgence for me as satisfying as any bakery treat in their store. As he began talking I quickly searched in my pocket for any scrap of paper that I usually carry for such an occasion. All I could find was a small dental appointment card, but I began writing feverishly. He was locating bakeries and recalling names that I had never even heard of before. While writing in the smallest print I could manage, I was able to record the names and historic locations of several that would serve me well as "leads" on a more recollected and calmer day.

What struck me most while listening to David MacArthur was his wide-eyed and yet measured pride in his family and in what they had achieved. His descriptions of other bakery families carried that same pride and that same sense of mission at the center of everything that they too had accomplished. While offering all of these crystals of accumulated knowledge he communicated other intangibles about the history of these bakery families.

Not only had many of the bakeries been bought and sold amongst themselves, and not only had they worked in one another's stores, *they had also been bound together as a larger family.* As an example, he even mentioned that he was a godfather to the son of one of his friends from another bakery family.

David's manner and tone throughout our conversation had been one of great pride, and his last effort on my behalf was to walk me across their spacious store so that I could see some of the McArthur family photos, particularly ones that showed their stores in different locations. And so, other pictures were beginning to form more clearly in my mind of *the bakeries of St. Louis.*

Perhaps the most gracious offer of help came when David told me that he would be happy to share an archive of fifty years of bulletins from the St. Louis Bakers Association. They were published and distributed monthly from the *Master Retail Bakers of Greater St. Louis.* With this offer I'm sure my face went into a very gradual but widening smile as I contemplated this treasure trove of information that might give historic substance to these pages.

So, I thanked him then, as I thank him now, along with Myndi and Jay Bearden and the young man who waited on me. I thanked them, of course, for their long-time bakery treats but also for the kindness and their gift to me of a Christmas miracle. Later, I came to learn that these fifty years of bulletins were not only sequenced by month and year in neat small binders, but that each month's bulletin was protected inside of a plastic slip jacket!

Someone who was unknown to me at the time had done the invaluable service of organizing these fifty years and protecting them as a primary source, perhaps with only the hope that they would be discovered and carefully used in the future! I learned later that this thoughtful person was a woman named Joyce Schwarz, the wife of one of St. Louis's well-known bakers. With this powerful send-off from the McArthurs I knew that I was about to launch a great treasure hunt! I had set-off to discover some of the *great bakeries and bakers of St. Louis!*

INTRODUCTION TO THE RESEARCH CHAPTERS

I had been waiting for the right day and moment to break into those three big boxes of archived bulletins sitting in our living room for nearly two years. Before I had become the custodian for these treasured materials I had been praying for a miracle so that I could find something that would break open the real story of St. Louis bakeries.

And, the miracle came in the form of a gift on-loan from one of the great bakery families in the history of St. Louis bakeries, the McArthur Bakery family, specifically David and Myndi McArthur.

At a follow-up meeting with David, he gave me the three boxes of archive materials. In it I found an exceptionally organized collection of resources. They were the monthly Retail Bakers bulletins published by the St. Louis Master Bakers' Association. These monthly bulletins were little time capsules all the way back from January of 1956 to 2006.

These rare finds that were made available to me had been organized by a woman named Joyce Schwarz, who had at least the same degree of interest in the topic as I did. But, she was also someone who had a great love for the *St. Louis bakery family*, so much so that she very carefully organized them for interested parties in the future!

It was as if these bakery bulletins were just waiting to be discovered by someone who cared about them. However, one thought kept me frozen in my procrastination. I had a bewildering fear at the thought of diving into these materials and not really knowing how I was going to swim across such a distance. One day my wife's words were an answer to my fears and a motivation to start the swim when she said, "You know, you'd better do this now because there are a lot of people counting on you!"

So, I concluded that the time had come for me to stop putting off this work as a potential book and begin making it into a real one. And then, I had an encouraging thought about beginning and sustaining such a swim. I had already experienced very enjoyable and even inspiring visits with some of the current bakers in St. Louis. So, I was beginning to get a sense of a particular personality profile among them.

Universally, they all seemed to have similar qualities in their responses. To this day, these interviewed bakers have all had the exact same enthusiasm and pride in talking about their bakeries. Each of them had an effervescent excitement to share their love for their own bakeries, their affection for their fellow bakers, and their enjoyment of their craft.

One other consistency has surfaced since I began this project. In talking with friends about "the Bakery Book Project" there has been a similar kind of excitement in hearing them talk about <u>their</u> favorite bakery from their youth. They have also invariably asked if they could help me do some of the research, especially in visiting the bakeries and in doing *their own taste tests as part of <u>their</u> research!*

PART 2

Stories and Wisdoms From The Bakers Bulletins of the St. Louis Master Bakers Association of Greater St. Louis

Introduction

There really is no way to describe the unique content of the Bakers Bulletins except to say that they always give a vivid picture of the times and a whimsically sage kind of advice to the bakers. Because of the personal style of the editor of these bulletins one also gets the feeling that he meant for his writings to reach out to us all.

The bulletins often give very practical instructions to the bakers about matters like economics, the business of baking, presentation of the bakery goods, and the day-to-day selling of the bakery products. However, sometimes the editor sounds more like a cheerleader, encouraging the bakers to hang in there with the physical demands of baking and at other times encouraging them to take some time for themselves and their families for rest and recreation. Most often these leisure times were ones that emerged from the bakery community itself, with countless kinds of social groups and events sponsored by the St. Louis Bakers Association. Singing groups, bowling leagues, formal dinners, dinner dances, banquets, and overnight trips were just a few of the countless activities that were offered to help the bakers remember that they deserved to have time with their families.

Within some selections of the quotable information the editor gives very concrete facts, but at other times he selects readings and even poems that are meant to be inspiring. In some instances he seems to choose ones that are meant to convince the reader of his rather preachy views. However, through all of the bulletins he has a very folksy, endearing, and soft style.

These samplings from the "Bakery Bulletins" proved to be as charming as I expected them to be, and the pictures that they gave of the *closeness* that I hoped to discover within the bakery community of St. Louis was far beyond what I even thought it would be!

In selecting the years that I did, I chose one or two years from each of the five decades that were available, and I attempted to give a picture of each year that would somewhat represent the period overall. I would urge you to read through the entries that were randomly selected here in order to get a picture of *the unique community* that was the St. Louis Bakers Association.

CHAPTER 4

"PARTNERS IN SWEETS"
SOME MORSELS FROM
THE BAKERS BULLETINS

From January of 1958
One of the Earliest Archived Bulletins

AN APOLOGY

"Oops, your editor made a slip. Last month the bulletin…mentioned the Christmas Party for the children of <u>all</u> of the members…Because of the error in the bulletin our allied members did not bring their children… Your editor blushes with humiliation at making so serious a mistake."

PRACTICAL

"Reference has been made in this bulletin about…increased labor costs. There is a limit to the production output per man per hour. A worker in a bakery will reach his greatest production efficiency in the second hour of work and can hold it for about 4 – 6 hours. Any overtime after 8 hours certainly should be considered only as an emergency."

PECANS

"Our retail bakers use pecan nuts every day without thinking much about the discovery of the pecan by…Captain Calieza de Vaca of a Spanish ship shipwrecked off the coast of Texas in 1533. He was captured by the Marianes Indians. Captain de Vaca later escaped, and he told of his being put to work by the Indians pounding these 'paccans' (the Indian word for the pecan) into meal. The early Americans sought out the pecan tree groves both for the food value of the nuts and the excellent lumber made from these trees."

LITERATE — THOUGHT HABITS

"We do not need to be urged to think; that comes as natural as breathing to all normal people...We should learn to form good thought habits.

THOUGHT HABITS

Sensible thinking is a habit acquired by carefully guided thinking over a period of years.

COMPLIMENT

"The December 1st issue of 'Baking Industry' referred to the coming New York Convention of ARBA, (the American Retail Bakers Association), as being as big as the one held in St. Louis in 1953! That is quite a compliment. It sets our St. Louis convention as a standard by which others are judged. It is a compliment to all of you bakers and allied men and women."

From February of 1958

"LITTLE MISS MUFFIN"

"We hope you have given out all your 'Little Miss Muffin' contest entry blanks...Some lucky girl between the ages of 6 and 10 years old will be selected to represent the St. Louis area at a national contest in New York. All expenses for this girl and her guardian for the trip will be paid by our local association...After New York, who knows what? A trip to Hollywood? A national T.V. show?"

On this same page the following AD appeared in a box.

Annual Card Party
Of the
Master Bakers Ladies Association

MONDAY, MARCH 3,1958

12:30 p.m.

Albrecht's Hall

3549 Arsenal

TICKETS ONE DOLLAR

NATIONAL RETAIL BAKERS WEEK

"This can be an eventful occasion for promotion. The American Retail Bakers Association has some excellent store decorations…You will find that dressing up your store for this occasion will have a stimulating effect similar to the effect that a new dress and hair-do has on a young woman! Plan now to make National Retail Bakers Week a SELL-ABRATION in your bakery."

EXTRA SPECIAL.

"Back in 1927 many bakers from all over the U.S.A. made a European trip together. There were about twenty-five from St. Louis on that trip. This year a similar trip is being organized which will include four important events, the ARBA, (American Retail Bakers Association), convention in New York, the World's Fair in Brussels, Belgium, the International Bakers Exhibition in Munich, and the 800th Anniversary Celebration of the City of Munich!

THIS N' THAT

Master Retail Bakers Annual Banquet, February 15th at Le Chateau Restaurant. There are currently 9100 people employed in the baking industry in Missouri.

From February of 1958

FROM THE BAKERS CO-OP

the Annual Report…showed the company (the Baker's Co-Op) to be in excellent condition financially.

CAPITAL STOCKS OUTSTANDING	1711 SHARES
DIVIDENDS ON STOCK	5133.00 or 3%
NET SALES, 1957	2,644,321.09

FROM THE BAKERS CO-OP continued
DISTRIBUTION TO MEMBERS

ON SUPPLIES	153,443.17
ON FLOUR	7,851.10
ON MANUFACTURED PRODUCTS	9,785.14

Author's Note: The Bakers Co-Op was a purchasing group that gave dividends to the bakers for using products from, and buying through, the Bakers Co-Op.

From March of 1958

A REVIEW OF ACTIVITIES IN 1957

January — Dinner meeting at Town Hall. Presentation of cake to Chuck Norman on T.V.

February — Stan Musial makes appeal for cooperation in the Crippled Children's Drive.

March — Bud Schwarz and 2 others present a cake to the St. Louis Hawks on T.V.

June — June 19th Stan Musial accepts a check for 1,149.27 on KSD-TV for the Crippled Children's Fund.

November — V. P. Leo Rozanek makes dramatic presentation on cost control in a bakery.

December — Children's Christmas Party

Author's Note: Bakeries and Bakers in St. Louis represented a huge family and a way of life for the bakers.

RECIPE FOR NEW ORLEANS BANANA CAKE

Bake one 8 inch chocolate layer. Slice into 2 layers so the top is 1/4 and the bottom is 3/4. Cover the bottom layer with custard cream. Slice 2 bananas in half and place on custard. Cover bananas with whipped cream, put on the top thin layer and finish with whipped cream. Garnish the top with pecans. Cherry or Pineapple cakes can be made in the same way.

SCHOLARSHIP AWARD

"The scholarship winner will receive 1,000 dollars to cover tuition, transportation, and living expenses at either the American Institute of Baking in Chicago or the William Hood Dunwoody Industrial Institute in Minneapolis. [Author's Note: What a bargain. One thousand dollars to cover all of this for an education in a trade!]

THIS N' THAT "

The Laclede Gas Co. will pick up the bill for our meeting
at Hotel Kingshighway on February 19th.

A bakery freezer is a shortage insurer, not a half-stale product refresher.

Author's Note: A very important historical fact and date. Back in 1886 we find the name of Jake Leibrecht who with Frank Meuser, T.H. Schmitthausler, August Gisler, Conrad Hagemeier, J.J. Meier, and John Rueckert founded *the St. Louis Master Bakers Association!*

It was this Jake Leibrecht who was the uncle of Louis Dreyer who caused 6 Dreyer brothers, all his nephews, to come to America...Luitpold was the youngest and the 7th son of the 7th son. As was customary in Germany at that time, the King of Bavaria became his godfather!

All six Dreyer brothers followed their uncle in the bakery trade, and all six successfully operated their own bakeries. These men set good examples for their children, and eight of them later had bakeries of their own.Quite an example of baking as a "family business and family pride." Obviously, bakery goods were a popular item in Germany. There must have been some excellent bakers there because of all of the generational learning!

From April of 1958

ECONOMICS

"The current business recession is actually more severe and deep-seated than we are led to believe...However, today the business slump is over-emphasized. Today some 71,500 of your St. Louis neighbors are jobless. Recession is an economic state — but it is also a state of mind, one that too often discourages normally healthy spending. For more than 110 years Boatman's Bank has encouraged saving...but Boatman's Bank is aware too that excessive saving can be as harmful as excessive spending. By healthy spending we can help to speed the inevitable return of full prosperity!"

Author's Note: On a smaller "scale," no pun intended, one of the bakers offers some practical and insightful economic advice.

Earl Schmidt said, "If you are selling a new product and have not had time to figure out the selling price, put the finished product on the scale and charge 3 cents an ounce."

Author's Note: Here is the ultimate bit of economic wisdom found under this heading. "Great industries are not built up by getting the best of someone else, but by giving goods and services that are worth more to your customers than the amount that they pay you in return!" G. Heath Clark

From May of 1958

STORE HOURS

"Sunday Closing — to close or not to close, that is the question. Changing shopping habits and the effect of supermarkets' store hours are causing many retail bakers to reassess their own operations... Back in the 1920's the Master Bakers Association had a Sunday closing law passed, but it seems that lawyers are seldom able to write a law without a loophole...Closing is no longer an Association problem. Too many of our Master Retail Bakers now have Sunday store hours."

PERFECTION

"The large wholesale bakeries which have experimental laboratories practically all agree that a bread dough cannot be properly fermented in less than 4 ½ hours, while in some retail shops the dough is divided into loaves about 30 minutes after mixing. Many bread doughs are considerably under-fermented. The resulting bread does not have the taste or keeping qualities it should have."

LET'S ALL GO TO A TEN HOUR WEEK!

"Labor 'leaders' are again talking about a shorter and shorter work week, 35 or even 30 hours a week. Why not 20 or ten?! How about a full day's work each Monday, then everybody enjoy a 6 day week-end?! In spite of the rabble rousers, the intelligent workman knows he can be paid only out of what he produces."

"IMPULSE" BUYING

"Packaged items <u>sell</u> from 18 to 300 percent faster than non-packaged ones. For every 3 items you plan to buy in a supermarket you'll buy 7 you didn't plan to buy. It takes you less than a second to make up your mind on whether to buy. Eighty percent of your purchases are based on the result of memory…After that first sale the product is on its own. Its freshness and quality either recommends it for another purchase or rejects it…If all bakers thought of each item they make on that basis they would improve the taste appeal all down the line. Freshness and taste appeal; that's it!"

From June of 1958

"LITTLE MISS MUFFIN"

"We chose Della Rae Moore as our St. Louis representative and still believe that she is tops in personality, poise, and ability…Even though she did not win the competition she certainly captured the hearts of those who saw her perform… But we accept WITH RESERVATIONS the opinions of the judges!"

BAKING SCHOOLS

"In America there are many schools that teach the art of commercial baking. However, there is quite a difference in these schools and the subjects in which they specialize. If anyone is interested in attending a baking school this fall, he should consult the officers of our association.

Author's Note: How nice it must have been to have 'many' schools that taught the art of baking at that time. Now, baking and pastry arts schools are very hard to find. There are only a few, and they are usually part of a larger culinary school.

SALES PROMOTION

"Last month a group of bakery women...spent a pleasant evening at
El Char restaurant...sponsored by the Master Bakers Ladies Society...
There was a dramatization of the failure of sales girls to make
extra sales simply by suggesting other products. This was followed
by a uniform show which the women naturally enjoyed!"

Author's Note: Consider the times, but I think some of these comments are definitely funny and reveal some changes in the culture! This entry was followed by the following ad in a high-lighted box.

BAKERS SINGING SOCIETY
ANNUAL PICNIC
SUNDAY, JULY 13, 1958
SHADY ACRES GROVE
DRIVE SOUTH ON ROUTE 61 TO RINGER ROAD.
TURN LEFT.

"THEY'RE HOME!"

"Our representatives are back from their air tour of Europe where they were attending the Bakers Convention in Germany. Emil and Frank forgot all about counting calories when they ate that delicious European bread...Carl carried a letter of greetings from our Mayor Tucker to the Mayor of Munich... read at the huge banquet at the German Bakers Convention in Munich!

CUSTARD PRODUCTS

At one time it was unlawful to make and sell whipped cream and custard products in St. Louis during the summer months. But now effective refrigeration has made that restriction no longer applied.

From August of 1958

JULY OUTING

"One of the most enjoyed outings the association has had in a long
time was at Green Acres last month. The card players and horseshoe
experts were on the job as usual. When inquiring about who was winning
in the card games it seems that everyone was losing! Nick Onofry,
the 'horseshoe professional,' was sliding his ringers in as usual!

Author's Note: Following is a little more of the Bulletin's folksy wisdom thrown
in — sort of like sprinkling sugar into a mixing bowl.

"IF YOU WERE"

"If you were busy being glad,
And cheering people who are sad,
Although your heart might ache a bit,
You'd soon forget to notice it!"

PEANUTS

"In baking, peanuts are most tasty when used <u>on</u> a product
rather than <u>in</u> a product...practically all good bakers prefer
to use other nuts as an inner part of bakery goods.

Author's Note: A good friend of mine, Bob, can confirm the incredible crunch and
taste of putting peanuts and butter smear on top of the classic "peanut rolls" in St.
Louis bakeries at that time!

From September of 1958

MODERN BREAD

"Now in the baking industry we hear from many sources about the excellent
tasting qualities of bread made from unbleached flour...Wholesale bakers'
bread is beautiful to look at. It is silky and white. But may I ask why it must be
silky and white? Whitenesss is no guarantee that it is flavorful. People have

been educated through advertising to look for extremely white bread. They can be taught to buy dark bread provided it has some plus value in taste."

Author's Note: How ironic that my wise old dad, "Old Maurice," grew up in eastern Canada, where the head of the Bakers Co-op had just traveled and experienced bread made from unbleached flour. Old Maurice worked as a young man in a bakery in Toronto and later became a pure foods advocate. He frequently preached about the important improvement in nutritional value of bread made from unbleached flour!

GRATITUDE
"The Master Retail Bakers Association of Greater St. Louis has been very fortunate in having a continuous line...of capable men who came forward over the years to hold office beginning in 1886.

QUOTES

"Get as many runs early in life as you can."
— STAN MUSIAL

"Have as many aspirations, ideals enthusiasms as you can."
— REVEREND NORMAN ZULAUF

"Lucky is the man who has failure early in life."
— ANONYMOUS

"What I am to be, I am now becoming."
— BENJAMIN FRANKLIN

ON PESSIMISM
"If it weren't for the optimist, the pessimist would never know how happy he wasn't!"

A FOLKSY QUOTE
The editor of this Bakery Bulletin wanted to remind us that, "Your PULL is developed by your PUSH!"

Author's Note: This quote is a flashback for me to another take on this folksy thought. To this day I can still remember at my own SLUH high school graduation our principal, Fr. Gerry Sheahan, told a story about a young boy who asked one of his Jesuit teachers, "Father, what does it take to really succeed in life?" The teacher paused and then said, "Tommy, go look at the word that is on the handle of that door over there." The boy went over, looked, and then said, "Oh, I get it, Father, you have to have <u>PUSH</u> in life!" The priest then said, "No, Tommy, look on the other side of the door!" Tommy pushed the door open and looked, and on the handle on the other side of the door it said, <u>PULL</u>!

It would seem that the bakers in St. Louis already knew that it took both PUSH and PULL to have great bakeries. They certainly had the PUSH in the mornings and hard work of long days, but they also had the PULL of their fellow bakers to pull them along and support them in their artistic craft! Notice the camaraderie and fellowship reflected throughout these bulletins as evidence of their close-knit bakery family.

From October of 1958

SWIMMING PARTY

"The afternoon swimming party that our president had at his home in Hampton Park in August was enjoyed by all. Virgil Ziegler in his bathing suit of the 1910 style was the comedy event of the afternoon."

GRANT'S FARM OUTING

"Our annual outing at Grant's Farm was enjoyed by a large number of our members and wives. It seemed that every table with red and white gingham table cloths in the courtyard of the Baurnhof was occupied. Otto Schutz's band entertained us as we sipped Budweiser and visited or played pinochle."

ABC

"Shortly after the Bakery and Confectionery International was suspended by the AFL-CIO, a new national union within the framework of AFL-CIO was organized...known as the American Bakery and Confectionery Workers. The members of the St. Louis local are very fortunate in having its own Retail Welfare Fund controlled by our own local and the retail employers."

THIS 'N' THAT

"Are you all set for that extra Halloween business that will come your way?
Plan for that!"

PATENTS

The U.S. government is now taking out patents for itself. The Department
of Agriculture obtained a patent for a process which would inhibit or delay
the process of things getting stale in yeast-made bakery products.

MISTAKES

"Don't get too provoked if one of your salesgirls fills a telephone order with the
wrong product. The telephone company reports many long distance calls to
Peter Rabbit for 'Cedar Rapids, Iowa' and Pepsi Cola for 'Pensacola, Florida'!

From November of 1958

FALL PEP

"Your customers are full of the zest and pep that these brisk Fall
days bring! This naturally increases one's appetite, and it is not too
difficult for an experienced salesgirl to sell that extra item!"

MORE THAN QUALITY

"Luckily, most of our bakers are fortunate in having a
wife who, through her years of experience in selling, has
acquired a workable knowledge of merchandising!"

From November of 1958

YOUR CAKE SHOW

"Don't forget the CAKE SHOW and DANCE of
our SINGING SOCIETY on Saturday, December 6, at the St. Louis House!"

"You have a CAKE SHOW, a VISUAL ART and a GUSTATORY ART
going on all at the same time, a DANCE going on at the show,
sponsored by none other than the SINGING SOCIETY!"

Author's Note: I felt that the make-up of this EVENT was one of the best examples of the ways St. Louis Bakers have always integrated the arts into everything that they do!

YOUR OPPORTUNITY!

"During the noon hour each weekday, Charlotte Peters, on T.V. Channel 5, features the birthday of some child who receives a free birthday cake. Charlotte Peters always tells the T.V. audience which baker is giving the cake that day. That is splendid advertising for the price of a delivered cake!"

THIS 'N' THAT

"A Prediction: The Annual Cake Show on December 6 will be a complete success."

Author's Note: Another "Cheerleader" Prediction! Could YOU HAVE PREDICTED the Cake Show's "unquestionable success?!"

FRUIT CAKE

Shapleigh Hardware Company is selling fruit cake to its dealers for re-sale to the public...a new twist, but at least it is not cheap, two pounds for 2.90!

BEGIN YOUR GOOD

"God sends the thread for a web begun, the words of an ancient proverb runs. So, whatever you hope to win, create, accomplish, or begin, step out boldly from where you are, beginning the task that you long to do! And, God will help you to see it through!"

WHY FLOUR BAGS ARE MARKED WITH THE LETTER "X"

"The reason why flour bags are marked with the letter 'X' dates back to a logical practice of those who sold it to the California miners. It indicated the price, and each 'X' meant that the bag was filled to exactly the value of 10.00."

TRANSITION

"The heights by great men reached were not attained by sudden flight, but they while their companions slept, were toiling upward into the night!"

Author's Note: Does this short rhyme not describe bakers perfectly? Perhaps not into the night, but rather into the wee hours of the morning?!

QUOTE
"Write it on your heart, that every day is the best day in the year!"
— EMERSON

From December of 1958

MERRY CHRISTMAS
"There is a real satisfaction and pleasure in recalling the happy associations
of old and new friends at this time...We want you to know we value yours
most deeply. And so, our heartiest good wishes to you and yours.
Sincerely, Your Officers

BETTER PRODUCTS
"The responsibility of having thoroughly trained shop managers rests
with the heads of the bakeries. Today there is no scarcity of baking schools,
not even a scarcity of scholarships. There are listed in the yearbooks of
our industry no less than 69 schools that teach baking in some form.

Author's Note: The dramatic change in the availability of training in the bakery and
pastry arts is evident in this important piece of data. From 1958 till the present
there is a vast difference.

THIS 'N' THAT
Annual Banquet, February 14th at Le Chateau
A Christmas Wreath Stöllen is made by filling a ring stöllen with
butter cream and diced fruit. Cut with a scissors, and fold back the
cuts to show the colorful fruit. Ice with pale green fondant.

A BARGAIN
The new 4 cent stamp for a 1 ounce first class letter seems to be quite a bargain
when we compare it with the rate that prevailed in the good-old days. Before
our railroads carried the mail the Pony Express charged five dollars in addition
to the regular postage from New York to the West Coast. William Cody, ('Buffalo
Bill'), a Pony Express rider, on one occasion rode 385 miles on one extended trip.
Even though he was quite a man, he must have been saddle-sore after that trip!

Author's Note: Although this would seem to be a pretty random piece by the Editor, it is also quite a compliment and show of praise in 1958 on the hardiness of our forebears! These past few pages contained only small samplings from the 'Bakery Bulletins' of 1958. Because it was one of the earliest years of bulletins from the collection I intentionally tried to be thorough in my overview of the samplings from 1958.

From January of 1959

PRAISE AND COMPLIMENTS

I would have the same kind of praise and compliments for the Master Bakers who have provided us through the years with so much joy and pleasure through their artistry and hard work.

THIS 'N' THAT

"In the November issue of "Fresh Baked A.R.B.A.," (the periodical from "the American Retail Bakers Association") made the suggestion that retail bakers have a phone answering service from the telephone company during the busy holiday season."

CROISSANTS

"The crescent rolls for which Paris and Vienna compete with each other as a breakfast treat, were first made in Vienna in 1696."

From March of 1959

THE FEBRUARY MEETING

What caused the extra large attendance at the February Meeting? Probably the many bakers wanted to greet Leo Rozanek at his first meeting as President. But, there was also an address by Mr. A.J. Cervantes, a candidate for president for our Board of Alderman. Author's Note: Mr. Cervantes later became the Mayor of St. Louis.

GROUP DYNAMICS
Some things to think about.

"Are donut and other specialized shops the coming thing in the retail baking field? How can we determine the shelf life of cookies, cakes and other specialty items? Does a retail baker lower his prestige by putting his products in a supermarket?"

From July of 1959

CHANGING TIMES
"In 25 years from now, (that would be 1984), many of the large supermarkets will undergo great changes. Some enterprising man will operate a T.V. market…and will take the housewife's order by telephone…and have it all ready to be picked up later. Some may even deliver it to her home! In fact, the housewife will buy most of her meals completely made up and frozen.

CHANGING TIMES
The large kitchen stove will be replaced by small infra-ray ovens… The meals will be scientifically balanced to give us all the food elements we need, which will cause us to grow bigger. Bed-makers will have to make longer beds, and the doorways will have to be made taller… Now, don't let this rambling get you down…These changing times will give the qualified businessmen unlimited opportunities. Prepare yourself. Prepare your *son!*"

Author's Note on the "Changing Times!" "Quite the predictions, and many of them right on target, but I don't think the editor really foresaw the changing times that would include the New Women's Movement, that was arriving even then and forward from 1959! He would soon have to say, "Prepare yourself, and prepare your *daughters!*"

Author's Note: He continues in this same issue with more soon to be outdated comments! He says, "What can we do to interest *young boys* to go to baking schools?" And later, he says, "How can the retail bakery better train *sales ladies*?"

FROM THE PRESIDENT'S DESK

"Stop a minute and think, we are the last of the hand craftsmen, dealing in edible products...we stand as a profession still dependent on talent and creative ability."

ATTENTION ALL BOWLERS

"The bakers' bowling season is about to begin...The fellows really have a ball in more ways than one. Why don't you join in the fun?!

HONOR ROLL

The following companies sell...goods or services to the retail bakers of St.Louis.

Anheuser -Busch Incorporated,
W.E. Beckman Co.,
Bakers Cooperative Association, Cahokia Flour Co.,
Case, Thomas, & Marsh, Hilker & Rletch Co.,
Jaudes Bakers Supply Co., Lange Topping Co.,
Purity Extract Co., Russel Schaumberg,
Shane Uniform Co., Standard Brands, Inc.,
Southern Products Co.

WHAT'S IN A NAME?!

(i.e. the difference between REAL BUTTER and Butter-Flavor)

"Butter to some extent was responsible for my entrance into the baking business. It was my father's suggestion that I became an apprentice, and he impressed upon my mind the importance of butter as the best flavor for quality bakery products, and I have used butter every day in my bakery!

Author's Note: How ironic to yours truly! My own experience while growing up with a German grandmother was extensive! Of course, I learned that, *all things are good in moderation,* but my German grandmother often pushed that limit with her Butter Cookies and Hungarian Butter Horns!

FROM YOUR PRESIDENT'S DESK

With a population of nearly 1½ million, people in St. Louis, and only 160 retail bakeries to serve them, let us discard the theory that we are competing with each other...the only threat of competition then is in our own shops."

Author's Note: "According to an article in September of 2007, by Scott Brandl, Chris Helfer was quoted as saying, 'The number of independent bakeries has dwindled over the years to fewer than 30 independent bakeries in the St. Louis area." Chris Helfer, co-owner of Helfer's Pastries also said, "We used to belong to the St. Louis Retail Bakers Association, but now the association doesn't even exist."At this time there is an informal estimate of about 14 independent bakeries in St. Louis. However, several small ones have been starting up thanks to young owners who have taken a new interest in the baking business.

TRUE VISION

"To progress, your mind must see more than your eyes do. Vision does not always refer to seeing. Deeper vision is a mental process!"

FORTY YEARS OLD

(Information on the History of the St. Louis Bakers Co-operative)

"On September 2, 1919 the first Board of Directors meeting of the St. Louis Bakers Co-operative Association was held at the St. Louis Turner Hall. At a special meeting on September 26, 1919, the new Co-operative Association purchased the Goetzman Brothers Bakers Supply Company, owned by Christian Jaudes. The price, $26,837.21. The new company officially began at 210 Market Street. Sales for the first month were 55,500 dollars. The first stockholders meeting was held on January 5, 1920."

GROUP DYNAMICS

"How can we get our 'sales *girls*' to live up to the name? Are women the answer to the decline of unskilled manpower?"

Author's Note: Today I think that the editor would get some big reactions to these comments!

From December of 1959

SPECIAL MEETING — CHRISTMAS PARTY!
Christmas Party — December 9th — 7:30 p.m.
At the Doerflinger Hall, 5431 Chippewa.
This is Family Night for Our Members!
Christmas Movies — Ernie Hellman, Magician — Santa &
Tree — Gifts for Children — and Refreshments.

From January of 1963

EDITORIAL
"Slow me down, Lord! Ease the pounding of my heart by the quieting of my mind. Steady my hurried pace with a vision of the eternal reach of time. Help me to know the magical restoring power of sleep...Teach me the art of taking minute vacations...Remind me each day of the tortoise and the hare.

KNOW YOUR WAGE SCALE
(A list of current wages and benefits in this issue for a week's cost to the owners.)

1st HAND BENCH
NIGHT WORK — 149.03 PER WEEK 141.81 PER WEEK
DAY WORK — 141.81 PER WEEK 134.61 PER WEEK

From February of 1963

THE ST. LOUIS BAKERS CO-OP ASSOCIATION
1961 REBATES
SUPPLIES — 6.78 %
FLOUR — 1.00 %
MFD. PRODUCTS — 11.50 %
DIVIDEND — 4.00 %

From March of 1963

FROM THE PRESIDENT'S DESK
(George Eipper)

"The Spirit of St. Louis is on the march in March of 1963. The new wonder of the world, the Eero Saarinen Arch and the Mill Creek Valley clearance of slums...form a new hub for our city. From this hub the fast traffic arteries Daniel Boone, Mark Twain, and the Ozark highways step up the tempo of our city...Our association has been a part of St. Louis history from the earliest times, and now in our 79th year we must also catch the beat of this modern tempo of awakening.

PROGRESSIVE WOMEN'S ASSOCIATION
"WOMEN IN BUSINESS ONLY"

The February meeting was held at Miss Hullings Restaurant. Each member brought a product that is popular in *her* bakery.

Author's Note: Notice the growing awareness for the need to change attitudes towards women from earlier bulletins.

From April of 1963

THE MODERN LIVING SHOW

"The Bakers Booth was the most popular in the 1961 show, and it will be again this year. It will be a privilege to have pastries and party products on display before an estimated 80,000 people!"From May of 1963

LITTLE MISS MUFFIN

NATIONAL "LITTLE MISS MUFFIN"

Here we see Gail Gastorf, our National Little Miss Muffin, putting a coin on the Coin-Cake which collected so much money in the lobby of the Chase Park Plaza Hotel. Gail has been active in this coin collecting for the Crippled Children's Fund. This huge cake was decorated by the students of the bakery apprentice training class at O'Fallon Tech High School.

From June of 1963

THREE HAPPY TEEN-AGERS

"Here we see the shy winners of the Jr. Miss Muffin Contest. This contest was held in conjunction with the Modern Living Show at the Kiel Auditorium in April. These teen-agers baked cakes and cookies that were judged to be the best by the committee."

THE **B**AKERS **B**ULLETIN OF GREATER ST. LOUIS

JUNE 1963

MASTER RETAIL BAKERS

THREE HAPPY TEENAGERS
Here we see the shy winners of the Junior Miss Muffin contest. They are, from left to right, Mary Jane Haskell, 2nd prize; Renauta Gray, first prize and named Junior Miss Muffin, and Rosemary McCarthy, third prize.

Don McArthur looks very official as we see him presenting the TWA airplane ticket to the Jr. Miss Muffin at the Retail Bakers Cake Show last month!

From July of 1963

ICINGS

Icings are used for various purposes. As we all know a fondant-type is recommended for rolls, stöllens, etc. The product should be glazed with syrup immediately after baking and should be iced while it is still warm. That will give it that appetizing glassy appearance.

From August of 1963

TAN-TARA RESORT

It is not too early to make plans to attend the Missouri Bakers Association Annual Fall Outing at Tan-Tara Resort. George Buford has ordered us genuine Ozark fall weather.

From August of 1963

NEEDED, GOOD PUBLIC RELATIONS!

Our association needs a program to keep alive the fine reputation it frequently gains by way of intelligent public relations. Let us travel backward in our memories when the arena had its grand opening in September, 1929... when our "Neighborhood Bakers" booth featuring decorated cakes was the most popular. In 1954-55 our president, Rich Sattler, gained much favorable publicity through the Bakers Night at the Ball Park. In 1956 our president, Bud Schwarz, had our members pledge 12,800 dollars to operate an elaborate retail bakery at the Jubilee on the Riverfront. In 1957 Bud developed the T.V. program on the Charlotte Peters Show which brought many new customers into our bakeries. In 1958 our first Little Miss Muffin contest was held. It gained much good will. And then, there was Retail Bakers Week which was started in 1935 and 1936, and then presented each year until 1959. There were many other promotional programs during these years."

From September of 1963

"TIPS"

"Try egg-washing apple pies and sprinkling on a fair amount of cinnamon and sugar before baking. How many bakers go into the salesroom and look at their products from the customer's side of the counter. Try it occasionally.

From October of 1963

PENSION CHECK #1

"The Retail Baker Pension System is now fully in operation. In the photo we can see Walter Schmidt receiving a pension check from

Tom Grace, (an employer representative of the Board of Trustees) as Joe Windisch, secretary of Local #4, happily looks on! Walter Schmidt, a 50 year member of Local #4, was the first baker receiving his retirement check."

From November of 1963

Author's Note: An abundance of folk opinions and sometimes folk wisdoms occurs in some of the bulletins!

DOERS

"Enthusiasm for one's work and a desire to do a good job are the most valuable assets one can have as an employee, an employer, or as anyone engaged in any sort of work. It isn't always the most highly educated or the most thoroughly trained person who does the best job or wins top honors. Enthusiasm to enter one's work with a will to do a good job tops all others."

A LETTER TO TEEN-AGERS

The Police Chief of a small town was asked to address a P.T.A. meeting about "The Teen-Age Problem." He declined the invitation to speak, but he did send the committee this letter instead. In this letter he said, "Always we hear the plaintive cry from teen-agers,

'What can we do? Where can we go?' The answer is — 'Go Home!' Hang the storm windows, paint the woodwork, rake the leaves, mow the lawn, shovel the walk, wash the car. Learn to cook, scrub the floor, repair the sink, build a boat, get a job! Help the minister, priest, or rabbi, the Red Cross, the Salvation Army. Visit the sick, assist the poor, study your lessons. And then, when you are through and not too tired — read a book! Your parents do not owe you entertainment, although most of them try to provide you with some…The world does not owe you a living. On the other hand, you owe the world something. You owe it your time and energy and talents…so that no one will be at war, or in poverty, or sick or lonely again. In plain simple words, GROW-UP! Quit being a cry-baby! Get out of your dream world, and start acting like a man or a woman!"

Author's Note: The editor's connection of this letter to the bakery world followed with these words.

"In thinking about this letter from the Police Chief, we wondered if sometimes many of us in our relations with our association, in what we expect the association to do for us, and in what we do to help the association are pretty much like a lot of the teenagers he's talking about."

From December of 1963

DIRECTIONS FROM A HOUSEWIFE ON COOKIE-BAKING

"Light the oven, get out the bowl, spoons, and ingredients. Grease pans, crack nuts. Remove toys and blocks from the kitchen table. Measure two cups of flour. Remove Johnny's hands from the flour. Wash flour off of him! Answer doorbell. Return to kitchen. Remove Johnny's hands from flour again. Wash Johnny again.
Answer the phone. Dump all of the salt that Johnny put in the greased pans. Wash the pans. Look for Johnny.
Catch up with Johnny who is running away while knocking the mixing bowl off the table.
Wash kitchen floor, wash dishes, wash table, wash stove and wall. Wash Johnny! Call up your baker, and order cookies.
Take a nap with Johnny!"

THE GREATEST CRIME

Author's Note: Though the Editor of the Baker's Bulletins freely offers his obvious conservative opinions he also gives a good amount of balance and fairness as he shows in the following tribute to Samuel Gompers.

"Samuel Gompers was the Grand Old Man of labor unionism who served 42 years as president of the AFL. He was a great man whose ability was recognized by Woodrow Wilson who appointed him to the Peace Conference which met in Paris in 1918 - 1919.
The following is a quotation taken from one of Mr. Gompers speeches:
"Doing for people what they can and ought to do for themselves is a dangerous experiment. In the last analysis, the welfare of the workers depends upon their own initiative.

Whatever is done under the guise of philanthropy for social morality which in any way lessens initiative is the greatest crime that can be committed against the toilers. Let social busy bodies and professional 'public morals experts' in their fads reflect upon the perils they rashly invite under this pretense of social welfare."

From January of 1971

Author's Note: Here is the Editor's Happy New Year <u>wish</u> to all of his readers, but it seems to read more like a prayer than a wish!

HAPPY NEW YEAR!

"MAY YOU ALL have the good sense to take each day as it comes, accepting life's disappointments, and relishing life's better moments.

MAY YOU ALL find a smile or two to give away and a thoughtfulness to bestow on a fellow human being.

MAY YOU ALL remember that GOD IS NOT DEAD, but only in the hearts of some men, and look to Him for direction and understanding.

MAY YOU ALL remember that we are all in need of a kind word and a helping hand. We need one another.

MAY YOU ALL remember to look about at God's creation and never take it for granted.

MAY YOU ALL have the strength to carry on in times of adversity.

MAY YOU ALL have GOD'S BLESSINGS AND LOVING CARE IN 1971."

Signed: YOUR EDITOR and STAFF

WHAT IS YOUNG?

"What is young, and when is it?

Young is an attitude, a spirit. A way of looking at things, of responding to them.It is not an age. Not a hairstyle or a piece of clothing or a musical beat. Young can be a child seeing his first rose or Verdi at age 81 composing his first opera. Young can be a teen-ager swimming on a surf board or Einstein, in his 70's still working on his unified field theory, sailing his boat, or playing his beloved fiddle. Young is not a monopoly of youth. It flourishes everywhere, the vision has been kept fresh, the muscles of the mind firmly toned, the juices freely flowing. Let's not cater to youth for its own sake, for its slogans and styles of the moment. Nor scorn it for any of those reasons. Instead, let's respect 'young,' wherever it may be found, and whether the beard is soft and curly or stiff and gray. Spirit has no color. It is always translucent, with its own imaginative sheen. Youth should be listened to. But young should be followed.

THERE IS NO GENERATION GAP
BETWEEN THE YOUNG OF ANY AGE!
— Leo Burnett Company, Advertising

From February of 1971

Author's Note: The following item I must admit even surprised me that it was entered into the Bakers Bulletins! On the cover was a direction that said, "See Page 3 — Cissy Colpitts." So, I did that, and there I found a glamour-shot picture of Cissy with her measurements and below it another direction to "See Page 6."

   Much to my surprise, there was a full body photo of Cissy in a bikini! I immediately thought, "What is happening to the Bakers Bulletins?!"

The editor tells the story behind the picture.

CISSY COLPITTS — 38-24-34

(See page 6)

"Our cover girl, "Little Miss Muffin" from 1995. Marie Onofry said, "She watched Cissy grow up, and who would have thought little Cissy would have grown up to look like this?!" The picture was discovered by two movie producers, who brought Cissy to Hollywood. This past summer she was offered a contract by 20th Century Fox. She turned them down…She has recently taken a college major in film production, and she hopes to return to Hollywood… and find out if Hollywood has a place for a girl with her talents. We hope so, Cissy…Best of luck from all of the bakers…We are proud to have once been a part of your career, from "Little Miss Muffin" to Hollywood film maker.

From May of 1971

FROM THE PRESIDENT'S DESK

"I'm sure some of you have young people working for you…and sometimes it seems like an impossible task to train them. But, we seem to forget how our bosses felt about us when we had our first jobs. What I'm trying to say is this. "Are the youth of today different from the youth of yesterday? I guess everyone remembers what they did right but somehow forgets what they did wrong." from Your President, Paul Bretscher

From July of 1971

PROGRESSIVE BAKERS LADIES NEWS

"The Baker Ladies met at Perkins Restaurant…Shirley Bretscher and Kate Bolata brought the bakery items on display. Helen Lubeley won the free lunch…The nominating committee…to get new officers for the coming year are Mrs. McArthur, Mrs. Lubeley, and Mrs. Heimburger

SPECIAL NOTE

Author's Note: For anyone interested in a detailed history of the turning points of change for the baking industry in the mid-70's. I would direct you to the Bakers Bulletins from October, 1972 – June, 1973. In each of these nine bulletins. Leo Rozanek gives a lengthy summary and assessment of these changes and the state of the industry. He addresses everything from the volatile issue of raising the minimum wage to the controversial five point revolutionary changes to the Baker's Co-op in the February, 1973 issue of the Bakers Bulletins.

CHANGES TO THE BAKERS CO-OP

Author's Note: As a sampling from these nine lengthy letters from Leo Rozanek and because of their importance, the five points of change to the Bakers Co-op are summarized here. These proposals were made by the new president of the BAKERS ASSOCIATION, Bill Federhofer, and listed in the 5th Letter of the nine Letters titled "THE ASSOCIATION" by Leo Rozanek.

"FIRST. Facilities and financial assets of the CO-OP should be made available for an immediate establishment of an apprentice training school...

SECOND. There should be the establishment of a dynamic public relations and advertising program with professional management.

THIRD. There should be the establishment of a uniform bookkeeping and cost control program for all retail bakers, wholly managed and operated within the framework of the Co-Op's office facility.

FOURTH. There should be the establishment of a finance corporation for the purpose of granting loans and credit to young aspiring bakery operators, and also serve as a strike fund...Opportunity for investment shall be granted to retired members as well as allied members...

FIFTH. Last but not least, I propose the creation of an executive vice president office with full pay. His duty and responsibility shall be the supervision of these programs and simultaneously serve as business manager of the association...In theory — it all sounded ideal. For here was an opportunity to put the true meaning of a Co-Op in its full perspective.

Our new president's unquestionably sincere concern over the welfare of our industry certainly presented an exciting era. Suddenly, I had become involved!"

— Leo Rozanek

From January of 1981

MASTER RETAIL BAKERS CHRISTMAS PARTY

Well, our entertainment committee has done it again with one of our outstanding Christmas parties...It was held in the St. Louis Bar Association quarters on the 36th floor of the Mercantile Tower Building...Dance music was provided by Russ David's combo, and in between dances the accordionist and Imogene McArthur provided a sing-along with many Christmas carols!

From February of 1981

FROM THE PRESIDENT

"Well, I hope everyone enjoyed our annual banquet last Saturday...Three new officers were installed,... Randy McArthur, Larry Hofstetter, and Ray Blasé...I'm sure everyone is aware of the upcoming Miss Cheesecake Contest. We will have a group of thirty lovelies who will be making their debut, and Russ David will be there to emcee the program.

From May of 1981

THE AGE GAME

"I find it most engaging
To watch friends who are aging.
Some handle problems neatly
With subtle skill discreetly,

While others groan, and rant and rave,

And generally misbehave.

It makes me think as years go by,

I'm going to keep a watchful eye

On attitudes, which say far more

About you than your yearly score."

Corinne Geeting, Carmichael, California

From June of 1981

THE OLDEST COMPANY IN TOWN

Author's Note: Surprise, surprise! It was a bakery! News Article with PICTURE 1981 Bulletin. Below picture is a summary of the Article.

The Oldest Company In Town

"We're the oldest firm in St. Louis."

This is the proud boast of Fred Teutenberg IV, president of Teutenberg's Bakery and Restaurant and great-grandson of the firm's founder.

The first Teutenberg bakery, located at Second and Walnut Streets on a site now occupied by the south leg of the Gateway Arch, was opened in 1812 by Franz Teutenberg, an immigrant from Germany. In

1921 MODEL: Teutenberg boasted fast delivery.

"We're the oldest firm in St. Louis." This was the proud boast
of Fred Teutenberg IV, president of Teutenberg's Bakery and
Restaurant and great grandson of the founder.

The first Teutenberg Bakery, located at Second and Walnut Streets on a site now occupied by the south leg of the Gateway Arch, was opened in 1812 by Franz Teutenberg, an immigrant from Germany. In the ensuing 166 years five generations of the Teutenberg family have continued and expanded the business."

From September of 1981

CARONDELET HISTORICAL SOCIETY TO 'MARK' BAKERY BUILDING AND CHURCH

"The Carondelet Historical Society will place Historical Markers on two structures in Carondelet this Sunday, May 31st at 1:30 p.m....Marker 11 will be placed on Doerings Bakery, at 7726 Virginia Avenue, now the historic Carondelet Bakery.

From October of 1981

HAAS AND COMPANY

Author's Note: This is an exceptional article on an important historic company in St. Louis, summarized here!

HAAS BAKERY NEWS ARTICLE

"Joseph Haas Jr. remembers the days when South St. Louis seemed a city unto itself. He remembers when his father, a newly-settled immigrant from Vienna, would toil through the night baking...Since that humble one-night beginning at 7th and Hickory Streets in 1924, Haas Baking Company has grown into a firm with over 200 employees. Through all its growth, Haas is still a family enterprise. It is now, in 1981, the only independently-owned wholesale baking operation in the state of Missouri. In 1951 the younger Haas took over the business completely.

The company operated with one truck until 1959...the company later moved again to a four acre site on Reavis Park Drive in South St. Louis County...and expanded its routes to cover a three hundred mile radius.

Joe Haas remembers that during his childhood there was a retail bakery every three or four blocks. But, in the early 1960's the growth of supermarkets shook the industry. Many well-known bakeries couldn't stay competitive and eventually closed or sold out.

LADY DONNA CAKE

"Fairview Heights, Illinois Baker Charles Beyersdorfer, Jr. created his greatest masterpiece on the occasion of his daughter Donna's wedding. Beyersdorfer assembled the finished product standing nine feet tall and weighing more than four hundred pounds. Approximately 40 small layer cakes were used...The bride had to use a step ladder to cut the top layer for the traditional photographs!"

SMILE AWHILE
A Cake Joke

"Finding a piece of cake missing from the table a mother said to her son, 'Jimmy, there were two pieces of cake on the table last night when we went to bed, and this morning there is only one. How do you explain that?!'

'I don't know, Mom,' replied the boy, 'I guess it was so dark that I just didn't see the other piece sitting there '!"

From November of 1981

PRESIDENT'S MESSAGE from BILL TARVER

"Fall colors...signal the waning days of my term as President...There is one person...that I would really like to thank...who gave me my first job...it was in a Jewish bakery, working seven days a week, and you were finished when everything was finished...We made excellent bread and rolls, but terrible sweet goods, they were awful. I had a hard time being accepted there because I was not Jewish...after I had been there for a few years customers thought I was the boss's son, and I never told them anything different. That made things a lot easier...

In the thirteen years I was there I learned some very important lessons. One lesson I learned was...you can be the best baker in town and go broke if you can't run your business. The man I'd like to thank is Jack Lickhalter. Today he is retired enjoying the fruits of his labors.

From December of 1981

"IF I DON'T GO, I DON'T GET"

"In a remote area there was a man with a rowboat who would ferry passengers across a river for ten cents. When asked, 'How many times each day do you do this?' He said, 'As many times as I can because the more I go, the more I get. And, if I don't go, I don't get'." That's all you need to know — that's all there is to know — about business, economics, prosperity, and self-respect."

From December of 1982

DELLA RAE — MISS MUFFIN of 1957

"Born again Country Singer, Della Rae, one of the featured performers at the Chase-Park Plaza Hotel on New Year's Eve, is on top of the music world. She has had top bookings throughout the nation including gigs with Ronnie Milsap, Ray Stevens, and Mickey Gilley...She has recorded on the RCA Victor label. She and her husband now live with their two children in Affton, Missouri.

Della Rae

From January of 1991

ONWARD

"After seven years and four names — albeit just one owner — it'll be Auld Lang Syne after the holidays for the Federhofer restaurant on Chippewa Street at the River Des Peres. Bill Federhofer Jr., the famed bakery heir, will turn in his apron and one hundred hour work weeks to give his attention to food wholesaling.

ABLE BAKERS AND INDEPENDENT BAKERIES, STRUGGLE HERE

Author's Note: An important news article with significant historical information, by Jerry Stroud of the St. Louis Post-Dispatch.

"For the last 30 years, Walter Binder has stood in front of the oven at Lake Forest Pastry Shop, checking each stöllen, each cake, and each pan of cookies as it goes into the oven…But, Binder is also a member of an increasingly rare breed, a master baker who can look at a cake and tell what it needs.

St. Louis once had hundreds of bakeries, most of them family businesses with the father as the head baker…But, as of now, the number of full-line independent bakeries has shrunk drastically in the last twenty years. Bakers blame a variety of factors, including the growth of supermarkets, superhighways that speed customers past their doors, Sunday hours at most grocery stores, and even fast-food restaurants that serve breakfast.

Ed Federhofer, general manager of the St. Louis Bakers Co-Operative, said the Co-Operative had about one hundred fifty active bakers in 1968…Within a decade, the number of members who still operated their own bakeries had plummeted to fifty.

Bob Lubeley and his sister, Helen Murray, took over Lubeleys Bakery from their father in the mid-70's. At 37 Lubeley is one of the youngest bakers in the St. Louis area. Eight years ago Lubeleys moved. "It was rough at first," Lubeley said. But, he now believes the business is established at the new location, at 7815 Watson Road in Shrewsbury. Lubeley's more spectacular cakes have included a replica of Bagnell Dam, a huge Coca-Cola can for Six Flags, and a Boa Constrictor for St. Louis Zoo director, Charles Hoessle.

"Many people think of trips to a bakery as a luxury," said Lubeley's sister, Helen Murray. "But few supermarkets or wholesale bakers can match a family-owned shop in the quality and variety of baked goods or in personal service!"

BEST DOUGHNUTS

Author's Note: More Bakery Humor. There's much misinformation about dough-nuts. Doughnuts are the second largest member of the nut family, behind coconuts! Now then, back to our poll results: Dunkin' Donuts submerged Mister Donut by a margin of nearly four to one, while World's Fair Donuts rolled up from last year's fifth-place finish into the third place spot.

Here are the rankings from 1-10.

1. Dunkin' Donuts
2. Mister Donut
3. World's Fair Donuts
4. Donut Drive-In
5. California Do-Nut
6. Winchell's
7. Donut Hole
8. Lake Forest Pastry
9. Schnuck's
10. Danny Donut

A BAKER'S DOZEN

During the Middle Ages, bakers suffered severe penalties if they were caught selling loaves of bread that were below the legal weight. To avoid prosecution for any unintentional sale below this standard, bakers added a free loaf to every 12. So, a baker's dozen is really 13.From April / May of 1991

From February, 1992

BAKERY TRIVIA (From the Retail Bakers of America.)
What city displays the world's oldest cake and how old is it?

A food museum in Vevey, Switzerland displays the "vacuum packed" cake from the ancient Egyptian grave of Pepionkh. The cake is 4,000 years old. (Guiness Book) What was the largest pie ever baked in the U.S.?! There was a forty foot in diameter pecan pie, weighing 40,266 pounds that was baked in Oklahoma in 1989. (Guiness Book)

BAKERY TRIVIA continued

What dance, popular in the 19th century, was named for a bakery product?

"The Cake Walk," which was characterized by a high, strutting step with a backward tilted body position. A cake was awarded to the winner with the most intricate steps. (Academic American Encyclopedia)

MORE BAKERY TRIVIA

Name the top two record holders for donut consumption and their record-setting times.

James Wirth consumed 12 ¾ donuts in 5 minutes and 46 seconds, and John Haight downed 13 donuts in 6 minutes and 1.5 seconds, respectively in Canandaigua, NY, on March 3, 1981. (Guiness Book)

What was the length of the longest continuous loaf of bread?

It was 2,356 feet and 10 inches baked in 1987. About 200 people worked for 12 hours to prepare the bread. Baking took 90 minutes. (Guiness Book)

When was the first bakery established in America?

The first bakery opened in America in 1640. (American Bakers Association)

Name the state that celebrated its 150th birthday with a cake large enough to feed 300,000 people.

Bakers spread 30,000 pounds of vanilla icing over 20,000 layers of cake to produce the world's largest cake, weighing in at 90,000 pounds. In 1986 bakers in Austin, Texas mixed 31,026 boxes of cake mix. (Guiness Book)

Name 3 surnames that can be traced back to baking in Great Britain and France?

Foumier meaning baker in old French, who were specialists in pies and pastries. Flanns and Flawns, ancestors of the Flanners, who were specialists in baking flans or flawns. And, Baxter is derived from an old English term for a female baker. Eventually, the feminine term became "bakester" and then "baxter," a general term for bakers of both genders. (Bakers Journal, November, 1990.) Name the two U.S. cities where consumers spend the most on bakery goods. Buffalo, NY, and Portland, OR. (The food Institute, August, 1991)

STOPPING BY THE BAKERY ON A SNOWY EVENING
(With Apologies to Robert Frost!)

Whose cakes these are, I think I know.
His condo's in the city.
Though, he will not see me stop to stare
At every croissant and éclair.

My running shoes must think it queer
To pause with all these pastries here.
My diet's barely started — still,
I feel a weakening of my will.

The cashier says, "What would you like?"
Forgive me, exercising bike!
"Cream puffs, I think, just box up twenty.
Wait — one donut hole is plenty."

Whipped cream's luscious, white and deep.
But, I have diet vows to keep.
And, miles to jog before I sleep.
And, miles to jog before I sleep.

"911 BRINGS AID TO GINGERBREAD MAN"

A 4 year old boy in "Boyetta, Ohio alerted 911 when he recognized an emergency — his mom over-cooked the gingerbread man. In the 911 recording, the boy says, "Mom, it's the firemen, I told them it was an emergency."...The burned gingerbread man and five other cookies were taken to the 911 call center. "We just want to keep them for sentimental value," said the dispatcher, Roger Laird!

IT'S AS ST. LOUIS AS PEANUT BUTTER AND SLICED BREAD
(by Suman Bandrapalli of the Christian Science Monitor)

"We all know that ice cream cones were invented at the St. Louis 1904 World's Fair. But, here's a little more St. Louis Food Trivia. It was a St. Louis baker who improved on R.F. Rohwedder's mechanical bread slicer...In November 1928, a St. Louis baker named Gustav Papendia put the sliced loaves in cardboard trays to support them. In less than a year the bread industry was revolutionized."

From February of 1999

HOT CROSS BUNS

"What are Hot Cross Buns? Hot Cross Buns have a strong tradition as a Lenten sales item among Christian faiths...Hot Cross Buns are already being sold regionally throughout North America with success. Today's buns are a yeast-raised item, best made from a bun dough or a coffee cake dough. They contain raisins and diced fruit or a dried fruit mix...Spices such as nutmeg, cloves, cinnamon, and all spice may be used...Once baked, the buns are washed with a warm simple syrup. Roll icing or a fondant glaze is used to form the 'cross' or 'x' on the top of the bun once they have cooled."

From May of 1999

CAKES ACROSS AMERICA INC.
Uniting the Independent Bakers

"Cakes Across America, a membership organization uniting the independent bakers of America, has introduced a new 'gift of choice for all occasions' — a freshly baked, decorated cake, personally delivered by the local baker.

As a member baker, each independent baker has an exclusive territory in their locale. Any order received by Cakes Across America for delivery in this area must be placed with the member baker for baking and delivery. This is why the program is so unique — each cake is custom made-to-order. Orders are received from around the world for delivery anywhere in America via CAA's 800 service and through the internet.

Author's Note: From reading a good sampling of current reviews of Cakes Across America the service seems to still be in business, but the reviews over the years are very mixed. Some of the reviews reflect general satisfaction, but some of the reviews were pretty negative.

CAKES ACROSS AMERICA INC. continued

Specifically, the complaints were frequently about delayed payments for the cakes to the local baker. When trying to bring up the original website, cakesacrossamerica.com the search redirected to corporatecakes.com, and this website seems to mimic the service originally provided, but the location of the business did not seem to be available.

AMERICAN INSTITUTE OF BAKING —
MANHATTAN, KANSAS

Author's Note: In this issue of the Baker's Bulletins, there are listed course offerings from the American Institute of Baking — for "Resident Courses" and for "Baking and Food Production Courses" that are also part of the "Certified Baker Programs." For awhile a "Museum of Baking" was located at Manhattan, Kansas. The museum's holdings have been moved in recent years to the Grain Sciences Department at Kansas State University.

From July / and August of 1999

BAKE-MARK TAKES OVER ST. LOUIS BAKER'S CO-OP

"The St. Louis Bakers Co-Op has been owned and run by the Retail Bakers of the St. Louis area since 1886. It has been a thriving company for 113 years. This year we had an offer from the Bake-Mark Company out of the Netherlands. A few years ago they bought out Cahokia Flour Co., another St. Louis Supplier of bakery items. To all you customers of the St. Louis Bakers Co-Op, the Bake-Mark Company will continue to give you the same service and helpfulness as the Co-Op has done in all these years.

"ROLLING IN THE DOUGH"
From the Business Journal

By Cynthia Vespereny

"Sweet Encounters," a boutique bakery specializing in tiered cakes, just landed its biggest order ever. The bakery will create 350 individual wedding cakes. Each of the tiny two-tiered cakes will be different, each costing on average of $30.00 apiece for a total of $10,500.00.

Local bakeries say customers increasingly ask for expensive custom designs. <u>Modern Baking</u> recently found in a recent survey that median annual sales of full-line retail bakeries have climbed nearly 16 per cent in the past two years. Cakes alone sold by such bakeries now generate nearly one-third of sales on average.

McArthur's Bakery on Lemay Ferry Road expects 2.25 million dollars in sales this year (I assume that would be in 1999), "and 72 per cent of it was from decorated cakes," said owner, Randy McArthur, whose father began specializing in them in the 1960's. "There's more frequency where the cakes come up to $1,100. to $1,200," said Rick Torplay, the general manager of McArthur's.

McArthur said that their business has grown between 5 and 12 percent over the past decade, resulting in several moves to larger facilities. He finally bought a shopping plaza for 1.25 million dollars and moved the bakery there last summer, renaming the nine-store strip McArthur's Bakery Plaza. In the busy spring and summer months the bakery turns out more than 1,000 party cakes and 70 wedding cakes a week!"

DECORATOR TAKES THE CAKE FOR
BEING A SKILLED ARTIST

An Article, (condensed), From "St. Louisans At Work"
from <u>The Business Journal</u>

Name: Debbie Rhyne

Employer: Bob and Annette Garrett,
Lake Forest Pastry Shop

<u>Job</u>: Cake Decorator

<u>Duties</u>: Rhyne's basic task is to brighten up plain cakes by writing out greetings in icing for all kinds of occasions. She works freehand...She doesn't use a mold or template. "I write better on a cake than I do in real life," she said. She works very quickly...For a 10-inch round white cake one morning last week she laid down the strip of icing along the base in 14 seconds. In another 12 seconds, the top strip around the edge was done. The greeting...went on next...Then, she added 4 roses and 5 buds of icing, green leaves and stems. Elapsed time: 2 minutes, 21 and 35/100's seconds!

DECORATOR TAKES THE CAKE FOR BEING
A SKILLED ARTIST continued

Directly behind her is a collection of about 900 pictures of just about every image that's ever appeared on a cake in the United States in the 20th century. When customers request a picture, Rhyne uses a light projector called a "copy cake" that allows her to trace the outline of the image on the icing. Then she can fill it in with colored icing. In an average week Rhyne embellishes about 200 cakes of all sizes — about 40 a day. When demand is heavy during graduation season or before Mother's Day, she'll decorate 400 cakes in a week!

Most Famous Name On A Cake She Decorated.:
"It was for Chuck Berry, for his 50th wedding anniversary,"
Rhyne said. "When I did it, I didn't think about who it was,"
It said, 'Happy Anniversary, Charles and Themetta.'"

Experience: Rhyne started designing cake decorations for her son John when he was young. She realized she had a knack for the art and needed the income, so she began working in the National Supermarket's bakery center in 1990. After 2 1/2 years, she quit. Then she saw an ad for a decorator at Lake Forest. The owner then, Walter Binder, invited her in and had her decorate a cake. When he saw the deftness with which her hands moved, he hired her on the spot. She is the senior of two decorators.

What She Likes Best About Her Job:
She said that it was her freedom to create designs as she wants.
"I might get a wild hair and try something different,"

What She Likes Least About Her Job:
Getting up at 4:30 a.m., so she can leave her Metro East
home at 5:45 and arrive at Lake Forest by 6:30.

Conclusion To The "Samplings" from The Bakers Bulletins

It has been a nostalgic and sometimes sentimental journey for me with the "Bakers Bulletins" as my companion. Many of the pages made me remember some of the things that I loved about St. Louis and everyday America in those times. There seemed to be a mix in those days of sweetness and simplicity that I found in the pages of the bulletins.

There were times when I felt like I was on a quest to see if all of the things I *thought* were true about the noble profession of baking were actually present in the realities — that the bakers were a character profile set apart, that their motivations were as altruistic as I thought they were, and that their care for one another was unique in how they lived a communal life with one another.

I believe that they created for themselves a *"family of families!"* It was this ineffable quality that gave me the greatest admiration for them. I found them to be inspiring and hopeful as I looked through a window and saw a world of work, artistry, and loving service. As I shared the history of their baker forebears, with many of the current bakers that I interviewed there were always stories that reflected a caring work ethic, a refreshing energy of creativity, and an authentic love that saw their work as personal gifts that they gave to their customers.

It is my hope that the readers of these "Stories and Wisdoms" will be able to pursue many more of the archived pages of these bulletins. I also hope that you can eventually find these stories later in links and posts that will occur on the Bakery Book Project website called "How Our Hearts Were Stöllen."

PART 3

The In-Person Interviews With Twenty-Five St. Louis Bakers

An Acknowledgement

I would like to make a sincere apology to any and all of the St. Louis bakeries that were not included in the In-Person Interviews of this book. There were several reasons why this was the situation. In some cases there was no one who could be found who could give the history of a particular bakery. In other situations there was no one who was available to tell the story. And, for many wonderful bakeries there was just not enough space to include all of the bakeries that I would have wanted to include.

It is my hope in the future to include these bakeries in my pursuit of further research and the possibility of inclusion on a website on-line.

One thought about reading the Interview section of this book: Even though I was able to meet the interviewed bakers in person and one-at-a-time, I hope you can find these interviews as fascinating as I did! I would encourage you to read a few of them at a time rather than straight through. I would urge you to browse through them as you would on a relaxing walk!

Table of Contents
For the In-Person Interviews

- BRIDGE BREAD BAKERY
- CARONDELET BAKERY
- DIANA'S MEXICAN BAKERY
- EHNES PASTRY SHOP
- ELLERBROCK BAKERIES
- FEDERHOFER BAKERY
- HANK'S CHEESECAKES
- HAUSEL'S BAKERY
- HAUSER BAKERY
- HELFER'S PASTRIES AND DELI CAFE
- JAUDES BAKERS SUPPLY
- KNODEL'S BAKERY
- KRUTA'S BAKERY
- LAUGHING BEAR BAKERY
- LUBELEY'S BAKERY
- MARKLIN'S BAKERY
- MCARTHUR'S BAKERY
- NATHANIEL REID BAKERY
- PFEIFER'S PARTY PASTRIES
- SCHMIEMEIR BAKERY
- THE BLUE OWL BAKERY
- THE SWEET DIVINE
- WEDDING WONDERLAND
- WHISK: A SUSTAINABLE BAKESHOP
- WOLF'S BAKERY (WITH CONNIE WOLF)
- WOLF'S BAKERY (WITH RON and NOEL LADD)

Bridge Bread Bakery
Interview With Fred Domke

One night I had a dream that I was back at the homeless shelter and that I was making bread with the folks in the dining room. When I woke up in the morning I basically got up and said, "Thank you, Lord, I've got my instructions!"
— Fred Domke

RICH: Are you from St. Louis?

FRED: I am.

RICH: This Bakery Book Project I won't say is a "serious" project, but it's a very energetic and legitimate project.

RICH: You'll be my nineteenth in-person interview for the book, and I've been doing this for about seven years now. I've also done a lot of research on what you may not know much about, the St. Louis Master Bakers Association. The St. Louis Bakers Association was an amazing institution that held all of the bakers together with a glue of community and fellowship. They were very supportive of one another. It's a beautiful story! So, that will be in the book also. Of course, there's several other things that I still want to do, but pulling it all together is a daunting task. Sometimes I say it's like riding an octopus! But, I think that's enough about me. I know that

Mary Mother of the Church is one of your clients down in South County. That's how I heard about Bridge Bread.

FRED: Yes, baking for me did not start until Bridge Bread started.

RICH: So, there's a question that I'm sure you've been asked before, but I'd like to hear your answer myself. "What caused you, what motivated you, to start the Bridge Bread bakery?"

FRED: O.K., it was started pretty much as an action motivated by faith and then living out what I believed was my Christian faith. I had done some volunteering at a homeless shelter and wanted to do more than making people who were experiencing homelessness comfortable. Instead, I wanted to make them to be *not* homeless anymore. And, it was my belief that the best way to do that was to find a way to keep them employed. So, I had some familiarity, much less than I do now, with the population experiencing homelessness. And so, I thought about the question, "What kind of a business could you start that could employ just about anybody who is experiencing homelessness?"

FRED: So, that was a hard question! And, I know that my wife and I muddled about that for quite awhile. We made a couple of false starts with things like firewood bundles and gift baskets. And then, my wife went away for a week-end. So, I was the cook at my house, and I had never made bread, and I decided to make bread just to entertain myself. I made two small loaves of plain white bread, but they didn't turn out very well,. I often make a joke about myself and say that, "they were crummy." And, that's what I ate for dinner.

FRED: So, that night I had a dream that I was back at the shelter and that I was making bread with the folks in the dining room. When I woke up in the morning I basically got up and said, "Thank you, Lord, I've got my instructions!" So, I guess I started the bakery because I felt like I was called to do so!

RICH: Wow, what a great description of your experience.

FRED: We started one week later with no facilities and very little money and no permissions. We were using the kitchen at the shelter without permission of the shelter, with no license and no permits. We sold originally through my church, and then as time went on through other churches that also supported the shelter. And, that's how we got launched. In three months we had enough business from the churches who supported the shelter that we went to the shelter and said, "You know, we've been doing this in your kitchen anyway, so how about we make it official." And they did.

FRED: So, they made it into a program of the shelter, and that lasted for several years. Then, we went through a somewhat challenging "divorce" and became separate from them. They were eager to be separate from us, and we were eager to be separate from them. They have since gone out of business, and we have not. We have been independent for three or four years now.

FRED: Unlike many of your other bakeries, the fact that it was a bakery was not a goal. The goal was to have a social enterprise that could employ people experiencing homelessness, and the bakery came to me in a dream.

RICH: Yeah, yeah fantastic! I love it! That's a really neat story. Did you have any transition? I think you said you eventually took over the Black Bear Bakery's building.

FRED: Yes, in the fall of 2017.

RICH: Was there any transition from that, or was it just basically a business purchase?

FRED: They had actually gone out of business as a successful enterprise about a year and a half earlier. There had been a catering business run by one of their main people, but it had tapered off after he had a bad motorcycle accident. And then, there was someone who was making crackers, making gourmet crackers and selling them and using the facility, but that also had wound down. I have maintained a friendly relationship with one of the primary principals, Bobby Sweet, who was I think a founding member of the bakery.

FRED: Again, what I know of the Black Bear bakery is that it was essentially a social enterprise itself, but it was operated by a Missouri chartered collective, or you might call it a commune. And, this particular commune was called "the city of little bread." They believed that you should have a bakery where instead of having lots and lots of rules and structure, when people have disagreements you sit down and have a cup of tea and work it out. And, their efforts of trying to be in harmony with one another was a beautiful thing. They were able to operate for several decades in this and one other location. They had a previous store on Jefferson. They were able to operate here for about fifteen years at this location.

RICH: Yeah, sure.

FRED: They bought it, and resold it to us with a quick hundred thousand dollar profit for them. But, it was still a pretty good price for it.

RICH: Good.

FRED: We had removed most of the equipment in the kitchen, and either the prior owners took those things with them or sold them. In some cases I think they were junked.

RICH: I see.

FRED: We kept one piece of equipment from the Black Bear bakery. Probably one of the most salvaged pieces we have here, is the Middleby-Marshall rotating shelf oven, which is older than I am. I am seventy, and it's seventy-two, and, we use it every day! It's large. It's about the size of a Volkswagen bus, maybe even a little bigger, a little bit bigger round than a Volkswagen van. It has six shelves, each of which can hold three full-sized sheet pans. So, you can have eighteen sheet pans in the oven at a time, which means you can do about two hundred loaves of bread in about twenty minutes!

RICH: Two hundred loaves in twenty minutes?! Wow!

FRED: I can't sell two hundred loaves in twenty minutes!

RICH: [I break out laughing in amazement.] You know, I have a picture in my mind of having seen one of those somewhere.

FRED: They're very popular all over the world, and they're kind of like old Rolls-Royces! When they get old, people don't throw them away. They rebuild them and keep using them.

RICH: Wow, huh! They're good to maintain, right!

FRED: During the baking one of the things that's particularly cool about a Middleby-Marshall oven is that the combustion chamber is the baking chamber. So, the bread is baked over an open flame. The advantage of that is the combustion process. I'm sure you know, that when you burn natural gas it creates carbon dioxide and water vapor, actually creating a little bit of steam in the oven by having it be an open combustion chamber. And, that's good for the bread.

RICH: Yeah, I would think so! I see. The moisture content changes, right?!

FRED: Right!

RICH: I have loved doing this project because I learn so much! I'd love to share more of what I've learned with you! Also, there are amazing things around the country that are part of bakery history!

FRED: Just so that I don't forget, one thing that has become important to Bridge Bread over the course of the last four years is this. We used to have our bakery on South Grand Avenue, at Grand and Bates, and right around the corner lived a guy named Scott Wise. Scott Wise is a food scientist who works in the test kitchen and innovation center at A.B. Mauri in the Cortex Center of St. Louis. A.B. Mauri is the parent company of Fleischmann's Yeast and many other baking ingredient companies. Scott Wise introduced us to the management of A.B. Maury, North America, which is here in St. Louis. We've had a relationship with them, which has benefitted us with access to food scientists and their expertise!

RICH: Wow! Can you tell me the highlights of what you just said.

FRED: The company's name is A.B. Mauri, M-A-U-R-I. They're headquartered in the U.K. They're an international company, and their North American headquarters is here in Cortex.

RICH: Where is Cortex? And, what is Cortex?

FRED: Cortex is in the central west end, just north of highway sixty-four / forty near the Ikea store. Cortex is the city of St. Louis's innovation community. It is trying to foster innovation. It has many small companies, but it also has larger organizations like the research arm of Washington University.

FRED: Several large companies have their research centers there. Microsoft has a big research center there. As a matter of fact, their office rates there are higher than the ones in Clayton, and their vacancy rate is lower. It's a very booming district in the St. Louis area!

RICH: O.K., this is something I never knew anything about! [I laugh at myself!]

FRED: It used to be a pretty seedy warehouse neighborhood, and there are a few of those buildings that are left, but mostly they've been completely replaced by some very nice and shiny brand new buildings.

RICH: Yeah, and what would you say is the intersection that's closest to that?

FRED: It's just north of the intersection of I-64 and Boyle. It goes in-between I-64 and Forest Park, and it goes in-between Vandeventer and runs right up to the Washington University Med School campus on the west. So, it's sorta' nestled right between St. Louis University and Washington University Med School.

RICH: I see, O.K. That's really big, isn't it! [Laughing.]

FRED: It's a really important thing for the city of St. Louis. We also have the innovation center up north on Olive, north of where the old Monsanto was, now called Bayer. A German company bought this. That's the "plant science" area. So, that's also a high-tech, high innovation district!

RICH: Right. And, where is that?

FRED: That is on Olive and Warson. It's in Olivette and Creve Coeur, I think.

RICH: O.K. I know the area.

FRED: It has the north "plant science" center and things like that — it's called the "Plant Science Innovation Center," something like that.

RICH: I imagine the Missouri Botanical Garden has something to do with that, right!

FRED: True. They have some offices there. You bet.

RICH: Yeah, we were just at the Garden on Friday. It's awesome at this time of year. Yeah, we're really lucky in St. Louis. There are some very enlightened kinds of endeavors here now. Should I assume that your wife was kind of involved in the beginnings of the bakery, or no?

FRED: Before we started "Bridge Bread" I ran my own business. So, I had more flexibility in terms of the time that I could devote to "Bridge Bread." She worked for Bank of America, but over time I pretty much wound down my business, and she left Bank of America so that we're both full time on it now. We're both full-time volunteers. Neither one of us is paid.

RICH: Really?!

FRED: We're going on nine years working here for free. We both do. We work more than forty hours a week. This is my eighth day in a row, and I've got six more before I get a day off.

RICH: Yeah. Oh, my gosh. Well, I know that you sort of have a break day on this day. So, thank you for sharing some of your, whatever this time is for you on Mondays. so, you've been in business for nine years, right?

FRED: Yes, nine years on Labor Day. Labor Day week-end, 2011.

RICH: Do you feel there's any networking between you and other bakers or bakeries?

FRED: Primarily, that would be with the folks at A.B. Mauri. Not so much with other commercial bakeries at all, although there are a bunch of bakeries right here on Cherokee Street. I mean we're friendly, but we don't actually swap recipes or compare or anything like that. We're friendly competitors.

RICH: Did you say A.B. Maury was a German company, or did you say something else?

FRED: U.K. Their headquarters are in London.

RICH: Did you say they had part of their headquarters here?

FRED: They have their North American headquarters here. They have a headquarters on each continent. So, their headquarters for North America is here in St. Louis.

RICH: They must be enormous, right? Well, this doesn't really matter, but I'm curious to know how many people have been employed with your bakery?

FRED: Less than 50, but probably somewhere in the 40's.

RICH: So, how about now? How many would you say are actively employed?

FRED: In terms of paid employees, we have five. We have two, Sharon and I who are full-time unpaid. And then, we have several volunteers who work less. We are substantially diminished by the Corona Virus. We only hire people experiencing homelessness to be bakers. So, right now most of the social service agencies that serve the population of people experiencing homelessness are not having any direct contact with those people. Therefore, they can't refer any contacts to us for employment. We would like to hire more right now.

RICH: Yeah, I read that your business this year has been cut in half at least, right?

FRED: Well, it went way down, and then we found ways to put it back up. Originally, we sold through six channels. Previously, we sold through churches on consignment, we sold through our store, but then the store was closed, and we sold wholesale. We're a supplier of dinner rolls for all of the events at the Chase Park Plaza Hotel. They stopped having events, because of the virus. We did sell at farmers' markets, but they were completely shut down for awhile. They are back open now a bit. And, we sold through catering. We did catering to places like St. Louis University, which stopped having classes. Basically, all of our channels of sales went to zero in a matter of two weeks.

FRED: So, we had to reinvent ourselves, and the primary thing we've done to reinvent ourselves has been this. We are doing bridge bread delivery directly to people's homes. And, we are making bread for food pantries. We also have supporters who have donated the money to pay for the bread that we're making for the food pantries. In fact, we are just the contract bakers, if you will, for those donors to make bread for the food pantries because we're getting paid for what we do, and the money is being used to provide bread for hungry people.

RICH: Yeah, that's a great cycle, isn't it! Wow!

FRED: But, recently the farmer's markets have started back up, and we had a good week-end this past week-end. We were at both the Tower Grove Farmer's Market and the Ferguson Farmer's Market. We had a near sell-out at the Tower Grove Farmer's Market and a complete sell-out at the Ferguson Farmers Market! And then, we had a private sale for an event at a Lutheran church in South County that also did really well.

RICH: O.K., good. Those are signs of hope, right!

FRED: Well, we had to be kind of innovative in terms of not just lying down and dying. We had to figure out things. We made a little joke out of it. I don't know if you listen to pop music at all, but there used to be a song by the Chumbawamba group that went, "I get knocked down, but I get up again, and they're never gonna' keep me down."

RICH: That's good! That's a great theme song.

FRED: You can think of Paul Newman in "Cool Hand Luke," right?

RICH: Oh yeah, there you go. That's a good image. I can't help but think, isn't there another bakery called "Laughing Bear" or something like that?

FRED: There _is_ a bakery called "Laughing Bear." Yes, Laughing Bear makes pies primarily. It's run by a woman who, I believe, is a Buddhist priest, a delightful woman, and they use contract kitchen facilities at Centenary Church. She employs people who are ex-offenders released from prison. And, we employ people who are homeless, and there is a significant overlap between those two populations.

RICH: Is the church at Soulard, Sts. Peter and Paul, still a homeless shelter?

FRED: It is, and we've hired several of our bakers from the Sts. Peter and Paul Community Services. They're located right there on Broadway. Two of our bakers came from there, and one of them is staying there still.

RICH: Anyway, I was reading your biography, and it included some of your professional background. I can't remember what ties it all together, but it was pretty sophisticated stuff.

HOW OUR HEARTS WERE STÖLLEN

FRED: I'm pretty much a technologist. I was a chief technologist for a couple of companies. I taught information science at Washington University. I was in medical information, pretty much all of it high-tech, medical technology in particular, but high-tech in general.

RICH: I see, O.K. Well, that's amazing.

FRED: None of it had anything to do with baking or retail.

RICH: Yeah, that's amazing. Do you miss it at all?

FRED: I play around with technology actually, to keep the bakery running. I still write some software just to keep things going. As a matter of fact, while we're talking I'm using some software I have that helps me route all of my deliveries that I wrote myself.

FRED: You had a question about, "Were there any memorable people that we worked with?"

RICH: Yeah, I'd love to know that!

FRED: Well, let me share a little bit of that with you. A month or so after we started Bridge Bread we had a gentleman right up the street who literally was sleeping unsheltered, named Daryl Pitchford, and Daryl stayed with us until February of last year. He was a baker, he was a shift supervisor, he was a bakery manager, and he was a member of our board of directors.

FRED: When A.B. Mauri would have meetings of their corporate executives in St. Louis, very often we would bring them by the bakery, just to see it and they would say, "Here's a working bakery we have a relationship with." And, many of those executives, coming from all over the world would visit here. They would get to know Daryl, and Daryl would tell them his story.

FRED: This part of it is hard for me to tell. So, if I choke up a little bit, that's because it's sensitive. But, when Daryl passed away, I sent a message to A.B. Mauri letting them know that Daryl had passed, and they forwarded that to their Executive Team. Daryl got tributes from five continents! He had inspired people's lives.

FRED: Talk about whether people who are experiencing homelessness are worthwhile. Unless your book is a really big success, I don't think you or I are going to get tributes from five continents!

RICH: Whoa, I'm sure of that! [Loud laughter from me.] That's a great perspective, isn't it.

FRED: Those people were inspired by Daryl.

RICH: That's really neat. How old was Daryl when you found him and hired him?

FRED: He would have been in his late 50's because he was 65 when he passed.

RICH: So, he was with you the whole time, right?

FRED: He was with us until the time he passed.

RICH: Wow. You know, I'm still trying to figure out what A.B. Mauri does?

FRED: They make baking ingredients. Baking technology.

RICH: These are things that are huge, that are on a national and international level.

FRED: For the first five years we had no input. We just figured it out on the fly.

RICH: So you were learning on the job, right? Well, it sounds like you've learned well!

FRED: Our first "starter" we made at the advice of the guy that ran the kitchen at the homeless shelter, a guy named Alan Ramsey. And, he made me some "starter," and he looked around the kitchen, and he gave us what I thought were moldy grapes and dirty potato skins. Then, we put them in a big vat with some flour and water. And, we let it cook for a couple days. So then, we fished out the grapes and potato skins.

FRED: It wasn't until a year later that I realized those grapes weren't moldy. They were "yeasting!" That white stuff that forms on grapes was yeast, not mold! That was our first "starter."

RICH: Oh yeah! My gosh, do you keep using that? Now, does that stuff proliferate?

FRED: We never have to add anything except flour and water! We have two large vats of it now. Twenty-four quarts each!

RICH: Whoa! No kidding! Now, when you talk about your first "starter," are you shortening that? Is it starter yeast or starter what?

FRED: You just call it "starter." It's yeast and flour and water together, and the ancient way of baking bread is that you just take "starter." You take a glop of that, and you mix it with flour and water, you knead it, and you let it rise, and make bread. That's all it takes, flour, water, and salt.

RICH: Flour, water, and salt. [As I say in amazement.]

FRED: And, "starter," but the "starter" is the only thing you add in to the flour and water. It grows the rest.

RICH: Do you let that ferment for days, or how long?

FRED: Years! As a matter of fact, the Lickhalter "starter" that they used at Black Bear Bakery was rumored to be several hundred years old!

RICH: Oh, my gosh, I did not know that!

FRED: People even name their "starters," and they treat them like a pet! O.K. Let me take a gander through the Interview Questions and see what else there is that's particularly interesting. Well, it's good to know that from a business perspective, although we're a social enterprise, we make enough money from selling our product to pay all of our bakers' wages and all of their benefits. And, we can pay for all of the ingredients, and a little bit for the overhead. We do make some provision for a little bit of the mortgage and the utilities. The bakers can hold their heads high that they've *earned* their money, that it's not a hand-out, it's a hand-up!

RICH: Yes! Excellent!

FRED: And, I guess our signature products are probably our sourdough bread and our classic cinnamon roll 4-pack. Those are the things that we sell the most. They're probably not the most interesting. Probably things like our cherry pie cinnamon rolls and our fourteen grain and seed Burgen loaf might be more interesting, but they don't sell as well as the straight sourdough and the classic cinnamon roll 4-pack.

RICH: I see. O.K., that's awesome. Tell me about the cherry pie cinnamon rolls?

FRED: Yeah, sometimes I make a joke about it, and I say it's like a cherry danish and a cinnamon roll made a baby! That's what it is. You just basically have a cinnamon roll, and then you kind of hollow out a big scoop in the middle of it and put cherry pie filling in it!

RICH: Amazing, amazing!

FRED: There's an important step. The cherry pie filling has to be really hot, because otherwise, it would stay doughy around it from the cold cherry pie filling. It took us awhile to figure that out.

RICH: Wow! That sounds very inviting! I would be in there tomorrow if you weren't closed. [My laughter!]

FRED: We do home delivery. You can order on-line, and we'll deliver it to your house!

RICH: Well, we live in deep South County. I'd hate to make you do that.

FRED: We go all the way to Barnhart!

RICH: Is that right! Wow! What did you say was the, how many grain bread?

FRED: The fourteen grain and seed loaf, called Burgen Bread. It's a recipe from New Zealand.

RICH: That sounds really healthy!

FRED: It's got good stuff in it! It also has those magic enzymes, so that it stays soft and fresh for a few days too!

RICH: Nice! It sounds like you've learned a lot about bread, Fred.

FRED: I have, but I've learned a lot more about homelessness.

RICH: Yeah, I'm sure you have. Well, I don't want to keep you. I'm really happy that we were able to talk, and you did a great job of helping me with information.

FRED: Alright! Wonderful! And we're ending "on-time," so you get an A+ for that!

RICH: [My laughter!] Well listen, give me about a year, and I will try to get a book to you and everybody else that I've interviewed, alright? Thanks so much, Fred.

FRED: Alright! Thank you. Bye-bye.

RICH: Bye-bye.

The Carondelet Bakery
Interview With Linda and Bob Smith

You asked about the invention of the St. Louis gooey butter cake.
Well, it was "the yellow cake dough mistake!" You know, "the king"
of gooey butter got his recipe from us at Carondelet Bakery!
— Linda Smith

LINDA: Carondelet Bakery was sort of an old-fashioned bakery. My grandmother and mother worked for St. Louis Pastry Shop on Meramec. Later, my grandmother went downtown and worked for the Stix, Baer, and Fuller department store bakery.

LINDA: You asked about the invention of the St. Louis gooey butter cake. Well, it was known as "the yellow cake dough mistake!"

RICH: Maybe we can talk about that more later. But, for now what do you think is at the heart of <u>your</u> bakery goods at the Carondelet Bakery?

LINDA: That's easy — "the Golden Formula" — our coffee cake dough is at the center of almost everything we make. But, you know <u>our</u> gooey butter cake really comes more from a candy recipe than a cake!

LINDA: You know, "the king" of gooey butter got his recipe from <u>us</u> at Carondelet Bakery!

Author's Note: I assumed at the time that Linda was talking about Fred Heimburger as the king!

LINDA: On January 1, 1975 we bought what was then called Doering's Bakery. It was owned at that time by Ed Federhofer.

RICH: I know that many of the bakery families lived "above" the bakeries on the 2nd floor. Was that true for you?

LINDA: Yes, but did you know that there is a tunnel that runs between the two buildings that are here? The original building was built in 1872 by Jacob Daut. Then, there was a Bohemian owner during the 30's, and we still use their recipes. [At this time Bob Smith walks in from the kitchen after another hard day of baking and makes a few comments.]

BOB: I do remember a lot of the stuff about the St. Louis Baker's Association, in particular "The Singing Society." I also remember the St. Louis Baker's Co-Op. You had to be a member and a shareholder for you to participate. Ed Federhofer managed the St. Louis Baker's Co-Op for a long time. You know, Fred Heimburger worked at Carondelet Bakery for awhile.

RICH: Well, I'm curious, Bob — I'd like to know why you think the independent bakeries went out of business so fast during the 1950's and 60's.

BOB: Well, I agree with a lot of people that you've talked to — the supermarkets began their own bakeries at that time. But, I also think a lot of it had to do with the price of sugar that went from 21 cents to 68 cents in a very short time! The independents provided the best ingredients and the best products. Many of them owned their buildings, and if they wanted to stay in business, they had to do a lot of streamlining.

BOB: Also, the work ethic wasn't there among the young people anymore.

Linda: We tried to persuade our four daughters who worked in the bakery, but it was very difficult to get them up at 6:00 a.m., especially on a Sunday morning!

LINDA: One interesting historic fact was this — in the earlier days at Carondelet Bakery they would bake turkeys in the bakery ovens!

RICH: Yes, I've heard about this from several other bakers!

LINDA: In 1960 Herman Doering, Sr. and Ed Federhofer bought the bakery. They were brother-in-laws. In 1975 Bob Smith, my husband, bought the bakery when he was only 20 years old. Ed Federhofer financed the purchase for Bob.

LINDA: One thing that really affected the business was when Highway 55 was built. It pretty much split and broke up the neighborhood. In those days there were three bakeries in a three block area — Schmidt's was on the west side of Grand at Delor, Rozanek's, was also on the west side of Grand, and Eiper's was at Grand and Wilmington. It's a pizza place now.

LINDA: People don't really know how small our bakery is in total floor space. It is 150' long and 20' wide. And, it is now 140 years old. One of our best accounts was with Royal Orleans Banquet Center. We made wedding cakes for them for 25 years.

LINDA: A pretty important historic resource would be Violet Doering's book. She was the daughter of Herman Doering, Sr. She grew up at Carondelet Bakery, and her book is mostly about the Carondelet Bakery. She is a very bright and friendly person.

LINDA: A person to talk to about all of this is Ed Federhofer. He was on the board of the Baker's Co-Op and was its president for thirty years. The Co-Op was actually owned by about seventy-two bakers. The Co-Op built a new building in 1975 on the Italian Hill at 2701 Hereford, behind the Schnuck's grocery store on Arsenal.

How sweet it is

Carondelet Bakery has been rolling out pastries since the 1870s

By Jim Merkel
JMERKEL@YOURJOURNAL.COM

For half a century, Bernie Brown has stopped by the Carondelet Bakery whenever he had a taste for something sweet.

On this particular day, Brown, 78, could have chosen a butter cookie, a chocolate chip cookie, custard puffs or brownies when he stopped by the shop at 7726 Virginia Ave. Instead, he chose two danishes.

People have been making decisions like that since Jacob Duut took out a permit to build a storefront bakery in 1872.

Today, owners Robert and Linda Smith are carrying on the tradition Duut started.

"We still do it the old fashioned way," Linda Smith, 55, said.

Whatever the bakery sells — whether at the store or to restaurants — every recipe comes from a file box Robert Smith received when he bought the bakery on Jan. 1, 1975.

Smith started working

See Bakery on Page A5

Linda Smith cleans fingerprints from the front window of the Carondelet Bakery, 7726 Virginia Ave.

RICK GRAEFE | JOURNAL

Diana's Mexican Bakery
Interview With Anna Vasquez

And, what is that La Rosca that you make for January 6th?
It is a dough that has a lot of dried fruit on top.
In the middle of that Rosca we put "the BABY!"
That means the Baby Jesus, who is hiding. When you cut the Rosca
and you have the Baby Jesus on your piece of cake, that means that on
February 2nd you have to throw a party! It's like saying, "Thank You."
— Anna Vasquez

RICH: Now, are you from St. Louis?

ANNA: No, Mexico.

RICH: So, you're from Mexico. Our son does a lot of traveling, and he loves Mexico. He was most excited about visiting the town of Guanajuato. I want you to know that I'm very proud of our three children.

ANNA: OH-H-H! [Anna responds very quickly with delight.]

RICH: He said it was very beautiful. He said it was a very famous historic city.

ANNA: My husband is from Guanajuato!

RICH: Is that right?! Oh, my goodness! Are you from there?

ANNA: No, I'm from Michoacan.

RICH: Michigan?

ANNA: No, Michoacan.

RICH: Can I ask your husband's name?

ANNA: Refugio

RICH: Why did you name the bakery after your daughter? Just because you love her, right?!

ANNA: Yes, after we had Emmanuel and Daniel, she comes, and we named her Ashley Diana. Yeah, so I was like, I don't want a name kinda' like an American name because we are Mexicans. So, I would like to have something that represents us with a name or something that says, "Hey, here we are!" So, after she is born I'm like, "Ah, we're gonna' call the bakery Diana's Mexican Bakery, her second name!"

RICH: And, she is about twelve years old, right,?

ANNA: She's actually thirteen.

RICH: How are you interested in baking? Did you grow up with it?

ANNA: Not me. My husband. Just him, and then he used to work at El Chico bakery that is also over here on Cherokee Street. So, one day I asked him, "Can you teach me how to make cakes," and then he goes like, "But, we don't have whipped cream, we don't have beans." And I'm like, "I can go and buy all of those things at the store, and you can teach me." And then, when he started teaching me, I started making cakes at my home, from scratch.

ANNA: So, I learned how to make the cakes, and then we sold them to some of my friends and people that I know. And, I went with Emmanuel and Daniel and knocked on the doors of my friends and said, "Hey, this is the slice of cake that you ordered, and I'm bringing you your sliced cake." So, that's how we started the business, just letting the people know.

RICH: Door-to-door! So great! You had a "cottage industry," out of your house.!

ANNA: Yeah!

RICH: Our son lives very close to here.

ANNA: That's good. All of your children are married?

RICH: No, he is not married, and he's never married. We have two daughters, and they both have children. One lives in Kansas City, and one lives here, and they're both wonderful. At this time we have four grandchildren, and they're all wonderful!

ANNA: God bless your family.

RICH: Yeah, thank you! You too!

ANNA: Thank you.

RICH: We just finished a big Thanksgiving week-end. Our daughter and her family came in from Kansas City to visit, and I'm tired. [And, we laugh together.] I especially appreciate your meeting with me because I know it's your busy time of year. And your husband, Refugio, he must be busy. Did anybody in his family encourage him to go into baking? Or, did he just do it on his own?

ANNA: No, no. When he was young his dad said, "You're not going anymore to school. You're going to start making bread, and you have to come with me, to work with me." At the time he was sad because he would have liked to study, to go to school, but it was a decision that he could not say, "Yes or No." So, he started learning how to make the bread and cook.

RICH: And, what did his father do?

ANNA: He was a baker. and his father's father was a baker too. So, the grandpa was a baker.

RICH: He was? That's awesome! That's the way it seems, you know, many generations. You probably know some things about this, but it's a very proud thing in St. Louis, the history of bakers in St. Louis. Many St. Louis bakeries were a hundred years old, some were even one hundred fifty and one hundred sixty years old!

RICH: The bakeries were just passed on through their families! So, it's exciting! It's a great thing to be proud of. That's the way I feel about it. You probably do too. You seem to have very nice workers.

ANNA: [Anna laughs.] Oh, thank you.

RICH: You do! Well Manny, is he working for the bakery?

ANNA: Yes, he's a baker in the back.

RICH: What about Daniel? Is he too young?

ANNA: Daniel is our delivery guy.

RICH: I saw him, I think, going out the door last week when I was here.

ANNA: You came on Wednesday? Yeah.

RICH: Do you supply restaurants?

ANNA: Yes. We supply, umm-m, do you know "Mission Taco?"

RICH: Yes.

ANNA: O.K. we supply them, all of the "Mission Tacos." Yes, we have customers who drive like two or three hours to come and pick up bread on Wednesdays.

RICH: Wow! From other towns in Missouri?

ANNA: Yes, and also in Illinois. Some of them say that they come from Centralia, Illinois?! And, I don't know where else they say that they come from.

RICH: Anna, you know my wife and I stayed in a small town named Greenville, Illinois about a month ago, and we had a good time. And, they had this really nice Mexican restaurant next door. So, there's a really good Mexican restaurant in Greenville, Illinois. [Author's Note: I might have been suggesting at this point that Diana's bakery might want to see if this restaurant would like to become an account for the bakery.] But, that's big, that you supply Mission Taco. I ate at Mission Taco one time.

ANNA: Yes, we supply them with kind of like the French bread.

RICH: Are those sort of like rolls?

ANNA: Yes, kind of like bread rolls.

RICH: "Mission Taco," they have two or three places, don't they?

ANNA: Yes, the Soulard center, then Delmar, and then St. Charles.

RICH: You supply all of those? My gosh, that's a long trip. We like St. Charles. There's a brewery there that's really good! [At this time, we laugh loudly!]

RICH: So O.K., one thing I always ask is, "Do you have any things that you like the best that are your product? If you were going to pick one thing, do you think that there is a signature item? What do people like or buy the most?"

ANNA: Churros!

[At this point Anna sort of laughs with a giggle, and says,] Also, the flan and, the "Tres Leches Cake."

RICH: What is it called?

ANNA: "Three Milk Cake." Tres Leches Cake. That's the typical Mexican cake.

RICH: Can you tell me what's in that cake. I don't know what that is.

ANNA: In Tres Leches Cake, you bake the "bread," which is sort of a pound cake, and then you stick the cake into the milk, condensed milk, regular milk, and evaporated milk. And then, you can put filling or not put filling. And then, you just decorate it like a cake.

RICH: So, you immerse the cake in milk? And then, you rebake it or no?

ANNA: No.

RICH: So, is it kind of like a bread pudding??

ANNA: Maybe a little. The original is with no filling. It is the most cake that we sell here. We have like seven different ones, but that is the one that we sell the most.

RICH: O.K. Now I'm going to tell you what I really like. See, I know what they're called in French. And, I think you call them "palmers," but it's "palmiers" in French. The filo dough, are they made out of filo dough? They look like butterflies!

ANNA: Ahh-oh, "orejas!" We call them "orejas!"

RICH: Why don't you tell me anything that you can think of, that you want to talk about — in twelve years are there any stories?

ANNA: We started with a bakery, a super-small bakery. And then back then. we didn't have the cases where we could put the bread. When Daniel was little it was my mother-in-law, my husband, my sister-in-law, my mother's sister-in-law, and me.

RICH: Un-huh, does Diana help at all?

ANNA: Yes! She loves to help her dad in the back, making the bread! Not good in the front!

RICH: Is she too shy?

ANNA: Yes! She is super shy!

RICH: Do you have to get up early in the morning?

ANNA: For one year we worked from 3:30 in the morning until 9:00 or 10:00 P.M.! Seven days a week.

RICH: Are you now able to ever get away?

ANNA: Yes, sometimes.

RICH: Yes, it's good for you, isn't it?

ANNA: Yeah, because we wake up early every single morning. And then, when you think that everybody is coming to work, you get that phone call or that text that says, "Hey, I'm not going to be able to make it." And so then, *you* have to come in.

RICH: You have to cover for that person?

ANNA: Yes. Sometimes my husband doesn't have enough bakers during the day or night. And then, he has to cover both shifts. And, if I don't have enough help, I have to cover both shifts.

RICH: You do what you have to do, right? That's the thing of a business, isn't it?

ANNA: You're never free.

RICH: And, people have expectations, don't they? How are the holidays? Are they terribly busy? Like getting ready for Christmas?

ANNA: On Christmas we're super busy, also on Thanksgiving. On Thanksgiving we sell a lot of French bread. On Christmas, it is tamales! It's like everybody comes in for them. They will want to place an order. And then, we have too many orders on that day. And, that happens on Christmas Eve, December 24th!

ANNA: And then, we have January the 6th when we celebrate "Dia de Los Reyes."

RICH: The Epiphany?

ANNA: Kind of like that, yes. And then, we celebrate that with a cake, and we call that "Dia de Los Reyes," the Feast of the 3 Kings. That's when they bring to Jesus their gifts.

RICH: Diana, I want you to know — Diana, oh no, I called you by your daughter's name.

[And, we laugh together.]

ANNA: That's O.K. Everybody calls me like that. [And then, we laugh again!]

RICH: I'll bet that they do! I was a religion teacher in a Catholic school, so I know about the Feast of the Three Kings, and all of that!

RICH: The tamales, is that mostly to restaurants, or to individuals?

ANNA: Oh no, individuals, to the customers! For example, there are some big families, like of 12 or 15 people in the family, they come and say, "Can I have 5 or 10 dozen of the tamales for this day?!"

RICH: I know. They're good! I like them! And, you're open on Christmas Eve?

ANNA: Yes, but not on Christmas Day.

RICH: And, what do you make for Dia de Los Reyes on January 6th?

ANNA: We call it "La Rosca de Reyes."

RICH: I'm learning a lot! And, what is that, La Rosca?

ANNA: It is a dough that has a lot of fruit on top, dried fruit on top. In the middle of that Rosca we put "the BABY!" That means the Baby Jesus, hiding. When you cut the Rosca and you have the Baby Jesus on your piece of cake, that means that on February 2nd you have to "throw a party!" It's like saying, "Thank You."

RICH: You got lucky, right! That's very much like Mardi Gras, isn't it!

ANNA: Kind of.

RICH: That's great. It's a great tradition! Are those things all over Mexico?

ANNA: Oh, Yes!

RICH: Yeah, those are all feasts, right?

ANNA: You know, in Mexico there is no Santa Claus! We don't believe in Santa Claus. On December 24th is when we carry the baby Jesus and sing songs, and pass the Baby Jesus around the whole family! And then, on January the 6th is when de Reyes, [the 3 kings], bring presents to you when you are a little kid!

RICH: So, no Santa Claus at all, not even St. Nicholas?

ANNA: [At this time Anna laughs loudly, and says], "I think that now they do because you know how a lot of people came over here to America, and then they go back, and they go, "Ah, Santa Claus" — but no, when I was little, was when they bring you something.

RICH: You know the tradition of St. Nicholas, You put your shoes out or your socks out.

ANNA: Over there, [in Mexico], it's like you know, your mom or dad will buy those things, but if you're like super poor, you say, "I'm gonna take my shoe or my sock over to my uncle or my grandma, and see if they bring something to their house. So, on January 6th if you wake up and you don't find anything under the tree, you've got either your grandpa or uncles, and you say, "Oh, they brought something over here, not at my house, but I have something here."

RICH: That's really nice — yes, I have the same importance. It's about Jesus, it's not about getting presents and all of that. I have to tell you about my grandpa, who I went to Mass with almost every morning.

RICH: He pulled me aside one Christmas when I was a little boy into a very dark room and made me look out the window at the darkness, and he asked me, "Do you know why we have Christmas at this time of year?" And, I said, "No." And then, he said, "It's because it's the darkest time of the year, and now we need Jesus to come." And so, he explained how important Jesus' coming was, to be the light of the world."

RICH: And so, that was very special to me. So now, the winter solstice is very important to me because it means that our days are getting longer! [And, we laugh together.] You know, because we're going to have more light!

ANNA: I forgot to tell you about November 2nd. That is when we celebrate the "Day of the Dead," Dia de Los Muertos." You can even Google that. Have you ever seen the "Coco's" movie? Try to view it and see the most important things in there and keep them in your mind. It's like, for us when somebody dies, and then in November we put the flowers, the food and the drink, whatever they loved when they were alive. They say that the flowers bring them with the smell. They come and see, and they smell the food. I don't know if it's true or not, but we do celebrate every November, not October 31st, but November 1st and 2nd.

RICH: Do you have two "Days of the Dead?"

ANNA: Yes, the first one is for the babies, from zero months to twelve, the "Dia de Los Innocentes." The second one is when you're an adult, from twelve and older and someone passes away for some reason and that is who we celebrate.

RICH: Are there any other stories?

ANNA: Oh, like for us, May 10th is Mother's Day. It doesn't matter if it's a Monday or a Tuesday, Saturday or Sunday. May 10th, that's Mother's Day for us. Here in the U.S. it is the second Sunday of May, right?

RICH: These are all things I did not know. Do you still have your relatives working with you?

ANNA: My sister-in-law only.

RICH: Is the El Chico Bakery still in business?

ANNA: I think so.

RICH: I was just wondering if there are any relationships with other bakeries? We actually worked at St. Margaret of Scotland School with the mother of the girl who started the "Whisk" bakery down the street, on Cherokee Street. I haven't talked with her yet. There are so many specialty bakeries now, cupcakes and things like that, but I really was excited, when I came to your store last Wednesday, that you have a lot  of variety with so many different items. And, that's not true very often anymore. Are Christmas cookies an item for you?

ANNA: No, not really.

RICH: Well, everything here looks really good! But, I don't want to keep you. Is there anything else that you think would be good to know? The bakery is doing really well, isn't it?!

ANNA: Yes, thanks to God.

RICH: Yes, thanks be to God.

ANNA: The bakery used to be only half of what you see right now! We would bake in this part, where we are in the office right now. And then, we had a little fridge, and in front we had some cases, not all of what you see right now, there were only some of them.

ANNA: And then, we started growing more. This used to be a restaurant when we first came here. And, in the back there was a yard. So, the customers came in, in the back of the restaurant. So, we decided to expand the bakery to the back, and we made it fill the whole yard.

RICH: So, you built an addition!

ANNA: Yes!

RICH: Oh, that's important. I didn't know that either. Well, it made such a difference in what you could do, right! How many bakers are there?

ANNA: There are four. And then, we have somebody who bakes at night-time too.

RICH: So, four plus one at night-time. Do you do any cake decorating?

ANNA: My sister-in-law does most of the cakes right now, she's the one who makes them.

RICH: She's the decorator. So, you do some weddings?

ANNA: She does everything of the decorating. And, when she's not here either me or my husband makes them.

RICH: I see. Are there any other Mexican bakeries anywhere that you know of besides your own?

ANNA: The bakery store here at Cherokee and California streets. They just bake a little bit, but they don't go on deliveries. And, across from them is another one.

On the corner is Lilly's bakery. And, another one is still the big store, the Mexican grocery store. And then, El Chico bakery.

RICH: Well, if you think of anything else — I'm going to come back sometime to take pictures. And, I tell everybody this, that all of this is only positive. I will never put anything in the book that's negative, but you didn't even say anything that was negative. So, that's nice! [And here we laugh together]

RICH: I'm very positive about all of this, you know. I have nothing but love for bakers and bakeries! So that's all I need, I think. And, please say some prayers. I know that you are a religious person. So, say some prayers that all of this happens and that I get to publish this book! And then, Anna says, "I will, I will!" And, tell your husband thank you for giving you up at this busy time of year! [And here, again we laugh together.] That's great, Anna. Thank you so much. I hope you get some rest to get ready for the holidays.

ANNA: I will, I will try!

Ehnes Bakery
Interview With Dave Ehnes and Connie Wolf

You know, my dad would not throw anything away. He took anything that was left of the bakery goods either to the Loretto sisters or to the Little Sisters of the Poor.
— Dave Ehnes

Author's Note: There are some parts of this interview that were not completely focused on bakeries or baking. But, I felt the conversations between Dave Ehnes and Connie Wolf were very valuable as recollections between two children of bakers, both from family bakeries in the Shaw neighborhood.

RICH: You know, Dave, I've interviewed about eight major bakeries in St. Louis so far, and have edited about 40 pages of the best things I could find in the St. Louis Bakers Bulletins from fifty years of monthly bulletins. I inherited those bakery bulletins from the McArthur family.

DAVE: Mr. McArthur and my father were on the buying association's board together. They used to call it the St. Louis Bakers' Co-Op. When I was younger it was down in the vicinity of Theresa and Grand. They built a new one, maybe in the 1970's, and that one was in the vicinity of Arsenal and a warehouse district by the train tracks that go under Arsenal Street through a tunnel, right near where Home Depot is now in 2019.

RICH: Well Dave, do you remember the address of your bakery?

DAVE: 1807 South 39th.

RICH: I love that street because it goes by one of my favorite churches, St. Margaret of Scotland.

CONNIE: Yeah, so do I.

RICH: I work at St. Margaret of Scotland School. I've worked there for eight years now, at first as a paid teacher's assistant and now as a volunteer.

DAVE: Yeah, they win all kinds of awards for their school. That's where I went to grade school! I graduated in 1950. [With this information I calculated that Dave at the time of this interview was 82 years old, and I was 73 years old.]

CONNIE: Oh, I didn't realize that you were there, because I graduated in 1957.

DAVE: Yes, all four of us kids went there. Anyway, it was all nuns (at St. Margaret of Scotland) at that time. Well, one day we were all waiting downstairs in the church basement getting ready to parade down 39th street to go into the church for our 8th grade graduation.

DAVE: And, the nuns all decided that they were gonna' be part of the parade. At that time we must have had about twenty-three nuns! It was also interesting that the Park Avenue streetcar ran in front of the church on 39th street. Well, the streetcar came along just at the same time as the parade! And, I still remember the principal, Mother Florian. [As he turns toward Connie Wolf, he says,] "Do you remember her?"

CONNIE: [And, Connie responds], "I do remember her."

RICH: Well, Dave, I don't want to miss any important things. So, what do you remember about your family bakery? What are some highlights?

DAVE: We originally lived above the bakery, and my dad bought it from my uncle. He bought it in the 1930's. There were three buildings that were all joined together. One was a small supermarket called Flotkins. The bakery was in the middle, and then on the other side was the Paragon card shop. The buildings aren't there anymore.

DAVE: My dad sold it in the early 70's to a couple, and they operated a bakery there until 1979. They kept our bakery name, the Ehnes Pastry Shop. They took a two-week vacation, but they weren't getting along, and they never came back. So, my dad had to take the bakery back, and he decided then to have a big auction and sell everything. He did give some of the equipment to bakers who were friends of his.

CONNIE: Do you remember what year highway 44 went through, and didn't that hurt your bakery, because the bakery was sort of cut-off and placed on the north side of the highway which hurt the business? Isn't that when your father had to sell the bakery?

DAVE: Yeah, Highway 44 was very controversial, and they talked about it for years before it came into itself, but the highway actually had nothing to do with selling the bakery. When my father sold it the business district there was still going and viable. There was a really neat business district that eventually was lost between DeTonty and Lafayette. There was a Woolworth dime store, two drug stores, a hardware store, a little restaurant, and a cleaners.

CONNIE: So, those were knocked down by highway 44. But, your father's business, was it able to continue with 44?

DAVE: Yes. Well, by the time he sold it, they hadn't gotten that far. Yes, he sold it before highway 44 actually went through. Evidently, he was already thinking about all of that.

RICH: Ah, that is a good clarification. We thought that the highway ruined your family's business.

CONNIE: Yes, we went to Woolworth's too! But could you even get to Ehnes Bakery on 39th Street?

DAVE: Yes, because they channeled 39th Street under the highway, and it's still that way today.

RICH: Yeah, it's the only street in that area that goes north and south. It's an artery.

DAVE: Yes, my father went to a lot of meetings about Highway 44, and they were trying to push it farther north. But, the Italians didn't want it going through the Italian Hill. So, there was a lot of politics. [And then, we laughed together.] And you know, behind us was a movie show, the Shaw show.

RICH: Well yeah, that's reopened!

CONNIE: Do you mean as a movie theater?

DAVE: No, as an event center. My brother did some research on it, and he found out that it was built in 1913. They had a series of films on Saturdays. My mother would fix a big bag of popcorn, and we'd go over to see what Superman was doing or whoever was going to be there.

CONNIE: Oh, I'm sure we were there at the same time. We went all of the time.

RICH: Yep, that's what we did too. We'd go to those old neighborhood theaters. For me, mine cost 10 cents to go. My theater was the Melvin on Chippewa, and I think at Nebraska.

RICH: But, getting back to the subject of the Ehnes Bakery, what do you remember as the signature items that would draw people to the bakery — what did you emphasize?

DAVE: My father was a master baker, and he came to this country when he was seventeen. His uncle built those three buildings. He had built another bakery near Soulard before he built those. But, my father liked to make cakes.

DAVE: He made a lot of different kinds of cakes. And, Danish pastries, he made a lot of that too. By the time my dad sold the property he had eighteen employees. He worked around the clock, you might say.

RICH: Yep, that's what bakers did!

DAVE: You know, the guy who remodeled the Shaw Theater, he was a pharmacist. Kohlberg was his name. The one that was on 39th and Lafayette, that's what it was called.

DAVE: You know, that theater was originally "air-conditioned." They would have a big truckload of ice brought into the alley. And, there was a "sewer lid" there where the truck would drop the ice into the basement of the theater. And then, fans would blow over the ice! That was taken out of there later when they went to an electrical system.

RICH: So, the new "event-center" that was Shaw Theater is in the same location. Eighteen people was a lot of employees for your dad's bakery. This is great, Dave. Connie, were we talking about how dominant men were in the bakery business?

DAVE: Yeah, my mother had a lot of clerks working in the store. Well, no my father was not like that. Before he came to the United States he spent two years in a seminary. He was studying to be a priest, and then World War I started, and the area he was living in came under the French. And, everybody had to conduct business in French. That was another reason he decided to leave, especially because he had never studied the language.

CONNIE: May I ask — what about the children? Did they work in the bakery? Did you work in the bakery?

DAVE: I did in fact. I went to St. Louis University, and I did not do well. So, my mother decided that I should work in the bakery. I was going to work there for a year or two, and I ended up working in the bakery full-time for ten years. I did baking, and I made danish. At that time my dad had three bakers during the day, and he had some at night.

RICH: Were there any other family members that worked in the bakery?

DAVE: Well, "You had to make your money," my dad would say. So, when these special days would come along like Easter, Valentines Day, and St. Patrick's Day he would have extra people come in. He had this one brother-in-law who never did too well. So, he would come in like on Saturdays. When the bakeries were starting to disappear, my dad would hire some of those people for one or two days a week.

CONNIE: But, when we kids were in high school and even grade school, and when we were older we worked. The boys worked in the back with my father, and the girls worked in the front with my mother. We started when we were about five years old putting cherries on cookies. We worked, and I worked all through high school and college. So, did your brothers and sisters work through high school and college?

DAVE: They did. In fact, I worked when I was in high school. When I would come home after school, there would be a lot of business at the end of the day. We had a lot of business in the early part of the day and at the latter part of the day when people would be on their way home from work. And, remember we had the Russell bus, and it would let people off at 39th and Russell.

CONNIE: But, I think an important part of St. Louis bakery history is how the children especially would work running the bakery with their parents. To me that was significant in my growing up in a really good way. It was wonderful.

DAVE: Well, my mother would always have, what you would call today, nannies around. So, my younger brother was practically raised by a black lady that my mother had hired, and she stayed with us for about twenty-five years.

CONNIE: Well, did your mother work in the bakery? She was probably the head store lady like my mother was.

CONNIE: And then, she had one woman who was there when we started, and she was there when we left. That was another thing that I think was significant in that time. People stayed. You know, we had people for years.

DAVE: My grandfather was a small man like me, but he was very well-muscled. He would have been my mother's father, and they made a baker out of him too!

I just read the other day about St. James the Greater school closing. I guess they just couldn't support the school financially. When we went I don't remember us paying any tuition.

RICH: It was all kind of on a trust relationship from the collection basket at Sunday Mass, wasn't it? Isn't that something? Times have changed.

DAVE: Well, I'm thinking that was the only way that a lot of women were going to get an education. I think that was one reason why they became nuns. There's one of our relatives who comes to most of the family get-togethers, and I can tell the way she talks that she is a feminist.

CONNIE: Yes, a lot of the nuns are, but that's the beauty of you writing this history, is to bring out some of those things that were so much a part of us, like kids working with their parents. Maybe it's still true today, but you just don't have the small businesses. I mean, where are you going to find people who are willing to get up at three o'clock in the morning and work that hard? I know the owners made enough money, but the bakers themselves were not highly paid.

DAVE: We had a couple of men that worked for us, but actually they were farmers. They decided that farm life wasn't for them. So, they came to the city, and became bakers.

RICH: Wasn't there a movie theater on Cherokee Street?

DAVE: Yeah, I think it was called the Princess? That was too far away for us to go to the show. We had a show that was on Grand and Shenandoah. It was called The Shenandoah.

[The author thinks there was another show on Cherokee Street called "The Ritz."]

RICH: You know, Dave, I added something onto these "Interview Questions" just this afternoon. And, that was the question, "Do you know of any other bakers that would want to talk to me?"

DAVE: Well, you know the Federhofers. Have you talked to them? You know, I saw the senior Mr. Federhofer during the Christmas holidays, and I always buy a stöllen. This was one of the two brothers.

RICH: Yeah, I talked to one of them on the phone. Dave, I'm so grateful that you're willing to talk to me.

DAVE: Well, I'm trying to think. My dad was very good friends with the Ottenads, and they had two bakeries. They had one on Lafayette near Jefferson. there were two brothers. And, they had one just across from the Schnuck's store on Hampton and Gravois. And, what about Missouri Bakery?

RICH: You know, I interviewed one baker in Florissant, and I love this man. I've met so many nice people. This man's name was Chris Helfer. He has a beautiful bakery and delicatessen, and it's still doing really well.

DAVE: But, you're lucky that you've got those "Bakery Bulletins." You could see if any of these people we've talked about would be in those bulletins.

RICH: You know, this project could get so big. I interviewed Roy Schmiemeir. He was such a gentleman.

DAVE: Yes, he sold his store on Manchester, but it's still going. He sold it to one of his bakers. It became Clayton Bakery, and now it's Bello's.

RICH: And then, there were the Ellerbrocks, and they were in North County. I've become good friends with two of the Ellerbrocks, Rita Ellerbrock Andres, and Mary Kay Ellerbrock Turner. They thought Ellerbrocks had something like thirteen bakeries.

DAVE: Yeah, I remember Ellerbrocks and Warner-Knoll were bakeries that had a lot of branches. But, I remember my mother put her foot down and used to say, "We do well with one, but we'll do poorly with five."

CONNIE: Was that the same Warner-Knoll that became a florist.

DAVE: Well, that's a good question. There was another bakery that was very good — I think it was Rozanek's.

CONNIE: Yes, one of my nieces, one of the Landholt girls worked there when it was on Grand near Bates.

RICH: Yes, Carol Landholt. I taught her. We were good friends.

DAVE: The bakery across from the Tower Grove Bank, when it was on Grand, used to be Rozanek's, and then it became Bretscher's. What's there now is a restaurant. But, it would be good if you could get in touch with the Hausels. I know they're retired. They might be interested in talking to you. There are two brothers.

RICH: So, you think the two Hausel brothers might want to talk.

DAVE: Yeah, well they don't have anything else to do! [And, we all laugh together!]

DAVE: Their father worked for my father.

RICH: You know, I came up with a solution to a dilemma that I had. I thought, "I wish there was somebody who was really smart and who could put together a family tree of bakeries in St. Louis." I don't think I could do it because I couldn't be comprehensive.

RICH: I can't get to everybody, but I can do something else, and I love the idea. I could make a map of locations for all of these bakeries, where they were located!

Author's Note: Eventually I did put together a Bakery Map and a list of locations for historic bakeries in St. Louis. These can both be found in the Appendix.

RICH: Well, I can tell you it was like being in another world when I was reading those bakery bulletins. It was unbelievable. They give such a full description of everything in those times. I have fifty years of those St. Louis Baker's Bulletins. It's my hope that those bulletins can eventually be given to the Missouri History Museum if the McArthurs agree to that. The History Museum could take care of them. They have that archive location now on Skinker. As far as I could find out, they don't have anything on the topic of St. Louis bakeries.

DAVE: My dad was a Bakers Association officer for awhile. So I'm sure his name is in those bulletins somewhere. You know, my dad would not throw anything away. He would take anything that was left-over of the bakery goods either to the Loretto sisters or to the Sisters of the Poor.

CONNIE: That's interesting because my father was really big on giving away bakery goods too. He'd send some of the kids to take the Grand Avenue bus or streetcar down to some of the convents. And, my mother used to say that she thought he over-baked because he liked to give bakery goods away! [We all laugh together!]

RICH: You know, Roy Schmiemeir told me about one of the bakers that he knew, whose son went to California. He ended up starting a business. He makes all of the hamburger buns for a whole area of California for McDonalds. Can you imagine that!

DAVE: It's amazing how many people there are like that. I've got a classmate, who is a multi-millionaire. He invented the fountains for drinks that you go to for soft drinks. Oh yeah, the Russians approached him, and he set-up the first McDonalds in Moscow.

DAVE: My father's first name was William Ehnes. His first son's name was William also. My mother's name was Frieda. Did your sister, Mary Lou Wolf, work in the bakery too?

CONNIE: Oh yes, all of the girls did.

DAVE: I thought she was in the convent for awhile?

CONNIE: No, Ginny was the one that was in the convent for awhile, and she was the only one that didn't work in the bakery. She was in the Medical Mission Sisters.

DAVE: Yeah, they were in our neighborhood on Grand. We had the very top house on Flora Place that sat partially on Grand.

RICH: Yeah, we support the Medical Mission Sisters. They have trained doctors and nurses. They do really important work.

DAVE: Well, when do you think your goal is to finish?

RICH: Oh boy. I've really pushed hard this winter, and I'm still pushing now. But, the topic is so big that I could go on forever. I don't know. It's too important a story to just stop, but I do have to "rein it in" sometimes.

DAVE: [At this point there was a lengthy discussion of the Lubeley Bakery closing, and then Dave went on.] My mother used to play pinochle with the senior Mrs. Lubeley.

CONNIE: That's interesting because my father always played cards with Mr. Lubeley.

DAVE: Yeah, there was a Master Retail Men's Association, and there was a Master Retail Women's Association. They would meet once every quarter, and they would have cake and coffee. And then, after that they would play cards.

Author's Note: I don't remember anything from the "Bakers Bulletins" that described two separate organizations for men and for women. But, they did have some separate functions and events for the men and the women inside of the Bakers Association.

CONNIE: Well, my father passed away in 1984. So, he was probably quite a bit older than your father and wasn't in the group that played cards together.

RICH: You know, some of those kinds of things are all in the "Baker's Bulletins!"

The Ellerbrock Bakeries
Interview With Rita Andres and
Mary Kay Ellerbrock Turner

Oh my gosh, my friends would always say,
"I can remember your birthday cakes,"
because my dad would always make me mine.
Like, one year I had a Beatles cake. Another year I had the "little doll
in the middle" cake, and he'd make the little cake around it.
But, then, my grandmother who wasn't even with
the bakery would also make me a cake.
So, I always had to have at least two pieces of cake!

Mary Kay: The Ellerbrock Bakeries started, I think, in 1889, and it was William Ellerbrock who came from Horn Germany, a town close to Muenster.

Rich: Was he the original owner?

Mary Kay: Yes, it was William Ellerbrock, and he met his wife, Dina, our grandma who was from Muenster.

Rich: And, what was her name, her maiden name?

Rita: Janning. And, I can help you with that, with a family history.

Mary Kay: And there was kind of a history written, the story of it, (and I love the title), "The Gay, Glorious, and Glamourous Years!"

Rita: Glarmorous?! I don't get that! [And we all laugh.]

Rich: They had a flare for words, didn't they!

Mary Kay: Yes, and I'm thinking that Grandpa always said he wrote "The Bakery Song," but I really think that Grandma Catherine did!

Rich: But, who did claim to write it?

Mary Kay: It says his name on there, my grandfather, William Bill Ellerbrock, the first owner's son.

Rich: Can you make me a copy of that?

MARY KAY: But, my grandmother was the poet-writer in the family. William Bill Ellerbrock was actually president of the Missouri State Bakers Association for 1953, 54, and 55. My dad worked for William Francis Ellerbrock, the 2nd owner.

MARY KAY: Grandpa sold the Cass Avenue bakery in 1966 to Warner-Noll. My uncle Ralph then decided he wanted to work for the Stix, Baer, and Fuller department store, and he worked for them until it became Dilliard's. Then Dilliard's decided they weren't going to pay his retirement after 25 years, and that was the end of that.

MARY KAY: My mom never got into the bakery business. She did take us to two or three different stores at Christmas, and we would decorate them. So, that was my big thing.

MARY KAY: And then, I would also go down and sit in the decorating room, and grandpa would wash my hands. Then, I would take apart all of the dried fruit they would use for decorating. So, I worked at the bakery too, but I never got paid! [Loud laughter!]

RICH: Oh yeah, I'm sure! So, you decorated the store windows?

MARY KAY: That was a lot of fun.

RICH: Oh yeah, bakeries were so important to the spirit of the community and of the neighborhoods.

RICH: You know, Warner-Noll Bakeries bought out Ellerbrock Bakeries in 1966.

RITA: After my grandmother wasn't in the bakery anymore, she would make 100 stöllens a year, and she would give them to organizations like Our Lady of Good Counsel nursing home. She made all of their Christmas stöllens for them. Yes, she was always cooking. This would be Bill's sister.

MARY KAY: People would also come up to my mom and tell her that they really liked that they could come buy a sandwich at a stand-up bar inside the bakery, you know, so they could get a quick bite to eat and then get to work.

MARY KAY: Now, I'm not trying to say anything or brag, but my dad, Malachi Ellerbrock, was a friend of Fr. Dismas Clark, the "Hoodlum Priest," and I have pictures of dad giving him pies and other baked goods. And do you know what? Dad was invited to the premier showing of the movie, "The Hoodlum Priest," a movie about Fr. Dismas Clark.

RICH: So, did he bring food, like bakery left-overs to the halfway house?

MARY KAY: Yeah!

RICH: Wow, that's wonderful!

MARY KAY: Yeah, he would bring them by once or twice a week, whatever the bakery had. You know, they didn't throw things away. They tried to give them to people.

RITA: After my grandmother wasn't in the bakery anymore, she would make 100 stöllens a year, and she would give them to organizations like Our Lady of Good Counsel nursing home. She made all of their Christmas stöllens for them.

MARY KAY: Yes, she was always cooking. At one point she was the main cook at St. Joseph's Shrine. This would be Bill's sister.

MARY KAY: One Christmas I wanted a real baker's stöllen, a German one, so I went to a Schulte bakery in Washington, Missouri.

RICH: Why there? Where did this Schulte baker come from?

MARY KAY: He was an apprentice in the Ellerbrock bakery down on 13th and Cass. William Francis Ellerbrock was married in 1926, and they lived above the bakery. I have a picture, but that is one that I can't find.

RITA: I think my dad was born above the bakery in that building, but I'm not sure.

MARY KAY: They all could have lived real close, because they all went to church at St. Joseph's Shrine. It was our family's church.

MARY KAY: In fact, uncle Ralph played the organ there for 66 years, and Pope Benedict sent him a kind of recognition. When the pope found out how long he had been the organist there he wrote and asked, "How old is this guy?!" He started playing there when he was 14!

RITA: The story goes like this. When he was fourteen the person who played the organ got sick, and they didn't know what they were going to do. So, Ralph's mother, Catherine, told them that Ralph could play. And, it was an intricate organ!

MARY KAY: Oh my heavens, he didn't have a degree in music or anything. The person who is there now, I think, has a doctorate and is teaching at St. Louis University!

RICH: Wow! Now, let's get back to the bakery stories!

MARY KAY: When St. Louis went through its bicentennial year in 1964, and right before they closed the bakery, grandpa made a cake that was a whole block long!

RICH: Really?!

MARY KAY: Yes, they put it together with icing of course, but I can remember him cutting pieces of cake for people, while I was watching him on T.V.

RICH: Can I hear more about the 1964 cake?

MARY KAY: I saw it all on T.V., but here is a picture of it.

RICH: [While looking at the picture I said], "I know that building. That's the Old Post Office!"

MARY KAY: Yes, it was across from the Olive Street store. And, there was grandpa in all his glory!

RICH: [I then told Rita and Mary Kay about the archived bulletins that I researched from the St. Louis Baker's Association and showed them one. The following are some of their comments about what they saw in this bulletin.]

WEDDING CAKES
Bill and Helen Ellerbrock
May 31, 1949

MARY KAY: I know my dad use to make wedding cakes, but in this picture here's my grandfather showing the bride how to cut it. Eventually, my dad started taking pictures of all the wedding cakes for a catalog. That was one of my big things in life, to go down and watch them bake the cakes.

RICH: Yes, as a kid I'll bet you were pretty amazed!

MARY KAY: They used to deliver these wedding cakes to the Chase Park Plaza Hotel, the Stadium Club, and all of these places before they even had air-conditioning. Because they didn't have air-conditioning the cakes would start to melt. So, he'd go to these places, sit there and redo parts of the cakes.

RICH: Talk about service!

MARY KAY: Yeah, he felt that was part of his job! I forgot to tell you about one thing that was part of my job when I separated the dried fruit for the bakers.

MARY KAY: Before I even got started, my grandpa would tell me every time, and he would make me wash my hands three times and dry them. That was my job, and he would have to show me how to do it every time. When I'd forget something, he'd say, "Nope, we do it this way!"

RICH: When the independent bakeries started to go down in the 50's or so, and I've asked people's opinions about this, <u>why</u> did they start to decline?

MARY KAY: Well, I can tell you why. It wasn't just the unions. It was the fact that in the stores you had Betty Crocker come in, and as a girl I used to always want to have those little Easy Bake Ovens, and my grandfather said, "You do realize if you continue to play with that, it's going to be the death of the bakery industry." That was true, but also the cost of the supplies — you couldn't use the best ingredients because it was getting so expensive.

RICH: The Bakers Bulletins always talk about the economics of the bakery business because it was published to help the bakers. So, I would love to hear more of your thoughts on this. There seemed to be so many things that affected the decline of the independent bakeries. About 15 years ago I overheard someone say that there were only about 12 or 13 of the independents left in St. Louis. Now, some new ones have started up again, many of them begun by young people.

MARY KAY: Yes, like the specialty cupcake businesses. That's very different from having to have a large variety of things to be made every day. The number of hours that bakers had to work was significant. Like my dad, he had health issues, and he wanted to have a life and time with his family. He was just working constantly.

RITA: But, my aunt Valera had really bad legs, bad veins. She would get home so late because she had to close the store down. And, I can remember at Christmas we could never have Christmas until later.

MARY KAY: I never saw some of my family for two days. Because it was Christmas they were working constantly. And, in our family we all had the same kinds of issues with our backs and legs. We all kind of hobbled around. I had trouble with my feet and legs and scoliosis, and I know where I got it!

RITA: And, they never really were able to stop. I remember everything had to be perfect. I remember my grandmother would call me when I was first married, and she would ask me, "What are you having for dinner?" Well, if I was having some kind of mediocre thing, I would lie to her and say, "Oh, I have the roast in the oven with the potatoes," because If I didn't, she would say to me, "Now, Rita, you know, you better have a nice meal for your husband."

MARY KAY: Well, that's the way they were, but who could afford that every night?

RITA: Yes, you could never cut back on anything that had to do with food.

RICH: Well, several people have told me that the boxed cake mixes had a big influence on the downfall of the independent bakeries. Their conclusion was, "Why would you spend four times as much money on a made item at a bakery when you could make the same thing at home?" When they said that, I would be thinking, "But, you can't make the same thing at home!"

MARY KAY: Oh my gosh, my friends would always say, "I can remember your birthday cakes," [laughter and agreement from Rita], because my dad would always make me mine. Like, one year I had a Beatles cake. Another year I had the "little doll in the middle" cake.

MARY KAY: My friends called it the Barbie Doll cake, but it wasn't really a Barbie Doll, and he'd make the little cake around it. But then, my grandmother who wasn't even with the bakery would also make me a cake. So, I always had to have two pieces of cake!

RITA: You know, on your Interview Question Sheet that you gave us for homework, [Laughter], it asks us, "What were some of your signature items?" I think one of our items was our caramel nut stöllen.

MARY KAY: Yes, stöllens were the thing, and wedding cakes and cookies and French donuts. And, I used to bring the cookies, to story time in the kindergarten.

MARY KAY: Well, when I would go to my other grandmother she'd always have Wonder Bread! [We all laugh!] I used to always think it was really a treat to have Wonder Bread, and my dad would say to me, "There's gonna be a day," and with him pointing to the handmade baker bread, when you wish you had this bread." Well, by golly, that day has come and passed many times because I wish I had some of it!

RITA: Didn't they also have gooey butter cakes?

MARY KAY: Yes, they did – that was later on. I could eat all of that stuff!

RICH: You know, there are several bakeries that all claim to have invented the gooey butter cake. I talked to the owner of the Carondelet Bakery down on the south side, on Michigan, across from St. Boniface Church, and they said that it was invented because of a mistake in the baking. Whoever invented it didn't cook the cake long enough. Somebody called it "The Great Cake Mistake!"

MARY KAY: Yeah, I remember hearing that too.

RITA: You know, I've done that with Brownies, and they're much better too!

MARY KAY: That's how you get the chewy ones [More laughter].

RITA: Oh, and cream puffs. We had the long ones with cream coming out of the ends.

MARY KAY: Those were actually called cream horns. And then, all of us together say, "Yes, those were delicious!"

RITA: These are such good questions on your Interview Sheet.

RICH: Well, it's just fun to think about all of this, isn't it?!

MARY KAY: Well, I'm just tickled. We don't spend enough time on history, folks! It makes me so mad that we spend so much time on other things, yet there are so many lessons to be learned.

RITA: I know. When I think about all of the goofy novels I've read, I think if I would have read all of this history I'd be a whole lot smarter!

RICH: Well, we'll meet again.

MARY KAY: I've got about ten binders. That's the nice thing about all of this in that I can start putting things in different files and then into those binders.

RITA: Can I give everybody a little bit of the bakery treats?

RICH: Sure! By the way, do you think the total number of Ellerbrock bakeries was thirteen?

MARY KAY: Well, there was one main branch, and then they would deliver everything out to all of those other stores. And, that's what my dad did.

MARY KAY: I can also remember around 1945 my dad went to the Dunwoody Technical Institute in Minnesota.

RICH: Yes, that was the really big bakery school. That was the bakery school. Some people felt that it was the most important one in the country!

RITA: [While reading from the prepared questions Rita says], "What do you remember about the 'punching of the dough,' the business and nitty gritty of baking?"

MARY KAY: My mom would say that when my dad worked in the summer time he could lose as much as 20 pounds just in water weight. But, maybe that was an exaggeration.

MARY KAY: The Dunwoody School was mostly about the science of baking, the science of how bakery goods actually work to get the best quality.

RICH: I learned from the McArthurs that the Dunwoody School closed. So, I asked them, "How do bakers get training now?" Their answer was that, "Now it's all about apprenticing. It's all about learning on the job." Maybe the two of you can get together and figure out what were all of the locations of the Ellerbrock bakeries. And, you know, if you could put together a family tree, that would be great!

Author's Note: Rita and Mary Kay eventually did identify all of the Ellerbrock locations, and they are posted on the list of historic locations in the Appendix.

Federhofer's Bakery
Family History
Composed by Cheryl Federhofer

*Personal gifts of the bakery for us were the wonderful smells
of the bakery and how it provided a good life for all of us. Our
bakery friends were great and very hard-working people.
There were many wonderful memories and stories.*
— Cheryl Federhofer

Author's Note: Because Cheryl was unable to meet with me in an interview she was very kind in putting together this Family History of the Federhofer Bakery.

Family History

1. The Federhofer Bakery location has been at 9005 Gravois Road in Affton, Missouri. The bakery was open seven days a week from 6am to 11 pm.

2. Bill Sr. and Merle Federhofer bought the bakery on October 16, 1965.

3. Cheryl bought the bakery in February of 2017 from her parents.

4. Bill Sr. and Merle Federhofer started the bakery in 1965. Bill Jr. and Cheryl worked at the bakery all through high school. Bill Jr. was a cake decorator for a while after college.

5. Cheryl returned to work after college and then took a ten-year maternity leave (as my mother called it) to raise her sons.

6. Cheryl returned to work as the boys started school. Robin and Danny worked at the bakery at some times during and after college. All three of Cheryl's boys Justin, Tyler, and Bryce May worked there through high school. They all three returned to work at the bakery after college.

7. A few of the other grandchildren have worked there as well. Tyler and Bryce continue to work here and are learning the business to eventually take over.

8. So right now we have the 3rd generation learning and successfully running the business. The great grandkids love to come to the bakery for special treats and even a cupcake decorating birthday party.

9. Bill Federhofer Sr. is still working every day at the age of eighty-two. We have a few other employees that have been with us for twenty-five plus years also.

10. Doering's Bakery — Bill's sister married into the Doering family, and eventually she and her husband owned the bakery. They became partners with Bill's brother Ed who ran the Baker's Co-op. They were very close friends with the McArthur Bakery family. Don McArthur built cake depositors that we still use today. He nicknamed them after Danny (Zip) Federhofer,

the Zip Machine. Lubeley's were close friends also. Bill Sr. was on a bowling team with Bob Jr.

11. At Mid-Continent Paper company Bob and Marge Grommet and their son, Bob Jr., became very close friends. We would go fishing and horseback riding at their home.

12. As for Ole and Ginny Johnson, Ole was a salesman, and they became Merle's godparents when she turned Catholic. There are many more wonderful memories and stories. They were great and very hard-working people.

The Bakery

1. We have grown our business to a full retail one with some wholesale accounts by offering fresh baked goods. We keep up with the trends of cake and cookie decorating, while keeping the prices within reason. We have twenty-eight full-time employees and two part-time employees. Through the virus we have been able to keep our doors open with everyone still employed. We even had to hire more help. In fact, business is better than it has ever been.

2. When they opened the bakery they used the money out of their kid's piggy bank for their start-up money in the cash register. As time went on we changed the hours from 6:00 am – 11:00 pm. to 6:00 am – 9:00 pm, and then finally to 6:00 am – 6:00 pm. The flow of traffic over time on Gravois Road changed due to large factory closures in the area.

3. Business was much better on Sundays before the grocery stores opened up on Sundays. When they purchased the bakery there were over 100 bakeries in the Saint Louis area. So there was a lot of competition with other bakeries. Two strong memories were the hard work and the long hours. We are non-union now. Bill Sr. used to be one of the negotiators for the Bakers Union.

4. It was easy to get what we needed. We would get rebates on most of the products we purchased from the Co-Op. Bill's brother Ed ran the Co-Op. Bill Sr. was on the board of directors for the Co-Op. Some personal memories were Christmas parties at the warehouse, a really bad Santa, and pony rides in the warehouse.

HOW OUR HEARTS WERE STÖLLEN

5. Bill was president of the Missouri Bakers. They would meet monthly and hold social events, some of them at Lake of the Ozarks, with lots of mixed drinks, bingo and square-dancing. There was also the "Baker's Dozen Club" that had 13 members. The only way to get into this club was if someone dropped out or died. Bill Sr. became a member and they met monthly at different bakeries each month. They would bring a product to taste and would share the recipe with the other bakers. There was also the Salesmen Production Club that met monthly.

6. The salesmen would take the bakers out to dinner and would host other events both in St. Louis and at conventions. These salesmen called on each bakery every week to get their orders. It was a very social club of gentleman.

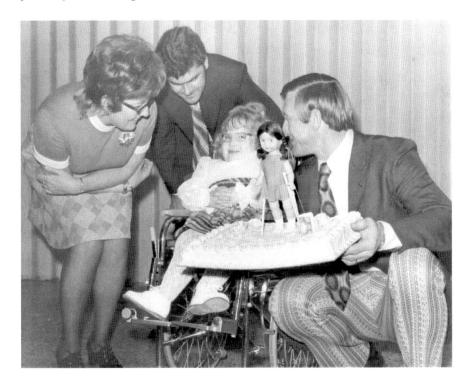

7. The Bakers Association was also involved in the Easter Seals Society. They would collect and donate money to the Society. Last but not least, there was the Ladies Bakers Club. They also met for lunch monthly and would share stories of hiring, customer service, products, and many other helpful ideas for running a business.

Highlights

1. We have remodeled three times in fifty-four years. The extremely large neon sign is original. We had it restored several years ago. When they removed the panels to replace them, the Mueller's Bakery name was still visible. It costs several hundred dollars to maintain the neon on the sign each year.

2. My mom always said she could write a book on all the excuses some employees could come up with for why they could not come into work or why they had to leave early on a particular day. Debbie Rapp calls herself the best store girl we ever had. She still tells the story of a customer who said they were told they could get a discount, because they were very good friends of Bill and Merle Federhofer. Obviously, they really didn't know Bill and Merle Federhofer very well. We had a baker who would work at night alone. He left but several years later he returned through the roof of our freezer to try attempting to rob us. He set the alarms off. He broke out the front door to get out. He didn't get anything. Then he proceeded down the street to break into Kenrick's Meat Market and was arrested. Many of the older bakers, their wives and children came to work here at the bakery when their bakeries closed. Some of them were Sam and June Wolf, Paul and Shirley Bretcher, and Carl and Delores Berry.

3. Some of the bakery's signature items were Grandma's, (Bill Sr's. mom's), Custard Pie, Mr. Doering's Springerles, and Bretchers Bakery's (at Grand & Arsenal) Deep Butter Coffee Cake.

4. Personal gifts of the bakery for us were the wonderful smells of the bakery and how it provided a good life for all of us.

5. Signature items for us were Swedish Crumb Loaf, Gooey Butter Cakes, Christmas Cookies, Springerles, Poppy Seed Stöllens, Pecan Danish Rolls, and Decorated Cakes.

Final

1. Carl Mueller owned and built the bakery in 1958.

2. Bill Sr. and Merle Federhofer bought the bakery on October 16, 1965 from Mr. Mueller. Amazingly, Bill Sr. was twenty-seven and Merle was twenty-four. At that time they had three small children and one on the way. They worked for Mr. Mueller prior to purchasing the bakery.

3. Bill Sr. worked at Doering's Bakery as a child along with his siblings and their mother. He started working at the age of nine for ten dollars a week. He would give his mother five dollars each week to help support the family. He would work afternoons after school cleaning the bakery and scraping floors. On Saturday nights he would go to the bakery by 7:00 pm and go right to bed. Mr. Doering would wake him at midnight to work for ten or twelve hours each Saturday.  He would fry donuts and do other odd jobs. He worked at several bakeries and supermarkets prior to purchasing the bakery.

4. Bill Sr. and Merle raised four kids Cheryl, Bill Jr., Robin, and Danny whom they put through Catholic schools and college.

5. Merle Federhofer passed last year at the age of seventy-eight, in June due to colon cancer.

6. Cheryl bought the bakery from her parents in February of 2017.

7. At age eighty-two Bill Sr. continues to come in a couple of times a day to check on us. He also has taken over as my office manager

"Hank's Cheesecakes"
Interview With Hank Krussel

"There used to be a drugstore in New York city called Lindy's, and somebody came up with the Lindy's cheesecake. If you just left a piece of this cheesecake sit on a plate until it comes to room temperature, and as it gets a little bit warmer, it leans over just a little bit more and more! It never quite melts completely, but it should be very, very soft. And, the flavor of it is just outstanding!"
— Hank Krussel

RICH: So anyway, I read a little bit about your story. That's mostly what I'm interested in, how you see the story and the development of the bakery at the beginning and just what it was like. So, that's kind of where we're going. I've been working on this for quite awhile. You'll be my 22nd in-person interview. So, I'm really excited about this project. I've done a lot of research and archive work on the history of St. Louis bakeries. So, I'm hoping to put a book out in the next year or so.

HANK: O.K., let me know so that I can get a copy.

RICH: Good! Yeah, that would be great!

HANK: And, are you going back to way-back-when with the old bakeries that were around?

RICH: I am. I have been focusing on the heyday of St. Louis bakeries which was anywhere in the 20th century, but they were doing especially well during the 1950's and 60's. I had heard that there were over 500 independent bakeries in St. Louis, and now there are many fewer than that as you know.

RICH: Most of the great bakers were German, weren't they?

HANK: You've got it! That would be me as well!

RICH: Right! I figured that! But, you have a specialty, and that's really interesting. Getting "leads" about other bakers to interview from bakers that I'm currently interviewing has been a really good way to pursue this research, because that way people trust me and they trust that I'm doing something that's serious and intentional, you know. So anyway, I read some of your story on your website, but I'd really like to hear how you describe the story of the beginnings and how you were motivated to do this, and so on.

HANK: Uhh-h-h, it's kind of a long story.

RICH: O.K., well I've got time. [And, I laugh here.]

HANK: I got a job to earn me a little money, and finally decided that I'd like to go into computer programming. So, I took all of the courses they had at Forest Park Community College and finished that up in May of '81 or '82? And, I said to myself, "Before I get a real job, I need to enjoy one last summer." And, I loved to go out to the mountains backpacking. So, I spent the summer doing that, and the more I was out there by myself the more I felt like, "I can't go back and work for somebody. It's just <u>not</u> gonna' work for me." So, I needed something to do. While I was working at my first job in Louisiana there was a woman working for me, and she found some cheesecake recipes somewhere. And, she would make one and bring it into the office. And, I thought, "My God, this is good!"

HANK: So, I had the recipes, and I enjoyed baking. I would make them, and it seemed pretty easy to do. And, after I got out of that job, if I was invited to dinner to somebody's house or a potluck or whatever, I'd take along a cheesecake. And, people would say, "Why don't you open a shop?" So, that seemed to be my only recourse.

HANK: That was the only thing I could come up with that I might be able to earn a living at. So, I worked out of my apartment, messed around, and did that for three years. And then, a caterer I sold to was moving out of a small space that he was in, and he said, "If you want the space I'll talk to the landlord. I can leave some equipment behind for you, and you can get started."

HANK: And, I figured after three years it was either time to quit or to do it right. So, I moved into that space. It was only about 750 square feet, and so after about a year I sort of outgrew it.

HANK: Do you remember or know about Cyrano's?

RICH: Yeah, I sure do. I think I was in there one time!

HANK: A long time ago it was on Clayton Road, down in a basement. That place burned, and there was a Shakey's Pizza Parlor right around the corner, and then they moved in here. While I was down at my first location there was a man who bought the Cyrano's name. They were still doing business in this building. He bought the Cyrano's name to keep the restaurant going, but this building was actually too big for Cyrano's. There was a lot of extra space, so he asked me if I would do his wedding cake for him and if I would like to move into this building and rent the extra space that he didn't need. So, we came up with an agreement, and this is where I am now. I've sort of outgrown this space, but I don't feel like moving again. That's the story!

RICH: Right, right. Sure. Yeah, when I was in it I guess I was in the original Cyrano's on Clayton Road. Didn't you have to go down in a basement kind of area?

HANK: Yeah, but I don't remember much about it.

RICH: Yeah. Who was the Cyrano's owner that you did the wedding cake for and who owned Cyrano's?

HANK: I cannot think of his last name offhand. His first name was Frank, oh yeah, O'Donnell. He was a nice man, but I think he just didn't enjoy doing that business. So, he got into other business ventures. Somebody else owns it now.

RICH: So, you rented that space from him at first?

HANK: Oh yeah, I did, but I told him, "If I rent from you, I want to be able to buy this space if you ever choose to sell. So, after some years he said, "Yeah, I want to sell the building if you still want to buy it." So, I own the building now, I pay myself rent, and I rent out the restaurant part that was Cyrano's.

RICH: O.K., has that changed names now?

HANK: Yeah, Cyrano's is down in Webster Groves now, and Del Pietro's is now the restaurant in this building. Yeah, the parents originally had a restaurant down on South Hampton, and now one of their son's, Michael Del Pietro, runs this Del Pietro's.

RICH: I knew the South Hampton Del Pietro's pretty well. You know what is in there now is "Salt and Smoke," a very popular barbecue restaurant. Things change fast, don't they?!

HANK: Yes, they do.

RICH: O.K., I can see your motivations in there because you were impressed with the flavors from the lady who made your first cheesecake for you.

HANK: Yeah, and I think I started out with one of her recipes, but based on that recipe I came up with a few others. Then, after I had done some of my own recipes I started to be creative. That was the fun part of it. I came up with the recipe for a good number of the cheesecakes that we sell these days. But, I also had a guy working for me when I first moved into the shop who was very creative, and he came up with a few recipes of his own.

RICH: Can you tell me about this employee that helped create some of the additional recipes?

HANK: His name was Keith Stewart. He had worked with a French chef who was in charge of the corporate dining room for one of the major banks in St. Louis.

HANK: He was very good as a chef. So, I hired him to do the mixing and the baking, and for a little while it was just the two of us doing all of the work. Then I hired somebody else, and the business grew from there. Keith liked being creative, and he came up with some new ideas. Then, I would make a few changes to fit my taste. One of them that he came up with was the key lime, and it is one of our most popular cakes! Turtle was another popular one, and he and I worked on that together. Plain and white chocolate-raspberry were the other two popular cakes, and I came up with those recipes.

RICH: Yeah, well those are all great flavors. Those four would have to be the best-sellers. So, you hired Keith, and then did you hire more people to do the mixing and whatever else needed to be done? Key-lime is such a distinctive flavor.

HANK: That was all his work. I'm sorry to say that I didn't have anything to do with it. Yeah, while I was at the first location I probably hired a few people, many of whom did not work out very well. Let me throw this in too, my mother would come in and wash dishes. She had a lot of free-time, and she enjoyed coming in, doing dishes, seeing what was going on, and seeing how well the business was doing and all of that. I owe her a great deal just for all of the volunteer work she did, though she is no longer with us.

RICH: Just like a mother, right! That's a neat part of the story, Hank, especially since my wife and I knew her personally! She was a very sweet lady, very nice. She was very popular with our whole parish church really. Everybody loved Catherine.

HANK: Good. Yeah, I recall you mentioning that.

RICH: Well, all of those things you talked about tell me a lot. How many people are employed now? I hope you have more help than you did at that time.

HANK: I've got nine employees right now.

RICH: That says that business has been good, right?

HANK: Yes, these days my wholesale sales to restaurants are way down because of the virus. But, we are retail, and that's the thing that's keeping us going.

RICH: Do you sell in any grocery stores like Straub's or anywhere else?

HANK: We do sell in Straub's, the four stores that they have. We also sell at Provisions Market over on the Delmar Loop. Those are the only stores that we sell in. But, before the virus hit we probably had sixty or seventy restaurants that we sold to. And, they're slowly coming back. We don't have near those numbers right now.

RICH: Wow, that's a big change, isn't it. Do you feel like you've been able to somewhat weather the change?

HANK: Yeah, so far. We actually closed down completely, and then shortened our hours for a few weeks. Then, the retail business started growing. So, I brought everybody back. I got a little bail-out money from the government. August has been a little on the slow side, but it always is. And yet, I really can't complain. We'll get by for a few more months, if not weeks.

RICH: Well, maybe Halloween, Thanksgiving, and Christmas will help, huh?

HANK: Oh, yeah. Easter was good this year. Mother's Day was very good. We normally don't do very well for Father's Day, but this year we did alright.

RICH: Good, that's great! Now, I don't know if this is a pertinent question or not, but are there any employees that stand out in your memory as being distinctive at all?

HANK: Yes. there are three in particular. The first was Keith who I mentioned. The other two work for me at the present time. There's a guy who doesn't bake the cakes, but he finishes them once they're out of the ovens and they come out of the pans. Most of them get toppings, and then we send them to restaurants or people pick them up. He's very good at what he does, very organized and knows how to schedule things.

RICH: What could be better, right!

HANK: Yep! It took me awhile to find some really good employees, but the people I have right now, if they choose to stay for the rest of their lives, that would be good!

HANK: The third guy works with the guy I just mentioned. Ken is the first guy's name. This guy's name is Tyree. The two of them together seem like they read each other's minds, and what the one doesn't get done the other knows to get it done. They really make a great pair.

RICH: That's neat, isn't it! And, is Tyree also a finisher?

HANK: Right.

RICH: If you came into your store as a customer, what do you think would be your favorite?

HANK: My favorite? I think our best cake is our tiramisu. This is also a cake that Keith came up with. But, for my money it's better than ninety percent of the tiramisu you may find around town. It's really a good combination of flavors!

RICH: That's neat, very neat. So, what would the flavors be? Chocolate, and is there a cream filling in there?

HANK: There's a bottom layer that's made of a chocolate crust, and it has a cappuccino flavor. But, before we make the actual cheesecake we bake a ladyfinger layer and just lay it on top of the espresso layer. It gets a bunch of rum soaked into it, and then there's a layer of vanilla cheesecake on top of that. [I just laugh with unbelief at how good this sounds!] Then, when we finish the cake each slice gets a big dollop of chocolate on top of it! And then, we sprinkle a layer of cocoa all over the top! Between the espresso, the cocoa, the chocolate, and the rum, it's just wonderful!

RICH: Oh, my gosh! [My laughter!] It is really good to hear your description! You know what I'm most attracted to, I just love plain creamy cheesecake, and I'm going to ask you to reminisce with me. Did you ever have Famous-Barr's cheesecake?! You grew up when Famous-Barr was located at Kingshighway and Chippewa, right? [Famous-Barr department stores later became Macy's.] They had a creamy cheesecake, and I have to ask you if that was a New York style cheesecake? It was a soft cheesecake.

HANK: No, I never had that. Well, let me tell you a little story here. There used to be a drugstore in New York city called Lindy's. They had a counter, and I guess you could sit down and have a sandwich or whatever, and somebody came up with Lindy's cheesecake. And, Lindy's cheesecake was the ultimate, the penultimate cheesecake.

HANK: I read an article thirty or forty years ago, and it was about Lindy's cheesecake. The person who wrote the article said, "Here's how you tell if you have the very best cheesecake. You put the slice on a plate, and the tip of the slice, which is the center of the cake, doesn't sit there perfectly. It kind of falls over a little bit because it's soft."

HANK: And then, he said, "If you just left the piece of cheesecake sit on a plate until it comes to room temperature, and as it gets a little bit warmer, it leans over just a little bit more and more! It never quite melts completely, but it should be very, very soft. And, the flavor of it is just outstanding!

RICH: [With my mouth watering], I say, "Oh my gosh, that's a great description!"

HANK: So, that's the kind of cake I like to bake, but a lot of times when you sell cake like that, people often bring it back and say, "Oh, this cheesecake isn't done." So, I try to keep my cheesecakes on the creamy side but bake them a little bit longer.

HANK: These days nobody makes them that way. There's this place called Lindy's in New York on Times Square where they sell this god-awful cheesecake. Nothing like the real thing as far as I'm concerned. Tourists stop in there, and they eat it, and I don't know why. And, most of the New York style cheesecake that you find in New York City is not creamy. I think it's over-baked, and it doesn't hold a candle to the old Lindy's cheesecake. You know, if you travel around the country it is difficult to find really outstanding cheesecake.

RICH: Yeah, I believe you, Hank. What would you call that cheesecake, just creamy? I mean, the original Lindy's, was that called the New York style cheesecake?

HANK: I think that's where it started. And, what they make in New York tends to be a little bit like a Lindy's cake. A Lindy's cake was a little taller than I make. Lindy's cheesecake had a pastry crust. It didn't have a crumb crust. That was a little bit more involved.

HANK: Though I haven't been to New York for a few years now, most of what I found on my trips up there was a slightly taller cheesecake and denser. The longer you bake it, the denser it gets. If you bake it less, it will be creamier and tastier. I think Lindy's was the original New York style cheesecake, but I don't think you can find it anymore.

RICH: Well, that's really interesting stuff! I feel like I finally learned what that creamy cheesecake was! They had a pretty good bakery at Famous-Barr at the Kingshighway and Chippewa location. It was memorable.

HANK: I wonder who has the recipe for that now.

RICH: Well, I guess I want to ask you the economics of your whole project, the business that you had there. Did it grow pretty consistently, or were there some up and down times?

HANK: I would say the biggest down time was during the recession some years back. Most people consider the recession as occurring in 2008. It certainly didn't kill us, and we came back from that. Business in the first couple months of the virus was considerably worse, but after those first couple of months we started coming back. It really wasn't terrible. We had a lot of new people coming in.

HANK: I just hired a person to take my place here, and I should have hired somebody for that several years ago. He's working on building up the business. The last several years I've just gotten very tired. As far as what I've accomplished, I was happy, or I should say that I was satisfied. I wasn't really happy, but I was satisfied. Here's a bad thing about the economics of our business. Do you remember Raskas Dairy at all?

RICH: Yeah, I do.

HANK: Raskas Dairy was a St. Louis based company. They made cream cheese, they made butter, and they made sour cream. In the last ten or twenty years they didn't make the butter, but they made the sour cream and cream cheese. My father was a pipe-fitter. He worked for a small business that did refrigeration service. He would work on their pipes at Raskas Dairy, and then, he would bring home cream cheese. They would give him a three-pound loaf of cream cheese, for the hourly rate or whatever he earned for his work.

HANK: Raskas had a great cream cheese. They were really nice people, but they weren't great business people I guess. I worked with them, and I could buy cream cheese from them. I'd just go to the plant, and I think it was on North Taylor. I'd pick up a load of cheese and pay them, and it was great.

HANK: The problem is that in the last several years the price of cream cheese has just gone up and up and up. When I first started out you could buy cream cheese for about 80 cents a pound. Now it's closer to 2.60 a pound or more.

RICH: Wow!

HANK: I like to sell things at a reasonable price. I hate paying high prices. So, I try to keep prices low, and that is the biggest problem in this business right now. It's about trying to buy quality ingredients at a reasonable price and providing my customers with a wonderful product. It's difficult to do. I'm just old-school, and I don't like the price of everything going up every year. The last four or five years I think I've raised prices every year!

RICH: Yeah, because you had to, right!

HANK: Yeah! I mean, I have to pay insurance, I have to pay taxes, I have a license from St. Louis County, I have to get a license from Richmond Heights. If we deliver into the City of St. Louis, St. Louis wants me to buy a license from them just to drive into their fair city and drop-off cheesecakes! Sales tax keeps going up, real estate tax keeps going up! I could go on and on.

RICH: O.K. I think that was also in the bio information on the website.

HANK: O.K. Sometimes I would like to see some negative things about certain things, as long as they don't impact me! It's hard to say positive things about some things! [I laugh loudly at Hank's honesty.]

RICH: [With me still laughing I say], "Well, thank you for your honesty!" [And, still laughing I say], "That's me too! I would love to see some negative things said about negative things!"

RICH: Hey, a big thing that I noticed in your story on the website was your embracing of sustainability, which I thought was really cool! And, I want to tell you that I just interviewed a young woman on Cherokee street who has one of the new bake-shops in St. Louis. There are specialty bakeries as you know. The name of her bakery is "Whisk," and the formal name of her bakery is "Whisk, A Sustainable Bakeshop."

RICH: It was really interesting to hear her talk about that and how committed she is to purchasing local from local suppliers, vendors, and farmers, and those sorts of things. Can you talk at all about that, you know, coming to that conclusion? Do you know, when?

HANK: Well, I mentioned earlier that I love the outdoors. So, I have always been an environmentalist. I went to school at Georgetown, and Shenandoah National Park was a little over an hour outside of D.C. So, I got out there a few times hiking and camping. My first job location was in Arizona, and I was just in heaven in Arizona, New Mexico, Colorado, and Utah. The best times I've ever had in my life were when I was wandering around in the mountains. Along with that comes a dedication to keeping the environment safe and clean.

HANK: There's a range of mountains in Wyoming called the Wind River Mountains that runs over a hundred miles. If you get on top of a tall peak in the Wind River mountains you can see the Grand Tetons which are sixty or seventy miles away. I always wondered, "What would it have been like to see that a hundred and fifty years ago when there was no smog. There was very little in the way of forest fire smoke, and you could see clearly for long distances. What would it have been like to see that?"

RICH: Yes, exactly!

HANK: Recently, I found out that there's a company that is working with St. Louis and St. Louis County to install "solar" at a reasonable price. Right now I'm looking into that for the shop and for my house. And, I'm seeing about it to install solar. It might cost a little money. It's more economical, but that's not my reason for doing it. It's also a little something I can do directly to affect and improve the environment, and I'm willing to pay a little extra for that. I didn't think I could afford to pay this out-of-pocket, but you get tax-breaks and this and that. It seems like a pretty good deal. So, I'll see what I can do with that.

HANK: As far as buying locally, it's very difficult. There is a local cooperative dairy, and they make cream cheese. And, I had an opportunity to buy some at a low price recently.

HANK: But, before I decided to buy some I wanted to see how it acted, how it behaved if you try to make a cheesecake out of it. We bought a few eight-ounce packages at Schnuck's and made a couple cakes with it, and it tasted different. If you eat a bite of that alongside of a bite of Raskas cream cheese cheesecake there's a definite difference between the two. That's not to say that this dairy is bad. It's just the flavor of the cream cheese depends on what sort of a cream cheese culture they put into it. And, there are all kinds of cream cheese cultures.

RICH: Yeah, right.

HANK: So, if I wanted to buy locally, and that's what I used to do from Raskas, I would drive a few miles, pick-up what I needed, and bring it back. Now, I can't do that anymore. An eighteen wheeler has to bring it in, and I buy a lot of cheese. It has to be transported two hundred miles.

RICH: Yes.

HANK: We do buy sour cream and whipping cream from Prairie Farms. We don't use a lot of produce like restaurants do. That's something that can be bought locally, but it's not something we use. Oh, there is a local company that makes vanilla, Lochhead Vanilla Company, and they have a very good product. We buy from them. We buy spices from McCormick Spice Company, which is located in the area. There is also chocolate, but we have to buy that from out-of-town.

HANK: The major ingredients that we buy, they're unavailable from local producers. Yeah, and if I want to put out a product I'm less happy with because I bought locally, I don't know if that would make any sense.

RICH: Right, sure. I think that's a big thing. The two things have to be taken into consideration. Well, that's really very honest, and I appreciate that. You really describe the dilemma that your store and many stores have to deal with. You know, if something is not available you have to get what you need that makes your product a quality product.

HANK: Right. I think that restaurants can get very good meat and vegetables locally.

RICH: I understand completely what you're saying. Well, I don't want to keep you too long. Is this one of your days off, or do you get *any* days off? [I laugh a little.]

HANK: Yeah. When I feel like not being here, I do as little as possible those days. That's why I hired this new person, because I don't devote time to this business that it should have. I may have mentioned this, my niece was supposed to take this over, but she got sick. So, I think I'm back on the right track again. And, this guy is very capable. So, I'm working with him.

RICH: Yes, for all bakers a consistent theme is that it is tremendously hard work and can really wear you down.

HANK: And, I have sometimes said that if I had known what I would have to go through with the government and problems that arise, employees, and everything else, if you'd look at all of what was in store for you, I'd think differently about the whole thing of being in business.

RICH: Huh! [I laugh a short laugh.] That is very honest also!

HANK: And, let me say one more thing too. Put this in the book! The FDA, the Food and Drug Administration, with all of the increased security, they passed the Food Safety Act, or whatever it was, some years ago to protect America's food supply from being contaminated. Well, I am a small company. I don't know if I've ever done over 700,000 dollars in sales in a year.

HANK: And, before the Food Safety Act, it was, "Write all of your ingredients on the cake box." Well, if you didn't sell more than "x" number of units of each individual product, you didn't have to do that. So, we had to register and then every year send in a report that we sold this number of this cake and this number of that cake, and on down the line. And, if somebody wanted to know about ingredients they were free to ask.

Author's Note: At this time, Hank said one of the funniest things I heard in all of the interviews. *You know, if you eat this cake and you're worried about calories, <u>don't buy this cake! Eat an orange</u>.* I loved this comment, and I burst out laughing.

HANK: And now, with this Food Safety Act the FDA sends an inspector in, and inspects this place like we're the Kraft Foods Company or some other huge food manufacturer. And, they say, "Do this, do that." or "You gotta' clean this up, you gotta' clean that up. You can't have this, you can't have that."

HANK: I've been in business for almost thirty-five years, and there's never been a single problem. I'm not here to put out a crappy product that I know is going to harm someone or make them sick. And, I have nine employees. "Don't you have bigger and better things to worry about than me?!"

HANK: The government passes these laws, and I don't know if they look at the consequences of what they're doing, but the FDA is the biggest thorn in my side. It really is.

RICH: I understand both sides of this, but I will try to put that in the book.

HANK: And again, I'm old school, and I guess the people growing up with it now, put up with it. The guy I hired doesn't have such strong feelings about it, but I certainly do.

RICH: Well, this is not an unusual comment either. I mean, I've heard similar kinds of things from other bakers.

HANK: And then, they want you to write down if someone gets sick from eating one of your cakes, how do you do a recall? You'd have to keep track of every one of your cakes, when it was baked, what ingredients went into it, and do that for every cake you bake. I could hire another person and pay them thirty thousand dollars a year to do that and make absolutely no money from that person's work. It's really insane. And again, I could go on and on.

RICH: Well, Hank, I'm so appreciative of your time and your candor, and I've really enjoyed talking with you. So, if you're a praying man, please pray that I get this book out sometime within the next year or so. [And, I laugh with a hopeful laugh!]

HANK: I will do that.

RICH: Pray to your mom. I know she's in heaven.

HANK: Will do. But, you've been doing this for so long, I admire your dedication as well.

RICH: Thank you.

HANK: I would certainly like to see this thing published. I would enjoy going through it!

RICH: It's just a great story that I want to tell. It's a beautiful story, honestly! I mean, the similarities between bakers, what you've had to deal with, and the dedication that you all have to making people happy! Really! That's what it's all about! [I laugh with admiration here!]

HANK: Yes, that really <u>is</u> what it's all about!

RICH: [And, I almost shout this!] "Hank, you make people happy! Remember that!"

HANK: I don't make the FDA happy though!

RICH: And, they don't make you happy, obviously! Well, thanks very much, Hank. And, I hope to cross paths with you again sometime.

HANK: I wish you great, great luck in finishing this!

RICH: Take good care of yourself, Hank. Thank you.

Hausel Bakery
Interview With Mark Hausel and Connie Wolf

My dad must have fired me a hundred times! I was such a smart aleck. I was nineteen, and I thought I knew everything. A couple of times he fired me, and he told me to come back in before I even made it to the door!
— Mark Hausel

RICH: Thanks for meeting with me, Mark.

MARK: Hopefully, my brother will come up with some stuff. We kinda' split it up.

CONNIE: Was he a baker also?

MARK: No, he's a pharmacist. He worked in the bakery, the one my dad and I owned, for a little while on Saturday mornings, at Christmas time, and some other times. You'll obviously cross-reference what I say with what other people say because my timelines aren't sure — I could kick myself for not asking more questions of my dad.

CONNIE: I have heard so many people say that.

MARK: Yeah, my grandfather passed away when I was about eighteen or nineteen, and I was just getting into the business. So, I never had a chance to ask enough questions.

RICH: I want to say here that Connie Wolf has been a tremendous help, and I appreciate her being along for the ride. One of the things that has really helped is that Connie has known some people that can introduce me to other people. And, if you can think of people that you know later, let Connie know. The first thing that I don't want to miss is the address of your bakery. Did you have one location or more than one location?

MARK: Oh, Hampton Avenue. It was between Itaska and Neosho. Right in the middle. I can't think of the address. And, just one location. We had a second location for about a month and a half, but I don't even want to get into that. It didn't really amount to anything except a loss.

RICH: Well, how many generations were involved in your bakery?

MARK: Just the two, just me and my dad. My dad bought the place from a guy named Elmer Blatz, and here's a little history note about him. The bakery he owned before was on De Baliviere Avenue. It burned down from a fire. So, he retired, and he didn't like being retired. Then he opened up this little place on Hampton Avenue. My dad retired around 1986 or so. I had gotten married in 1977. So, my wife and I took the bakery over in 1986, and we had it until 1995.

RICH: So, what was your bakery known for? What would it be if you had to pick one thing that you were proud of?

MARK: We made an assortment of small dessert pastries. There were six different kinds, and we sold them to quite a few wholesale accounts. Butler's Pantry and a catering business were the two biggest ones. That was definitely a specialty that my dad and I had.

RICH: Yeah, that's exactly what I was looking for because it seemed like every bakery had something that they would feature.

MARK: I never made a loaf of bread until I worked for Lubeley's. We didn't make bread down where I was.

MARK: See, my dad had high blood pressure, and he had to get out of owning his own business because the stress was too great. So, he did other bakery stuff for quite awhile. Then, he found this place because there was no night work. There was no bread, there was nothing like that.

MARK: I had done other things after high school, and none of them worked for me. So, my father said, "Let's go into business. The owner's lease is up. We'll take a three year lease. If you don't like it, you'll be twenty-two, and you can go back to school or do whatever you want." And, here I am at the age of sixty-two, and I'm still doing it.

MARK: And, just between the three of us and the fencepost, my dad must have fired me a hundred times! I was such a smart aleck. I was nineteen, and I thought I knew everything. A couple of times he fired me, and he told me to come back in before I even made it to the door! [At this point, we all laughed!]

RICH: Was your wife or your mother involved in the business at all?

MARK: My wife didn't get involved until later. We got married, and then we had kids right away, and she probably got involved when the kids were about four. She started working then, and by the time the kids got into grade school she was full-time at the shop, you know, working mostly in the store. Yeah, eventually she was involved.

MARK: Has anybody mentioned John McHenry? Well, he never owned a bakery, but he worked at the Fav-Rite bakery with my dad. He knows a lot of people, and a lot of what happened. He was an instructor at the O'Fallon Tech school. I'm trying to find his phone number. It didn't even dawn on me about Mr. McHenry until just this morning. He worked for my dad when he owned the Fav-Rite bakery with Joe Klingel down on Cherokee Street. My dad and Joe Klingel bought it from a guy named Bagee.

RICH: There are actually some new bakeries coming in down there.

MARK: Well, that actually is still a bakery. It's a Mexican bakery. Has anyone mentioned Elmer Klund's bakery? They were on Gravois, a half block south of Loughborough on the west side of the street.

Author's Note: Later, I discovered that the Klund Bakery was owned by the grandfather of Jason Siebert, who with his wife Jenna now owns the bakery in Soulard called "The Sweet Divine".

RICH: This is so interesting because of all of our childhood experiences. At that time everybody had a family bakery that they were loyal to, and mine was the St. Louis Pastry Shop on Meramec Street at Virginia, cattycorner from Winkelmann's drug store. It's so interesting because the joke has always been that there were four things on every corner in South St. Louis — a tavern, a gas station, a confectionary, and a bakery.

CONNIE: And, a church! [And, we all laugh together in agreement.]

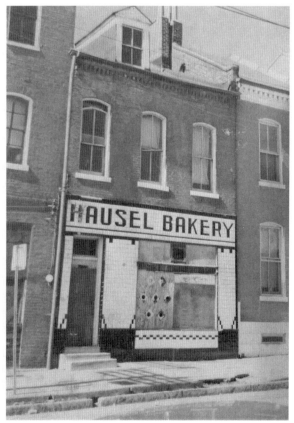

RICH: And, what was the location for the Hausel Bakery?

MARK: It was at 9th and Geyer the first location of Hausel's Bakery. It's a condominium now.

MARK: I have my grandpa's naturalization papers, but they're buried somewhere at my house. That would have been when he left Hungary and then came through Ellis Island. He was a baker when he came here. I don't know what he did over there. His name was Mike Hausel, and he bought a bakery for my dad to work in because my dad worked too hard to be a jobber. I think it was the Melba Bakery on South Grand?

RICH: Was it in that arcade with the Melba Theater?

MARK: No, it was on Grand Avenue about two or three blocks south of Tower Grove Park on the west side of the street.

RICH: Was that the old Bretscher Bakery location?

MARK: That was the building. I'm not sure whether Paul Bretscher bought it from my grandfather or not. It seems like that is what my dad told me. My grandfather was Michael Hausel, and my grandmother was Susanna, and she was from Romania. They spoke pretty decent English by the time I was growing up.

MARK: He started a bakery at 9th and Geyer. [At this time there might be a recent bakery that's located there called, "The Sweet Divine."] His dad and his brother were both marble workers. So, where the bakery business came from I don't know. They started that bakery in the mid to late 1920's.

MARK: Somewhere in there they had to sell that bakery on 9th and Geyer because my grandfather got sick, and they told him he shouldn't own his own business anymore. So, then he "jobbed out," and worked at Moellinger's and a couple of other bakeries. And then, they did the Melba Bakery thing, and then I think he sold that one to Paul Bretscher. Later in the fifties my dad ran the Famous-Barr department store bakery downtown, the department store that later became the downtown

Macy's store. My dad managed the plant down there for all the Famous-Barr stores that had the bakery stuff, until he bought the Fav-Rite Bakery with Joe Klingel.

RICH: So, do you have any idea when the Melba Bakery was bought, the one that became the Bretscher Bakery?

MARK: I would venture to guess in 1947 maybe? And, he only kept the bakery a short time. That's when I think he sold it to Bretscher. Paul Bretscher then sold it to a man named Dieckman, but he kept the name as Bretscher's for a long time.

MARK: I'll tell you, the person you need to talk to is Ed Federhofer. Ed could tell you more about the bakeries in St. Louis than anybody, because he ran the Baker's Co-Op.

MARK: I think Ed Federhofer would probably talk your ear off. I'll hit the computer and see if I can find him and his phone number. Bob Lubeley might even have it. He might have it, because he and I were pretty close. Ed Federhofer could tell you where he worked, but then he ended up running the Baker's Co-Op. You'd have to ask him about it, but he and my dad had something to do with the union and putting it in the bakers' contracts that they could only work five days a week.

RICH: This is probably a good place to tell you this, but I've been working about five years on this project, and it doesn't look like the end is in sight. I inherited from Randy and David McArthur three ten-ream paper boxes of the Bakers Association's monthly bulletins for about fifty years. Somebody kept them in perfect sequential order, and I think it was a lady named Joyce Schwarz who was associated with one of the bakeries.

MARK: I was actually working part-time for McArthur's, not for Randy because he doesn't own it anymore. But, I've been icing cakes over there on Saturdays to supplement my health insurance.

RICH: So, how long have you worked for The Blue Owl?

MARK: Two and a half years. I hope to retire there. I know that this doesn't have anything to do with the bakery business, but if I forget, my father would shoot me if I didn't bring it up. Connie, my father-in-law bought a newspaper route from your brother, John. He knows more about your family.

CONNIE: Oh, I'd love to talk to him. I'm kind of getting a book together on my family.

[Author's Note: Connie Wolf was the youngest of sixteen children in the Wolf Bakery family.]

MARK: Like I said, I want to get some stuff from my brother. I can't really think of anything else except what's on that piece of paper. But, don't be afraid to text me with questions. Another bakery that was near us was across the street from Ted Drewes.

MARK: Grau's bakery was in a single free-standing building, sorta' cattycorner from Ted Drewes. It shared a parking lot with the Catholic Supply Store. Oh, and then there was Schmidt's Bakery on Grand, Earl and Ed Schmidt. Yep, and Rozaneks bought the Schmidt's bakery. And, the Schmidts were related to Ron Jaudes somehow.

RICH: I've been told that Ron Jaudes is an important person to talk to, if he's around.

MARK: Oh yeah, he's around. His son owns a work-out place. You'd never know that Ron is as old as he is. He is in such great shape, physically and mentally. And, he is a really good guy. Yeah, they had three generations of Jaudes Bakers Supply down on Broadway.

RICH: They only closed recently, like in the last couple of years, I think?

MARK: Well, they sold their stuff to Bono-Burns. It's probably been eight or ten years, but Ron has just recently retired. Ron retired right before I left Lubeley's. Yeah, between Ed Federhofer and Ron Jaudes they'd be able to give you the run-down of every bakery since forever. They are the two people that you are definitely going to want to talk to. So, I will take these Interview Questions, write some stuff down, make some notes, and call some people.

RICH: If you could do an expanded timeline that would be great!

MARK: Well, my brother is four years older than me. So, the things that happened when I was very young he'll remember better than I will. He's working out of town, but he said when he gets back he'll be looking up a bunch of stuff. We'll get together and figure out some timelines for our personal stuff.

RICH: Mark, how long did you work for Lubeley's?

MARK: Twenty-one years. I'll never forget it, but he didn't even need the help when he hired me. This isn't braggadocious, and I don't mean it to be that way, but he didn't want to let me go. He knew that since I had owned my own business, he knew my work ethic, and he knew some of my work. And, I belonged to the Bakers Association, the same with Bob and everybody else. It worked out great because he knew I could work in the back, and I could decorate cakes. So, I could do the whole thing, the things no one else could do, except for him.

MARK: I had hired a similar guy who came from the Fav-Rite bakery, and he was really good at the time. He could do the whole thing, decorate cakes, bake stuff, mix. He could do the whole ball of wax. So, when you get somebody like that you don't want to let him go even if you don't need him at the time. You find a way to fit him in.

RICH: O.K. And, his name was Joe Klingle?

MARK: That's the guy who owned the business with my dad. And then, my dad sold it to Joe. My dad's reasons for selling it were about his health as much as anything else.

RICH: Sure, sure. Well, that's been a consistent reason for retirement in the bakery business for a lot of people.

MARK: Alright, well I'm gonna' have to scoot. We'll keep in touch. And, if you want to get together again, and whatever you want to do with pictures let me know.

RICH: I will come back to you, O.K.? It's been great of you to meet with us.

MARK: Well, it was a pleasure. I was so excited.

RICH: We were excited too. I mean, honestly, this is a work of love.

Hauser Bakery
Interview With Jane Hauser Leonardelli

I can give you an example of the family thing.
On Friday nights my two younger sisters and I would
have to bake buns for the bakery and slice
bread for Saturday. We did resent it at times, but
we all liked to sing, and so the three of us would
take turns picking songs, and we would sing and harmonize.
That was a very fond memory I have, of working with my sisters in the bakery.
— Jane Hauser Leonardelli

RICH: So, your dad's name was Albert Charles Hauser

JANE: Yes, Albert Charles Hauser.

RICH: Well, your grand-dad was really something too, wasn't he! Did you know him?

JANE: It's interesting, my grand-dad was quite a character, and my father was very much like his dad. He was very active in the community and very helpful to the poor families in the area and the religious organizations that needed his help. But yeah, my father had more of a consistent career. My grandfather had worked all over St. Louis in the baking fields. So, it was kind of fun to remember all of that.

RICH: [While referring to the bio information I found on the internet I said], "You know, I was really impressed with everything that your grandfather achieved."

JANE: Oh, what did it say?

RICH: Well, I can tell you the highlights. It gave the addresses of the bakeries, which is important. But, it also said that he was president of the Retail Master Bakers Association for awhile. And, he was on the boards of directors for the Baker's Yeast Company and the St. Louis Baker's Co-Op, which is a really important organization in the history of baking in St. Louis. And then, he was very involved with the St. Vincent de Paul society, a Catholic organization that serves the poor.

JANE: Well, that kind of sounds like my dad. Are you sure? What year did he pass away according to that?

RICH: That was 1988.

JANE: Oh, that was my grandfather. Yeah, my dad passed away before his dad. He passed away in 1986. My grandfather was quite active in the baking community.

RICH: I have to tell you just a little bit of _my_ story about the "Bakery Book Project." I received fifty years of archive material from the McArthur bakery family. They were monthly bulletins from the St. Louis Retail Bakers Association. I've gone through those, though not all of them. There's one for every month for 50 years!

JANE: Oh, good Lord! Really!

RICH: Yeah, reading them was beautiful. One of the impressions that I got from reading those bulletins was that _as a community they were really good to one another. They were a family, they were an extended family, almost like a clan from 1900 to 1960,_ *and probably during the 1800's too, though my records don't go back that far. It's an amazing story, honestly.*

JANE: I am fascinated by that because even what I've read in this history that my aunt gave me, it does sound like they were *a community*, but of course everybody was more of a *community* then. *The families were closer together, the extended family of the bakers. It was a different time, I guess.* But, why are you writing about bakeries?

RICH: Why am I writing about bakeries? [I laugh!] Ahh-h, maybe because I love bakery goods! [I laugh again, and then we laugh together!] But, no. I grew up in St. Anthony of Padua parish, the Franciscan church on the South Side.ˋ

RICH: I was an altar boy, and I went to church almost every morning with my grandfather. After Mass we would go one block west to the St. Louis Pastry Shop, which was a remarkable bakery, and we would bring home treats for the family. We were a multi-generational home at Keokuk and Minnesota.

JANE: That's wonderful.

RICH: Yeah, I'm a pretty religious person. In fact, I taught in the Religion Department at Notre Dame High School for almost 40 years.

JANE: Wow!

RICH: So, I don't think I've ever said this in any of the other interviews, but it all went together for me with Eucharist. You know, you break bread at church, and then you break bread with your family!

JANE: Oh, that's wonderful, and it's true! Well, isn't that what the Eucharist is all about anyhow?! Isn't it about being <u>with</u> family and breaking bread, if the last supper tale is to be believed as it was told to us!

JANE: Oh, my dad sold the bakery to a young man named Jim Grundsinger, I believe it was in 1979. So, they were at 624 Holly Hills from 1927 until 1979.

RICH: Sure, sure! You know, I had friends in that neighborhood when the second location of your bakery was on Holly Hills. I suspect that their families went to the Hauser Bakery. When did that bakery close? That's important to know.

JANE: He moved in 1927 because the first Hauser bakery was on Arsenal Street across from the State Hospital. It was in 1923 that my grandfather bought that bakery. That's part of the history that I didn't know because there was a man named Vitale who wanted to sell that bakery.

JANE: According to my aunt, my grandpa and grandma purchased the bakery on Arsenal Street for five hundred dollars. At one point the hospital approached them and said, "Would you be willing to hire wards from the hospital to work at the bakery?" So, grandpa did do that until a time when he was held at bay by one of the wards with a knife. They decided then that it wasn't safe anymore for them to do that. So, they didn't, and then he ran the bakery himself.

FIRST BAKERY - 5315 ARSENAL STREET

RICH: Yeah, I see. Well, that would do it, wouldn't it?

JANE: Yeah, it sure would. Then, in just four years grandpa needed a larger space. His business was expanding because of the growing business from the Italian people on "The Hill." It was very Italian at that time in 1923. They respected grandpa and the baked goods. They would even invite them to weddings, and such. Grandpa's business grew in that way. So, they needed a larger space, and that's why they ended up moving to Holly Hills.

RICH: So, they sold the bakery on Arsenal in 1927?

JANE: I guess they sold it. They moved away from it. I don't think they had two locations operating at the same time.

RICH: Now, do you know that there is still a Vitale's Bakery on the "Italian Hill?"

JANE: I do know that! When I read the name today, I said, "Really?!" They have wonderful bread! Yeah, I love bakeries too, by the way!

RICH: Yeah! You almost have to say, *"Who doesn't love bakeries,* right?!" [A lot of laughter by both of us!]

JANE: Well, maybe people who are "anti-carb!" But, you know, it's in my blood-stream! I've got to eat it!

RICH: Yeah! I just interviewed Hank at Hank's Cheesecakes, have you heard of him?

JANE: Oh, of course, of course!

RICH: So, I just interviewed Hank about two weeks ago. We were actually in high school together at St. Louis U. High. He might have been in your husband's class.

JANE: He was! Oh, they're good friends!

RICH: Oh, there you go. That's right! That's how I got you as a contact. It was through Hank. Yeah well, Hank had a funny quote. He said, *"If people wanted to stay slim and eat greens all the time, you probably wouldn't like Hank's Cheesecakes!"* [And, we laugh at the quote!]

JANE: You know, I think that's true! He's right! I'm a sourdough bread baker now, not for a business just for us, but I've really gotten into it. So, I'm always trying to find people to give a loaf to, and I have to ask them, "Do you eat carbs, carbohydrates?" And, a lot of them say, "Oh, we don't eat bread." And, I say, "O.K.!"

RICH: That's really something. I've got a good friend named Jim who bakes and cooks, and he does these things just as hobbies. He makes great bread! He specializes in bread. It's wonderful that _you_ are still baking bread!

JANE: I'm a quilter. One of the other quilting people in our group and I created a sourdough starter. I thought I could do that. And you know, it has developed into a fabulous starter. I've made new starters for both of our sons, and now they're occasionally baking bread and garlic knots, and whatever.

JANE: But, it amuses me that my kids are also into baked goods. They're both boys and they both like to bake and cook, which is great!

RICH: That's really neat!

JANE: The bakery on Holly Hills was originally on Kansas Street. I don't know when they renamed it Holly Hills, but it was Kansas Street when everyone first moved there.

RICH: Really?!

JANE: They called it Kansas Street in Carondelet. We do have an old map of St. Louis that also has Kansas Street on it.

RICH: Oh, my gosh. Isn't that something! Well, I imagine that the Holly Hills area was developed kind of as a whole neighborhood at that time.

JANE: I think you're right. Well, it was part of the Carondelet neighborhood, and Carondelet was kind of like a mini-city in St. Louis.

RICH: That is interesting. I think Carondelet was the first settlement in St. Louis, wasn't it?

JANE: Yes, it was.

RICH: Because of my teaching at Notre Dame High School I found out about that, and I had Sisters of St. Joseph of Carondelet in grade school.

JANE: Yes, at Notre Dame you were geographically close to Carondelet. Well, I was at St. Mary and Joseph's parish, right across from the "Carondelet Sisters of St. Joseph's" motherhouse. So, naturally we had CSJ's.

RICH: Oh, isn't that neat! It's great to make all of these connections because earlier I interviewed Linda Smith at Carondelet Bakery, I don't know if you know where that is.

JANE: Was that close to River des Peres?

RICH: Yes, it was close to St. Boniface church on Michigan Avenue. It had a different name before it became Carondelet Bakery. It was Doering's Bakery before that.

RICH: But, the Smith family was there for a long time. I taught all four of the Smith's girls at Notre Dame.

JANE: Really?!

RICH: They were a very neat family. I do have a treat for you. I would encourage you to go to You-Tube and watch a video called "Bob, the Baker!" It's really touching and really inspiring. The featured baker on the video is Bob Smith of the Carondelet Bakery. It's kind of a tribute to bakers. It's really beautiful!

JANE: I love it! I'm sure I'll love it!

JANE: Bakeries were big when we were growing up. I mean, there was one every so many blocks. It was really amazing how many bakeries there were in St. Louis! And then, large grocery stores came in, and bakeries became less of a thing because you could buy your bakery goods from a grocery store.

RICH: Sure, of course. I remember all of that. That's actually a major mystery and question in the book, *"Why did the independent bakeries diminish in number so quickly during the 1950's?"*

JANE: Yeah, for sure. I think that's what started to happen. And then, they had to start looking for different ways to keep their businesses going.

RICH: You know, the best answer I ever got to that question, was from an early interview. This person said that supermarkets were a big part of the downfall, but boxed cakes also came in during that time! Isn't that interesting?!

JANE: I didn't even think about that! Sure, the ones that were on the shelves, the Pillsburys and things like that.

RICH: Right, yeah. It was so much easier and cheaper for people to make stuff at home. You know, I really do enjoy hearing about the family bakeries that had so much family history connected with them.

JANE: Yes, I was thinking about my dad's ownership of the Hauser Bakery after my grandpa retired and how much of a family event that was, how my brother worked in the shop in the back and the girls, there were five of us altogether, how we worked in the front.

JANE: At Christmas time my dad would always make special novelties called marzipan, and the whole family would work on that together, on the Sunday after Thanksgiving. We all had our special jobs. It was just a beautiful process, and it was definitely a family affair. And then, for holidays my Aunt Ruth would come in and help out. Sometimes my uncles would come in. It was really kind of fascinating. So yes, it was a family deal not only from generation to generation, but within the generations.

RICH: Yes! What was your brother's name?

JANE: My brother's name is Al, Albert.

RICH: So, he worked in the back with your dad?

BAKERY 3/20/26

JANE: Yes, he's Albert Paul Hauser. My dad was Albert Charles, and his dad was Albert Frank.

RICH: Right. O.K., I've got it. That's great. And, you say you had five girls in the family.

RICH: *That's really neat. So much of what bakeries did was give people a sense of the seasons, festivities, holidays, and all of those kinds of things.*

JANE: Absolutely! I have to say, that's a really interesting point that you give because, of course, the novelties that we made were all seasonally-related. You know, you have the consistent things that people needed to buy every day, but the seasonal stuff, I believe, was transitional to life! I celebrate every season, every holiday. You know, I make a big deal out of everything, and people are like, "Why are you into Halloween so much?" [My laughter, because my family also celebrates Halloween in a big way.] I think it's all because of the bakery! I just love celebrating everything, and it always gives you something to look forward to!

RICH: Exactly, exactly! I have to tell you, the virus quarantine and the isolation is kind of getting to us, just feeling like claustrophobic, not being able to have the freedom to go into stores, visit with our friends, celebrate at restaurants, and so on. So, my wife said, "We need to get out the Halloween decorations!" We change our decorations in our house with every season!

JANE: [Jane laughs here with enthusiastic agreement.] Good! I love hearing that. I love it! [And then, I laugh loudly with her.]

RICH: We just finished summer, you know. So, now we have to take down all of the summer decorations!

JANE: Well, good for her. I'm one hundred percent there!

The Goblins are Coming

RICH: *Like you say, for some reason it's important! The seasons are real, and I guess nature is very important to the rhythm of our lives!*

JANE: Oh, absolutely, absolutely! Wow, that is so cool! Yes!

RICH: Yeah, we're very lucky to have all of those things as part of our lives!

JANE: Yes, to make them important. I'm not really sure, but the building is certainly older than one hundred years old. I'm sure someone else had a bakery there because the oven was already there. So, what I don't know is who they bought it from. Wait, I do have a name. The building and business were purchased from Mr. and Mrs. Rehme.

JANE: You know, I'm kinda' curious about how old that building was when they got it, because it looks to me like it's over a hundred years old now. It was part of that established Carondelet area.

JANE: There was a coal-fired oven there. My brother said that it was coal-fired, until the city said that the coal was polluting the city too much. So, dad had to convert it to gas. But, the coal deal was a big deal because they had to stoke it constantly. You could never turn-off the oven because it would cause cracking in the oven and make it unusable. So, they never got to take vacations because they always had to stoke it and remove the clinkers until it was converted to gas.

RICH: My gosh, isn't that something!

JANE: This was at the one on Holly Hills.

RICH: Yeah, that's a significant piece of St. Louis history, that coal problem, you know.

JANE: Yes.

RICH: Did they have any down times, any financial struggles, maybe during the depression?

JANE: My aunt said that the depression was hard on the bakery. But, it says here, in my aunt's notes, that "they had disasters with various things, and the depression hit the bakery pretty hard." But, my grandparents were into donating a lot of stuff. So, what wasn't sold ended up being donated to Catholic communities like St. Joseph's Boys Home, St. Vincent de Paul food pantries, St. Mary and Joseph's parish, and the poor families in the area. So, they used to do that. they used to make a lot of donations of things that were left over.

JANE: But, I remember the day of the "Bay of Pigs" in the early 60's, was a significant challenge for my father because it was the first time that I ever heard him have concern and say, "I had no customers today at all in the store because people were afraid with the whole 'Bay of Pigs' incident."

JANE: My brother said that he thought the most cataclysmic thing that happened to Hauser Bakery was Interstate-55 because it tore right through the neighborhood. There were a lot of businesses that highway 55 took out, and Holly Hills was even closed for awhile. People could not access the bakery very easily.

JANE: So, my brother said that the saving grace for my dad at that time was the fact that my aunt, who wrote this book about our family, was the purchasing agent at St. Vincent's Hospital or home up north. She worked there. So, she made it possible that all of the bread and pastries were supplied by my father. She had them purchased from my dad, and that was his saving grace during the building of Interstate-55.

RICH: I see.

JANE: My brother said that the building of I-55 was a pretty significant destruction to dad's business.

RICH: So, basically I-55 tore the Holly Hills area apart, right?

JANE: Well, because they had to shut down Holly Hills, and there were businesses there. I think there was a Herman Knoll's florist on Holly Hills, and there were other businesses. I remember all of this as a kid because we used to play at Carondelet Park all the time. That whole block of businesses was just destroyed. They either had to relocate or do something else. I don't think they ever recovered from that because once they take your whole business away what do you do?

RICH: Well, that makes total sense. Oh yeah, did your family live by the store?

JANE: Yes, we lived <u>above</u> the bakery! We moved there in 1947. I was born in April of 1948. They moved there when they were pregnant with me. I'm the middle child. I'm right after my brother. There are two older sisters, my brother, and then myself. And, we lived there from 1948 to 1978.

JANE: That's when mom and dad moved out, when they sold the bakery. Yeah, we were right there above the bakery, which was both a plus and a minus. Then the bakery did become our life all of the time. We really couldn't get away from it, and it was hard on my dad.

RICH: That is also very familiar. Did you ever hear of Wolf's Bakery? Well, Connie Wolf was the youngest child of that family. They had their bakery that I think was one block south of Our Lady of Sorrows church on South Kingshighway. Later, they had several other locations. Anyway, they had 16 children!

JANE: [Here we pause in amazement, and then Jane says,] "Oh, my goodness gracious!"

RICH: So anyway, I was able to become friends with her, and she actually helped me with a couple interviews. She's a wonderful person, and her name is Connie Wolf. She was the youngest child of those sixteen children. They lived over their bakery! Can you imagine?

JANE: Oh, my goodness! I hope it was a huge place for all those children.

RICH: Well, Connie said that, because of the age range, some of them had moved out, that it was never all sixteen children living there at the same time. Usually, it was about twelve.

JANE: Oh, thank goodness! We thought we were crowded with eight of us living upstairs over the bakery! My brother had his own room, and the five girls slept in one room. My parents had a bedroom, but we never had a dining room. We had a living room. That was it, one bathroom.

AL - CLARA - JOHN - RUTH - MARCE - VINCE - DOT PAUL - EMMA - DAD

RICH: Well, let me ask you, I know your grandfather was a very responsible person in the sense of taking leadership in the St. Louis Master Retail Bakers Association, and then on the Board of the Baker's Co-Op.

RICH: Do you know anything about his participation in those organizations? Was your dad involved in those kinds of things too?

JANE: I'm sure my dad was involved with the National Retail Bakers Association. And I know that when the Gateway Arch was built the St. Louis Bakers Association had different bakers from the community go downtown and do demonstrations. I know my dad was involved in that. It was kind of an Arch dedication month. I remember it being a big deal for my dad to go down there. And, my brother went down and helped him.

JANE: Dad was very active in our parish community. He was president of the St. Vincent de Paul Society, a Catholic service organization focused on helping the poor. I guess he carried on like his father did and did a lot of good works for people in the community. I think it took some attention away from the baking organizations for him to be able to do that.

JANE: Grandpa and grandma had three children, but mom and dad had six. So, their attention was on their children and their children's activities, the church community, and the religious organizations that they supported in the area. So, I think the baking organizations became less of a thing for dad.

RICH: Right, right. Actually, the Bakers Association stayed in existence until around 2005, but I think it probably diminished during your dad's time.

JANE: O.K., that might have been part of why he was not as engaged.

RICH: Right. And, you probably never heard him talk about the Baker's Co-Op or anything like that, did you?

JANE: I didn't hear him speak about the Baker's Co-Op because I didn't really work with him in the shop, and by the time I was old enough to ask the questions or even think about them, it was after my children were able to negotiate on their own a little. I couldn't really talk with him about all of this. Now, I would love to go back and ask a trillion questions.

RICH: When you were growing up was your parish Sts. Mary and Joseph?

JANE: Yep. And, I'll tell you, it breaks my heart that they tore down the school, but I <u>have</u> been in the church since then. When we moved back to St. Louis three years ago I wanted to reconnect with some of the people in my high school class. So, I went to the Carondelet Historical Society and found out they were doing a Fall Festival that year. Of course, I went.

JANE: I'm not very religious anymore, but I'm very emotionally connected to this community. I was able to go to the church, the Mass, and a supper afterwards. And, I reconnected with a few of my friends from grade school and a second cousin. It was a great experience, and now I want to do some volunteer work at the church. They use it for weddings and things sometimes. They call it Sts. Mary and Joseph Chapel now.

RICH: I understand. Was your dad also involved in the St. Vincent de Paul Society?

JANE: Oh, my dad was president for many years. He was also in the Holy Name Society. Yes, very involved, even when he moved parishes out to Assumption Parish, after they sold the bakery. He was very engaged in the St. Vincent de Paul Society.

RICH: That's great! I was at Notre Dame High School for almost 40 years. My wife was a teacher also, and when she retired she got an assistant job at St. Margaret of Scotland School in the city. And then, I also got on there as an assistant. Anyway, the St. Vincent de Paul Society is very active in St. Margaret of Scotland parish, because of their location. There are a lot of people in need in the area.

JANE: Absolutely. My husband, Michael, grew up in St. Margaret of Scotland parish, and he always loved this neighborhood.

JANE: So, that's why we live pretty close to St. Margaret of Scotland. We wanted to live in an integrated neighborhood. We like urban living. I love St. Louis. I have strong roots here from the 1700's. So, I feel it is *my* city! Yes, I am very happy here.

RICH: That's very neat! Now, I'm gonna' sound like I'm selling you on St. Margaret's, but I want you to know that I am so inspired by the people of that parish! We've been involved with them for about nine years, and I'm just blown away by their incredible attitudes towards diversity, helping people, and caring for one another.

JANE: You know, that doesn't surprise me. We had CSJ's, (Catholic Sisters of St. Joseph), there, and I think the St. Joe order had a more inclusive and open attitude. I've always been proud that those were the people that I respected the most.

RICH: Yes, exactly! They passed on some important things, didn't they?!

JANE: Yes, very good values!

RICH: We get the magazine for the Carondelet Sisters of St. Joseph. They're even more compassionate and intentional than ever in their values. They are willing to put themselves out there. It's very inspiring!

JANE: I love that! It *is* inspirational.

RICH: Now, here's the great St. Louis question, where did you go to high school?

JANE: I went to St. Elizabeth's Academy on Arsenal Street and Louisiana.

RICH: Sure, that makes total sense.

JANE: Well, my Aunt Ruth had gone there, and my father thought that St. Elizabeth's would be good for his daughters. And then, my mom got a teaching job there. So, all five of us graduated from St. Elizabeth's Academy.

RICH: Oh my gosh, your mom taught there! I am really taken by that! I immediately thought about that. "How did she do that being a baker's wife and being a mother of six?!" She was pretty incredible!

JANE: Well, she didn't go back to teaching until my sister Rita, who was the baby, was in kindergarten.

RICH: Oh my gosh, I would be so proud of her.

JANE: I <u>am</u> overwhelmingly proud of her! She taught French, but English and Latin were her two majors. French was the third until they got a French teacher.

RICH: Were there any "characters" that were memorable as employees or anybody who had the most longevity in the bakery?

JANE: My dad was the primary baker for so long, but he had a variety of different people who worked for him. A lot of the women who worked out front were long-term employees. Catherine, Juanita, Louise — all of those were wonderful women who worked there for a long time. But, you know, we girls worked there too.

JANE: Oh yeah, as a young girl working in my father's bakery, he did hire a lot of high school boys. And, because we went to an all-girls high school we really liked the fact that there were boys working there!

JANE: So, we had a lot of fun. There were a lot of flirtation things going on, and for us as young women that was a pretty cool thing. If we asked my two younger sisters and myself what we remember the most. That would be what we remember, a lot of young guys working there that we got to tease with and flirt with, and whatever, you know. It was fun, it was a good time.

RICH: That's very cute and very cool!

JANE: I can give you an example of the family thing. My two younger sisters and I are each eighteen months apart. So, the three of us on Friday nights would have to bake buns for the bakery and slice bread for Saturday. That was every Friday night. We did resent it at times because sometimes we wanted to be with our friends. But, we all liked to sing, and so the three of us would take turns picking songs, and we would sing and harmonize.

JANE: *That was a very fond memory I have, of working with my sisters in the bakery. It was a great thing to do. It was very bonding. The three of us still have this strong bond.* Again, there were eight years between my oldest sister and my youngest, and we were considered the younger kids.

RICH: That's really a neat story.

JANE: Yeah, we worked there longer than anybody else, though I think Catherine, Louise, and Juanita might say otherwise. But, they worked there a long time too. I just can't fix it in time.

RICH: Oh no, that's fine. And, can you tell me again the names of you girls, the "three amigas." It was you and your two younger sisters, right?

JANE: Yes. Joan is the one right under me, and then Rita was the one right under her. So, it was Jane, Joan, and Rita. It was fun. Don't get me wrong, we loved our older sisters, but they *were* older than we were. So, they did what people did at their age.

RICH: Yeah, that's the neat part of the story, close-knit sisters, right!

JANE: And, we still are! We still talk all of the time. We mean so much to each other even now.

RICH: Well, I'm gonna' jump to something else here. This is an important question. I think it might take some thinking, but maybe not. Can you remember any signature items? What were people's favorite things that you can remember?

JANE: I asked my brother this question, and I challenged him on his answer, because I didn't necessarily agree with him about all of this. He said that dad was known for his rye bread, that his rye bread was a really great product.

JANE: I said that I thought my father had a crusty hot bread that came out at noontime every day, and there were things called "bread ends," and crusty horns, and then French breads. People would kinda' hang-out waiting for those to come out of the oven. That was a big deal. My father also made potato flour donuts, and that was a Thursday specialty. He was kinda' known for those. Of course, the specialty items at Easter were the panorama of eggs and bird's nests, rabbits and chickens, and eggs of all sizes. Those were his Easter novelties. Dad started taking orders for those like a month in advance!

JANE: My brother said he thinks dad's fruit pizza was one of the first fruit pizzas in the area. It would be a round flat dough with either just fruit on top or divided into sections. One was a section that was cheese, a section that was cherry, and a part that was apricot. The fruit pizzas were a popular item for a long time.

JANE: And then, there was the marzipan. I just paged through my aunt's booklet, and apparently marzipan was big for her too. We were a German bakery. So, things that were kinda' German were pretty successful. Gosh, there were so many things.

RICH: Sure, sure. You know, there's a distinction that people make. There are now a lot of specialty bakeries that have opened, and they only do cupcakes and cookies, and things like that. But, Hauser Bakery was a "full-line" bakery, right?

JANE: Oh, yes, yes! Oh, by the way, dad got a lot of wedding cake orders! If you lived in South St. Louis you'd ask people where they got their wedding cake. They'd say, "Hauser Bakery!" Yes, he had every-thing, and I appreciate that. Now, I think Federhofer's is one of the only places that does the same thing. They offer a little bit of everything. I'm sure you've been to Federhofer's.

RICH: Yes. Actually, I taught Cheryl Federhofer at Notre Dame High School!

JANE: I love their bakery goods because they remind me so much of my dad's.

RICH: Yeah. Well, McArthur's is still pretty close to a "full-line" bakery.

Above, bakery owner Al Hauser mixes cake batter.

JANE: Yeah, they're a delicious bakery! And, Lubeley's on Watson, when it was in business was also one of those kinds of bakeries.

RICH: Oh, those are just phenomenal bakeries. I was so sad when Lubeley's closed.

JANE: Me too! It was like, "What happened?" We weren't living here at the time, but it was like, "Oh, no!"

RICH: Yeah. I interviewed Helen Lubeley, and that was a wonderful interview.

RICH: Her description of their closing was really unbelievable. She said that they felt a responsibility to let their customers know about their closing ahead of time, to not have it be a shock to them. So, they let them know three weeks before their closing, and she said that those three weeks were both miraculous and a nightmare.

JANE: [Jane is laughing at this time.] Because people wanted to order all of this stuff, I'm sure!

RICH: They said that eventually they had to limit the purchases to something like two cakes and one side or smaller item, you know like donuts or something like that. It sounded like they had to bake almost round the clock, for three weeks! So, that was touching that they cared enough about their customers to let them know.

JANE: Why did they close? Was it just age?

RICH: She said that they just couldn't do it anymore. They were just too tired. They felt physically they couldn't do it any longer, and nobody in the family wanted to take it over, you know, which is a common theme.

JANE: My brother talked about that. He said, "Fortunately, if we knew then how much was involved," but we may have still considered taking over the business. And yet, we probably would have had to specialize. You know, both of us enjoyed so many aspects of the business. It's not what our life-careers would have been, but it would have been something special to do, you know?

RICH: Oh yeah, absolutely. It's kind of like when someone sees a person that they would have married or something like that, and they say, "If I was only fifty years younger..." [And, we laugh together!] "If I was only fifty years younger, I would have bought that bakery!"

JANE: Right, right! I know! "Or, if we could go back and do it now, we probably couldn't even get the oven started!" Wow!

RICH: There's just a tremendous amount of information I've been privileged to receive from people, you know!

JANE: Well, it's charming that you're doing this. When are you going to get this book done?

RICH: [I sort of gasp at the question, and say], "That's a tough one. I hope within a year or so." But, I'm very excited to tell you that you're my twenty-third in-person interview!"

JANE: Oh my gosh, that's awesome!

RICH: Yeah, I'm actually shooting for twenty-five in-person interviews. So, I'm almost there. And, I hope eventually to add-on to those with on-line research for important bakeries where I couldn't find anyone to interview.

JANE: That's amazing! No wonder it's taken you this long to do it, right?

RICH: Yeah, I have a big need for somebody, if you know of anybody, who is extremely creative, a design person. I am still kind of awe-struck by the task of putting it all together.

JANE: Oh yes, it's a daunting task, I'm sure. You just need your "through-put." You need your thread that's going to put all of it together! And, I think you know what that is. *St. Louis is the focal point, and these bakeries were some of the spokes that bound St. Louis together as a community.* Bakeries were important to that sense of community. Nathaniel Reid is a fabulous bakery. Have you been out there?

RICH: Yes! I interviewed him, and I have enormous praise for him as a person!

JANE: Oh, my gosh. Well, I don't know what he's like as a person, but I respect everything he creates! I mean it! I go out to Nathaniel Reid's, and I buy an almond-filled croissant for three dollars and seventy-five cents, and it's ginormous!

RICH: Do you know anybody involved with, or have you been to, Union Loafers?

JANE: I used to buy their bread until the virus took over. And then, I started to make my own bread. So no, not really.

RICH: You know, a bakery that I wish was still there for you in your neighborhood was Bretscher's Bakery on South Grand. He had a great reputation, but I personally don't know anything about him. I have to find out something because I don't know if there's anybody around, I don't know if you've ever heard of him.

JANE: I can remember the name. Where on South Grand? Was it down south in the Carondelet neighborhood or towards that neighborhood?

RICH: Oh, no. He was probably just south of the Rooster restaurant. Yeah, so apparently he was a nice man and had a great bakery, but I don't know anything else about him.

JANE: Rich, are most of these bakers that you've interviewed of German descent?

RICH: [I laugh quietly.] Oh, yeah! Definitely!

JANE: I'm curious about that too. Hmm-m-m.

RICH: Oh yeah, that's a very common thing. I don't know if you know Nathaniel Reid's background, but he could work anywhere in the world.

JANE: Yeah, so why did he choose to settle here?!

RICH: I asked him that same question, and here is a direct quote from him. *He said that he loves St. Louis! He grew up in Farmington Missouri, he went to the University of Missouri, and he loves the Midwest!*

JANE: Really!

RICH: Yeah, he's a world class baker. He's worked with nothing but five-star pastry chefs around the world and got his schooling in Paris! So, he's the real deal!

JANE: I think I read that part about him, but I didn't know he grew up in Farmington. I really do think that we are lucky to have him here.

RICH: Oh my gosh, yes! He sent home some samples with me. So, here's a cute story. He gave me one of his lemon raspberry pound cakes. And, it was my wife's birthday coming up in about a week. So, I said to him, "Oh, I'll save this for her birthday." And then, he said, "Oh no, you won't! You're gonna' eat that now. I don't want you to wait a week to eat that." [With that story, Jane and I laugh thankfully at how seriously he takes the quality of his bakery goods.]

JANE: And for a man of his reputation you would think that he'd be off-putting, but he's not!

RICH: No, he's not at all. He's got a young family. He has two little ones. No, I found him to be nothing but humble.

JANE: Well Rich, is he doing well out there, did he say? I mean, is that a good place for him?

RICH: I think so. He talked about how they do everything from "scratch." He said, "Everybody says they do things from 'scratch'," but then he said, "we actually <u>do</u> things from scratch." [And, I laugh in amazement in thinking about his honesty at that time.]

JANE: Did you happen to taste any of his sandwiches?

RICH: No, I didn't, but he sent home a jar of his Fig Raspberry Preserves. My favorite is his Palmiers, you know the butterfly cookies. He sent those home with me. They're enormous, and they were <u>so</u> good! [Jane is laughing in the background the whole time that I'm telling these stories!] It was so much fun! He was so nice. He gave me all of those things to take home!

JANE: Wow! How generous! It just makes me want to run out there and shop tomorrow!

RICH: Please tell him that you talked to me because we have a really nice relationship.

JANE: That's lovely!

RICH: Well, let me see, [as I look at the list of Interview Questions], You've been in town for about three or four years, is that right?

JANE: I think it'll be three years on October the 10th.

RICH: Ahh-h. Well, we're glad you came back! [I laugh with gratitude here.]

JANE: You know what? I am *too*! We considered going back to North Carolina where we lived for a long time. But, I think there's a pull of St. Louis for me, you know, I think it's just in my blood.

RICH: It's wonderful to talk to you, Jane. I really appreciate your meeting with me.

JANE: Thank you, Rich. It's enjoyable to talk to you too. And, maybe after the virus is gone you can come over and have some sourdough bread with me!

RICH: Ooh-ooh, I would really like that! There are so many things that we share in common, and it's just gratifying to talk to people like you. I don't want to give this up. In some ways I don't want the interviews to end! I love doing them.

JANE: Your book is a great concept. I love it!

RICH: Well, I've started telling people that I interview, "If you're a praying person, please pray for this to take hold and to bear fruit, you know, that I actually get it published." [We laugh.]

JANE: Well, I think you will once you hit your "through-put" line on this. That's gonna' be the thread that's gonna' pull it all together. I think it's going to fall into place. I really do.

RICH: Oh, thank you! That's very encouraging.

JANE: So, it's a great project. I'm glad you're doing it. Thank you so much for pursuing this.

RICH: O.K. Well, thank you, Jane. I appreciate it, and keep all of this in mind, and prayer too. Thank you. Bye-Bye.

JANE: You're welcome. Keep yourself in good care. Bye-bye.

RICH: You too!

Helfer's Bakery
Interview With Chris and Kathy Helfer

*Your question about the St. Louis bakery community, you asked if we were
a close-knit community and whether we took care of one another.
The answer is, "Yes, absolutely!"*
— Chris Helfer

CHRIS: Well, what do you want to know?

RICH: Well, Chris, thank you so much for meeting with me, and I guess my first question would be, "Were you the only owner of the Helfer's Bakery?"

CHRIS: Yes, my wife and I. We started in August of 1977. I was twenty-two, and my wife was twenty. I started in a part-time job with Dierberg's grocery store. Dierberg's owned a small bakery named Marie's. I would pick-up bakery goods from Marie's pastry shop, and deliver them to Dierberg's, and then they moved to a bakery shop in Westport. Dierberg's then sold Marie's pastry shop to a man named Norton, and I stayed on and worked for him.

RICH: Is that where you learned the bakery business?

CHRIS: Yeah, he was separated from his wife, and she moved down to Florida. Not too long after that, he passed away, and there was really nobody to take over his bakery. So, I took it over, and I really had no business doing that, but I kept all of the employees and contacted all of the suppliers and told them that I would pay them in cash if they would continue working with me.

CHRIS: And like I said, I really had no right to do all of that. Then, about two weeks later his wife came back from Florida, and she took the bakery back over. And, I kept working for her.

CHRIS: Then, I bought a bakery down in Arnold named Grbac's. It was a very small bakery, and that was in 1977.

RICH: That wasn't the bakery that became Harter's, was it?

CHRIS: No, they were further down the road. Harter's has always been there, and they're still there. So, I kept the Grbac Bakery for about a year and a half, and then it became Helfer's. Then, I bought another bakery out in Ballwin out on Manchester Road, Shatkin's Bakery from Paul Shatkin. That bakery was about four times bigger than the one down in Arnold.

HOW OUR HEARTS WERE STÖLLEN

CHRIS: When we bought the bakery in Ballwin, we still kept the smaller bakery down in Arnold as a storefront. Then, we also bought the small building next door to our current bakery up here in Florissant and used that as a storefront. I don't know if you noticed the A-frame building next door that now has a barbecue place in it, but we used that one too as a storefront or a "cold spot."

RICH: So, you had two storefronts.

CHRIS: Yeah, we had two storefronts plus the main bakery in Ballwin. We eventually shut down the one in Arnold, and in 1993 we moved into the larger building up here in Florissant, the present location we're in now. At that time we did not yet have the deli part going. We began that in 2005. So, that's the history of the bakery.

RICH: That's a pretty good history there. That's a lot of work.
[And then, we laughed together.]

CHRIS: [Chris shrugs diminutively, and while laughing he says], "We do alright."

Author's Note: *At this point Chris said some very important things. I believe he was saying some things that are true for all bakers. In his own words he talked about some feelings that I had heard in only an implied sort of way from other bakers. He spoke with a unique pride about his special career, his calling, his one-of-a-kind business, and his love for what he did in his life of baking for others.*

RICH: I do have some other things that I wanted to ask you about.

CHRIS: *Sure, I'm very happy to talk about all of this! This is exciting for me! I love to tell my story!*

RICH: Chris, that is so great!

CHRIS: *I could have you here for hours! I could tell you my story for hours!*

RICH: I'd be glad to come back. How does that sound?!

CHRIS: Whatever you want to do!

RICH: You know, Chris, I've learned so much from doing this, from talking to so many bakers, and I've tried to put into words one particular thing. Here it is: *The extended bakery family in St. Louis in all of its history has seemed to be a sort of "bakery clan," one big "bakery family!" [I sort of laugh here in trying to express something that is hard for me to put into words, but then I try.]*

RICH: *The big bakery family in St. Louis was amazing. They all worked so hard in serving their customers and each of them in their own individual stores. But, the most amazing thing was that they seemed to be so good to one another. They were pretty good to one another, don't you think?*

CHRIS: *Oh, absolutely! I want to tell you what, when we first went into business there was this guy, a salesman for Mid-Continent Paper Company. His name was Oly Johnson. He took it upon himself to drive us around to all kinds of different bakeries and introduced us to the owners. He just took us around!*

CHRIS: *You know, your question about the St. Louis bakery community, you asked if we were a close-knit community and whether we took care of one another. The answer is, "Yes, absolutely!"*

Author's Note: Chris then told a story that perfectly illustrated his belief that *the St. Louis bakery community was a close-knit family of bakers.*

CHRIS: *You know, there was a time when I had to deliver a wedding cake to a reception in South St. Louis, and in those days people liked to use fountains at their receptions. Well, we didn't have any that worked. So, I got on the phone and called Bill Federhofer, whose bakery was down on the Southside, and I asked him if he had a fountain and if I could borrow it. What meant a lot to me was his response. He didn't even hesitate, and he loaned me his fountain!*

CHRIS: I know I'll sound like an old codger, but baking is not an easy life, and it doesn't seem like each generation wants to work as hard as we did. *You know, I love my business. I just love to work on my business!*

Author's Note: The following information about "other contacts" I believe is another indication about how the St. Louis area bakers were colleagues and not competitors.

CHRIS: Oh yeah, I've got a couple other contacts for you. Bob Grommet, Tony Balota, and especially Mary Balota over at Mid-Continent Paper Company. And then, there's Ben Duke's bakery in Alton and Jim Kruta's bakery in Collinsville.

CHRIS: You know, my grandpa was a baker, and he would play cards at night. But, I remember he always had to leave early and go home at 9:00 o'clock so he could get home to get some sleep.

RICH: Chris, what about the St. Louis Bakers Co-Op? When I was reading through the monthly bulletins of the St. Louis Bakers Association I came across references to the Bakers Co-Op. That seemed like a really great idea and something that helped the bakers. I had never really heard of this kind of structure that gave the bakers an economic buying power.

CHRIS: Yeah, it was a really good thing, and there weren't that many of them around the country.

RICH: Well, how did it work?

CHRIS: See, you bought shares in the Co-Op, and then you would buy most of your supplies from the Co-Op. It was very well run, and the person who headed it was Ed Federhofer.

CHRIS: Also, the Co-Op had a board, and I was on the board when it closed. But, at the end it was forced out of business by a Dutch company that bought up the Co-Op.

RICH: What do you mean? "They 'bought up the Co-Op'?"

CHRIS: They tried to buy-up all of the different parts of the Co-Op. They were trying to create a "vertical monopoly." The Co-Op closed sometime in the 1990's.

RICH: Chris, are there any other bakeries on the North Side of St. Louis that I should know about and include in my search?

CHRIS: Yeah, Knodel's Bakery. You know, they were a little different from us, but they were very dedicated. Yeah, I've got a little story that will tell you how dedicated bakers are. I had a semi-retired baker named George. I can't remember his last name. Well, George had a heart attack one night and passed away. Do you know what? His wife called me in the middle of the night to tell me that he wouldn't be coming in to work in the morning.

RICH: Kathy, you seem like you have always been committed to the bakery business and to your bakery as much as Chris has been.

KATHY: Well, yes I am. My grandmother did some baking. Maybe I got some of it from her.

RICH: You know, one of the questions I always like to ask the bakers that I've talked to is this. "What would you say would be your signature items? What would you say Helfer's bakery is best known for?"

CHRIS: Oh, I would say our strawberry and whipped cream items. We make a variety of these items. There are two things that I want you to know about these, and that is that we always use only *fresh strawberries* and only *real whipped cream*! We are also known for our PACZKI items. They are a Polish item pronounced POONCH-KEY. During the two weeks before Lent we sell around a thousand dozen!

Author's Note: My time with Chris and Kathy Helfer was enormously enjoyable. They were two of the most pleasant and gracious people I have ever met.

Ron Jaudes Interview
of Jaudes Bakers Supply
With Connie Wolf

*As a kid, I would ride in the car on Saturday mornings with my dad and my grandma.
We'd go down to the South Grand bakery, and I'd have an apricot
danish or a white iced jelly. I was six or seven years old.*
— Ron Jaudes

Author's Note: This interview with Ron Jaudes was one of the most valuable sources of information that I experienced. Because he, his father, and grandfather sold bakery supplies to so many of the bakeries in St. Louis he had a wealth of information that he freely shared with me, at times with a very dramatic and animated voice!

RON: We had Jaudes Bakers Supply. My grandfather, Leo Jaudes, Sr., started the family business. I was the last owner, and we existed for eighty-four years. Leo, Sr. passed away when he was 96. My grandfather borrowed 5,000 dollars to start the business from his grandfather back in 1924. That was a lot of money. At that time his grandfather said there was only one provision. He had to pay the money back in two years. And, my grandfather said to himself that he had to at least try because this was the only chance he would have. That was the beginning.

RON: My grandfather had two sons, and after the second childbirth his wife passed away. So, he had to raise two boys without a wife and start a business. In those times there used to be over six hundred retail bakeries in St. Louis. Yes, six hundred and twenty-three retail bakeries. That would have been back in the 1940's and 50's. When I was a little kid, my mother's mom and dad owned a bakery on Grand and Walsh, in South St. Louis, just south of St. Mary's High School.

Author's Note: Because of Ron Jaudes wide-ranging knowledge, and because of his giving of a specific number of 623, this may have been the most accurate estimate of the number of bakeries in St. Louis during this period.

RON: My mom's mom and dad were my grandma and grandpa Schmidt and all of the people who worked there were relatives, uncles and cousins, and all of them bakers. They made everything from scratch, and it was just sensational. As a kid, I would ride in the car with my dad and my grandma. On Saturday mornings we'd go down to the South Grand bakery, and I'd have an apricot danish or a white iced jelly donut filled with "Rex" jelly! I was six or seven years old.

RICH: Let me understand the lineage here. That bakery was not Doerings. Doerings was the bakery that preceded the Carondelet Bakery.

RON: Two blocks down was Rozanek's Bakery. And, on the other side of the street was Ehnes Bakery. So, in one block there were three bakeries. Then, a short distance away on Holly Hills my other uncle, Al Hauser, had a bakery there. *After grandpa passed away, Mr. Hauser's wife died. So, my grandmother and Mr. Hauser got to know one another. And then, Mrs. Schmidt and Mr. Hauser, they got married!*

Author's Note: *When Mr. Jaudes said this his eyes got very big, and he was very emphatic in his voice! He was very dramatic in describing this!* Remember the Hauser Bakery interview was posted earlier in this publication. *What is important here is the inter-marrying of these two families!*

RON: *On my gosh, was that ever a mess! With the Jaudeses, with the Ladds, with the Hausels, with the Wolfs, and with the Schmidts, if you got them all together on Thanksgiving, you had a couple hundred people! Well, you can just imagine with all of those people! If you asked me why my grandfather wanted to get into that, I imagine that he thought, "All of these bakers that we know in the family, they're gonna' have to buy their supplies from somewhere!"*

RON: You know, I wrote down some of the different companies that I could think of that were in the bakery supply business. *My grandfather told me that the first bakery supply company in St. Louis was Guggenheim.*

RON: So, my grandfather who had borrowed 5,000 dollars, started a business, and raised two little boys, was one tough little son of a gun! He was a tough guy. I don't even know how he made it, but he did. And, at the end of the two years he didn't have 5,000 dollars to pay his grandpa back. What do you think he did? He went to the bank to get a small business loan to pay his grandpa back. [At this time, Ron laughs loudly!]

RON: At that time if you didn't hit the markets right, on the shortening market, the oil market, the sugar market, flour, he bought all of that stuff, you'd be in trouble. He told me that one time he bought a whole truckload of sugar, and the market went down, and he lost everything. He went broke twice!

RON: So, he was good friends with Ed Gruenfelder. *Ed Gruenfelder and my grandfather then <u>started</u> the Baker's Co-Op.* Even though he had a business of his own, my grandfather started the Baker's Co-Op.

RICH: That was Leo Jaudes Sr., right?

RON: Yes, Leo Jaudes, Sr. and Ed Gruenfelder.

RON: And, Ed Federhofer *ran* the Baker's Co-Op. Let's push the clock way ahead maybe forty years. On this one day Ed Federhofer called me in to see him when the Baker's Co-Op was going to sell-out, along with Cahokia Flour Co., to a company named Bake Mart.

RON: They called me down there to the Baker's Co-Op, and along with Carl Zimmermann from Cahokia Flour, the three of us sat there, and they said to me, "We want you to go in with us. That would be Ed Federhofer, Carl Zimmermann, and Ron Jaudes, the three of us, "and sell-out the St. Louis Bakers Co-Op to Bake Mart." I said, "No way." My grandfather and my dad, they were gone. I said, "They would not think very much of their grandson or son, if he did that." And then, Ed Federhofer stood up, went over to the safe, in the corner of the Baker's Co-Op, and said, "I want to just show you something." And, he showed me the originating indentures of the Baker's Co-Op. And, they were the <u>competition</u> for the Jaudes Bakers Supply.

Author's Note: While thinking about this at a later time, I wondered if these indentures were just one more piece of evidence that showed the cooperative climate and relationships of the bakery community.

RON: I went around and sold stuff for my grandpa and my dad after I came out of college. My grandfather would often say to me, "You're wasting your time calling on Lake Forest Bakery on Clayton Road with Walter Binder. He's a big Co-Op member. He won't buy anything from you. So, I said to him, "Well, I don't have anything to lose. I may as well try." So, that's the attitude I had to take as a salesman.

RON: I went into these bakeries, all over St. Louis that were members of the Bakers Co-Op. We also had competition from Cahokia Flour and from W.E. Beckman Company. There was also a St. Louis Fondant Company. They made all of the icings.

In fact, when St. Louis Fondant Company went out of business, Bakers Co-Op bought all of their equipment, and they began making all of their own crunches and icings there.

RON: That was really a smart move. Oh yeah, there was a company called Greenlee, and Greenlee Products was the company that handled all of the frozen products. Nobody else had enough refrigeration. So, Greenlee had all the frozen fruit and all the frozen eggs. He had a monopoly. His name was Tucker.

RON: Then, there was Mid-Continent Paper Company owned by Bob Grommet Sr. He's been gone for years, and now his son, Bob Grommet Jr., passed away about two months ago. I went to Bob Grommet Jr. about fifteen to twenty years ago, and I wanted to merge with him and have it called Mid-Continent Bakery Supply.

RON: I would be working with Bob Grommet, but he thought I was joking. So, I sold my company to Orville Middendorf of Middendorf Quality Foods. After eighty-four years I was the final owner. Everybody else was gone. So I was by myself.

CONNIE: And, you were ready to retire, right?

RON: Well, not really. Orville Middendorf was in the process of buying a whole string of businesses. I was in the Chef de Cuisine with him. I belonged to that, which was a good connection with all of those country clubs.

RON: And then, one day we were sitting at a dinner at Sunset Country Club, and I said to Orville Middendorf, "So, how is it going with the sale of your company?" And he said, "Oh, it's going along good." And then, I said to him, "Did you ever consider having a bakery supply division?"

RON: And, he says, "Well by golly, no, why?" And, I said, "Well, you've got everything else." And he says, "You know, I'm the 'center of the plate' as the meat man." He had produce and everything else, dairy, grocery, paper. And then he says, "By golly, you and I have to talk." *So, he bought Jaudes Bakers Supply Company." And then, I worked for him for five years until he sold Middendorf Quality Foods to Performance Food Group.*

RON: *Have you ever heard of them? They're the number three distributor of food products in the United States. Sysco is number one, U.S. Foods is number two, and Performance Food Group out of Richmond, Virginia is number three. So, I became a part of Performance Food Group.*

RICH: Did he keep the name, Jaudes Bakers Supply, for the division?

RON: Yes, for five years, until he sold out. Then, I worked for Performance Food Group for a year, and they said, "Well, you know we're nationwide, and you're the only bakery supply division that we have in the country. So, we're gonna' eliminate that." So, I said, "O.K."

RON: Well, you know, what was I going to say? So, they terminated me after about a year. I turned in my laptop, and I thought, "What am I gonna' do now? I'm too young to retire."

RON: So, Bake Mart was there at the time, and I didn't want to go to work for them. The only other possibility was Dawn Distributing. Jerry Burnes was part of Bono-Burnes. That's the name of the company that is in the bakery supply business now. They're in Maplewood. Bono-Burnes, Jerry Burnes.

RICH: O.K. So, Bono-Burnes is a partnership, right?

RON: So, I went in to see Jerry Burnes down in Maplewood unannounced. I came to the front desk and asked, "Is Jerry Burnes here today?" And, the receptionist answered, "Who wants to know?" So, I told her, and then she called over to his office to let him know I was there.

RON: In about two minutes he came around the corner with a funny look and says, "Yeah, that's him." And then, he says to me, "What the heck are you doin' here?" And, I said, "I just came in to tell you that Performance Food Group just let me go, and I was wondering if you'd be interested in any of my customers." Hah, he lit up like a Christmas tree. [After Mr. Jaudes told this story, he laughed loudly.]

RON: He didn't believe me. So, he picks up the phone, and he calls up to Performance Food Group and says, "This is Jerry Burnes down in Maplewood from Bono-Burnes, Dawn Distributing. Did you just let Ron Jaudes go?" He didn't even believe me. And they say, "Yeah, we just terminated him, but he's a good guy. We just didn't need that position."

RON: And then he says, "O.K., Jaudes, let's talk." So, we talked for about 20 minutes, and then he says, "Glad to have you with me. You're on the payroll right now." So, I went right out to St. John's Mercy Medical Center, (they're called Mercy Hospital now). That was my first order for him. I started bringing in orders and overwhelmed Bono-Burnes. They had just been selling to donut shops pretty much. They sold Dawn Donut Mix. That's where Bono came in. This guy Bono, he was a sales rep for Dawn Products. Dawn Products is the largest bakery supply company in the world. They're international.

RICH: Where did they start? Are they an American company?

RON: Yes. They're from Jackson, Michigan. I believe my figures might be inflated, but I think that Dawn Distributors, from east to west has 28 distribution centers across the country. After I was there for five years, the distribution center here in Maplewood went from about twenty-third to become the third largest in the United States. I brought the Schnucks account to Jerry Burnes, a huge account, the Dierberg account, another huge account, St. Louis Bread Company, Companion, and on and on. I could talk to you for an hour about each one of those accounts. *It's been an unbelievable ride in my life. I can't even believe it.*

RICH: That's a great story.

RON: And, that's only the beginning. I worked for Jerry Burnes for fifteen years, and I just retired a year ago in 2018. They grew to become the third largest in the whole United States. I brought them so many large accounts. Some of the others were Bellerive Country Club, the Chocolate Factory at 44 and Kingshighway, and Butler's Pantry, a catering company. That in itself was a whole new business. I thought I'd go to work for Jerry Burnes just for a year or two just to phase myself out of that city traffic. It was crazy. So, now I'm trying a new profession. It's called retirement. It's different.

RICH: It's probably because you loved your work for so long, and it was an intense kind of job, right!

RON: *All the people that you know, that's what you miss, and you knew exactly on a Wednesday at one o'clock, you knew exactly where you were supposed to be. The people would expect you to walk in. I called on a lot of my customers in person. A lot of the sales reps now, they get on their computer or on their phone and say, "Hey, if you need something give me a call, or text or fax your order in." You'd be surprised at how much better you can do when you sit down and talk in-person to someone, like Rich the baker, (as he's referring to me), and get the order. When I would talk to you, I'd say, "You need all of this too!"*

RON: I used to meet my grandfather, Leo Jaudes senior, for lunch at Grone's cafeteria. Now there's only one cafeteria left in St. Louis, Miss Shari's in South St. Louis County.

RICH: I taught "Miss Shari" at Notre Dame High School, a great all-girls high school. That cafeteria was named after the owner's little girl. That's who I taught, and she's still with them.

RON: Yeah, I know, and the other sister is in Indiana. They have another restaurant over in Indiana, and it's named after their grandma. Ron Amann is the owner, and his mom's name is Rose. They call it "Rosie's." One of his other daughters, Debbie, and now Shari, is over there at Rosie's place.

RON: They actually opened two places over there. They used to call me in St. Louis and ask me if I could ship to Indiana, and I'd say, "No." because Dawn had restrictions that you could only sell so far in an area. So, there was another distributor over there for Dawn that they had to call.

RON: *Until now, nobody would ever believe it, no one would ever believe my life story.* [Ron laughs loudly to himself at this time.]

Author's Note: Later, I assumed that this interview and the publishing of it might have given Ron a chance to tell at least a part of his life's story.]

RICH: Well, that's what I want to write down. So, when did your dad start in the business?

RON: My dad, Leo, Jr. and his dad Leo, Sr. had this bakery supply business. So, his dad gave him this "mortar book," (meaning his sales book), and he said, "get out there, and call on all of these bakers." So, he went into Schmidt Brothers Bakery on South Grand Avenue, and there was a "store girl" in there waiting on the customers. That was Dorothy, my mother. He married her!

CONNIE: Is that how he met her?! Oh, isn't that funny?!

RON: Yes, by calling on her father the baker! All of my mom's brothers and cousins used to give me all kinds of trouble. They used to say, "Jaudes, do you know that you were conceived on a bunch of sacks of flour in a storeroom?!" They would say that to me all of the time! [Of course, we all laughed together at this!]

RON: There was my uncle Vernon, my uncle Bob, and my uncle Ed. My uncle Ed was the one who sold the bakery to Sam Wolf.

CONNIE: Oh, really? [Coincidentally, Sam Wolf was Connie Wolf's brother.]

RON: I could go on, and on, and on.

CONNIE: Oh, no. But, did you sell bakery products to Sam?

RON: Oh, sure!

CONNIE: But, you didn't sell to my father. Your father sold to my father, right.

RON: My dad started working for my grandfather around 1942.

RICH: O.K., when, would you say, was the earliest that you started working for them?

RON: Oh-h-h, I started working there when I was in high school. I used to work there in the summer time, loading trucks, sweeping the floor, cleaning out the toilets, whatever. So, I was about twenty-one years old when I started full-time there.

RON: I went to college in Kansas City, at Rockhurst. I was already working part-time during the summers calling on people. My first account that I ever had was up on North Lindbergh. It was a Holiday Inn. At that time nobody ever called on schools, churches, hotels, or country clubs.

CONNIE: Well, where did they get their supplies?

RON: You know, probably from Allen Foods, way back then. I would go in there and be talking to one of the chefs, a big black man. I'd go in there every week, and one day he gave me an order. That was fifty years ago. I could hardly wait to get downstairs to the lobby of the Holiday Inn, to put my quarter into the pay phone, to call my grandpa and give him the order. [At this time, we break into a laugh together!]

CONNIE: I'll bet he was proud of you! So, where did you get your stuff, like if you sold cherries?

RON: We bought stuff from all over the world. Sometimes people, like a stock broker, would come into the office, and he would talk to my dad or my grandpa, and he would say, "Hey Mr. Jaudes, we've got a good deal for you to invest in a bond or a stock."

Ron: And, my dad would say, "All of my money is invested in this warehouse. I buy thousands of dollars of pecans. I buy sugar and shortening. Everything I've got is out there in this warehouse. I don't have any other money. When the sugar man comes in they want the check. It was a tough-go in those times, you know.

RICH: What year was it when you were twenty-one? What year would that be?

RON: Uhh-h, 1963 I think, when my son was born. And then, I had a daughter who came along a couple of years later. She's a senior flight attendant now with Southwest Airlines stationed out of Scottsdale, Arizona. My son went to Mizzou, and he majored in food and nutrition, and physical education. So, he's an expert in nutrition.

RICH: My dad would be so happy to hear about his emphasis on nutrition. My whole life I grew up with this pretty strict diet. And, organic foods was everything to him. So, he would go into grocery stores, into the produce section, and he knew the answer to the question before he even asked it. So, he would ask, "Do you have any organic vegetables?" And, they had no idea what he was talking about. Yeah, he would be so happy now because everybody has organic vegetables!

RON: Well, he was ahead of his time! Have you ever been in that Plant Science Center at the Missouri Botanical Garden? That's really hot right now. Big time!

CONNIE: I was part of that when it started. I was working at the Missouri Botanical Garden. So, I was in on that because I used to go to meetings. I'll bet that's been about twenty years. It's nice to see that it's been successful.

RON: Well, they're coming on strong now. And, I think that Todd Schnuck is the CEO of that place.

RICH: What was the Miss Shari's Cafeteria connection to bakeries? Why did we start talking about that?

RON: Ron Amann called me, and he said, "Ron, I'm gonna' open a cafeteria restaurant, and I'm gonna' make some pies. I need three recipes, one for an apple pie, a pecan pie, and a coconut cream. Could you get those for me? And, I said, "Sure." That's what we started out with, and then I did business with him for forty years. Every time I came in there, he gave me an order, every time. At one time, they had three cafeterias.

RICH: I love eating at that cafeteria.

RON: Well, it's been a senior citizen place. They've got good food. I took Ron Amann, his son, and his grandson to a ballgame last year. Well you know, they closed the one at Warson Woods. So, the people from there all came over to the Southfield location on South Lindbergh. He said that their business went up twenty percent.

RON: Here's another sideline story if you want to know something more about Miss Shari's. Their location at Warson Woods wasn't their original spot. They were in the parking lot of Dierberg's down on Manchester Road. Ron Amann built a cafeteria there, and then Mr. Dierberg came in and said, "I want that spot. Would you be willing to move your cafeteria down on the other side of the parking lot? I'll give you this much money." Then Ron Amann thought, "I think I will!" [Ron Jaudes said this with his usual dramatic voice!] And, he moved further down the road.

RON: The same thing happened to him on Watson Road, across from Garavelli's. St. Louis Bread Company came knocking on his door saying, "We'll give you this much money for that spot." And he said, "Oh, O.K." That's why Ron and Doty Amann have a place in Florida on Marco Island with a big boat! [Ron laughs loudly at this point.]

RICH: Well, I want to get one more fact. Was there one location for Jaudes Baker's Supply or more? Could you tell me the addresses?

RON: It originated at 422 south 6th street. That's exactly where the Cardinals play baseball now, at Busch Stadium. The city of St. Louis came to us, and they used the "Right of Eminent Domain" to get the property.

RON: They told us that we had to get out of there. My grandfather couldn't quite figure that out. Finally, they came back a third time, and said, "Mr. Jaudes, you're gonna' see a big crane coming down the street with one of those big wrecking balls on it. If you're still in here we're gonna' start swinging and knocking the building down. So, you better get out." [And again, Ron breaks out laughing loudly.]

RON: They paid us. They offered us a figure, and it was take it or leave it. So, we had to move. We moved from there to 1440 South Broadway, about a half mile south to a location in the Soulard neighborhood. The building is still there. When I retired and sold the business we sold the building and all of the ingredients. My grandfather was from the "old school." You'd do it his way and no other way.

RICH: Yours was a German family?

RON: Yeah, Jaudes is German and French, mostly German. We just had those two locations.

RICH: And, when did that move take place?

RON: We built the building down there in the Kosiusko Redevelopment area. I don't know the year, but it was when they built Busch Stadium, the "round one" with the arches and all.

RICH: You know, sometimes I forget to ask some of the essential questions because I get so interested in the stories. I tell everyone I talk to that all of this is nothing but exciting for me. My grandfather and I would go to Mass every morning, and then afterwards we'd go to the St. Louis Pastry Shop catty-corner from Winkelmann's drugstore on Meramec. I think Al Langer was the owner. So, that's where my love of bakeries grew. Everybody I talk to loves to talk about their childhood bakery!

RON: There were a lot of good bakeries in St. Louis. *Now* there are very few.

RICH: Recently, I discovered McArthur's Bakery on Lemay Ferry Road, and I got to know David and Randy.

RON: Well, have you talked to David McArthur recently? He's now the sales manager down at Bono-Burnes. I worked with him, and he's the one I told that I was going to retire. And, he said to me, "By God, Jaudes, it's about time!" And then, he said, "Good for you."

RON: My dad worked until he dropped over dead. My dad died at the Baker's Co-Op. My grandfather started the Baker's Co-Op, and my dad died there.

RICH: [As Connie is leaving to get to her job, I say], "Alright, it's great to see you again, Connie." [And then, I turned to Ron Jaudes and say to him], "She has been a tremendous help and source of encouragement. I interviewed her about two months ago. She's as excited about this project as I am."

RICH: You know, I usually ask bakers, "Did your bakery have a signature item? Did you have something that you were especially proud of?" And, they always did. I don't know how to translate that question to your business, but when you think of your business, what do you think was the center of it. I know you were very proud of your business!

Old-Fashioned Success
Lake Forest Pastry Shop Still Using Tried And True Methods

RON: *I would say that the key to the eighty-four years in our business was in a good way that we sold ourselves. Everybody wanted to buy from Ron or Leo. They just wanted to buy from us! At the beginning of a sale you have to sell yourself,* even to people like Walter Binder from Lake Forest Bakery. My grandfather told me, "Oh, don't even waste your time going in there."

RICH: What was he like?

RON: He was pretty interesting. He watched over that business very carefully, and when I came in he considered me a distraction. He thought I was distracting his people who were working there, and that was costing him money. When I would come in, he'd be standing there at the oven. But, he turned out to be a very good account.

RON: When he'd see me come in, he'd turn around and turn his back to me. I'd just say, "Hi, Mr. Binder, it's Ron Jaudes, and I just came by to say hello and see how everything was going." So, I learned. After calling on him for a few months I would have a little sheet of paper, and I would write down something like, "Skim milk powder and the price, or cherries or something," and always just three items.

RON: And then, I'd say, "Mr. Binder, if you don't mind, check these prices when you get home, and see if there's anything I can do to save you some money." And, he'd say, "O.K." Well, that went on for over a year, every week. So, finally one time he called me, and he said, "Mr. Jaudes," Mr. Binder would always pronounce my name as Yaudes in the old-time German, and he'd say, "Is that price on milk powder still in effect? Fifty pound bags, you know."

RON: And, I would say, "Yes sir, it's still in effect." And then, he'd say, "Well, could I get a delivery of that on Monday?" And, I said, "Yes sir." And then, he'd say, "Send me five bags." And then, I said, "Thank you so much!"

RON: Then, the next time I'd have something, maybe Libby's pumpkin in the fall. And he'd say, "Are you sure that's the Libby brand?"

RON: And I'd say, "Yes sir, that's one year old." You know, you'd always buy it one year old because it makes the pumpkin age, and it makes you get an extra pie out of each can. And then he'd say, "Well, send me ten cases of that pumpkin." And, that's the way it went on. And, it turned out that every single time I went in there for twenty-five years he'd give me an order, and it would always have between five and ten items on it. And, my grandfather would sit there and say, "I have no idea how you did that, but we'll make the deliveries." And with all of that, Walter Binder was one of the main shareholders in the Baker's Co-Op, who was one of our competitors. So, that's just one little story.

RICH: Yep, that is a great story!

RON: And then, down the street was Pfeifer's Bakery.

RICH: I just interviewed Rosemary Pfeifer. She's wonderful.

RON: She's a nice lady. There was Carl Pfeifer and Rich Pfeifer. Rich Jr., their son now works for Straub's Bakery on Kingshighway next to the Chase Hotel. Walter Binder's bakery was Lake Forest Bakery on Clayton Road. And now, it's a health spa for women. Things change. Kitchen Conservatory is now in the location where Pfeifer's Bakery was. I think the Pfeifers still own that building, and they get a rent check. And, I know Rich, Rosemary's husband, told me that he made more money doing nothing and getting that rent check than he did when he was baking!

RICH: Well, he had to work a lot less, right! You know, Mark Hausel was very helpful, and he was very complimentary of you.

RON: That's very nice to know. He's a wonderful man. He eventually went to work for Bob Lubeley, and he worked there for fifteen or twenty years.

RICH: I just interviewed Helen Lubeley Murray. They're all nice people, just like her.

RON: She's priceless, and I'm sure she misses the business terribly, the baking business, and all the people that she knew. Bob is still pretty young, about sixty. Now he's delivering car parts.

RICH: A lot less stress, right?! And, better hours!

RON: But, Helen Lubeley, Sr. passed at 102. She and "Papa" worked their whole lives together. I'm sure it was tough for Helen, Jr. and Bob to close that family business.

RICH: Helen Lubeley told me the story about their closing. She said that they didn't want to just close and not give their customers a chance to get used to the idea. So, they told them about two or three weeks ahead of time. She said the business they had for that next three weeks was so big that they could not even keep up with it.

RON: I know, I know. I was their salesman, right to the last day. I knew Bob and Helen's dad, Ed Lubeley. I used to call on him! So, I'm really old. [Laughter.]

RICH: No, you're not. We're not! I just turned 74.

RON: Oh, you're young!

RICH: Yeah, sure!

RON: But, it just shows you how long we've been around. It's amazing. Like I said from the beginning, driving down South Grand on Saturday mornings up until now, all the stuff that's taken place nobody would ever believe it. And, you're just getting the little bits and pieces.

RICH: Yep, just skimmin' the top! You know, there's an important question I have to ask each person I interview, "Do you know any people that you can introduce me to or do you know of any more contacts with bakers?" I tell people I just "follow my nose," you know, as in "what's the next step?" One of those things that comes out of that approach has been to get referrals for additional interviews. For example, Mark said that he was going to get me in to see Ed Federhofer.

RON: His daughter, Karen, has worked the front desk at Bono-Burns, Dawn Distributing for fifteen years. And, she's still there. Bill Federhofer's daughter, Cheryl, has been running the bakery on Gravois. And now, her two sons are running that bakery. Yes, those are the grandsons. I would call on Bill Federhofer at the bakery on Gravois.

RON: I remember one time I was there at Christmas time, and Christmas time in a bakery is really busy. Bill and his wife Meryl were there, and they wanted me out of the way. So, to make some conversation I had to say something. So, I said, "Meryl, I hear you're going to Florida. When do you guys leave?" And, she said, "I'm leaving Monday morning with him or without him!" And then, he said, "Oh yeah, I'm going."

RICH: Let me check something out. The Schmidt bakery on south Grand. Were they relatives of yours?

RON: Yeah, that was my grandpa and grandma. That's where my mom lived. That's where my dad met my mom as a store girl. That's where they said I was born on the sacks of flour in the storeroom. And, I spent my entire youth there, every Christmas, every Thanksgiving, every Easter. Our Easter took place in the bakery on the benches in the back. That's where we had our Thanksgiving dinner, on the benches with all of the bakers. My grandmother would do all of the cooking and everything.

RON: Next to the bakery they had their own chickens where they had their own eggs. They grew their own vegetables. That's the way it used to be.

RON: Downstairs in the basement of the bakery that was their storeroom. They would buy dried apricots for apricot coffee cake. They would buy ten boxes at a time, and put them down in the basement. They would buy them from Leo, my dad.

RICH: Was the Schmidt bakery any other bakery, ever?

RON: No. The corner is gone. They tore it all down. There might be some kind of a business on that corner, I'm not sure. But, it was at Grand and Walsh. It was never another bakery. They were there until they all passed away. And then, my mom's brother, Ed Schmidt, the oldest one, he moved out to Grasso Plaza. And, Sam Wolf, Connie Wolf's brother, bought Ed Schmidt's bakery when he retired.

RON: *So, like I said, in the bakery business all of those families knew one another. Then, the biggest event in my memory was when my grandmother was at the Schmidt Bakery on South Grand, and her husband passed away. Then, Mr. Hauser's wife passed away. He had a bakery down on Holly Hills. Well, Al Hauser and Emma Schmidt got married! Oh my goodness, I was an altar boy at their wedding! It was crazy!!*
[As Ron told this story he proclaimed all of these things in a <u>very</u> dramatic way!]

Author's Note: This joining of families in marriage seemed to be one more example of how close-knit the "bakery clan" was in St. Louis!

RICH: Were you really an altar boy for that wedding?! That's great. That's great stuff really.

RON: I forgot all about being an altar boy in my grandparents' wedding.

RICH: You know, there are a couple bakeries I would like to get to know. And, I wondered if you knew anybody that could connect me to them. I can't get a connection or find anybody who knew Fred Heimburger. Do you think there's anybody who is still around?

RON: No, I don't think so. Fred and Audrey Heimburger sold that corner at Baptist Church Road and South Lindbergh to a bank. Fred built a big home down there by St. Anthony's Medical Center, [Now it's called Mercy Hospital South.] His wife passed away, and his two kids weren't interested in the bakery. So, Fred Heimburger went into the banking business, and he started his own bank across the street from Federhofer's Bakery on Gravois! I don't know what you have to do to get a charter for a bank, but Fred had a lot of money when he sold that corner.

RON: He had enough money to start his own bank. And then, he joined Sunset Country Club. All of his friends were there, and he told them that he wanted them to bring their money to put into his bank. He said that a lot of them did! And, when his bank got its assets up to enough money another bank came in and bought him out.

RICH: Somebody told me that the Heimburgers owned that entire intersection on South Lindbergh, all four corners. Now, if you think of anybody who can make that connection to Heimburgers let me know.

RON: I'm sure his daughter and his son are still around. I can't remember what his son's name was, and the daughter was as beautiful as her mother. The bank might know where they are.

RICH: Another bakery that I'm interested in is Warner-Knoll. Somebody just told me that they had multiple locations.

RON: Yes, Fred Heimburger worked for Warner-Knoll. You know, he always told me that he invented the gooey butter cake, but a lot of people used to say that was baloney. How many people have invented the gooey butter cake?! [And, we laugh!] There are probably twenty bakers in St. Louis who said that they invented it!

RICH: Do you know Roy Schmiemeir?

RON: Very well! He and I went to bakers school together. He used to work for Fred Heimburger. He would be a guy who could tell you about Fred Heimburger, [Ron says this in a very excited voice.] All of his sons work for Mid-Continent Paper Company. Roy and I are very good friends! He's a really nice guy.

RICH: You know, I might have to go back to Roy to get Fred Heimburger's story. Roy told me that his sons are all in administrative positions at Mid-Continent Paper Company now. I interviewed Roy Schmiemeir, and it was great to talk to him. He's a delightful person. He's such a likeable man. You and he are a lot alike. Well, the story about Roy Schmiemeir retiring is this. He told me the story in this way. He said, "You see that woman in the other room," as he's referring to his wife, "she told me to 'get out of the business, and retire or else'!" So, he retired early!

RON: Yes, he did. And, he was after me for another fifteen or twenty years for me to retire, because we were supposed to retire together. But, I was stuck down at Dawn Foods working for another fifteen years after five years with Middendorf. They all thought I was crazy. I guess I was.

RICH: Helen Lubeley gave me a possible connection to Cynthia Knodel of Knodel's Bakery.

RON: Sure. They closed their bakery after almost one hundred years. Both of the owners, Ned Inglish and Marlene Knodel, passed away. But, look at this!

RON: [As Ron leafs through some papers he brought along he says], "Here's Knodel's Bakery! There's Rich Miskell's cell phone number, Cynthia's husband, if you want to call him." Now, their name is not Knodel, it's Miskell, but they ran Knodel's. Cynthia is the daughter of the Knodels. She's a really nice and interesting person.

RON: You just tell him that I told you to call him. He'll be thrilled to know that I thought about him! They sold the bakery up there in Ferguson to some real estate developer from St. Charles, but he's not even a baker. So, they're just going to use the property. It's been about six months now. Rich is a really nice guy, he's a good guy. He's a Knight of Columbus in the Catholic Church. We used to talk about White

House retreats. He'd be a good connection, especially for Knodels. He could give you all of the information that you would need to know about the Knodels, Ned and Marlene Inglish, and all of the Knodels because that was a one-hundred-year-old bakery, just like the Lubeleys, you know.

RICH: And, Ned and Marlene were the parents of Cynthia, right?

RON: Yes, and they were one of my clients. It seems like since I retired there have been about seven places that have closed, like Lubeleys, Knodels, and Party Pastries.

RICH: You know, somebody else I interviewed was Chris Helfer. Do you know Chris Helfer? Chris is such a nice man. I have honestly loved everybody I've interviewed,

RON: Yeah, he's still in business. Yes, Chris Helfer and his wife, Kathy. They were with Dierbergs at the beginning of Dierberg's Bakeries. He worked for Marie's Pastry Shop in North St. Louis years and years ago, and then he opened his own place rather than going to work for Dierberg's.

RON: Marie's Pastry Shop was at the beginning of Dierberg's bakery. There are so many names going back. It's just amazing.

RON: There were a lotta' bakeries! I'm sure I can't remember all of them or even half of them. When I was a kid I used to go along with my dad in the car. He would drive around and make his route and call on all of the bakeries, and I would go in and just listen and watch. It was quite an education for me as a little kid. I would watch him and his techniques and his methods.

RON: When he would come into a bakery people would just want to give Leo an order, and I could see why because everybody liked him! Whether it was Bettendorf-Rapp or Schnucks or National Super Markets, Miss Hullings Cafeterias, Pope's Cafeterias, or whoever it was, my dad sold to all of them. We had one heck-of-a business! It was big time! We were tremendous competition to Cahokia Flour Company, to W.E. Beckmann, and to the Baker's Co-Op.

RICH: Do you remember King Arthur Flour.

RON: Yeah sure. That one was a specialty flour, and I think Bono-Burns has King Arthur Flour on a palette if you want some. [I thought, "Why would I ever <u>want</u> some King Arthur Flour?!"]

RON: If you'd ever go into Bono-Burns down in Maplewood they've got three big warehouses. They're pretty much the only game in town, bakery-wise!

HOW OUR HEARTS WERE STÖLLEN

RON: There's no Baker's Co-Op. There's no Bake-Mart. There's no Jaudes. There's no Beckmann. The only other ones around are the big grocery companies like Cisco, U.S. Foods, and Performance Food Group. Those three companies, as big as they are, they don't carry any bakery supplies. I mean if you were in the restaurant or grocery business like your dad, and he wanted to buy almond paste and he called on those companies, they wouldn't have almond paste because they don't call on anybody who uses it! They don't sell sweet condensed milk or macaroon coconut, the things like that, you know. There are so many specialty items in the bakery industry.

RICH: Now, what does David McArthur do at Bono-Burns?

RON: David is the sales manager. He's the boss, and he has five salesmen under him. He calls the shots. And, Reed Burnes is the son of Jerry Burns, who was the owner but now he's sorta' stepping out of the picture. Reed would be the one that you should contact. He's the new owner of Bono-Burns, and it's up to him to make that continue.

RON: They have a tremendous distribution. Bono-Burns distributes about twelve million dollars a year just to Schnuck's grocery stores. They're the number one purveyor to Schnuck's. As long as Schnucks stays in business in St. Louis and somebody doesn't buy them out, Bono-Burnes is their number one supplier to their bakery. They buy tons and tons of stuff from Bono-Burnes. Most of it is from Dawn Foods. Just to give you an idea on one item, when Schnucks runs brownies in their ad for their one hundred plus stores they'll buy fifty of the two hundred and fifty pound bags of Dawn Brownie Mix, just one item from Bono-Burns. [At this point Ron laughs at the amount.]

RON: And then, the next week it might be carrot cake. Then, the next week it might be gooey butter cake. And then, the next week it might be pumpkin. I used to sell all of this stuff to Schnucks. You know, when bakers buy pumpkin, it has to be Libby's pumpkin. They'll say, "If it's not Libby's pumpkin, we don't care what your price is."

RON: Also, when I sold them apple sauce, when they made apple sauce cake, they only used Musselman's apple sauce. They would say, "We don't care if you've got brand X apple sauce."

RICH: Well, I want to tell you, I think Schnuck's has some very good bakery goods!

RON: Oh, they're outstanding! What do they have now? They just took over another eighteen stores from Shop n' Save? They have about one hundred and twenty stores now. Can you imagine? Have you ever been in their bakery up there on Page Avenue? It's the old National Supermarket distribution center.

RON: They made a complete bakery out of it. Their bakery goods are outstanding. You go in there for their gooey butter cake, and they have it in those little plastic things. It's the best! It's better than Fred Heimburger's, and he said that he invented it! [And then, we laugh!]

Author's Note: At this time, Ron Jaudes reflected affectionately on Fred Heimburger's ability to tell "tall tales," about his being the inventor of the gooey butter cake and other claims he would make. He seemed to agree with Roy Schmiemeir's similar descriptions!]

"The baker said that the bread wasn't too fresh . . . so I got cream puffs instead."

Knodel Bakery
Interview With Cynthia Knodel and Her Husband Rich Miskell

RICH M.: I wish Ned and Marlene, Cynthia's parents,
were still around. They would be happy to talk to you.

CYNTHIA: We are thrilled to talk to you.
I know my mom and dad helped the Helfers along the way to get started.

— Cynthia Knodel and Rich Miskell

RICH: You know, this is a labor of love, I love doing this. The people I've met, like Chris Helfer and his wife, who also own a northside bakery, have been so helpful.

CYNTHIA: Yes, Chris is great.

RICH G.: See, I don't know anything about the northside bakeries. So, please tell me anything you know about places up north. And, if you think of any bakeries that were important on the northside, please let me know.

RICH M.: Well, Helfers is a big part of the northside. You know, we don't have a lot of pictures. We do have some photos, and we do have stuff like that. We may have left some things when we sold the bakery.

CYNTHIA: We do have a plaque, a newspaper plaque from when they did a story on us.

RICH M.: Before Marlene passed, Jennings had a "Jennings Bakery Day." I mean, Knodel's Bakery was a staple, oh my goodness, in that area since the 1950's. And then, prior to that —

CYNTHIA: — we were in the city.

[I thought it was very touching how Cynthia and her husband would finish one another's sentences during the interview.]

RICH M.: Yeah, it still was on West Florissant, right?

CYNTHIA: Yes, it was on West Florissant the whole time —

RICH M.: — since 1901 from when Cynthia's great grandfather started the bakery.

CYNTHIA: And then, Sidney eventually met my grandmother, Margaretha, but she went by Marge. She was also German. They continued on with the bakery, and that was during the depression. They actually did very well during the depression because they sold bread, and you know people <u>had</u> to buy bread. My mother was born during the depression in 1928. She was actually born above the bakery at the first location on West Florissant. They were still so poor that they couldn't afford a cradle. She used to sleep in a dresser drawer.

RICH G.: I've heard similar stories. That's great. I don't think she was the only one at that time. [Laughter] O.K., where was your location, the 2nd location?

CYNTHIA: Our location for 67 years was at 6621 West Florissant, and my father actually designed the building. [At this point, Cynthia and her husband, Rich, had a conversation about multiple locations in addition to the one at 6621 West Florissant.] They had several locations. When we were thriving in our business we did bread, all kinds of breads, we did coffee cakes, all the pastries, basically a full-service bakery.

RICH M.: Pies and cakes and wedding cakes, everything! One of the things that they didn't do — *they didn't waste a thing*. So, when you would wind up having a mix of left-overs, or you would wind up having cakes that would get crumbled and then mixed with other things, they would make what are called "fruit rocks." And then, they would take the fillings that they weren't going to be using, and they would mix it all together and make "fruit rocks." So, a lady at our church, we're at St. John Bosco church, and she's going back forty years now, asked, "Do you guys still make 'fruit rocks'?"

RICH G.: O.K., how do you make "fruit rocks?"

CYNTHIA: You just take everything that's left over from the week, and throw it together, and put in some filling, and bake it up! It might be different every week.

RICH M.: So, as far as recipes go and things like that, we'll have to call "Baker Bob."

CYNTHIA: Yes, we have a baker that worked for us from the age of 16 until he retired at 65, His name was "Baker Bob," Baker Bob Greaves!

RICH M.: And, not one day longer, 65 and he was gone!

RICH G.: You know, there was a video on You Tube called, "Bob the Baker," about

Bob Smith, who was the owner of the Carondelet Bakery. This video is of a different person from your Knodel's baker. It's really a beautiful short video! I taught all of Bob Smith's daughters at Notre Dame High School. I actually taught several bakers' daughters at Notre Dame.

RICH G.: These interviews have all been very comforting because I've been so encouraged by what I've learned. My theory behind the big story is that the St. Louis bakery community was a very unifying thing because almost all of the bakers knew one another.

CYNTHIA: Yes, they did, especially through the Baker's Co-Op. Everybody knew everybody through the Co-Op. They even had social events together, and they had them all of the time! My parents and grandparents went to the events of the Co-Op all of the time. That's why when the Co-Op died it was so sad. The man who led it was Ed Federhofer.

Author's Note: Cynthia seemed to merge the Bakers Co-Op with her overall memories of the St. Louis Bakers Association.

RICH G.: I taught Bill Federhofer's daughter, Cheryl. She's now a partner with her brother as co-owners of the bakery on Gravois, and it seems like it's doing well!

CYNTHIA: So many of the little bakeries have closed.

RICH G.: Do you know Roy Schmiemeier the past owner of the bakery that used to be on Manchester?That bakery is still open, but not by him. It became Clayton bakery, and now it's Bello's.

RICH M.: Bello's! Have you talked to him? Oh my goodness, he is a lot more modern than everything you're talking about. Let's see, where is he from? Oh yeah, the Ukraine?

CYNTHIA: No, I think Greece.

RICH G.: Well, I'm glad it's still going. Did you know Roy Schmiemeier at all.

CYNTHIA: No, but my parents did.

RICH G.: Cynthia, how long did you work at the bakery?

CYNTHIA: Me personally? Well, I worked there all through middle school around 1976 or 77, then high school. Then, I went to college. After that, I got another job. And then, I worked at the bakery after my mother enticed me to come back.

RICH G.: Now, did you know Connie Wolf, or any of the Wolfs who owned the Wolf bakery? They had sixteen children and lived above the bakery. She has become a good friend, and she was supposed to be here today, but she's a dog sitter, and had to do that. She's the youngest child of the sixteen. I interviewed her, and she got so excited about this project. She's been very helpful, and encouraging. I did learn that the Co-Op was important.

CYNTHIA: Yes, really important.

RICH G.: Yes, because they bought in bulk, right? They represented all of the bakers who belonged to the Co-Op. And, part of it was that there were dividends at the end of the year based on how much you spent? I think it was such an ingenious idea!

Author's Note: I did learn later that the Co-Op was started much earlier.

RICH: Oh yeah, when did you close, Cynthia?

CYNTHIA: This past August. We had a lot of good customers.

RICH M.: There were a lot of really good folks down there, a lot of really good customers. As we were going out of business we got so many hugs, even from people we didn't know. We had seen them in the bakery, but didn't really know them until the end of the business.

RICH G.: Well you know, this book is going to be a "tribute to bakers." I hope it all happens. It's hard to know how it's going to end up because I have so much information. I wanted this to be a "coffee table" book, lots of pictures and some information too. We want people to read it and enjoy it, you know. But, it's been an ongoing question for me about how to give so much great information a place and keep this book short enough for people to *want* to read it. We'll see!

CYNTHIA: Well, we evolved when the big stores were taking over a lot of the bakery business into a place for cakes, wedding cakes, and specialty items. We quit doing bread, and we quit doing pastries. We did mainly cakes, cookies, cupcakes, and that kind of thing.

RICH M.: Bob Greaves would be a great source to fill in some timelines for that kind of stuff. We had stacks of catalogs of our cakes, and they were done by theme. When Cynthia would meet with a specialty or wedding cake person, she would use these catalogs.

RICH G.: Did you do the decorating? [Question to Cynthia.]

CYNTHIA: I decorated. No, I don't bake, at all. Rich is the baker.

RICH G.: I guess it was Roy Schmiemeir who said, "If you were a baker, you had to love the work, and it was very satisfying because it was very artistic."

CYNTHIA: It <u>was</u> very artistic, and during my whole life I liked art a lot. [While looking at a photo album, Cynthia commented,] "That's my mom and dad's wedding cake." We used to do parades. [And then, looking at a picture of the first bakery location she said], "This is actually where the bakery was when it was brand new."

CYNTHIA: [Then, looking at another photo, she commented,] "And this was when town and country had their anniversary. We did a lot of parades.

RICH G.: You know, I've never asked anybody this. How hard is it to work with fondant?

CYNTHIA: It's not hard if you know what you're doing.

RICH G.: It's sort of like laying stuff on, right?

CYNTHIA: Yeah, you just roll it out and drape it on.

RICH: How does it hold?

CYNTHIA: You just use a light layer of butter cream. It's like an edible glue.

RICH G.: So, what was 6715 West Florissant?

CYNTHIA: That was a location we had.

RICH M. So, I guess that was in 1944 and 1945 which was prior to being at 6621 West Florissant.

RICH G.: [While looking at one of the cakes in the cake catalog, I commented], I like this one. It's so fancy!

CYNTHIA: Yeah, that's really pretty. That was made with fondant, with fondant bows.

RICH G.: [And, looking at another photo of one of the cakes in the catalog, I commented], "I think this is really classy. It's really beautiful."

RICH G.: Was it hard to close?

CYNTHIA: Yes and no. Too many problems. Yeah, and so tiring, but I do miss it.

RICH M.: You know, it's funny. I do miss the customers.

RICH G.: You know, Helen Lubeley was very descriptive of her feelings about what it was like to close their store. She said, that they didn't want to just close. They wanted their customers to have some notice. So, they announced it three weeks before, and she said that those three weeks were unbelievably busy.

RICH M.: Oh, I was down there during those three weeks. Because they were so busy Helen passed off four or five wedding cakes to us. I went down to their bakery on two or three occasions to pick-up samples of their pound cake or their amaretto cake, so that I could kind of match them. And, it was during that time period when I saw that there were lines out the door!

RICH G.: So, who were the family members involved in your business? You and Rich, and who else?

CYNTHIA: My parents and my brother. My parents are Marlene and Ned Inglish. And, my grandparents were Sidney and Marge Knodel. Our marriage name is Miskell. And then, there was my great grandfather, who was Carl Knodel.

RICH G.: Well, we know how it is with sick or injured people. And, you have a daughter who's disabled, right? I have a mother-in-law for whom my wife has given care for over fifty years, first after a car accident that left her brain-damaged and lately slowing down just from aging. She's a sweet, sweet lady.

CYNTHIA: And, that was part of the reason that we closed the business too. My mother and father were aging, and they were both needing care. We have a daughter with disabilities, and there's a lot of care needed there. We do have nursing, but there are a lot of doctor appointments and this, that, and the other. And, we weren't able to attend to the business like we needed to. So, the sales weren't what we needed.

RICH G.: So, first things first, right? Family first?

CYNTHIA: First things first.

RICH G.: You know, there is a really helpful thing that I need to ask you. Do you know any other people that I could talk to? These interviews are really helpful, and they sometimes give me the next step of someone who had a bakery that you know personally.

CYNTHIA: You spoke with Helfer's, right? Did you want new bakeries or old bakeries?

RICH G.: I'm focusing mostly on old bakeries, but I'm open to new bakeries too.

CYNTHIA: Well, there's Mike at Wedding Wonderland.

RICH G.: That's good to know. Where is he located, and how do you know him? Did he ever work for you?

RICH M.: Actually, the gentleman who won the title two years ago of "America's Next Great Baker" was Al Watson, and he worked at Wedding Wonderland. His wife worked for us, and he worked for us for the longest time. Now, he is mostly out of the bakery business. Now he's an electrician! You win "America's Next Great Baker," so then you become an electrician!

RICH G.: After getting that award where can you go next, right!

RICH M.: So, Al and Heather, who is Al's ex-wife, both started working at Knodel's in their teens, I guess. Yeah, Al is a cake decorator, beyond compare. Very talented, can you imagine, he won a national T.V. baking show! [After looking it up on his cell phone, Rich says,] "Alright, it's also known as 'Cake Boss, Next Great Baker'."

RICH G.: Do you think he'd be willing to talk to me?

RICH M.: I'm sure Al would be willing to talk with you.

CYNTHIA: I have his number. I do feel comfortable giving you his number. Actually, let me call Bob Greaves who was one of our bakers to see if he'd be willing to talk to you.

RICH M.: Yeah, "Baker Bob" would be a wealth of information as well.

RICH G.: I don't know any bakeries on the Northside other than Helfer's and Ellerbrock's. I have talked with a good friend, Rita Ellerbrock Andres and her cousin, who is part of the Ellerbrock family. They are both wonderful people. I talked with them a couple of times. So, I know the Ellerbrock's story. Are there any more Northside bakeries that you can think of?

RICH M.: So, Wedding Wonderland is a Northside bakery. Cynthia knows all of the old bakeries, much more than I do.

RICH G.: I'm getting a picture now of bakeries on the Northside. Were there any other bakeries?

CYNTHIA: Bob would be able to help you with that better than me because I was younger. He's a good ten years older than me.

RICH M.: Yeah, since he started with us when he was sixteen he knows the whole thing. What about Porter Louis? Because he was an African American they used to go out and buy Porter his food because he couldn't go to the restaurants.

RICH G.: That's crazy!

RICH M.: But, Porter Louis was a baker! Bob Greaves would often say, [Rich Miskell said the following with an impersonating gravelly voice], *"You know, Porter Louis can bake anything!"* He would say, "That guy, just knows it!" Porter's probably 75 or 80? He retired. [Then, Cynthia's husband said to her], "But, didn't he pull you out by the woodshed one time,?"

CYNTHIA: Oh, he took me in the back, and he told me that I was being disrespectful.

RICH M.: Didn't he spank you?

CYNTHIA: No, but he came close. He was like my dad, and I had about twelve dads!

RICH G.: [While laughing], that's what it sounds like!

RICH M.: You were probably pretty young, right?

CYNTHIA: Yes. He took me out in the garage.

RICH G.: I'd love to talk to him.

CYNTHIA: Oh, and there was Aunt Jewel, Julia Jungerman. Aunt Jewel was a vital member of our family. She lived with my grandparents, and she was our head decorator.

RICH G.: But, she wasn't a relative, right?

CYNTHIA: No, but she was my godmother. She decorated, and she taught me how to decorate. She kept the decorating part of the bakery afloat.

RICH G.: She taught you how to decorate?

CYNTHIA: Yeah, when I was about five years old, making roses!

RICH G.: Well, she must have taught you well. You did beautiful work.

CYNTHIA: Thank you. And, she worked all the way up until eighty something. She's passed away a good fifteen years ago.

RICH G.: What would you say your bakery was known for? I ask this question to all of the bakers, and some people have said, "for everything!"

CYNTHIA: I would say cakes. Decorated cakes.

RICH M.: And, I would say that has been true even until recently, especially for the last twenty years. If you would go back further, I mean, you were talking about going to the bakery in the morning after Mass. Baker Bob would get up on a Saturday morning for what we used to call "store cakes." So, the bakery would sell eighty to a hundred on Sundays and all of the pastries, and all of the stöllens, just on Sundays. On Sundays everybody would go to church, and after church come to the bakery. [There seemed to have been a pattern here with my own experience!]

CYNTHIA: Yeah, "store cakes" were the two-layer eight-inch cakes. Some were lemon, some were chocolate, some were caramel. Oh, they would go in and out.

RICH M.: Cynthia's father, Ned, was always a big experimenter. So, he would say, "Oh yeah, we're going to be doing lemon cakes now, and then lemon cakes would die off. Or, we would be doing whatever.

RICH M.: [And then, Rich M. says to Cynthia, "That was your dad, right, a big experimenter! And, they would run that series of cake for awhile, like orange cake." Oh my goodness, dreamsicle, orange cake. You know what dreamsicle is, right. I adjusted that recipe. We did an orange cake that had a cream cheese filling with whipped cream icing.

RICH G.: Wow! My wife loves the dreamsicle flavor! And, you called it an orange cake?

CYNTHIA: Yeah, a dreamsicle cake.

RICH M.: You know, the best cake right out of the oven, but it loses its umph fast, is pound cake. On the top of a cake when you bake it, especially like a wedding cake, you get what they call a "sugar ring." You can even see the sugar browning out of there. Well, you know you're going to have to cut off the top of that cake to get the upper layers to sit flat for when you're doing a wedding cake. So, I can tell you what happened on the wedding cakes to most of those tops. [And, as Rich pats his belly, he says], "That sugar ring on the top, it's better than bread right out of the oven! No frosting, no icing, no none of that. But, when it's still warm, oh yeah!"

CYNTHIA: It's delicious.

RICH G.: Wow, that's really interesting. It's like the turkey slicer on Thanksgiving Day, they get the first tastes of the turkey!

RICH M.: They get the good stuff! The orange cake was done with white cake, because when you do it with yellow, it doesn't look right. The orange and the yellow just don't mix out right.

RICH G.: So, was that a late or recent specialty?

RICH M.: So, I talked to Marlene about bringing back the orange cake, and I changed it up a little bit. She was like, "Oh my goodness, yeah you know, twenty-five years ago we had a three year run with orange cake, and then we just quit. So, things just ran through their natural cycle." It had orange zest and a puree kind of thing inside the cake itself. The puree came actually from a kind of "fruito" type of mix.

RICH G.: What was that like, the fruito?

RICH M.: The fruito is an orange concentrate, and it would be mixed into the batter. You can get it at Dawn Foods, the baker's supply distributor.

RICH G.: [As Cynthia comes back into the room, I say to her], "I was just learning how to make an orange cake. I was just asking your husband about orange fruito."

CYNTHIA: Orange cake is delicious. But, I don't know what orange fruito is. I'm not a baker. I'm more of a chef because I don't like to measure. I like to just throw stuff together. When you bake you have to measure!

RICH G.: Our son-in-law is a chef. He's a professional chef, a personal chef, and he works for families. Fortunately, they moved back to St. Louis with our daughter and grandson. We also have two little granddaughters in Kansas City. So, we're very lucky, we're very blessed.

RICH G.: When you think of the history of the Knodel Bakery that's a long time, isn't it? I would think you'd be very proud of it.

CYNTHIA: Yes, that is a long time. and, I am very proud of it!

RICH G.: That's been a consistent feeling for all of the bakers I've interviewed. If you are a baker how could you not be proud of what you've done?!

CYNTHIA: I wish I could have continued to let it be open and stay in business, but we just couldn't. We owned the whole block. So, we had to decide when we got an offer to sell, to go ahead and sell. You know, we were lucky to get out, really lucky.

RICH G.: And, to get something for it, right?

CYNTHIA: We didn't really make much, but it was lucky just to get out. It was really sad. What was really sad was that we lost so much of our stuff when we left. But, we still had two weeks of wedding cakes and some decorated cakes to do. So, even though I wasn't supposed to do anything because of my back surgery, of course I did. And, losing all of our stuff after we sold just broke my heart. Just watching all of our stuff go, it was just breaking my heart.

RICH G.: I understand.

RICH M.: I understand too, but I'm a little more pragmatic. I was like you guys are gonna' need some of that stuff, but "It's your animal now." We had amassed sixty to seventy years of stuff.

CYNTHIA: Yeah, and all of the "cut-outs" that we had?

RICH M.: I think they thought that they weren't going to be doing cut-outs, but they wound up doing them anyway.

RICH G.: Now, were those cut-outs things that you had purchased?

CYNTHIA: No, we made them, we drew them ourselves. We had like "Thing One" and "Thing Two," you know from The Addams Family. We had so many.

RICH M.: We had a box of cut-outs that customers could just go through, like the "Hulk" and all of the kid's characters.

RICH G.: They were like stencils, right, that you used to decorate the cakes?

RICH M.: More or less. So, what we did was this. The image got drawn out, and then we'd cut that out. Then, it got placed over a full or half sheet cake. And then, we would cut that out. If you wanted to cut out the cake you would just put that on top, and then you'd trace around it with a knife. For things like Spiderman buildings and Mickey Mouse and other things that you would have, it was a stencily kind of thing.

CYNTHIA: A lot of hard work went into those.

RICH G.: Whoa! [As I'm looking at the photo of the cake that we were all looking at], I ask, "How did you prop up those layers with those little pillars? There's something inside of those cones, right?"

RICH M.: Yes, I think those ice cream cones were filled with Rice Krispy treats. But, there was icing inside of them too. So, those Rice Krispy treats were a structural support themselves.

RICH G.: So, it supported some of that weight. Oh yeah, I was going to ask you, "Who did you have to do your finances? Was it you, Cynthia?"

CYNTHIA: No, we had an office manager. Yeah, she was very good.

RICH G.: Then you didn't have to bother with that part of it.

CYNTHIA: No. It was Heather. She was invaluable.

RICH M.: Oh yeah, Heather. Well, Marlene, Cynthia's mother, did it forever before Heather. Marlene was the business manager. Cynthia's brother, Darren was technically the CFO, the Chief Finance Officer, but he was very hands-offish. Once in a blue moon he would look over everything, tell everybody how to do stuff, and then go back to Colorado.

RICH M.: Marlene did all of that forever and ever, and then she brought Heather along the way. Heather was invaluable. Heather was "Miss Caterer." She was "Miss Icer," "Miss Decorator," "Miss Office Manager." She was amazing as long as she didn't have to really involve herself with customers. She couldn't handle the stress of customers very well. But, with everything else, she was on it. I always said, "If I could have ten Heathers, I could rule the world!"

RICH G.: I believe you. It sounds like she was great!

RICH M.: Yeah, Heather was phenomenal. Heather was Al Watson's wife. He was at Wedding Wonderland when he won the title of "America's Next Great Baker!"

Author's Note: My interview with Cynthia Knodel and her husband was very touching.

At this time the tape recording ran out of tape, but we continued talking for awhile longer.

Kruta's Bakery
Interview With Paul Kruta

There were such good feelings
amongst the bakers.
Yeah, we still do some of that.
...they might say,
"Oh yeah, we're out of this.
Do you have any extra?"
And, we'd say, "Oh yeah sure...we'll be here,
and you can get us next time."
Yeah, it's wonderful!
— Paul Kruta

RICH: I just wanted you to know that McArthur's Bakery started me out on this Bakery Book project. They were wonderful to me. I don't know if you know David or Randy McArthur?

PAUL: Oh yeah, yeah. They actually came in quite a bit and would talk with my dad. They're both reps for different companies now, and so we actually have a lot of dealings with them. So, they're good friends of ours.

RICH: Oh, good! I'm glad to hear that. They're really nice people. David, I think, is with Bono-Burnes, right? And, is Randy with somebody too?

PAUL: Yeah, Randy is with Dawn Food Products.

RICH: What is the address of your bakery?

PAUL: Yeah, at this location the address is 300 St. Louis Road, Collinsville, Illinois.

RICH: So, Kruta's Bakery just celebrated their one hundredth year anniversary in 2019.

PAUL: Yeah, last year! The anniversary party was on August 18th!

RICH: Wow! I've interviewed at several other very old bakeries. So, is your dad still involved with the business?

PAUL: Yeah, yeah. He's technically retired, but he's here every day! [Paul laughs.] He <u>has</u> stepped back a little bit, but he's still kind of involved. He's still the guy that we go to with all of the questions and everything.

RICH: Was that Frank Jr.?

PAUL: No, Frank Jr. was his uncle. My dad's name is Jim. Jim Kruta is my dad. His dad was Tony Kruta, and he's the one who built this specific location.

RICH: It's always so great when I hear that people are carrying on their family bakery.

PAUL: And, Tony's dad was Frank Sr. He's the one that started the whole thing. He's the one that came from Russia. I've actually got his immigration papers right here. He was born in the Ukraine, in Russia.

RICH: So, Frank Sr. was the first. And, what about the uncle? Who was he?

PAUL: So, Frank Sr. had five kids, Joe, Casey, Tony, that was my grandpa, Frank Jr., and Estella. Frank Jr. was the youngest boy. So, he was my dad's uncle. All of them were involved with the bakery at one point or another. Frank Jr. worked at the East St. Louis location his whole life up until it closed. And then, he came over and helped my grandpa over here.

RICH: How long were they in East St. Louis?

PAUL: The East St. Louis bakery started in 1919, and they closed their doors in 1974. So, they had 55 years in that location.

RICH: So, in 1974 did they move here right away or did they take some time for the transition?

PAUL: Yeah, my grandpa had decided that he was going to put one in Collinsville for his son. He wanted his son to be able to carry on. He wasn't sure at that point that he wanted to stay in East St. Louis. So, he thought, "We're gonna' put one up there in Collinsville. Then, we'll have two places going. So, I'll be here in East St. Louis, and they can be over there in Collinsville." Then, it just got to be too much. So, it was just, "Well, we'll go and help Tony in Collinsville."

RICH: So, Tony was the one who was in charge of this bakery, right?

RICH: I love gathering this information, and I don't really want to give this up very soon. So anyway, the Mc Arthurs gave me these three 10-ream boxes filled with fifty years of bulletins. Apparently, this one lady organized all of this, and I think her name was Joyce Schwarz. It was so organized that I tried to take each decade, and take samples from each decade. *It's just a great story, and I want you to know that the bakers were so cooperative with one another and so kind to one another!*

RICH: *There were such good feelings amongst the bakers.* For example, they were godparents for one another's children, they inter-married, they bought one another's stores, they worked in one another's stores, they shared goods when someone needed something.

PAUL: *Yeah, yeah. We still do some of that. Yeah, we've got a couple of bakeries on the East Side, and they might say, "Oh yeah, we're out of this. Do you have any extra?" And, we'd say, "Oh yeah sure, come and pick it up. We'll be here, and you can get us next time." Yeah, it's wonderful!*

RICH: *And, that's really become the main story that I want to tell! How good the bakers were to one another. They were almost like a little tribe that took care of one another! [At this point Paul agrees saying, "Yeah, yeah!" while laughing and nodding his head!]*

PAUL: Did Randy or David McArthur ever tell you about the "Baker's Dozen?" Yeah, it was his dad and my grandpa and other bakers. They were pretty guarded with their recipes and what not, but they would always be helping each other out! Actually, Randy was the one who told me about those things.

RICH: Yeah, they had kind of a little club, didn't they? I have to learn more about that

PAUL: This is a little bit more about my grandpa. Tony, took over when he was sixteen because Frank Sr. got really sick pretty young. So, Tony who couldn't even drive, would walk around to other bakeries, and they would help him to get his footing because he was a kid, you know. Sixteen year olds back then were a lot different from sixteen year olds now, but still he was a kid. Yeah, he had a strong drive to keep everything going.

RICH: Paul, are you one of the decorators here?

PAUL: Yeah, I decorate, and I do kinda' like the finishing work in the morning. So, actually I don't do any baking or mixing. I can do a few things, but I'm not as well-versed on that as my dad would be. So, after everything comes out of the oven me and a couple of other people, we ice it all up, get it ready for the store, and put it out in the cases so that when we open at 6:00 a.m. it's all ready for people to look at and smell and buy!

RICH: Wow! So, what's your sleep time like?

PAUL: Well, I've got a five year old. So, that can kind of vary. [Paul laughs.] But, I try to get in bed by 8:00 or 9:00 o'clock. and then, I'm in here around 4:00. So, I'm one of the last people in as far as the early morning guys are concerned.

RICH: Really?! Do they come in even earlier?

PAUL: Yeah, the guy that runs the ovens and gets everything started up in the morning, he's here around 2:45. And, that's on the weekdays. On the weekends it's like midnight.

RICH: Yeah, you just got finished with a busy time over Thanksgiving didn't you?

PAUL: Yeah, Thanksgiving and Christmas. It was nuts. We had to take a week off after Christmas. It's a lot of hours.

RICH: Oh my gosh, just the cookie demand probably? You do cookies, right?

PAUL: Yeah, we've got just a few different kinds of cookies that we have every day in the store. Chocolate chip, sugar, oatmeal, and cinnamon and sugar. That's pretty much it. And then, we've got decorated cookies.

PAUL: But, for Christmas our big cookie time, we make a pound tray of assorted butter cookies. That's a lot of work. We've got a whole assembly line of people packing and doing stuff to get those out. We just sell them in the box. We don't sell them individually. And, that's it, because if we try to break them up, there'd be no hope for us! [At this time Paul laughs!]

RICH: Yes, that's a lot of labor! But, cookies are a big seller at Christmas for a lot of bakers, right? You know, I'm really glad to see somebody your age hanging in there. I want you to know that there are a couple other young bakers in St. Louis.

PAUL: Yeah, sometimes I kind of go, "Oh man, can I do this?" Yeah, I can do it! I kind of have to realize that maybe I wouldn't be able to. [At this time Paul breathes a heavy sigh.] *You know, like you were saying, "There's a lot of love, and there's a lot of ache in baking too because like at the holidays I don't see my family, my wife and my son, very much. You know, like the week of Christmas and leading up to it, I don't really see them at all, except in passing. It's almost like we're roommates for a week rather than husband and wife. So, that's interesting and difficult. But, the more I think about it, I think, "Man, I couldn't* do *something else. This is what I am."*

RICH: *It's your life, right!*

PAUL: *I have to tell everybody who asks me about it, "It's like everything I have, it's because of the bakery! So, I couldn't walk away from it! There's no way!*

RICH: I'm really glad to hear that! There's a guy up in North St. Louis County, Mike Temm. He's got a bakery called Wedding Wonderland, and they do nothing but cakes. He's about your age, and he is completely committed to the bakery business. So, that will be there, and then hopefully Federhofer's will stay, and I hope Missouri Bakery stays.

PAUL: Yeah, they've got good cake!

RICH: Yeah, we've gotta' keep the doors open! [Paul and I laugh in agreement!] Yeah, so are there any stories that you can think of that stand out?

PAUL: Oh, so yeah. This is one that I would pretty much hear every Christmas. In East St. Louis the train went right by our bakery building. They were right by the station, on Eighth Street and Exchange. So, the store is just packed, and there's a line out the door because it's the holidays. Everybody has got to get into the store to get their breads and their pies, hustling and bustling. It's Christmas Eve, and a guy comes running in, and he says, "I got the conductor to stop the train. All I need is a holiday bread." And then, just like the red sea, the line parts, and they let the guy up. He buys his holiday bread, and gets out, and then he says, "Thanks, and Merry Christmas!" And then, everybody is right back at it. They always bring up that story!

RICH: Wow! What a great story!

PAUL: Yeah, but I don't know how that would go nowadays!

RICH: Yeah, people are so rule-oriented now. People just don't seem like they can make exceptions to stuff when they could choose to be kind.

PAUL: Yeah! I can just imagine somebody running in and saying, "Oh, I've only got five minutes. Can I come to the front of the line?" And, I would say, "I don't know, we've had people waiting an hour and a half." I don't know how people would feel about it now because everybody is in such a hurry.

RICH: Are there any stories connected with your family members, like your uncle, or your grandpa?

PAUL: Very, very little. My grandpa passed when I was three. He always called me "his little buddy!" But, my dad always talks about how <u>fast</u> my grandpa was, just how quick he could do things because when they started they didn't have all of the machines that we have now, all of the different things that could cut things out in just a couple seconds.

PAUL: If you look right behind you there's one of our donut cutters. So, they sit on a wheel, and it rolls the dough, and my grandpa could cut the donuts out faster than that would go. So, my dad would tell me, "Yeah, he'd get fed up with the machine, and he'd just start cutting them out himself."

PAUL: To me that's just like my dad. He's so much faster than anything I can see. And, to have my dad tell me, "Oh yeah, my dad was so much faster than me!" It's like, how fast were these mutants?! [And then, we both laugh together!]

RICH: How could that be, right?!

PAUL: It's just like a super-human ability to turn it out!

RICH: That's amazing! Did you have any other employees that you remember that weren't family and that stood out?

PAUL: Well, right now our guy who comes in at a quarter to 3:00 in the morning. He's been here since he was sixteen or seventeen. He was just a kid. Basically, he's been working here for his entire life. So, he's practically family.

PAUL: Yeah, he's definitely put in his time. He's actually going to retire after Easter. So, Mike has been a part of my whole life. Right now I work next to him. And then, Yvonne was our decorator for years and years. And her brother Danny works here still. He married my mom's sister and so, he's my uncle, and he's family now.

RICH: So, how old would you say Mike is?

PAUL: Oh gosh, I should know this. I'd say he's in his sixties. I'll have to ask him.

RICH: So, how many decorators do you have now?

PAUL: We've got me and another guy. He does all of the flowers and what not, and I do all of the writing and all of the drawings. My dad can do all of that too. If he needs to help out he can, but it's mainly me and Jason.

RICH: Did your dad go for formal training anywhere?

PAUL: Oh, I'm not sure. My uncle Frank, Frank Jr. did. He went to the Wilton school.

RICH: Oh, that's good to know. There's a place in St. Louis that's still a school, O'Fallon Tech, and they had a baker's program. Then, there was a very important school up north somewhere called the Dunwoody Institute, which was like a national training center for bakers. I've heard of the Wilton school. That's a brand name for equipment, isn't it?

PAUL: Yep, it's kind of their thing. Their main goal is to be able to have affordable baking equipment for anybody. And so, they sell their stuff at discount department stores. Not like their big equipment, but all their decorating supplies and everything, books, and even courses.

PAUL: The hobby stores like Hobby Lobby, Michael's, and Joann's, they feature Wilton training. Yep, I took the "flowers course" there. You could pick-up the book. It's like seven dollars. If you go to take the course, then you bring the book to the course, and they walk you through page by page on how to do it. It was something like five weeks. My wife and I both did it.

RICH: Right now there doesn't seem to be many places that train bakers. People just seem to learn on the job.

PAUL: That's how I did it, most of mine. Yeah, most of my learning was "hands-on!"

RICH: Exactly. Well, this is great information. Another important question is, "What do you think Kruta's is best known for? Are there any signature items?"

PAUL: Oh yeah, sure. I'd say definitely gooey butter cake, cream horns, and one more, the "Fudgie," which is a chocolate cake, a really rich chocolate cake, and then it's topped with a chocolate Fudgie fondant. So, it's a tiny bundt cake basically, and it's really popular. So, I think those are our big three every single day. Oh yeah, and donuts, glazed donuts.

RICH: Yeah, glazed donuts. You can't really beat 'em,, can you! It seems like there's only a few places that make them the right way. I'm sort of afraid to say this, but I think maybe the taste or the crunch is directly related to the amount of grease in them. [We both laugh in agreement!]

PAUL: Well, my dad is pretty particular about how they come out! Yeah, they have to be just right. If they're too greasy they're just like "ugh"! But, if there's not enough, they just don't have the right flavor. You gotta' fry them in the right stuff!

RICH: Yeah, exactly! And, the crispiness of the glazed icing! That's funny! But, tell me again what those chocolate things are called?

PAUL: They're called "Fudgies!" So, here's kind of the evolution of the "Fudgie." When we first started out we made a large one, a Fudge Torte Cake.

PAUL: So, basically it was the same thing as when you make a pineapple upside down cake. You grease the pan with a caramel smear so that it bakes into the cake and makes it really rich. So, we did that with chocolate, and then when we turned it out, we topped it with our donut icing and put chopped pecans on it! People really like them, and we sell some of them every single day. Then the left-over batter we throw into muffin tins. And, we sell those, maybe a dozen every few days.

PAUL: At one point cupcakes just kind of took over the market. So, we stopped selling the larger Fudge Tortes, but people were buying "Fudgies" by the dozen. So, now we make between six and eight dozen on a regular day, and it's sometimes about twelve dozen on the week-ends. Yeah, people will buy a lot of those!

PAUL: So, our signature items would be glazed donuts, Fudgies, and then cream horns and gooey butter. I'd say those are our big four everyday items.

PAUL: We've got a Cranberry Nut Bread which is like a "quick bread." It's almost more like a batter than a dough. So, it's got more of a cakey consistency to it.

PAUL: It's cranberry, nuts and sugar — and oh, they're so good! [At this time Paul just laughs and revels at the thought of the bread!] So, we make those at Thanksgiving and Christmas. I think they're talking about making them for Valentine's Day too!

RICH: Well, there's a guy I want you to know about because he's young like you, and he's in the St. Louis area too. His name is Nathaniel Reid. *He said that having his bakery here was what he wanted to do. He loves the Midwest, and he loves St. Louis. And then, he said, "I could be anywhere, but this is my love, this is what I want to do, this is where I want to be."* Yeah, he's worth looking up!

RICH: Is there any other question on the "Interview Sheet" that catches your eye?

PAUL: Yeah, the question, "What were the greatest satisfactions of baking?" I can tell you that right now. This is actually something my sister told me when we were talking about our history. This was one of the things she said last year for our big 100th anniversary, "We really get to know our customers, because we've got a lot of repeat people. There are people that order from us for every holiday, every birthday, every special event. We've literally got life-long customers."

Author's Note: At this time Paul talked about how much he had been given on a personal level from being a baker for his customers.

PAUL: Their entire lives, we get to be a part of it! And so, it's really a unique thing! I get to know our customers because I've been working here my entire life and even when I was a kid too! So, there are people that I've gotten to watch grow up from behind the counter. "Man, I can remember when you came in with your dad, and he lifted you up so that you could see the donuts. And now, you're lifting your kid up so that they can see the donuts!"

PAUL: It's a really special thing that I get to be part of all of that. So, that's definitely one of my greatest satisfactions, getting to watch other people enjoy what I've done my whole life and have that be a big part of their life too.

PAUL: We're on Facebook, and everybody else is on Facebook too. And, they'll post messages, "Oh, Kruta's is such a special memory for us." And then, we get people who have moved away messaging us out-of-the-blue saying, "I wish we were in St. Louis so that we could get x, y, or z from Kruta's for our holidays, but we live here now!"

PAUL: So, we get stuff like that all of the time. *It's really great knowing that we've made that much of an impact on other people's lives!*

RICH: Yeah exactly, because you have affected <u>their</u> history!

PAUL: It also puts a burden on us to make sure that we <u>keep</u> doing a good job!

RICH: I'm sure they love you for sure! I think they'd be pretty forgiving if sometimes things didn't turn out so well!

PAUL: Yeah, we get that too. Sometimes they'll let us know. "Hey, I got a cake last week, and it didn't quite measure up." And then, we'll tell them, "Oh, bring it back, and we'll fix it for you. We'll get you a new one."

PAUL: You know, Randy and David McArthur are in here pretty regularly, and they're reps for their companies now. We get to talk to them a lot. We get to chat, and it's pretty cool!

RICH: Would you mention me to them because I know David pretty well, though I haven't seen him for several years. If you see them, tell them that the things they gave me, the boxes of bulletins, are absolutely safe in my living room! They're a pretty important record of baking in St. Louis, and they're already so organized.

PAUL: My response to the interview question on the sheet that says, "Were there any particular characters in your bakery's story that stand out?" That would be my Aunt Joyce, who was Frank Jr.'s wife. She was kind of the family historian. She was so alive, and was the one who had a story for everything. She was a story-teller and a font of knowledge for the family.

PAUL: Hmm-m-m, "What were the economics of the bakery business in this particular bakery." [Again, Paul is trying to answer some of the questions on the Interview Questions sheet.] A pretty good question for me. So, like any business you've got your ups and downs, your slow times and your strong times.

PAUL: So, Christmas was really big, but January is really slow because everybody is on their new diets! About the third week they start coming back in!

PAUL: And then, Valentine's Day is really big. But there is a story from the early days of the bakery. During the depression they managed to keep the doors open and keep people fed. So, it was good that they were able to keep going through such a crisis.

PAUL: So, the story goes that my great grandpa would put a silver dollar in the batch of dough for one of the breads. So, if you got the loaf of bread that had the silver dollar in it, that was kind of a way that they kept people buying bread. It was like a little lottery! We couldn't do that now because there's all kinds of health regulations and what not.

RICH: Yes, definitely!

PAUL: And then, during prohibition the rum-runners would come in and make deals with bakers to get their sugar and their ingredients so that they could keep producing! Depending on who you talk to in the family, my great grandpa either told them "No" or told them "Yes." And, there's a bit of uncertainty about which way he ended up.

PAUL: And then, Frank Jr.'s son was telling us the story about how his dad, my great uncle, would sleep on the sacks of sugar so that when the bakery was closed they couldn't come in and steal it. He was like a human burglar alarm because the house was connected to the bakery.

RICH: Would they offer to buy supplies or would they just take them?

PAUL: Well, it was kind of both. If you turned them down, they'd break in and steal them anyway. Like I said, depending on who you would talk to, that was the question of whether or not my great grandpa caved into them.

PAUL: If you want, I can give you a little time-line of the beginnings of Kruta's Bakery. So, Frank Sr., my great grandpa, came over from Germany.

PAUL: In 1906 he came to America through the Galveston, Texas port. Then, in 1910 he became a citizen. After that, he moved to Indiana, and I think he and his brother Jim started a little bakery. Then, when they moved to East St. Louis around 1919, that's when they started the Kruta's Bakery in East St. Louis.

RICH: And then, in 1974 they opened here in Collinsville, right?

PAUL: Yes, 1974 was when they opened in Collinsville. So, my great grandpa and his brother Jim started the Kruta's brothers' bakery in Buckner, Illinois sometime after 1912. Then they moved to East St. Louis a few years after that. They moved to 8th Street and Exchange.

HOW OUR HEARTS WERE STÖLLEN

PAUL: Goose Hill was the name of the location, not the bakery. The area was called Goose Hill. That's where a lot of the Eastern European immigrants lived. There were a lot of job opportunities there, like stockyard work and things like that in the early 20th century. Yeah, for a lot of the customers English was a second language. Another fun story that my dad told me was about his grandma — she was the decorator who wrote on all of the cakes.

PAUL: But, she couldn't speak English very well. So, she would have a note to show her what had to be written on the cake. She would write on the cake, and if she got to the end of the cake and didn't leave herself enough space because, you know if you get through "birth," and then you don't have enough room for "day," she'd just leave it off because she didn't know. But, half the customers didn't speak English either. So they didn't really know the difference! [We laugh together.]

RICH: Wow! There were limitations, weren't there!

PAUL: Yeah, people were really forgiving of all of that because again they all knew that it was just the way it was! Nowadays, if you misspell somebody's name, you gotta' give 'em a free cake! [Laughter.]

PAUL: Oh yeah, I thought of another question from the Interview Sheet, "How do you think the retail chain stores affected business? What was it like when the superstores had their own bakeries?" Yeah, that was a hit. Our bread sales aren't even half of what they were ten years ago.

PAUL: You can buy a big loaf of bread from one of the "big box stores" for just a buck. Ours are almost three dollars. And, if you buy the loaf of bread that's got all of the preservatives, it'll last you almost three weeks before it goes bad. Our bread will last a few days before it'll start drying out and become "toast" essentially! So, we took a big hit on bread. The fact that we still sell any bread is sometimes amazing to me!

PAUL: The other issue we have now is that we've got all of the coffee shops selling bakery goods, and we have all of the high-end bread companies. They'll sell a loaf for five bucks, and people will be saying to themselves, "I'm getting something great because it's expensive." Or, on the other end of it, "I can go to the superstore and get it for a buck!" That kind of puts us in an odd position, because we don't get to say, "Our artisanal bread," because they'll go to the artisanal shop! All they do is score it differently and bake it with flour on the top!

RICH: Yeah, so you're getting hit on both ends!

PAUL: Yeah, and they get to charge an extra two bucks for it!

RICH: Exactly! There are just so many sources of baked goods now.

PAUL: We still sell pretty many donuts. We're still cheaper than donut shops, but ours are just as good, and people know it. With the grocery store donuts, I think you really get what you pay for.

RICH: There's a difference, isn't there.

RICH: Several other bakers have also said that. You know, this is kind of an interesting side bit that I asked a relative of an important baker. I asked him that question: "What caused the decline of the independent bakery?" His answer was, "Superstores for sure." But, then he said, "You know, something that nobody thinks about that is just as important — is the beginning of *cake mixes*. Because people didn't have to leave their homes, and since the mixes were a lot cheaper they felt, "Oh, I'll just make my own cake at home. Then, I don't have to go out, and I don't have to spend twice as much."

PAUL: Yeah, that makes sense.

RICH: I know. And, it came in at about the same time, in the 1950's. So, Betty Crocker and others had a hand in it too.

PAUL: That's one thing, I'll say, that makes us special is that we don't use mixes. We still make our own batter for our cakes.

RICH: That's great!

PAUL: But, I'm certainly not gonna' fault other people for going to a pre-fab mix because there's a lot more consistency. You know exactly what you're going to get.

PAUL: One thing I think that's really affected our business, and this is a very recent development, is the trans-fat ban from the FDA. Trans-fats are a huge ingredient in a lot of shortenings. So, the production companies had to reformulate everything. They had to redo all of that. It really changed how pastry would rise. It would change the flavor. It changed all of that. Thankfully, now we've got it where we need it to be, and I think our icing is better than it ever was.

PAUL: But, for awhile there were a lot of people saying, "Hey, this icing is different!" And, we'd say, "Well, yeah it is." And, they'd say, "You had to change your recipe?!" And then, we had to say, "Well, we were forced to change our recipe."

PAUL: So, we've got some old-timers now who say, "You know, Kruta's just isn't the same as it was anymore." And, we had to say, "Well, it's not really our fault. We couldn't really help it. The government regulation said that we can't use this ingredient." They said, "This ingredient is kind of like red dye number five." And now, legally we can't use different trans-fats.

Author's Note: The following is one of my favorite quotes from all of the interviews.

PAUL: "This is kind of a big gripe for me because everybody says, 'Oh, it's unhealthy, it's unhealthy'." *"Well, it's sugary bread cake covered in sugary icing! We're not making any claims that it's a healthy cake! If you eat a whole cake, you're gonna' get a stomach ache, and if you eat too much, it's probably not going to be too friendly to your body."*

RICH: Yeah, this is not rocket science. You know, that's really interesting because that's the second thing that I heard like that this year. Another baker felt there were other effects from some other regulations.

PAUL: Also, there's kind of a limit on what we can do for decorations. If I just decorated, sure, I'd definitely practice up on some different things.

PAUL: I do try to push myself as much as I can with my designs, but I don't do any shaping or molding or sculpting or anything. It's all kind of drawing and air-brushing art.

PAUL: So, I wouldn't say that we've lost a great deal of business, but yeah there's definitely a little bit of a pull from people that can affect you. For example, there's a Facebook group, and every now and again somebody will say, "Oh, can anybody make me a cake like this?" And then, some other people will respond and say, "Oh yeah, Kruta's Bakery can!" And, I'll have to say, "Oh, I can't really do that. I don't really have the ability or the equipment to do anything like that."

RICH: Yeah, because they can probably do stuff like the photographic transfers to a cake?

PAUL: Oh, we can do that! But, sometimes they want something that's super elaborate. I always try to work with people, but sometimes I do have to say, "Oh, I can't really do that one." So, there's not necessarily so much lost business as lost opportunities, I guess. I think there are other bakers that can either charge less or they've got more time to do a fancier cake like that.

PAUL: If they're only doing four or five cakes a week they can devote all of their extra time to making the special stuff. But, I gotta' be able to do four or five cakes in an hour! [Paul laughs.]

PAUL: But, I would rather see somebody go somewhere and get what they wanted than come to me and be disappointed and then have that be a bad mark on my business and reputation.

RICH: Yeah. sure. Exactly! You mentioned sculpting, and I don't even know what that means!

PAUL: So, there's cake-shaping. That's where you cut the cake or you have a specific kind of cake mold that puts it out into different shapes. And then, there's sculpting where you've got, for example, modeling chocolate, where you get it into a consistency like dough. It's almost like Play-Doh or clay, and you can sculpt it into different shapes.

PAUL: And then, there's a lot of tricks for those big "Ace of Cakes" and "Cake Boss" shows. One of their big tricks is to make things out of a Rice Krispie Treat kind of stuff. And, they'll sculpt that into the big elaborate shapes.

PAUL: Then, they'll cover that with fondant so that it's still part of the cake, but it's not actual cake. So, then it's not gonna' fall apart when it gets to be delivered. That kind of thing is just not in my technical abilities. If it was, I'd probably be more willing to take on stuff like that, but that's a whole 'nother craft almost.

RICH: Yes, I'm sure! And, it would be time-intensive, don't you think?!

PAUL: Yeah, another thing that's really affected our business is cable T.V. There are those baking shows that are not very realistic, because they can edit things down to where a cake that takes literally a week and a team of people to make it can get made so that it fits into a forty-five minute episode!

PAUL: So, some people could come in and say, "Can you do anything like this?" And, if the answer is "Yes," then it's, "Yes, but it costs maybe eight hundred dollars!" That's not what I would do, but at another specialty cake shop, they would get this huge sticker shock! They'd probably say, "Eight hundred dollars for a cake?!" And, the shop would say, "Yeah, you're getting a team of laborers to work on a piece of art...that you can eat!" [Paul laughs!]

PAUL: So, you'll get disgruntled people that way. Yeah, "sticker shock" is the biggest thing that can come from those shows because they don't tell you how many thousands of dollars it costs to get the "Ace of Cakes" to make your cake!

RICH: Well, I interviewed a baker that you might like to get to know. Mike Temm from Wedding Wonderland bakery, is worth getting to know, because he's kind of in your age range. He's a very nice man. He's been there thirty-eight years, and he's totally committed to it. He started with an Easy-Bake oven when he was six years old, and he's still got it in his store in kind of a shrine!

PAUL: Oh, that's great!

RICH: He's really cool! He's up in Florissant. Anyway, he was telling me that he had a guy who he sponsored for a show on the Food Network, and he won the title of "America's Next Great Baker!" The baker came out of his shop, and he's got his name on a banner in his shop. His name was Al Watson. But, he told me that the reality T.V. thing, was really kind of frustrating, because he had to pay for the lodging for two people for six weeks while they were in production!

RICH: He had to pay for all of their expenses until they were in the finals. He said that it was a big cost. And he said, "That's just the way it is." If you want to be involved, and if you want the publicity and recognition, you have to pay.

PAUL: Yeah, we've gotten a few calls in the past couple years where someone will say, "Oh, you know we're gonna' be filming a cookie bake-off. Would you be interested in applying for it?" And, that's not a guarantee to be on it. And, I say to myself, "I don't have time to take six weeks off of work to do that, and I might not even be on the show." And I'll tell you, there are really talented people out there who would probably kick my butt, [Paul laughs loudly!], because like I said, I'm not even one of the bakers. I'm one of the finishers. But, I mean my dad's not gonna' do it, and my brother doesn't have time to do it. We've got a shop to run!

RICH: Yeah, there's not enough time in the day for that kind of thing. Well, I don't want to keep you any longer. This was a great experience, Paul!

PAUL: Oh, it was a pleasure for me too!

RICH: Good, I'm glad! You know this project is really very inspiring and encouraging for me, and I'm not just saying that. I think it's because people like you are so proud of their history! It's a chance for bakers to tell their story! So, that's my goal! It's great being with you really! Enjoy your day off!

PAUL: Oh, I've got one more story that my dad told me. It's not really bakery related, but it's family history related. My great grandmother who would leave words off of cakes, was an immigrant. She became a naturalized citizen, but she wasn't born here. So, she was so nervous when she was going to take her test, she forgot all of her English. She couldn't speak it. Well, the judge looked at her and said, "You know these answers don't you." And, she nodded her head. And then, he stamped her papers and she got approved for citizenship.

RICH: Thank God for the graces of our times, right! There's a lot we complain about and stuff that we kinda' shake our heads about, but we're very blessed, aren't we! Sounds like you're blessed with creative and meaningful work, and with your family!

PAUL: Yeah, we've got one son, and he's five. My son loves coming in to the store, and when he does he gets a chocolate donut with sprinkles! Lately he's taken to running out into the store and wanting to sell things to people! He says, "I wanna help out in the store, daddy!"

PAUL: And then, I have to say, "You're five, and I can't really let you out there! He'll say, "I want to sell one of these!" He'll grab the cupcake decorations and run out into the store and say, "Would you like one?!"

RICH: Oh, you want to keep that going, right! You don't want to discourage that! That will be good for business! You might want to get his picture on your literature! [Paul and I laugh together!]

PAUL: Yeah, we did put a few things up. I have a nephew Jim, who is sixteen years old now, but there's a picture of him when he was a baby that we actually have out in the store. He was crying because he couldn't get a juice box that they had in the trunk of their car. So, he was pouting and pouting, and my sister was snapping lots of pictures of him. And, in one of the pictures he's got this one perfect tear coming down his face. We put that picture out in the store with a quote bubble that says, "But, I wanted a Kruta cake!" It's great, and it's been out there for about eleven years now!

"But I wanted
a Kruta cake!"

RICH: Oh, my gosh, that's a great image. Perfect! Kids can sell anything, right! [And then, we laugh together!] Thank you very much for talking with me, Paul!

Laughing Bear Bakery
Interview With Kalen McAllister

…Our ex-offenders are so proud of what they do! I have to tell
you that one woman was so excited because she made her first
cherry pie. She went running around the building going,
"Look at this, I made this, I <u>made</u> this!"
— Kalen McAllister

RICH: You know, I wanted to tell you that your bio on your website is wonderful! You seem like a person who loves to do many things, and that's similar to me.

Author's Note: It may be important to know that Kalen McAllister is an ordained Buddhist priest.

RICH: O.K., before we get started, I wanted to tell you just a little bit about the "Bakery Book Project" because it's really <u>your</u> story that I want to hear and focus on. So, this is something that I started about ten years ago after I retired from teaching. I want you to know that you will be my twenty-first interview! This whole project has been nothing but a joy. I've been gifted.

RICH: There have been two main parts to the research I've been doing — the first source was my diving into the archives of the St. Louis Bakers Association and then after that doing the twenty-five in-person interviews. In all cases I've been privileged to hear some incredibly inspiring stories. Actually, this project has ended up being a ministry for me, because I was able to talk to people who loved telling their stories and because I loved listening to their stories. The other part of it, the archive part of reading the bulletins, was an amazing experience of discovering a "community" that the independent St. Louis bakers had, especially during their heyday, during the 1950's through the 2000's in St. Louis.

RICH: So, hopefully that's what this book is going to be about. And so now, I have to figure out how to make a lot of material fit into an entertaining book.

KALEN: [As we laugh together, Kalen says in an encouraging way —] "You can do it!"

RICH: Well, thank you. That's really helpful! [Again, we laugh together!] Yesterday a friend of mine said, "You know, tell me about one of the bakers." So, I told him about one of the bakers. Afterwards he said, "When you told me about that baker your whole face lit-up, and that's what your book should be about! Maybe you can publish the interviews on the internet or something like that, but you want to take the best ideas and talk about how they touched you!"

RICH: So, this interview is about your story. So, I'm going to stop talking, but I think I have an important starting question, "What in the world got you going in the direction of your project?"

KALEN: Well, I was a prison chaplain, and I was in a male prison, level four. Level five is the highest. The guys would come to me about a week before they would be released, and they would say, "You know, 'Chap' (for Chaplain), we don't even want to get out of prison because we won't be able to find a job. And, we'll be right back in prison, you know, because we'll have bills to pay and all of that."

KALEN: So, when I decided to retire I told them, "I'm going to do something about this. I'm gonna' create a business out there that would hire ex-offenders." So, I retired in 2015, and I started thinking, "Now, what am I going to do? I know there are a lot of jobs out there for guys coming out of prison, but they're really dirty jobs.

KALEN: These are jobs nobody wants to do." There's one guy who does floor refinishing, and he's exposed to those fumes all day, you know that kind of thing.

KALEN: So, I wanted to do something nice, that was enjoyable, that when you had your finished product it was great. You know, I love to bake. My background is actually in chemistry, and I was never taught as a proper baker. But, you know, there's so much chemistry in baking. And so, every fall I would get into this baking mode.

KALEN: So then I thought, "Why not start a bakery?" But, I didn't have any funding. So, I put out a letter to all of my friends, and I said, "I'm going to start a bakery for ex-offenders. Could you send a donation?" And, I raised 2,000 dollars. That was in the summer of 2015. Well, I found a bakery that might be familiar, Carondelet Bakery?

RICH: Oh-h-h, I taught all of their daughters at Notre Dame High School!

KALEN: [Kalen laughs heartily.] I'll be darn.

RICH: Yeah! Bob did retire, but he has since passed away.

KALEN: After they closed Carondelet Bakery was doing an incubator bakery. So, we started out in November of 2015, and I hired two people. Within two weeks we were absolutely broke. We had no money. We did make payroll, and we got supplies, but we had to buy mixers. Luckily this guy heard about me, and he was a CEO of a company. So, he called me up and said, "Look, I want to buy a pie for each of my employees for Thanksgiving!" And then, he says, "I want to pay you up-front." So, with that we managed to get through. He saved it. I mean, it would have gone down the drain, and he saved it!

KALEN: The Sisters of St. Joseph are in that neighborhood of Carondelet near the Carondelet Bakery location. And, in January we managed to get a grant from them. We actually made a pie, a French Silk pie, and we called it St. Joseph's French Silk Pie!

RICH: Wow, great! [And, we laugh together!]

KALEN: And, that got us through to summer. With the coming of summer we started doing markets and things like that. So, we were at Carondelet Bakery from November to August of that year. And then, we actually needed a bigger space and more freezer space. So, we found this church downtown. Again, it was an incubator, a health-approved incubator. So, we moved in here.

KALEN: You know outreach is so important, getting your products out. It's kind of like putting your book together. It's kind of like the big challenge. We had one of our board members who managed to get us into Straub's grocery store. And, we got into the Smokehouse.

KALEN: And then, we got into Dierberg's, but we actually pulled-out when the virus hit because if people can't sample your product, no one is going to know what it is and buy it, you know. So, that door is still open if things settle down.

KALEN: But, we've been struggling. We did get a couple of bigger grants from a company up in Boston, and that supported us in going to more days a week, higher salaries, and the purchase of a delivery van. However, the bakers are amazing. You know, we interview people, but we don't require any baking experience. We'll teach that! But, one person that we hired used to bake all of the time, and his parents were Lebanese. So he can make Lebanese baklava. I mean this guy was incredible. Now, we have a woman who has kind of taken his place, and she's incredible too!

RICH: Fantastic, right!

KALEN: So, we've gotten really good help coming out of the prisons. I think the important thing to realize here is that these jobs are more important to them than they might be to an average person, because it's really hard to get a job right now anyway. It's always hard to get a job, but if you have a prison record attached to it, that makes it even more difficult.

KALEN: You know, we pay pretty well, we pay higher than minimum. We're still part-time, we're not full-time yet, but it's a pleasant working environment. *And, they're so proud of what they do! I have to tell you that one woman was so excited because she made her first cherry pie. She went running around the building going, "Look at this, I made this, I made this!"*

RICH: That's wonderful!

KALEN: The recipes are from older and more experienced people. We want the best! We're not settling for anything that's just average, you know, and not something that you could put together fast. And we do things from scratch! For example, we make key lime pies where we zest the limes, and then we squeeze the limes. Our eggs we bring in from the country, and they're free-range eggs.

KALEN: The one thing about interviewing me on the phone, rather than being here, is you're not able to taste all of this stuff.

RICH: Oh, yeah! I miss that too! [Here is where I "groan."]

KALEN: [Then, we laugh together!] Yeah, you'll have to come down someday! But like today, this one woman is a cheesecake maker!

RICH: Oh, my gosh!

KALEN: So, today she's making dreamsicle cheesecakes. Do you remember dreamsicle, the ice cream?

RICH: Sure.

KALEN: Well, today she's making a cheesecake. It's called an Orange Creamsicle Cheesecake, and it tastes just like the Dreamsicles, but with a graham cracker crust. It is so good! But, the people come in from different places, like this one woman was from Mississippi originally, and she can make the best sweet potato pie you've ever eaten!

KALEN: I wasn't even a sweet potato pie person, but I am now! So, people come in, and they work together, and they help each other out! I think that's the most amazing thing about the bakery. For instance, sometimes people come in for the interview, and they don't even have bus fare to get back to their house. And, our people will go, "Hey, I have an extra bus pass. Here, let me give it to you."

RICH: Oh, my gosh! Yeah.

KALEN: And then, people on the outside donate clothing and household items.

RICH: Yes! You've got quite a variety of talent coming in, don't you!

KALEN: Oh, so much, so much. and you know one person, and this is kind of a funny story, but I asked this woman if she had ever used scales before to weigh things, and she kind of gave me a look. And, I asked her, "Well, do you know how to "tare" a scale?" And, she said, "Shut up and give me the stuff. I'll weigh it!" She obviously had a background in "weighing things," you know. [And, Kalen laughs heartily at this!]

RICH: Yeah, yeah, I get it. I was picturing that, a pretty clear picture, right?!

KALEN: Yeah, it's a very creative project. I mean, the thing I noticed as a chaplain was that people in prison actually have nothing, and they're so creative with nothing. It makes me feel stupid because they see possibilities here and there that I don't see.

RICH: Yep, well, they have to create hope out of something, right?

KALEN: Right. And, you know, they just have to get along and they have to survive. In prison you have nothing. You're given about seven dollars and fifty cents a week. And, you have to buy your shampoo and your deodorant, which is why a lot of guys shave their heads because they can't afford the shampoo, toothpaste and all of that, you know.

RICH: Yes, that's an insight all its own!

KALEN: Yeah. That's a whole 'nother story. The bakery has been very successful. I think we've had twenty-seven people go through here now, and of that number only two have gone back to prison.

RICH: Yeah, I was gonna' ask you about that. "Recidivism," as in how often are there "repeat offenders?" And yes, that's a very good percentage. You're doing well!

KALEN: And, we have an amazing board of directors. Actually, we have George Lombardi on our board. George was the Director of the Department of Corrections of the whole thing, and he retired.

KALEN: I also have my past boss who was a deputy warden, and he's on that board too. And then, we have other people, like we have a banker and a lawyer and an Indian chief. [Kalen is joking here.] But, we have these people who have direct experience in working with people in prison.

RICH: Yes, I read about George Lombardi. I don't remember everything, but he seems like a very faithful friend, right?

KALEN: Oh, he is incredible. He is so supportive, yes! And you know, we have this one rule. We've been on a lot of T.V. shows, and interviews, and things like that. The one thing I don't ever encourage, and I tell the people when I hire them, "No one will ever ask you what you've done, from here." And, if the news people come in, I tell them that they're not allowed to ask any of the workers what they've done. And, I tell the workers, "If they persist and ask, you don't have to answer that question. That's your personal information, and no one cares from this day forward. We're working from now and into the future. And, the past is gone."

RICH: That's beautiful, and so redemptive! Very neat! I saw that you had a place called Plantasia, and I don't know if you owned it or not. You had a landscape company?

KALEN: [Kalen laughs here.] Yeah, that's true. I've done everything! I owned a landscape company in 1980. And then, I worked for Trailnet ("Gateway Trailnet" — a Rails-to-Trails organization for bike riding). I was a project manager for the Chain of Rocks Bridge renovation, and then, a prison chaplain. And now, I'm a bakery mom!

RICH: I have to tell you, I've ridden the Chain of Rocks Bridge bike trail, when it was open! We went across the bridge. "Nice job!" [I said, as I congratulated Kalen on her work on the Chain of Rocks Bridge!]

KALEN: I'm glad it got used for what it was meant to be used for! I was one of the ones who started the Eagle Days, the viewing of migrating eagles in winter time, particularly from the bridge.

RICH: Oh, my gosh! Yeah, that's right. That's really an interesting spot with the spillway and the curve in the bridge there!

KALEN: Oh yeah, it is. I also did a promotion. We did the first wedding on the bridge. They did a Route 66 theme, lining the bridge with the old cars, and then we had a stretch '57 limo to bring the bride over, and they got married right there at the curve in the bridge.

RICH: Oh, my gosh. How symbolic, right! [We laugh heartily together!]

KALEN: Yeah, right! It sorta' said, "Hey, your life is gonna' change!"

RICH: That's right! It's gonna' be going in a new direction! So, Kaylen, we have a lot in common. By the way, what is your e-mail address?

KALEN: Sure. It's <u>kalen1@charter.net</u>. Another thing I want to touch on here is the future of the bakery. We are looking at this point to get into our own building, and we're looking to rent something probably with a hood in it. You have to have a hood as a safety feature, and they're so expensive. You could easily spend fifty thousand dollars on a hood, [I gasp.] and another fifty thousand to install it!

KALEN: With the holiday season coming up we do a lot of pies. It would be nice to maybe do two shifts or something like that. So, if you hear of anybody with a reasonably priced bakery or restaurant with a hood in it, we would be interested!

KALEN: And, we kinda' need something on a bus line because the workers are just out of prison, you know. So, they're riding busses.

RICH: Sure, I understand. I don't suspect Carondelet Bakery would be a possibility, would it?

KALEN: They had it for sale, and they were asking half a million for it, but it was so out-of-date. So, it would probably cost two or three million to bring it up-to-date. I mean, they were still using wooden tables, and that's against health department regulations. It's probably grandfathered in, but it's against health department rules right now because you have to have stainless steel.

KALEN: Have you interviewed Hank from Hank's Cheesecakes?

RICH: No, I haven't.

KALEN: I delivered for him at one time, way back in history, but he has really good cheesecakes. And, he's down there on Big Bend off of Clayton Road, between Dale and Clayton.

RICH: That's a great idea. You've just answered one of my Interview Questions that says, "Are there any other bakers you know who I could interview?"

KALEN: Yeah, I would definitely say Hank. He's a sweet guy.

RICH: I think his last name is Krussel, isn't it? Well, it is a small town to say the least. I went to St. Louis U. High with him. I sat next to his brother and played trumpet in the band with him. And then, his mother was a parishioner in Mary Mother of the Church parish down here in South County. She was a sweet lady. So yes, it's a small town.

KALEN: I would love for you guys to come down here. Bring your son with you and come down and try these new cheesecakes, these creamsicle cheesecakes!

RICH: I don't know if I said this, but that is one of my wife's favorite flavors! I think Steak n' Shake used to have a milkshake that was a Dreamsicle milkshake.

KALEN: I think you're right, yeah!

RICH: Now, this will be an interesting thing. It really occurred to me that I loved the description of Victoria in the background information on your website. She was the Native American woman, and I wondered if you ever thought that you might be like Victoria, and that's why you named the bakery that way!

KALEN: No, Victoria just did so much to help us get going. She did all of the paper work that I just hate doing. She got us incorporated. She got us so many things, and then when she passed away, I just wanted to honor her. And, I just couldn't name it Victoria's Bakery.

RICH: Here is a follow-up question, "Was she a real person?"

KALEN: Oh yeah, definitely. In fact, she gave me a Native American name. She called me "Mochaween." And so, I asked her, "What does that mean?" And, she said, "Dirt Woman," because you work in the dirt all the time, with your landscaping business.

[And, we laugh together!]

RICH: Quite a name! Yeah, thanks a lot, right! But, her meaning was very rich and wonderful.

KALEN: Yeah, she was quite a person!

RICH: The picture that is on your website, is that her?

KALEN: Yes, that's her. She was a Shawnee woman.

RICH: She was a pretty lady really. My goodness.

KALEN: She was beautiful.

RICH: Your description of her was beautiful. I love the qualities that you saw in her. I also wanted to ask you, "If you were to come into your bakery as a customer, what would be your first choice?"

KALEN: For the food? Hmm-mm-m, what was the latest thing? I mean, a week ago we were making Mango Key-Lime pies, and those were terrific. And then, Emily came and she says, "I do cheesecakes." So, I fell in love with these Dreamsicle cheesecakes.

KALEN: But, one of our best-selling products is "Bear Candy," which is sold at Schnuck's. It's a puffed corn, not popcorn, and it has no kernel on it. It's coated with caramel, and it's baked three times. It just melts in your mouth. People call it crack, [We laugh together]. Of course, I'm not talking about the people here.

RICH: Oh, no. I hear you.

KALEN: The people who taste it, they go, "Oh my gosh, I can't stop eating this." Just so you know, it's at the Webster Dierberg's. Actually, it's at all of the Dierberg's! But, I also like our chocolate chip cookies.

KALEN: This is a very fun story. We have a man named Orville working for us. Well, we were making chocolate chip cookies. But, Orville kept making them really big, and we said, "Orville, make 'em smaller. Use this scoop, and not that scoop." So, he would use a smaller scoop, but he would really fill it up. And so, after working with him for a month trying to get him to make the cookies smaller, we gave up, and we said, "O.K., make 'em big, and we're gonna' call them the 'Big-O's' after Orville. So, now we have these "Big-O" chocolate chip cookies. You know, we use Ghirardelli chocolate, and we have sea salt on top. They are delicious!

KALEN: And then, we have one of the women we call our cookie-maker. We invented a cookie called the "Hearty Lombardi" after George Lombardi. It's a cake cookie. It's filled with pecans, with pecans on top with a dried cherry in the middle. It's our own recipe, and it's very good.

KALEN: And, we have root beer cookies. We also have peanut butter cookies with chocolate chips in them. We have oatmeal, white chocolate, and cranberry cookies. We go through a lot of sampling, and if it doesn't make the grade, it's outa' here!

KALEN: We were making some mango upside-down cakes. they were good, but they weren't great. *For things to stay around here, they gotta' be great!*

RICH: What a great motto.

KALEN: We had a chocolate, bourbon, pecan pie! Because of the bourbon we kinda' switched that out. So, now we're making cranberry pecan pies.

RICH: Well, they both sound good! What was the cookie called that Orville created?

KALEN: The "Big-O!" [We laugh naughtily!]

RICH: What a great name! [I laugh again!]

KALEN: We like to get the baker attached to it once they've created something!

RICH: You know, one of the questions on the "Interview Questions" asks, "Were there any memorable employees?"

KALEN: As far as memorable employees, I think all of them are for one reason or another! You know, apple pie season is coming up for fall, and this same guy would come in at 2:00 in the morning and make all of the crusts and get the apples ready, so that when we got in later we would be able to put the pies together and get them cooked for that day.

KALEN: But yeah, I think all of them were memorable. Orville was also memorable in one other way. One of the health department rules is, "No cell phones in the kitchen." And this makes sense because you've got your mouth up against the phone all day. It's dirty, so very germy! All of the employees know that you can't have a cell phone in the kitchen. Well, Orville would take off any chance he would get and go hide some place with his cell phone. He was a great cook, you know, but I would open a cabinet door, like in the hallway, and there would be Orville! So, I have memories like that too.

RICH: He found a way, right!

KALEN: Well, on his next job, there were two or three guys from here that went to a place that employs guys and pays pretty good. It's like factory work, and they came back and visited. They said that when Orville got there the first thing he did was pull out his phone, and he was on his phone the entire time! So, I guess if you've been in prison for so many years without a phone, there's that.

RICH: I'm sure they're sometimes starved for social interaction too.

KALEN: Oh, and there was one guy, on his first day he came in, I told him to go in the back and get something. Well, it was thirty minutes later, and he never came back. So, I went back to find him, and he was standing there staring. And I said, "You know, you're so high." I said, "You know the rules here. No drugs." And then, I said, "Just leave, O.K." And, he said, "Oh, I'm not high." And, I said, "Yeah, get outa' here." So, he left. So, there are a couple stories like that, but most of them are just positive, really positive.

KALEN: A lot of these people have never had anything positive in their lives. They come from families who are not supportive. And then, they have a group here who are supporting them and encouraging them, and that's made a world of difference.

RICH: Yes, I'm sure! You know, another name comes to mind. I really am a strong believer in networking, and I'm sure you are, of course. Do you know Steve Campbell from Doorways? He started out in St. Francis de Sales Church.

KALEN: His name sounds familiar. Oh yeah, he and I became the best of friends. He invited me to join him, and I went to a Mass, a special Mass, and it was wonderful.

RICH: Oh, good. I want you to know about Steve Campbell, because he's a kindred spirit to you and a like-minded man. He's been involved with the poor, and Doorways was started as an AIDS project. And, I think the name, it either used to be or it still is called, the Peter and Paul Community Services.

KALEN: Oh-h-h, [Kalen sort of gasps with surprise!], we deliver pies to them! Someone donates pies to them every winter!

RICH: Isn't that neat! I didn't know that!

KALEN: Yeah, we take hundreds of pies to them or they come in and get them. We give 'em, to that Peter and Paul group! They're wonderful. The women who come to pick up their pies are just so warm and friendly. They're really neat people!

RICH: Yeah, Steve is just a dedicated missionary or minister, whatever you want to call him, and he's been doing that for forty or fifty years.

KALEN: Wow, that's incredible!

RICH: So, I want you to know about people that you'd enjoy and find a network with.

KALEN: Yeah, that's a good group. Doorways was a good group. Way-back-when during the AIDS epidemic I would deliver food to guys with AIDS, and I think that was connected to Doorways.

RICH: Yeah, my wife was involved for quite a few years with Food Outreach. So, I don't know if you were familiar with that.

RICH: Well, I guess the questions just keep coming. I'm curious if you do anything more with your Buddhist ministry?

KALEN: Yeah, we actually have a room in the same church as the bakery where we have a Zen center. And, recently with the virus epidemic we've been meeting on-line, you know, with the Zoom thing. We're kind of half moved out of here and looking for a new place for the Zen center. But, we're not panicked yet because we can't meet anyway.

KALEN: But, I'm what's called a "Dharma Transmitted" priest. In fact, I'm leaving tomorrow to go up to the monastery. Yes, we have a very active monastery up at the border of Minnesota and Iowa. And, I have students here in St. Louis too.

RICH: To be "dharma transmitted," is that a special training or certification that you have?

KALEN: Well, in Buddhism, it's kinda' like when the Buddha stood up one day before he died, and he held up a flower, one of his disciples smiled because he understood that the buddha was saying, "Everything is encapsulated in this one flower." And so, this person who smiled, he became the next person in line when the Buddha passed away. So, that's called "dharma transmission."

KALEN: So, through that person after him, and then the person after him, and down to my teacher, and then he transmitted to me. So, I have a paper that traces my name to my teacher, all the way back to the Buddha.

RICH: Oh my goodness, that's wonderful, isn't it?!

KALEN: Yeah, it's like you're not supposed to be able or allowed to teach until you're "dharma transmitted." So, I went to Japan to the founding temples, Heji and Sogigi, and I had to stand up and do the service in Japanese.

KALEN: Yeah, the founding temple, the Andoggan's Temple doesn't have electricity or anything. In the winter the monks are sitting there, and you can see their breath. So, the service started at like 3:30 in the morning, and the temple was built on the side of this hill. It was built in the 16th century. And, they had these Japanese lanterns with candles in them, Yeah, it was very beautiful.

KALEN: A lot of people, you know, think that we fly off of our cushions and levitate and stuff like that. And, I said, "If anybody ever does that, I'm outa' here!"

RICH: Yeah, that's another group. They're called "magicians!" [And, we laugh together!]

KALEN: The thing that really attracted me to Buddhism was that it's an everyday practice. And, Christianity is too. But, what really hits you in the face with Buddhism is that everything you do is part of "practice," you know. Everything can be a form of prayer, right!

RICH: Yes, exactly! I feel very fortunate and thankful for the prayer and spirituality group that my wife and I are in. It's eleven people, and we meet once a month. We take a year to read one book. We take about two chapters at a time and then share among ourselves. It really feeds our souls, as I'm sure you know.

KALEN: Yeah, that is great.

RICH: Yeah, so we have a lot of things in common! I've really enjoyed talking with you.

KALEN: Well, once the virus goes away or gets solved, or we get the vaccine or whatever, if you ever want someone to come down and do a meditation with your group or talk about meditation, I'd love to.

RICH: What a great and gracious invitation! I'm really hoping that we can again start doing some of these creative things that aren't so restricted because of the virus. That's a great offer, and I'm writing that down. You know, I've got it on tape, and I'll hold you to it! [Then, we laugh together!]

KALEN: Well, I feel very fortunate in having met you on the phone. I hope someday you'll come down and try some of our products.

RICH: I promise you I will, and I'll bring my son with me. Thank you so much, Kalen.

KALEN: Thank you.

RICH: Bye-bye.

Lubeley Bakery
Interview With Helen Lubeley Murray

*When we would go to the Baker's Association meetings everybody would
bring something and then share their recipes...that was part of the fun!
It kept the camaraderie going...
People are in the bakery business because they love it. They love the smell, they love
the feel, they love the recipes. They love seeing that everything is produced well.
They love that the customers like it!*
— Helen Lubeley Murray

HELEN: You know, all of those bakers were really messy! They'd throw flour all around and all over the floor. [Laughter.] Well, you want to hear a funny story? At one time our bakery was located near a dentist's office. The baker at that time would say, "You know, you guys are really good for my business, because when they're finished with you they always come to us next door to get a treat." You wouldn't think that a dentist office would be so good for us. I guess we sort of worked together!

HELEN: There was a baker lady named Mrs. Shatgens, and she sort of mentored my mother, Helen Lubeley, Sr. Mr. and Mrs. Shatgens were very good bakers, but I think their bakery had to close because of the building of highway 44. You know, there were two bakeries in Kirkwood that were right across the street from one another.

HELEN: There was Martin's Bakery where my father, Edward A. Lubeley, worked. And then, there was Obermeyer's Bakery where my mother, Helen Lucille, worked. Helen Lucille was a Maret.

HELEN: So, after Martin's Bakery closed my father then moved across the street and started working at Obermeyer's Bakery, and that's how my mother and father met. Then, the depression hit, and that's when my father and mother decided to open their own bakery near Christy and Kingshighway. After that they moved to Maplewood in the mid-1940's.

HELEN: They were married twelve years before they had their children. They were just trying to get established at first. At that time Maplewood was quite the hub.

HELEN: Adrian Koch, who developed Yorkshire shopping center and built a lot of small brick houses just west of the shopping center approached my dad and asked him if he would be willing to move to the Yorkshire location. Of course, we knew that the exposure would be better for us. That was the time when people were moving that way.

HELEN: Also, Crestwood Plaza was being built at that time. So, my father did move to Yorkshire, and that was when there were only the first three buildings on the west side. There was also an arcade underneath with businesses. In the first three buildings there was our bakery, Tommy's hardware store, and I think a Tom-Boy grocery store.

HELEN: Then, my brother Bob came along. Adrian Koch then decided to develop that whole half-circle at Yorkshire, and my dad told him where he wanted to be. At that time there was an IGA and a Kresge's dime store that moved in there. The time for those two locations of Lubeleys combined to be about thirty-four years.

HELEN: The shopping center wasn't being very well taken care of, and access to get supplies into the store was very difficult for the bakery at the first corner location of Yorkshire. There was something like an underground alley to Yorkshire where trucks would have to drive in order to deliver. Eventually, a big plot of land for the most recent Watson Road location was sold by the Archdiocesan seminary to Dierberg's, and that's where the bakery finally moved. So, the address of the first Yorkshire location was 8021 Watson Road and for the second, and last location, it was 7815 Watson Road. You know, I worked at these bakeries for fifty-two years, and Bob worked at them for forty-eight years. My sister was there for fewer years because she came in later.

HELEN: So, that was quite a blow to Mr. Koch that my father wanted to move on up the road. I personally didn't want to move up there because I thought that was a no-man's land. Nothing was up there except Happy Joe's Pizza. So, when the seminary sold all of that land to Dierbergs we thought, "O.K., all of that means that progress is coming."

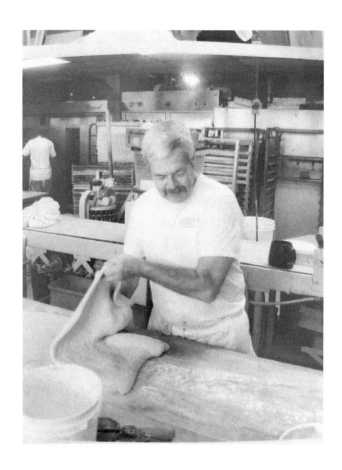

HELEN: So, we bought the building, fixed it up, and moved sometime in the eighties. One of the other reasons we moved was because we were squashed between those two buildings, and we didn't even have a place for our supplies. It wasn't big enough. And, there was that added inconvenience in not being able to get our supplies very easily when they were delivered.

HELEN: You know, we were the first bakery in St. Louis to put in a deli.

RICH: The first?

HELEN: Yeah, we were the first. At the time there was a buzz going around that this was the thing to do. There was, of course, Panera's, and at that time it was still being called St. Louis Bread Company. That's when Bob's wife came in. So, by trial and error we had to find out what were the good providers for a deli. This wasn't the bakery business. This was something new. After about three years we had it figured out. We knew what we wanted to do. But, we had researched it, and everybody seemed to like what we were doing. Everything there was homemade, and of course we had our own breads! In our later years I sorta' wished we had expanded into some different things. You know, you can kinda' get in a rut.

HELEN: And then, there was a whole new series of things that came in. You would have your meat inspectors because you're buying meat from the farmer and you had to have it inspected. And then, you had your OSHA people because you've got a bread slicer and a meat slicer. There were only certain people who could use them and certain ages of people who could use them.

HELEN: And then, you had the Health Department. They were pretty much O.K. about the bakery, but they were very picky about the deli. The soups had to be a certain temperature. They had to be made a certain way. And then, we had to be careful about heating things up.

HELEN: We didn't serve anything <u>hot</u> unless someone wanted something heated up in the microwave. And then, they were concerned about exhaust fans. You know, they go by a textbook. They don't go by common sense. [Laughter.] Anyway, that was something new that we all had to go through as well.

HELEN: You know, I told my brother I can't believe how small the bakeries are now. Our bakery was probably three times as big as most of them, and we always made sure that the bakery was full of product. You know, at the time that we closed and retired several other bakeries asked if we wanted to work at their places. And, we said, "No, do you know this is our very first Christmas that we can be together?"

HELEN: Here's my sister's photo book that she put together for us of the last day of the bakery. And, here's a picture of my mom.

RICH: She was beautiful. She was very pretty.

HELEN: Yeah, she had such pretty long hair before they were married, and then after they were married she cut it. I guess she figured she couldn't have long hair in the bakery business.

HELEN: *When we would go to the Baker's Association meetings everybody would bring something and then share their recipes. And so, they could either put it in their bakery or not. And, that was part of the fun! It kept the camaraderie going. You know, you could call somebody and say, "You know, I'm out of this, and our supplier is closed. Do you have any extra?" And they would say, "Sure, I'll send it over now."*

RICH: You know, all of the bakers I've talked to say that exact same thing. The same things are also said throughout the Bakers Bulletins! *The St. Louis bakers had such a close-knit community.*

HELEN: Yes, it was! You know, all of the prices of the supplies were rising so badly, especially about the time we were trying to retire. Bob had a heart problem. I had a heart problem.

HELEN: My dad, especially in his later years, had started getting these terrific ulcers in his legs, and that was because his veins were no longer able to pump the blood up into his legs. And, my brother had the same problem.

RICH: Do you think that was because he was on his feet all of the time?

HELEN: My brother also had carpal tunnel. The doctor told him that if he didn't get off his legs he was going to lose them. So, his wife told him that he'd better consider what he was going to do. Then, after my mom died we had to decide how long we wanted to stay in the business. So, we waited three years. And, during that three years we looked around to see if we could find somebody who wanted to buy it or go into it.

HELEN: So, a lot of the bakers that we talked to would ask, "Why would anyone want to go into the bakery business?" You could make so much more money doing so many other things, like computers or selling cars or whatever. In the bakery business you weren't going to get rich quick. So, it didn't happen. A few people wanted to buy our bakery, but they didn't understand that they weren't going to make it just selling cookies and cupcakes.

RICH: So, you're saying that they would have to have a "full-line" bakery.

HELEN: Yes, they wouldn't be able to pay the mortgage or anything.

RICH: So, you're also saying it was mostly health problems that pushed the decision to close?

HELEN: Yes, mentally and physically. It was just the time to call it a day. And, I have a lot of arthritis in my feet, my knees, and my hands. When we were in our thirties we could just stay up till midnight, and bake and talk shop, and get things ready for the next day. And now, maybe we can wobble out of there! [Laughter.] All of the bakers will tell you the same thing, that it takes a lot out of you.

RICH: I'm sure it's a great relief for you to be retired.

HELEN: And, you don't really know the future. It was hard leaving, and it's still hard. People are in that business because they love it. They love the smell, they love the feel, they love the recipes. They love seeing that everything is produced well. They love that the customers like it.

HELEN: And then, the last ten years we were doing mail orders and internet orders too. It got a little bit overwhelming. It got to be, "Whoa, we can't have retail and on-line and people asking us to mail locally." It wouldn't have been enough to hire a person full-time to do it, but it would have been too much for one person to manage the people, the deli, the kids, and all of that.

HELEN: You know, the bakeries were one of the places where you could have a job for the teen-agers. But, they could be a pain in the neck because it's their first job, and it's not their real job. Yet, they also had a chance to learn responsibility! They learned to show-up, to show-up on time, to be honest, to be understanding to the customers, and it was a good place for them to start! And, when they graduated from college some of them would even ask us for references.

RICH: Yes, these were very important and conscientious values. These were some of the same things that Roy Schmiemeir said about hiring, that their workers learned responsibility. He said that the bakery gave him a chance to hire not just young people but even some adults with special needs, people who couldn't handle a more demanding job. Now, you mentioned the Inglishes, the Inglish family of the Knodel Bakery. Tell me about them.

HELEN: Well, we were always South, and they were up North. You want to get ahold of Marlene Knodel Inglish and her husband, Ned. They are in their 90's, but their minds are very good. I will call you with Cynthia Knodel's cell phone number. And, you could tell her what you're doing and ask her if you could come up and talk with them. Yeah, they started in 1905. I'll get you Cynthia Knodel's phone number and Mark Hausel's phone number.

RICH: Now, what did you say about the Hausel Bakery?

HELEN: Well, Mark Hausel came to work for us years ago. His bakery closed, and then he may have moved into Blatt's Bakery. Mark Hausel's dad had the bakery, and his dad had it before him. Mark was an excellent baker, and I'll get you his number too. I'm trying to think, Blatt's Bakery was at Bates and Gravois, and I'm thinking Hausel's Bakery had to be in that area too. I think he moved to Hampton, and then Blatt's Bakery may have taken over the one on Gravois.

HELEN: Did you know anybody from Rozanek's Bakery? I think they were down on Grand and Bates.

RICH: No, I haven't. There are some bakeries that I haven't been able to connect with. Heimberger's is one of them.

HELEN: Yeah, that's interesting. His dad was a grocer, and he owned all of that land around South Lindbergh and Tesson Ferry Road. Fred was a typical old baker, fat and round.

RICH: Yeah, Roy Schmiemeir worked for him and said that he was the easiest and nicest person that he ever worked for. Oh yeah, somebody else said that Fred claimed to have created the gooey butter cake. And then, this person also said, "Yeah, Fred said a lot of things!" [Laughter.]

HELEN: Yeah, they talked about that when my dad was still around, and my brother Bob seemed to think that Fred Heimberger <u>did</u> create the gooey butter cake. We tweaked it a little bit, but people would say that our gooey butter and Fred's were pretty close. It seems to me that gooey butter has been around since the late forties. So, I don't know.

RICH: You've given me so much already, I don't want to interrupt you. I love listening to you.

HELEN: Did you ever hear of Matachek's Bakery?

RICH: Yes, a long time ago. Where was that?

HELEN: That was where Hampton Road and Watson split. I think there's a pancake place there now.

HELEN: But, I remember they had this expensive neon sign that said "Matachek's Bakery, Home of the Whipped Cream Cakes." And, I always

wanted to go in there when I was a kid. And, I thought "That's a rich bakery. Look at that big sign that they can afford!"

HELEN: So, my dad was very good friends with some of the ethnic bakers. I can remember John Pulaski. He was in the city. John was Polish, and he had a heavy accent. And, if you know anything about the "old world," there was a pastry that was so thin that you could see through it?

HELEN: It was a European Strudel, and he would start with a dough, and he would work it and work it until it was as big as a twelve foot by six foot table. One man did this. And then, he would cut it, and he would have his apples and spices. Then, he would roll it, and the dough would have those thin little layers.

RICH: This wasn't a puff pastry, and it wasn't a phyllo dough or anything like that. So, my dad thought John Pulaski was amazing with his craft. And then, there was Otto Lang. He had a bakery in the city too. But then, he ended up buying some land in Washington, Missouri and became a farmer.

RICH: Good for him, right! Yeah, Roy Schmiemeir retired pretty early. And then, he went to work for Mid-Continent Paper Company. Now, his three sons are all there. He offered to have me talk to his son Kevin, but this research is so big that I don't know where to stop, and I have to stop somewhere. I'm trying to focus on the independents. That's my real love.

RICH: You know, I taught Cheryl Federhofer.

HELEN: Oh, you did! Well, there was Ed and Bill Federhofer. Bill bought what was called Martin's Bakery, a different Martin. Then, Bill and Meryl wanted to retire, and they offered the bakery to David, but that deal didn't work out. So, they waited awhile, and then they offered it to Cheryl.

HELEN: You know, I have a sister, a sister who wasn't in the business right away. My sister, Susie Lubeley Suardi, was in charge of decorating. She and my oldest brother both had a real talent in the arts. She became one of St. Louis's best decorators. She came in a little later, but the timing was right because she freed up Bob to concentrate in the back.

RICH: What do you think were your signature items? I know personally that your bakery was so good at everything!

HELEN: Well, you know there was so much there. If you focused on our cakes I would have to say our Dobos Torte. If you focused on our cookies I would say our butter cookies, and I would say our decorated ones with the butter cream icing. Those were very popular.

HELEN: And then, we had some of the best donuts around, I think. They didn't have a lot of grease in them, and they had a very good taste.

[Author's Note: It was very easy to notice Helen's legitimate pride in Lubeley's Bakery!]

RICH: And, you had such a nice variety of donuts.

HELEN: And then, the stöllens. Bob had at least ten trays of four stöllens each. Even when we were leaving, in the last days he had that place completely filled with product every day.

RICH: I loved your small hand pastries.

HELEN: You mean our danishes. Yeah, everybody had a favorite.

RICH: I loved your twists!

HELEN: Yeah, you mean our almond twists and raspberry twists.

HELEN: And then, everybody wanted those artisan breads until people started hearing that you shouldn't eat so much bread, and they were hard to chew. Then later, people went back to the bakery breads because they tasted good and were wholesome, and they weren't hard to chew, and they were good for sandwiches! So, like my dad said, "everything comes and turns around." It really does.

HELEN: Oh, and about the Dobos Torte. Torte means "many layers." And, the Dobos was a particular kind of semi-sweet chocolate that was in-between all those layers.

HELEN: Well, you know they had these St. Louis Baker's Association meetings, and we'd all get together. They always had the social part first, and we'd all trade stories. The men didn't gossip, but they really talked about what was going on in the industry. And then, they'd get down to the business part of the meeting. Sometimes they'd talk about a new product and say, "You know, I tried this new thing, and I had to add this to it." Or, they'd say, "Don't waste your time on this one."

HELEN: I don't think my dad knew Roy Schmiemeir. My brother Bob did. My dad knew some of the old guys. You know who I should get ahold of is Bill Bender. His dad was Walter Bender. Walter was the owner of Lake Forest Bakery, and he said he was a fourth generation baker. So, Walter is gone, but his son, Bill, would have a lot of information. I've got to find Bill Bender's phone number. He would go way back!

HELEN: It's interesting. Marlene Knodel married Ned Inglish. He left an architecture job to become a baker, and she left a very lucrative pharmaceutical sales job in order to take over the Knodel Bakery. She would be my generation. She's even younger than me.

RICH: You know, Connie Wolf of the Wolf Bakery family has been a big help to me.

HELEN: Yeah, good for Connie! She seems to have a heart for it.

RICH: I really wanted to get in touch with you all, and I was so glad that she knew you. She told me that your dad and her dad played cards together.

HELEN: Ohh-h-h yeah, the "card games!" They played poker and drank! [Laughter.] They had a good time. Yeah, I remember those poker games because we weren't allowed to go downstairs.

HELEN: They'd have some of the employees and some of the other bakers there. And they'd say, "Boy your dad, the more he drinks the more he wins!" And, I would say, "Oh gee, don't tell my mom that!" [Laughter.]

HELEN: You know, then they had all of these culinary arts schools, and they'd think fancy pastries was the way to go, the stuff that they'd serve at the hotels and banquet centers. And then, they'd say, "Well, let's go over to France and learn about French pastries. But then, they weren't making the good German pastries anymore. That was the stuff that sticks to your ribs, and when you bite into it, it's good and you want to

HOW OUR HEARTS WERE STÖLLEN

eat it, instead of a flaky, buttery, chocolate thing that's wonderful, but you wouldn't want to eat that every day.

HELEN: [At this point Helen goes into some very nice personal memories about her mom.] I remember my mom. We would always have these little white bags on the table, and my mom would come home after her shift at the bakery. I remember before she'd go back to the store to make sure the evening girls got there she would have her danish roll and coffee and read her paper even before she would eat her sandwich! It was in her blood, she just loved sweets! [Laughter.]

RICH: First things first, right?!

HELEN: She would never gain any weight. She was ninety-two pounds all of her life. Dad, on the other hand, he went up and down, in and out. [Laughter.]

Author's Note: At this point, Helen Lubeley was very candid about the closing of their bakery and the interest that others had in purchasing it.

RICH: Now, I don't want to forget to ask, "Was there any interest from anyone for buying the business when it closed?"

HELEN: Yes, there was. They wanted our name. They wanted all of our recipes. And, they wanted us to keep working for them, for at least a year. But, we knew that they really didn't know what they needed to know. They didn't know anything about the business. And, we could have sold it to them, and the bank would have taken the place back, and they would have gone into debt. And, we knew it.

HELEN: They were not happy with us for not selling it to them, but we kept telling them, "We know that you like to bake at home." But, they didn't know how to do bakery baking. They knew how to do cookies and cupcakes, and they made beautiful things. But, we told them, "You're not going to be able to pay all of these insurance things that you'll have to pay, all these other things that you'll have to pay, and the bank. You're not going to make it." And so, we backed out of the deal.

HELEN: The other thing was that physically Bob was hurting, and I was just bushed. So, the idea of working for them for a year and helping them get on their feet just wasn't possible. At that point Bob said that he couldn't do it. He couldn't do it full-time anymore. Bob said to them, "You don't understand, we're doing you a favor." He meant that we didn't want them to get into something that we knew they couldn't handle. They didn't really see it that way.

HELEN: Another contender for the purchase was from Webster. She remembered coming into Lubeley's with her family when she was a little girl, and she wanted to keep Lubeley's going. But, she wanted us to stay on-board and do what we had been trying to do for three years, and that was to actively find managers and bakers to take it over.

HELEN: But, we told her that anyone who is capable of managing a bakery is already working for somebody else. We don't have anybody. We couldn't find anybody, except ourselves and the ones who are already retired. And, they don't want to manage anymore.

HELEN: [At this time Helen gave a description of what an old-fashioned bakery involved.] You're talking about an old-fashioned bakery, where you have a mixing room, and there's just flour, water, eggs, bakery spices, and you have to make everything from scratch.

HELEN: You have to make your cake doughs, your donut doughs, your sweet doughs, your danish doughs, and your specialty puff pastry doughs. And, all of those have to "start," and then you have to have the craftsman that you give the "base" to — to weigh it, to roll it, to fill it, and to finish it.

HELEN: And then, you have the baker who bakes it up, who puts it into the revolving oven, and finishes it off, and then you finally give it to the public. [Notice that she used the word, "gives" it to the public as if this is not just a monetary transaction.] So, this is old-time baking. It's the real thing. People are just not interested in learning that.

RICH: You know how people talk, and they don't really know what they're talking about. But, just in the last week or so I heard someone say that they thought that Lubeley's had a mini thing going on and that they were going to do something different.

HELEN: Well, we hoped at one time to take some of our recipes and to have them in the grocery stores, but our place is really too big to make gooey butters, deep crumb cakes, and caramel croissants, or whatever is selling. But, once they have your recipes, you'll maybe make a nickel on your product. You don't really get anything. It's not really worth it.

RICH: So, is that what McArthur's gets on their gooey butters that they sell in the grocery stores?

HELEN: No, they make their own. They have a midnight crew that comes into their store, and that's all that they do is make their product that goes out to the stores.

HELEN: July is a good month for bakers to be less busy. Well you know, being a South area gal you don't get out much, and you don't have a clue about what's going on up North. But, North in its heyday was just as well done as South City. It was just spread out more. Yeah, my mom and dad said that there were over two hundred and fifty independent bakeries at the time of the depression. They all brought their crafts as immigrants when they came. They'd open up these little shops, and the mom and dad did all of the work.

RICH: I'm gonna' see if you can remember the addresses of the Lubeley's bakeries at Yorkshire center?

HELEN: That would be 8021 Watson Road, and I don't remember the other one. This address would be for the Yorkshire location at the corner of the center. So, there really were three locations at the Yorkshire area, one at the far western end of the shopping center, one at the corner of the Yorkshire Center, and the last location a couple blocks east on Watson Road. That address was 7815 Watson Road.

HELEN: The front of that location didn't always look like that. At one point my dad decided he would become an amateur wood worker, and he created some kind of sign that didn't work at all.

HELEN: And, I said to my brother Bob, "Oh my gosh, it looks terrible." So, when my dad passed away we changed it.

RICH: You know, I've got to tell you something that's kind of fun. Well, our daughter dated Ryan, your nephew and Bob's son, just one or two times.

HELEN: Aww-w-w, really?!

RICH: So, I had met Ryan, and I think I told Bob that. [As we're looking at pictures in an album, Helen points out a picture of Ryan.]

HELEN: There he is, and there are my two daughters. Here's Ryan working. Yeah, they all helped out at the very end. And, there are those raspberry twists that you liked! [Hardy Laughter] There's Susie, mine and Bob's sister, and the two head decorators.

HELEN: Well, it was very hard to get it started, but it didn't take much to close it down. And, we said to ourselves, "How do you close a business when we don't really want to and nobody else *wants* us to? And, we're really at the top of our game as far as people knowing who we are, and our recipes." And, we said, "How are we going to do this?"

THE LAST FEW DAYS

HELEN: We even contacted a consultant with that question, "How do we close a business?" We didn't want to just close it and not tell our employees and such. So, he talked us through it. I now understand why restaurants and such do that, and it's because they couldn't handle the influx of people who wanted to eat there for the last time. It was the same thing with us. We told everybody that we were going to close on a certain date, which was really going to be three weeks before we actually closed. That seemed like a mistake.

HELEN: Oh my gosh, we ran out of ingredients. So, the Monday after the Sunday of the second week we had to put up a sign that said, "CLOSED — We Need To Restock — Can't Open Till Tuesday." We needed a day to make the doughs, and prepare the apples and the fillings. We were out of everything. This was because everybody was used to having everything there when we opened up.

HELEN: We opened those days at 7:00, and everything was gone by 10:00. Finally, we had to put a limit on what people could buy. People wanted to buy three, four, and five dozen of the items, and we said, "No, there's a line of people waiting, there's a limit." And, the limit was pretty nice. We said, "You can buy a dozen danish, and you can buy two coffee cakes, and you can buy two stöllens, and no more than that." That was a lot. If they couldn't get what they wanted that day, they just came back the next day and stood in line!

RICH: I was tempted, and I thought about coming by, but I didn't want to make you suffer with another customer!

HELEN: Oh, once it was all out there all we really needed was to have people to get it to them. Susie's husband, Mark, stayed outside and gave everybody a number and directed traffic. My husband was smart and said, "I'll just stay out of the way."

HELEN: So, I don't know if this helped you or gave you any more information, but I hope so.

RICH: Yes, this was a great help. I loved meeting with you and talking to you!

Marklin Bakery

Interview with Richard and Marie Grosch Marklin

*Bakers would borrow yeast and other items from one
another when they were out of something.
One Friday night before the busy week-end Marklin's mixer broke down. So, he had
to call on Ellerbrock who saved the day and mixed the Friday night batch of dough!*
— Richard and Marie Marklin

Author's Note: This interview was <u>not</u> tape recorded, but was taken down in notes by the author. This was a very charming interview in the home of Richard and Marie Marklin who were very kind in their willingness to reminisce about their bakery and their family history! At the time of this interview they were both ninety years old. Richard and Marie Marklin had seven sons.

Richard and Marie Marklin met in 7th grade. Richard Marklin's mother's name was Bernardina, who was better known as Dina, and she was an Ellerbrock. Other Ellerbrocks included Bill, Clara, Hattie, and Ida.

Bill Ellerbrock and Albert Marklin each had a son, and they had separate bakeries. They had a friendly rivalry between the two brother-in-laws. Albert Marklin's bakery was known as "Marklin's Bakery — the Sweetest Spot in Town." He had that bakery for eleven years, and then his wife passed away. He then sold that bakery to Carl Hilbert. Richard worked for him for a few months, and then went to Ellerbrock's and worked there for about two years as a decorator.

Albert then built a bakery known as "Marklin's Pastries" at Delmar and Old Bonhomme in University City. Richard worked there as a decorator. Ironically, Albert Marklin was allergic to wheat!

Link's Bakery was on North Broadway near Riverview and they always had a cat in the window. [Richard's quick comment was], "My gosh, who would buy bakery goods from a baker with a cat in the window!"

HOW OUR HEARTS WERE STÖLLEN

Richard Marklin's family rented a bakery in Baden and lived above the bakery. In the 40's and 50's retail bakeries were very abundant and competitive, but very friendly. Bakers would borrow yeast and other items from one another when they were out of something. Albert Marklin would cook turkeys for their church in one of the rotating ovens. On one occasion the oven jammed because of an odd shaped pan. In telling this story Richard Marklin quipped, "and that was what you got for your charity!" [We all laughed at Richard Marklin's comment!]

One Friday night before the busy week-end Markliin's mixer broke down. So, he had to call on Ellerbrock who saved the day and mixed the Friday night batch of dough!

Bakers worked very hard, and sometimes they weren't always ready to share their recipes.

One day Richard saw someone copying from his recipe book. So, he stopped him and told him that he wrote down the recipes in some kind of code, and that if the other person would use them he'd have a mess!

At Christmas time my dad, Albert Marklin, would mix a lot of the stöllen dough with Valeria, Clara Ellerbrock's daughter. Then, Richard would make the stöllens. Hattie Ellerbrock, Clara Ellerbrock's sister, was the business person of the family.

For ten years Richard Marklin "moonlighted" in Ferguson at Stan Ozenkoski's bakery in Cool Valley. In 1975 at the Jamestown Mall and in St. Charles they had cake decorating contests. Richard made a "dummy" cake out of styrofoam. It didn't do well in St. Charles, but won a 1st place prize in the Jamestown Mall contest.

One year they made "Lamb Cakes," but because of a feature story in the Parade Magazine of the St. Louis Post-Dispatch newspaper, they had too many orders. Because of that they had "Lamb Cakes" all over their house on the 2nd floor because they had no storage.

There was a special problem with delivering wedding cakes. The wedding cakes would slide. So, oftentimes they would have to repair them. [This problem was described by several of the other bakers interviewed. They felt it happened sometimes because of the lack of air-conditioning during the hot weather of the summer!]

Richard Marklin then commented that, "We also had to adjust the amount of shortening during the summer months because we had no air-conditioning. We had another problem with putting layer cakes together because of the layers."

HOW OUR HEARTS WERE STÖLLEN

McArthur Bakery
Interview With David McArthur
and Myndi Bearden McArthur
With Some Comments From Randy McArthur

*Yeah, throughout the year the St. Louis Bakers Association would always
have stuff going on that everyone was invited to. They had bowling
leagues! They had the Bakers Singing Society. They had the Women Baker's
Singing Society. They had the German Bakers Singing Society.
And then, in the summer they had the yearly picnic.*
— David and Myndi McArthur

Author's Note: Chronologically, this was the <u>first</u> interview completed of all of
the in-person interviews. I am very thankful to David and Myndi McArthur, and
Randy McArthur for their willingness to share their information and to give their
personal encouragement for me to begin this "Bakery Book Project!" This interview was filled with information about the McArthur Bakery, the St. Louis Master
Retail Baker's Association, and their personal knowledge of many other bakeries!

RICH: David and Myndi, what caused so many independent bakeries to go out of
business? Many people say it was due to the beginning of the supermarket era.

DAVID: Sure, it caused florists to do the same, just like it did with so many others. You know, actually it was a combination.

DAVID: You know, you've got to remember the geographics of where bakeries were. Bakeries were on every other corner in the neighborhood, back when everyone lived in neighborhoods, and back before there were freezers. [At this point there was an interruption in the interview for a business question from David's wife, Myndi.]

RICH: [As I was pointing to an historic photo I asked,] "Where was that?"

DAVID: That was Federhofer's Bakery with the owners, he and his wife. That's going back about forty years ago.

RICH: Yes, I taught Cheryl Federhofer. She was from that family. She still works there and is an owner.

DAVID: Yeah, right. She's a year older than Myndi, and they both went to Notre Dame High School. And now, she runs the Federhofer Bakery.

RICH: On Gravois in Affton, right?

DAVID: Correct. Yeah, she's the only one of the kids left in the business. She runs it, and her boys work there. I see them sometimes. *Bill Jr. is my daughter's godfather.*

RICH: *Is that right! See, that's what is so amazing about all of this. I talked to somebody who was related to the Wolf family. It seems like everybody is related to somebody in the larger bakery family, either as really related, or by marriage or friendship!*

DAVID: Yeah, there were a lot of bakeries in St. Louis. I've heard that in 1960 there were around a thousand bakeries in St. Louis. You know, I've heard that number kicked around more than one time.

Author's Note: During the interviews there were several different estimates of total bakeries at any given year in St. Louis.

RICH: A thousand bakeries?!

DAVID: Correct.

MYNDI: [As she was paging through the Bakery Association Bulletins, (that they were going to give to me later in the interview), Myndi observed], "You know what you're gonna' like in here are all of the recipes that different bakeries submitted to the bulletins."

RICH: Yeah well, I could really put a whole section of those in the back of the book, recipes and featured favorites!

MYNDI: Right! Each one of the bulletins usually has a recipe.

RICH: Is that right?! That could be a whole 'nother book!

DAVID: Yeah, it could be! [Laughter all around.]

RICH: Hey, David, <u>you</u> ought to be writing this book!

DAVID: No, no. I don't have time! You know, I look at these pictures like I've said before, and I know all of the names. But, it's sad. They're all gone, so many of them. Not all, but most.

MYNDI: Well, like Bretscher's Bakery.

DAVID: Yeah, Paul Bretscher's Bakery, up at Hartford and South Grand. *Our gooey butter recipe that we have today is Paul Bretscher's recipe.*

RICH: Is that right?!

DAVID: Yeah, and we've been using it for about ten years. Yeah, Paul Bretscher taught me to water ski, off a pontoon boat we used to take up on the lake at Terre du Lac. He had a little property that we went to.

RICH: [After hearing David reminisce I thought to myself], *"There's that St. Louis Bakery family feeling again!"*

MYNDI: [As she is looking at another one of the Bakery Bulletins Myndi says,] "Oh yeah, this one talks about three proud graduates of the apprentice training school."

DAVID: Yeah, look at that. Bill Bender, Robert Shelton, someone I don't know, and Dale Paul. Dale Paul was the guy who worked for us up until 6 months ago. Yeah, he's semi-retired. Now he's a part time manager out at Lutheran South High School. He also worked for Federhofer's for twenty years. Then, he had his own donut shop. He sold that, then worked for Kirkwood Bakery, and then came here.

RICH: [At this point, I thought to myself, "You sure picked the right person to interview for great oral history about St. Louis bakeries!"]

MYNDI: But, does it say where they graduated from?

DAVID: Well, they went to the apprenticeship school at O'Fallon Tech High School in St. Louis. It was the St. Louis Baker's apprentice school at O'Fallon. It was there right at the school, and it was staffed by John Bath. He was the guy, one of the guys, and then a lot of the local bakers would go and donate their time. That's in this book of bulletins from '71 – '73.

RICH: Thanks, great! That's a good tip. And, that's funny because our daughter Katy taught French for 5 years at the Gateway magnet school, which is the school that O'Fallon Tech became. Now she's in Philadelphia having a baby.

DAVID: [While looking at another issue of the Baker's Bulletins David says], *"Yeah, the old meetings. Everybody used to take bakery goods and show off their stuff. And then, they had the recipes, and if you liked what they had, they would give you the recipes."* [Then I thought, "Wow, what a neat thing that they would freely share their knowledge, even about their best creations!"]

RICH: They would give their recipes away for <u>free</u>? Really?

DAVID: Yeah, it was <u>not</u> a cut-throat business, "I'm better than you are type of thing." Because you know, a guy who requested a recipe from another guy was essentially saying, "You know, you're doing a good job."

RICH: Yeah, that makes sense!

DAVID: It was kind of a compliment to a guy that somebody would ask for something that he had. *It was more than a competition!*

RICH: *More than a competition! What a great concept!*

DAVID: Yeah, right!

MYNDI: *That was like when we got married, we had five hundred people at our wedding because of all of the bakers who were there!*

DAVID: *Yeah, because I grew up knowing them.*

The Annual Mid-October, Missouri Bakers Convention was its usual rousing success.

RICH: *That reinforces everything that I've been hearing about the family feeling of the bakery community in St. Louis. The more I hear about this, the more I think it's like a big family, almost like a tribe!* [Everybody laughs.]

DAVID: *Yeah, it was. Through the years there were a lot of guys I knew where we went to their houses.*

MYNDI: Well, you had that Christmas thing and you had that formal dinner that we went to every year. I can't remember, what was that for?

DAVID: It was the Installation Banquet for the new officers.

MYNDI: And then, in the summer they had the yearly picnic. How long ago did they go to the Kirkwood Lodge?

DAVID: Oh, I don't know. But, this would be interesting, [David said the following things as he was looking at another one of the Bakery Bulletins,] "Here you go, wages. Here is the wage scale from 1963. First-hand baker night work, 132.00 per week. First-hand baker day work, 116.00 per week."

RICH: Wow!

DAVID: But you know, those are just some fun facts.

RICH: *Sure! You know, I had a question — if I quoted from this and gave credit, would I have to get permission?*

DAVID: *No, there's no association left. There's nobody left.*

RICH: *O.K.*

DAVID: *Nope. The St. Louis Bakers Association is essentially dissolved. We've spent all of the money, and we no longer file with the state of Missouri for a tax-free status.*

MYNDI: "Hey, I think that's your dad," [Myndi said as she was pointing to a picture in one of the Bakery Bulletins].

DAVID: Oh, dad's all over this thing. We would drive out on Route 66 over the Meramec River bridge at Sullivan Beach and go to Green Acres Park.

RICH: Where was the Kirkwood Lodge?

MYNDI: Oh, that was at Lake of the Ozarks. Yeah, we used to go there every October, from Saturday to Tuesday. *It was open to all of the bakers and the suppliers. But, throughout the year they would always have stuff going on that everyone was invited to. And then, wasn't it once or twice a year we would just do a dinner. And so yeah, I mean they were always getting together.*

DAVID: [While pointing down to one of the Bakery Bulletins David says], "Who knows? You may get into these, and who knows what you'll find!"

Author's Note: His prediction was absolutely true!

RICH: So, I've been wondering ever since I took these bulletins who actually put all of these in binders, sequenced by years, and protected in plastic sheet protectors?

DAVID: That would be Joyce Schwarz. Her husband was Armin Schwarz, and they were long time members of the Baker's Association. Their last bakery was on Clayton Road near Skinker.

MYNDI: You know, the Bakers Association also had bowling leagues.

DAVID: Yeah, they had bowling leagues! They had the Bakers Singing Society. They had the Women Baker's Singing Society. They had the German Bakers Singing Society.

DAVID: [As David's brother, Randy, was walking by, David asked him], "Hey, what was Bud Schwarz's last bakery's name?" [On hearing Randy's answer, he said], "O.K., it was Armin's Bakery. Huh, my memory's better than I thought. It was right on the corner."

RICH: Right on DeMun and Clayton, I think.

MYNDI: Here's a picture of the Men's Baker's Singing Society. This one just shows the men.

DAVID: A lot of those pictures you'll find in the backs of the bulletins with the announcements.

MYNDI: Oh yeah, you all did something else. What was that "Little Miss Muffin" thing? I remember that!

DAVID: [Again looking at a different issue of the Bakery Bulletins he says], "Oh, there's my mom there with Larry Wilson."

RICH: Do you mean Larry Wilson from the St. Louis Football Cardinals?

DAVID: Yeah, that was a fund-raising benefit. We used to put cakes on the counter, and then we had a little doll on crutches, and people would stick their change in the cake. We collected thousands and thousands of dollars doing that.

MYNDI: [Again, while looking at another of the Bakery Bulletins Myndi says], "Yeah, here are some pictures of the men's bowling league and the women's bowling league."

RICH: O.K. What was the "Little Miss" Cheesecake" contest or the "Little Miss Muffin" contest?

Miss Cheesecake Contest

Author's Note: There seemed to be several different names for the same contest, or there were several different promotional contests — Miss Cheesecake, Miss Cupcake, or Miss Muffin.

MYNDI: [Randy McArthur comes up to the table, and Myndi asks him], "Randy, do you remember what the 'Little Miss Muffin' thing was all about? This bulletin shows a few of the young girls."

RANDY: It was a contest that they had. There was no particular purpose for it other than just to promote the bakeries. So, they would have a contest. [David McArthur then introduced me to his brother, Randy, one of the owners of the McArthur Bakery.] The "Little Miss Muffin Contest," was mostly a PR thing, and now as I recall it, one year the "Little

Miss Muffin" even won a trip to Disney World, and flew there on TWA. I can remember the picture of her with a little TWA bag getting on the plane.

DAVID: It was like a kids beauty contest

MYNDI: Yeah, because in all of the pictures she's all dressed up and stuff.

DAVID: Oh, here you go, here's a picture of "Little Miss Muffin" of the National Retail Baker's Week, in the Bulletin of February of 1962. Under the picture it says, "Every bakery should have a 'Little Miss Muffin' contest. This creates local interest in the bakery which creates good will." Each bakery had a contestant.

MYNDI: One of these says that the convention was held at the Chase Park Plaza Hotel.

DAVID: Yep, I can remember one in '64 or '65.

RICH: Was that a national convention?

MYNDI: Yes, the ARBA, the American Retail Bakers Association, January, 1965.

RICH: What was your dad's first name?

DAVID: Donald, Don. The editor says here, "Don's mother contributed to the meeting by making the uniform. It was sure nice of Mrs. McArthur to help us out with this activity."

RICH: Could you all brainstorm with me about some of the other bakers' family names?

DAVID: Well, you had Sam Wolf. You had the Bretschers. He had two daughters. Sam and June Wolf. You had the Lubeleys, the Knodels there up on North Florissant. One of the daughter's names was Inglish. They're both still there.

RICH: Do they still have a bakery?

DAVID: Lake Forest Bakery was owned by the Benders.

RANDY: I was president of the National Association in 1998.

MYNDI: You got Bill and Merle Federhofer, but then you also have Ed and Jenny Federhofer who started Carondelet Bakery.

DAVID: Well, they didn't start it. They had it. Ed also ran the St. Louis Baker's Co-Op.

RICH: I'd really like to have a "Family Tree" of the different bakery families.

DAVID: Especially with Federhofers because then you had Doerrings. They married. You had the Doerrings and the Federhofers mixed in, because Herman Doerring and Ed Federhofer owned Doerrings Bakery, which is what Carondelet Bakery was then. And then, the Federhofer boys went into their own bakery.

DAVID: The other families — you had the Rozaneks, Leo's kids. They're bakers for Dierbergs, at the Dierberg's plant.

MYNDI: And then, there's the Helfers.

DAVID: He's first generation.

MYNDI: Yeah I know, but he's still there.

DAVID: Chris Helfer with Helfer's Pastries up in old Florissant. He does a nice job!

MYNDI: Kruta's over in Collinsville on St. Louis Avenue.

RICH: Is he still there?

DAVID: Yes, yes. Jim Kruta. His dad built that place. Kruta's and Federhofer's were almost identical buildings built in 1968. Kruta's was in Illinois, but they were still part of the Bakers Association.

RICH: Is it still there?

DAVID: Oh yes, it's still there. Kruta's and Federhofer's buildings were built <u>as</u> bakeries.

MYNDI: Who was the one that had Harter's?

DAVID: Yeah, that was in Arnold.

RICH: Is that still around?

DAVID: Oh yeah, the guy that owns it now is John, and he's Laotian. He started here, and he learned the trade here. *A lot of these guys if you want to talk to any of them, you can use my name. It'll help, because we're friends with all of these people. It would help to open the door.*

DAVID: Lubeleys could give you a lot of history. Helen Lubeley and Helen's mom is still alive. She's 100 or 101 right now. But she worked up until two years ago!

MYNDI: And, what about Schmiemeyers?

DAVID: That's now owned as Clayton Bakery. Clayton is the guy who worked for Lake Forest for years, Bill Clayton.

MYNDI: But, what about the bakery that we built out by Clayton and Woods Mill? Who took that one over?

DAVID: Umm, that was Party Pastries. Yeah, that was Schmidt's. Party Pastries was started by the Schmidts, the second generation of the Schmidt family.

RICH: Schmidt's was on Michigan in South St. Louis, wasn't it?

DAVID: Yeah, that's where my dad started. They had three places in the 50's. My dad started by washing dishes at Schmidt's.

DAVID: And then, you also had the St. Louis Pastry Shop back in those years.

RICH: Yeah, that was at Virginia and Meramec! That was my bakery when I was growing up!

DAVID: Yeah, that was owned by the Langers, Al Langer.

MYNDI: Hey now, what was the one that my grandpa Bishop owned that was by that all-girls school in the city?

DAVID: Yeah, there were so many of them, but see St. Louis Pastry Shop was big. That was the plant there on Meramec, Meramec and Virginia. They had three or four stores. My dad and him were best friends. I used to go over to their house all of the time as a kid.

RICH: Now, who do you think was the originator of the St. Louis Gooey Butter Cake? St. Louis Pastry Shop on Meramec was one of those that claimed to be.

DAVID: Well, who claimed it was Heimburger. Fred claimed to have been the inventor of it. My own personal opinion is that a gooey butter mix is so far from a cake mix. I think it's all baloney. It's not even close to a cake mix.

DAVID: *What is close to a cake mix,* and this is where I think it's just rhetoric, *is the deep butter cake. Deep butter is nothing but a very rich yellow dough cake, and deep butter is also St. Louis only. You've got gooey butter and deep butter that are both St. Louis traditions.*

DAVID: But, they say that deep butter was the screwed-up cake mix, and they added stuff to it, but gooey butter is so far from a cake mix it's not even close. No baking powder — tons of sugar, and tons of shortening. I mean, you would have had to been just "whacked out."

RICH: Not really a cake then, right?

DAVID: Heimburger was the one who forever claimed to have been the inventor of that, but Fred claimed to be a lot of things.

RICH: He had just the one bakery, right?

DAVID: Yep, right there on South Lindbergh. He used to say that he sold ten thousand pounds of Christmas cookies every year. I'm saying the man had a twelve pan oven. I'd say if he started in June or July and went twenty-four hours a day non-stop he might have been able to do that. Now, if he bought a lot of cookies wholesale and repacked them, I'm not going to say he didn't sell ten thousand pounds of cookies.

MYNDI: [While looking at another Bakery Bulletin Myndi says], "Here's another picture of the baker training place, the old O'Fallon High School program. This is from '68. And, this issue talks about Fred Heimburger too!"

DAVID: Fred? Yeah, that would have been about when he built his place.

RICH: So, did Bob Lubeley start Lubeley's?

DAVID: No, Ed and Helen did. Hey, Randy, what was Schmidt's first name, the person who dad worked for?

RANDY: Earl.

DAVID: Yeah, it was Earl Sr. and Earl Jr. Correct?

RICH: And then, there were only two generations of Lubeleys, right?

DAVID: Well, there's Bob and Helen, but the third generation is there now. Their son is there now.

RICH: Yeah, Ryan, right? Lubeley's hires a lot of Notre Dame High School girls over there, and so does Missouri Baking.

DAVID: Yeah, Missouri Bakery. You've got the Gambaros — Chris and Mimi are running it now. And then, oh God, I love them. They're good friends — all of them, but Leno was my favorite. He and I just had something click from the time I was a little kid. Yeah, they're still going. Now, Chris's daughter is in there, and she's working, and I think she's got some long-term aspirations of taking over the business.

RICH: That's a hard thing to do, right. I mean, getting the family involved in the business?

RICH: Now, weren't the Doerrings related to the Schmidts?

DAVID: No, I don't think so. Not that I know of. You know, I could be wrong.

MYNDI: Like I said, Ed Federhofer could tell you a lot.

DAVID: Federhofers and Doerrings were related. And, I could get you Ed's phone number if you wanted it.

MYNDI: He lives in the subdivision right behind mom and dad, right behind St. Martin of Tours.

RICH: I'd love to talk to him.

MYNDI: He could tell you a lot, because he had the St. Louis Baker's Co-op. He would know all of the bakeries, because he distributed to all of them.

DAVID: Bill and Ed Federhofer are brothers. Bill and Ed's sister married a Doerring... Yeah, there were five kids in the Federhofer family, and one of the sisters married Herman Doerring. So then, Herman Doerring and Ed Federhofer opened Doerring's Bakery, which is now Carondelet Bakery on Virginia, 7726 Virginia.

RICH: Yes, and Carondelet Bakery is said to be the oldest continuous running bakery in St. Louis.

Author's Note: I discovered in a later interview that the Bakers Co-Op was started long before Ed Federhofer.

DAVID: Well, he was the last "director" of it. It was started way back in the 50's, but he could give you the history of it! It was unique, because it was one of the oldest bakery co-ops in the country. It was owned by the bakers. It was a true co-op!

MYNDI: And it lists something in here, [referring to another issue of the Bakery Bulletins]. Here it lists how much money bakers spent and got back.

DAVID: I think you mean, what the dividends were that year. It wasn't the only one, but it was one of the only co-ops in the country.

DAVID: Our bakery that was originally on Arco, was built by the Hohm family in 1902, and dad bought it from them in 1954. Bill Hohm was his name.

DAVID: It was built and meant to be a bakery, a bakery and an ice cream shop. And, we lived above it. There were a lot of those old neighborhood corner bakeries, and the owners and families lived above them.

RICH: Yeah, I think the Smiths still live above the Carondelet Bakery.

DAVID: Well, at Missouri Bakery Lino lived above that bakery for years and years, up until he was about seventy when he finally moved out and built himself a big old house there on the Italian Hill. He got married like at seventy years old. Yeah, he lived there about twenty years.

MYNDI: [While looking at another Bakery Bulletin, Myndi commented], "See, here it shows that the Bakery Co-op gave back almost two million dollars in the past twelve years, and that was in 1965!"

DAVID: Yeah, see the more you bought, the more you got back. It was actually a rebate.

MYNDI: And, I read here too — that for flour and stuff it showed how much rebate you got back for what you bought.

RICH: What did they sell?

DAVID: Everything from frozen to refrigerated items, and they made their own icings and even did some toppings. They were a big-time supplier and manufacturer.

RICH: I didn't know anything about this. Another question I had was whether they had a baker's union?

DAVID: Yes. Still is, and at one time it encompassed both retail and wholesale. But, today it's just wholesale — like Schnuck's bakeries, Dierberg's bakeries, and Colonial Baking until they went out of business. So, I don't know who all you've got left. I don't know how the union can even be solvent anymore.

RICH: Were the independents involved with them at all?

DAVID: Yeah, a lot of the independent bakers were union. You know, some were, and some weren't. But, we always got along. My dad's bakery was never a union shop, but we always paid above union scale, at least most of the time.

MYNDI: Roland Hadler — did he have a bakery?

DAVID: Yeah, Hadler's Bakery. They had a place off of South Grand somewhere. I can't remember. There were so many.

RICH: Yeah, every corner, right?

DAVID: So many.

MYNDI: Yeah, because we'll drive around, and David will still say, "Uh-h, that was a bakery. You can tell that was a bakery."

RICH: Yeah, exactly. Can you remember the bakery right up the street on Broadway?

MYNDI: Yes, I worked there!

DAVID: It was Herman's.

MYNDI: Yeah, my sophomore year of high school I started working there!

RICH: It was really a small building, wasn't it?!

MYNDI: Herman Walkenhorst.

RICH: What I can remember from them was their peanut rolls!

MYNDI: Yes, and they would make a really big strudel! McArthur's strudel is long and thin, and theirs was wide. But, I think my favorite thing from there was their strudel!

DAVID: Yeah, so theirs was made from filo dough instead of puff pastry.

RICH: Is that right?!

DAVID: The really thin stuff when you put all of the layers down.

RICH: There's only going to be a few people who remember that bakery, but I really liked it.

Author's Note: The photo above is of a lighted wall decoration that is still displayed in the current McArthur's bakery and would seem to be the perfect message that bakers wanted to communicate through all of their bakery goods!

Nathaniel Reid Bakery
Interview With Nathaniel Reid

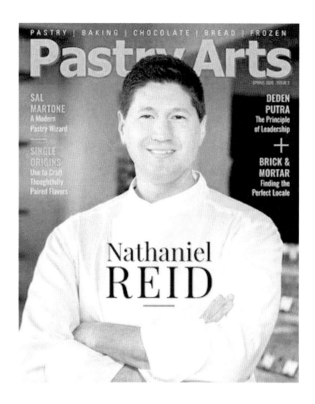

*I have been lucky to have been offered some pretty prestigious
positions and to be able to look them in the face
and say, "No," because they weren't what this was.
This is where I always wanted to be...
Some people would say, "Why did you move here?!"
You know, I take a lot of pride in the Midwest!
I LOVE IT HERE!*
— Nathaniel Reid

RICH: First of all, I think I heard someone say you and your wife just had a new baby!"

NATHANIEL: Yes we did. On Monday the 12th we had a little boy! And then on the 18th our daughter turned three! So, it's been an exciting time!

RICH: You're "in the business," right!

NATHANIEL: Yeah, between the time at home and here. Actually, at the time of our grand opening of the bakery our daughter was born a week after that! It's been an amazing time.

RICH: Your bakery is my fourteenth interview. It has been so great doing these interviews because they have revealed a love story that was created by the independent bakers of St. Louis. You know, I started out at McArthurs interviewing them. In addition to the interview they loaned three big boxes to me that were filled with fifty years of bulletins from the St. Louis Bakers Association.

NATHANIEL: Oh wow, that's pretty neat!

RICH: Those bulletins tell such a great story! The independent bakers during the 1950s to the 2000s were a very close community. They were godparents for one another's children. They sometimes married into one another's families. They "floated" everywhere, meaning that they worked in one another's bakeries. Many of them seemed to work in three or four different bakeries at different times.

NATHANIEL: What got you interested in this project?

RICH: Well, I grew up with a grandfather in south city, and there was a bakery on Meramec and Virginia called, the St. Louis Pastry Shop. He and I would go to Mass pretty much every morning at St. Anthony of Padua Catholic church. And then, afterwards we would bring home the bakery goods! Later as an adult, a friend of mine and I would joke about writing a book about bakeries because we loved donuts and we loved bakery goods. His name is Ed. He's a teacher and a great guy. Well, that's sort of my story.

RICH: I just did an interview at The Blue Owl with Mary Hostetter! She's as sweet as Mary Poppins, and she has this great vision. She has this signature item called "The Levee High Apple Pie."

NATHANIEL: I haven't had the pleasure of meeting her, but I have experienced

"The Levee High Apple Pie." I don't know how many apples are in there, but it is amazing.

RICH: In all of this project I have just tried to follow my nose! But, I love doing these interviews so much that I don't really want to stop!

NATHANIEL: Maybe you'll have to do a second edition or a second volume!

RICH: I think so, it seems like it! [And, we laugh.] Not only do I love listening to these stories, but the bakers seem like they love telling their stories. So many of them are retired bakers or they are about to retire.

NATHANIEL: It's nice that they have so much experience in life, and it gives them a chance to sit down and pause for a minute. Well, what led you to my place?

RICH: Somebody who lives in this area told me that I had to try Nathaniel Reid's Bakery. [At this time, since we were sitting by the door Nathaniel took a brief pause to thank two of his customers for coming in. He did this every time someone would come in the door and whenever someone would walk towards the door to leave.]

NATHANIEL: I find this interesting, with all of the rich history of bakeries that St. Louis has had, your friends led you to my bakery. Well, tell your friends that I said thank you.

RICH: Yes, I will tell them. Your address, is it 11243 Manchester?

NATHANIEL: Yes, that's it.

RICH: And, how many years have you been here?

NATHANIEL: Three years. August 1st of 2016 is when we opened.

RICH: Wow! You've done a lot in a short time, haven't you!

NATHANIEL: I think so. You know, it's great to see the responses to our bakery. I feel like what we do here is a little bit unique from what's been done before in the market place.

NATHANIEL: I left this area in 2003. When I left Missouri I was away for ten years and then when I came back in 2013 I didn't know exactly what would work and what wouldn't work. I wanted to do something that was a little bit new for the market, and I think it is new and unique to most markets in the U.S. Of course, whenever you do that you don't know quite what the reactions are going to be. You just hope for the best, and swing for the fences. We're very fortunate that we've had a great response for all of our products. And, all of the people telling their friends has allowed us to grow. It doesn't have so much to do with us. The customers are doing the hard work for us.

RICH: That's nice. But, there's nothing easy about what you do, right.

NATHANIEL: Yes, and it's interesting. We make everything from scratch. You know, through the years less and less is that the truth, in what "scratch" really means. There's a lot of places, they buy a product and bake it there, and they'll say, "It's made in-house or baked in-house."

NATHANIEL: You know, there's all of this wiggle room for what's the reality where some of the people you probably interviewed from forty or fifty years ago it was a different thing. They probably did bake from scratch!

NATHANIEL: What I like to do is I like to cook. I don't like to open boxes. I've done this for twenty years, and I wouldn't have started this if the job was about opening up boxes and scooping goop out of a bucket.

NATHANIEL: Everything we do here, we do it from scratch, all of the croissants, all of the bread, all of the macaroons, the jams, everything. We make it here, the salad dressings, the puff pastry, the pickled vegetables, glazes, finishes. The only thing we don't make is flour. I don't grind my own flour or mill my own flour. I don't grind my own chocolate. I leave those things up to the people who are more knowledgeable about them than I am.

NATHANIEL: But, what I do is I take raw goods and transform them into purchasable products that hopefully have a uniqueness about them. I'm very, very quality driven, having great basic ingredients to start with and then build from there. And then, we use our creativity, our ingenuity, our technical knowledge to make our product into something that's hopefully better than you can expect. We're always trying to beat ourselves and beat our customers' expectations.

RICH: My point in talking about Chris Helfer was that he said something about the two things that draw people to baking. He said that they are the artistry and the service.

NATHANIEL: Yeah, absolutely!

RICH: I really don't think you would work that hard if you didn't feel you were helping people and that you were doing something very important for people. That's the direction of the book. What a great service that you all do.

RICH: You know, I think it was Roy Schmiemeir who said that around 1960 there were something like five hundred bakeries in St. Louis. Maybe it's an exaggeration, but it seemed like during that time there were four things on a lot of street corners — a tavern, a gas station, a confectionary, which was like a little quick shop, and of course, a bakery!

NATHANIEL: Really? You know, it seems like two of those four are still on every corner! [We laugh together!] And, probably not the two that we really need! Wow — that's amazing!

RICH: So anyway, there was an enormous number of bakeries. And, one of the important parts of the story is in the question about "What circumstances hit in the culture that made it really difficult for the independent bakeries to go on?" And, I asked people that question who were much older than you are, and they'd say, "Oh well, that's easy. It was the supermarkets. The supermarkets really put us out of business." But, one person really had another good answer. He said that "It was the supermarkets, but it was also the boxed cakes!" A good answer I thought, because when Betty Crocker and other boxed cakes came in, people saved themselves some time and trouble from having to go out. They'd just make it at home, and they were satisfied with it. Besides that, it was cheaper. So, there were a lot of factors that came together at the same time.

NATHANIEL: And, it's still a fight today, you know! If you look at the technology and the quickness of what supermarkets can do, it gets better and better and cheaper and cheaper, and their purchasing power is higher. But, I think the difference in where I've tried to lead our establishment is in focusing on what <u>we</u> can do well. Not focusing on what they can do, but focusing on what I can do and on how we can differentiate ourselves from them through quality and service, taking the time with our customers and through the quality of the product. I mean, I know that no supermarket can compete in this arena where we are. So, I wouldn't dare try to compete with them in their backyard, and I hope they wouldn't with me in my backyard.

NATHANIEL: And, it's fine. There's room for both. And that's the thing. I feel that in the past when you look at the history of baking, there was this commercialization of the product through larger establishments, through mass-produced bread, through this supermarket thing. I feel like a lot of the smaller bakeries tried to follow and compete against them instead of staying grounded and saying, "This is who I am. Yes, we might be a little less profitable, but I'm gonna' make a higher quality product and stay in business." And then, we'll keep the loyalty of our customers during that transition time.

NATHANIEL: I've been asked this question by interviewers from Spain and from France and other places before. That's where the creativity and ingenuity, the quality of the products that we can afford to do are always going to keep us in business.

RICH: Yeah, I'm sure it will. And, you're in a good location because people in this area care about quality. There were a couple of very high-end pastry shops pretty much in the area close to Galleria, so pretty close to where you are now. Some of the buildings are still there. There was Andre's, there was Pfeifer's, and there was Lake Forest.

NATHANIEL: Most of our clients who come in talk about the older places. They talk about Lake Forest, and they talk about Andres. That's most of what I hear.

RICH: Yeah, they had a little bit finer products. Do you ever think about expanding eventually, or later?

NATHANIEL: Yes, sometimes. This is a marathon, and I think I'm meticulous about what I do in the pastries, but also in the business. For me, it's like if you buy a house or build a house you put the foundation in first and you find solid ground, right. So, this is my solid ground. We built this place. My dad and I actually built this whole place, every wall. And, my brother and I did this floor and all the way to the ceiling. He's a retired carpenter, and I pulled the favor of a lifetime.

NATHANIEL: I grew up doing carpentry with my dad, and my brother did too. I did that for six years with him, and he did me the favor of a lifetime in helping me build this place. You know, it was a labor of love. It has a sentimental value. It would be hard to walk away from this place for that reason too. And, that's part of the story. We did everything we could to open up our dream. For my wife and I this has been our dream business, our dream. From four years ago when we started, it was to do this someday, to have that real community-feeling bakery.

NATHANIEL: *I have been lucky to have been offered some pretty prestigious positions, to have been offered some once-in-a-lifetime opportunities, and to be able to look them in the face and say, "No." I've had multiple occasions, but they weren't what this was. This is where I always wanted to be. And, they weren't in that direct path to be here and do my own small business. They might have been opportunities of a lifetime for someone else, but they weren't for me.*

RICH: Wow nice, very cool!

NATHANIEL: I could have easily opened up other places and do all of those things, but it wasn't the dream. You know, if I had wanted to work at a multi-chain type of place, I have done that in the past. I had that opportunity, but there's a joy to this!

NATHANIEL: There's joy just staying small in a way. We will be bigger at some point, over the years. I've got another twenty-five years to work at least, right!

RICH: Please know that I'm not encouraging a pre-mature expansion for you at all.

NATHANIEL: I could see something else happening or this space developing when it's needed, but when *we* want it to. *But, in the end I think the question is, "What's happiness for you?" You know, what's happiness for me? For me, this is great, this is happiness, just being able to produce a product I love and doing it with a team I really enjoy being around.* Being able to have that contact with our customers and have engagement and get to know the community, and be able to affect the community, hopefully impact the community in a positive way through employment and through multiple community activities that we do, and charities and things. I mean, that's the fun part. And, I don't know if driving all around town, making sure people show up on shifts and managing, I don't know if that gets to be any more fun or not. So, at some point in life, is it more and better, or not.

RICH: Exactly. Yeah, I wanted to respond to you and tell you that the older bakers that I've talked to would tell you to pace yourself, pace yourself for economic and business reasons, but also for health reasons because they've always said, "It's really hard work."

NATHANIEL: It is work. It's stressful, and it's hard on everybody. It's hard on everybody around you, your family, your friends. So, you know what, how much do you need in this life? How much are you going to take with you anyway?

RICH: And, you know that from this little guy who just came, right! [Referring to the recent birth of Nathaniel's little boy.]

NATHANIEL: Yeah, yeah. I mean, at the end of the day maybe instead of having another business and the possibility of having more financial security, you have more quality time with your family. Yeah, that's the dream, and you have to have the thought, the dream, the vision, and then put a plan in to make those things happen.

NATHANIEL: And, that's where I am right now, you know, finding a way to make it all work together a little bit. Yeah so, sorry for the long-winded answer, but it's more than just a business decision to me because it is a family-owned business.

NATHANIEL: I'm lucky enough to be in a position to make decisions that aren't always based on economics, just like we're closed on Sundays every week. We've never been open on a Sunday, and we never will be open on a Sunday. It's a personal decision. It will never make us more money, but it doesn't matter. If you can't make enough money to stay in business six days a week, you shouldn't be in business at all.

RICH: So, I don't know if you're a sports person or not, and this is somewhat irrelevant, but an NFL quarterback just retired. He was an elite but injured quarterback. Did you hear about that? They say he left about a half billion dollars on the table, that he could have made during the rest of his career. And, he said, "It's not worth it. I don't care how much money it's worth."

NATHANIEL: But, everybody has their own perspective. I'm not saying that what I'm saying is right, but it's my truth. It doesn't mean that it's somebody else's. And, it's not meant to talk about anybody else's business model or anything that they do. It's just for me, and I've been doing this for twenty years now. It's about searching for what in this life is going to provide me with the best opportunity to do what I like to do in all avenues of life. So, that's a long-winded answer. I'm sorry.

RICH: No, it's a great answer, and I love talking with you about all of this. We have a son-in-law who is a personal chef. He's really good at what he does, and he loves what he does. [At this time Nathaniel says thank-you to two more customers who are going out the door.] But, he won't work for a restaurant because of the hours. He'll only do personal cheffing or he'll do catering for a special event. We have a grandson and our daughter in town because he chose to work here. And so, it's his family that's important to him. So anyway, I know you were in France for awhile. Can you give me some highlights?

NATHANIEL: Oh, I think I've had a very successful career. I was very fortunate to have a lot of great opportunities right away. I've made the most of it or tried to make the most of it. Right after culinary school I got hired by the Ritz-Carlton in Las Vegas. The chef there had just won the World Pastry Championship. That was the most prestigious competition in the world at the time. He won that about six months before I came, and he was the reason I applied there, to work for him. So, I was lucky to be hired there right out of culinary school.

RICH: You were at the culinary school in Paris?

NATHANIEL: Yeah Paris, at the Cordon Bleu. [At this time Nathaniel says hello to another customer saying, "Hi, doing well, thanks!"] It's interesting because Le Cordon Bleu just contacted me. They're having their 125th anniversary, and they're writing a book, and they wanted to have some alumni be in the book. So, they chose me to be in the book. Last month I just submitted all of the recipes and photos and stuff. So, it's pretty neat to have your alma mater recognize you for what you've done.

NATHANIEL: So, I worked for the chef in Las Vegas, for about a year. And then, he left to run a chocolate company. So, I'm there at the Ritz-Carlton in Las Vegas, and I never even wanted to go to Las Vegas, I never even cared to visit there. I went basically just to work for this man because he is really great at his craft. But, I'm in this flux of, "What do I need to do now" kind of feeling because he's the reason I had moved there.

NATHANIEL: And, it just so happens that he tells me about this famous chef opening up a restaurant in Las Vegas named Joel Robuchon. Do you know who Joel Robuchon is? He just passed away last year. There were three chefs who were named chefs of the century, and he had more Michelin stars than any chef has ever had, more Michelin star restaurants than any other chef.

NATHANIEL: Now, this isn't a normal thing at this time yet, that some big name French chef is going to open a prestigious restaurant outside of France. This was kind of the start of that kind of thing happening. So, he's opening this restaurant in Las Vegas, and people tell me that I should go to work for him. You know, there are several Three-Michelin Star restaurants, which is the top in the world that you can get. There weren't very many times that these guys left France and tried to open something like that outside of France at that time. Now it's more common. So, he was one of the first guys to try that, and he opened a place in Las Vegas. So, I applied there, and I opened that restaurant which had three Michelin stars.

NATHANIEL: And then, there was an existing hotel within the MGM Grand. It was called The Mansion Hotel, and it was rated the number one hotel in the world in 2004 by Conde' Nast. And, they basically replaced the kitchen staff there with our team, Joel Robuchon and myself. So, we went there to head the pastry team. So, I ran this hotel pastry team where the most expensive room night there was 35,000 dollars in 2006. And then, the cheapest villa was 5,000 dollars a night, and there were 36 villas. So, I had this amazing experience to be at these top-class places.

RICH: Another world, right?

NATHANIEL: Another world. Unbelievable. There was this one time, they call them "whales," the gamblers. Well, there was this one whale who had just been at the Wynn Hotel that had just opened, and there were a lot of big-time gamblers there. So, they were trying to win him back, to come back to the MGM properties.

NATHANIEL: So, they had this special dinner there, and we made a cake for the dinner. [At this time Nathaniel had several short conversations with his customers as they were coming in or leaving.] I worked for the MGM Grand. I worked for the restaurant. Yeah, it was called Restaurant Joel Robuchon.

RICH: I have to tell you. I think we're a lot alike in our feelings about Las Vegas. I took a really fun road trip when I was in college, and I drove through Las Vegas one night, in the town and out of the town. And, I didn't even get out of the car!

NATHANIEL: You saw enough, yeah?! [And then, we laughed together.] More or less I opened up those three places and had good experiences. I wasn't *the* pastry chef at those properties. I was the assistant. And still, I was in charge of that hotel at the end. So, I worked there for three years for him and got some great experience working with products. At that time dinner there cost almost 500 dollars per person, and that was without wine or anything. The tasting menu at the time was four hundred ninety-five dollars for the sixteen courses. I heard that it was the 4th most expensive restaurant in the U.S. at the time. It was a good experience, seeing things and touching products that you'll never see again. You work with truffles and caviar and lobster, that's just with every plate.

NATHANIEL: I worked with savory and pastry before. I went to school for savory and pastry. After culinary school I did mainly pastry and baking.

NATHANIEL: I went to culinary school at Le Cordon Bleu in Paris, but I went to the University of Missouri in Columbia, and I did Hotel and Restaurant Management there. While I was there I worked in the restaurants there. How I really learned to cook was there. The name of one of the restaurants was Chris McD's.

RICH: You know, my wife, Sue, and you are fellow alums of Mizzou.

NATHANIEL: Oh, did she go there? That's great. So, that was my first introduction to a kitchen. Before that I worked at the Alumni Club at the Reynolds Alumni Center. I was a dishwasher there. Like many people that was my first job in a kitchen. Before that I was a waiter at a restaurant there. So, I was being a waiter making good money, and I had a great idea that I wanted to get in the kitchen and be a dishwasher because that's the doorway into a kitchen! When you have no practical skills, that's a great entry way to get your foot in the door. People do that here, and they've been very successful. You gotta' learn the job, right?

RICH: You gotta' start somewhere, right!

NATHANIEL: You might start in the mailroom and work your way up, right? He taught me a lot at the restaurant. I'm very fortunate that somebody wanted to hire me when I had no experience but had the will to learn and the will to work hard. You know, I think that's sometimes enough.

RICH: Have you ever been interviewed by Feast magazine or Sauce?

NATHANIEL: Yeah. By Cat Neville. Yeah, she's a delight.

RICH: I want to make contact with her because I've got a lot of material, and I don't know if she'd be interested in it or not. She's pretty approachable, isn't she.

NATHANIEL: Yes, very. So, I worked there, and that was in Las Vegas. And then, I had an opportunity. And you know, things go back and forth, one door closes and another one opens. That happened so many times for me.

NATHANIEL: Actually, I had an intention of moving back to France because I had this world- renowned chef offer me a job, and then the visa paperwork didn't really work out. They told me I had to get a student visa. So, that would have meant that I'd have to pay for school. And, I'd already been to school for six years after high school. So, that was a way you could go and kind of skirt the system.

NATHANIEL: Then, there was this chef in California, and somebody put me in contact with him. He was a well-known chef around the world. He won the World Pastry competition as well. So, his assistant was leaving, and he was looking for another assistant, I mean like his right-hand man. So, I took the job with him, and that was in Laguna, California in Orange County.

NATHANIEL: The hotel was the St. Regis Hotel. There's the big one in New York that invented the Bloody Mary. That's their claim to fame. I worked for him and was his assistant for about a year. Then, he left to open his own school and offered me his job. So, my first job as the executive chef in charge was of this five-star, five-diamond resort. It was the "Un des Meilleurs Ouvriers de France" that he won. It's called the M.O.F. They have the red, white, and blue collar. He won this prestigious competition in France and also won the world competition of cooking basically. And so, my first job of being a chef was taking over for him. They were big shoes to fill!

RICH: Yes, I'm sure!

NATHANIEL: But, they saw that I did most of the job anyway. It was kind of relaxing in a way. It made sense for me to take it over for him. So, for the next three years I was the chef at that hotel, at that resort.

RICH: Who was the guy who you took over for?

NATHANIEL: His name was Stephane Treand. So, he was a great chef and showed me a lot of interesting things. And then, there were a couple more stops. When I moved to California I got tapped by this guy named Norman Love. He's kind of like an industry leader in chocolate and confections. He was in Florida, and he was looking for a chef to help build his brand and his business. At the time he only had one retail shop, and his idea was to really open up a lot more shops. He wanted to open up the pastry and baking side of his business, and build a gelato ice cream production part of it. So, he hired me to be the pastry chef there to help scale his business, open up new places, and open up a production facility, just everything. So, I moved to Florida. That was in Fort Myers, Florida.

RICH: Oh yeah? We were repeat visitors for twenty-five years to Sanibel Island, Florida, across the causeway from Fort Myers.

NATHANIEL: Oh yeah! That's great. Do you know Daniels Parkway? Have you been to dinner at Norman Love's? It's in the airport too. Like if you're coming from the airport and you go north it's right there where that road and Daniels meet.

RICH: We have three children. They're grown, but we found out that we didn't have a need to go anywhere else but Sanibel Island. They were so happy to go to Sanibel.

NATHANIEL: If there's not a hurricane, the shelling there is unbelievable. I liked the Ding Darling Wildlife Refuge also. That's a great place!

RICH: We loved it. I can tell that you have the same sensitivity as I do about things like that. There really are so many important and valuable places in the world like that, that make life better, ones that renew your mind, your spirit, and everything.

RICH: You know, I've been so fortunate to meet so many bakery people. I've met such a variety of people in doing this. For instance, Connie Wolf who does the interviews with me sometimes, her family's bakery was in south city, and she was the youngest of sixteen children. So, when I interviewed her, she got so excited about the "Bakery Book Project" she said, "Well, I could do a lot of things for you." So, there's just such a variety of people who I've met. That's been a great part of the fun of it.

NATHANIEL: Everybody's got different ways. You know, I think that's the fun part about life. And like they say, the drive and the adventure of it is sometimes better than getting there.

RICH: Oh yeah, exactly. Whenever you do anything creative, you experience that.

NATHANIEL: What are some of the other questions you have for me?

RICH: Well you know, maybe it's kind of an absurd question, but I guess the way I've asked people in the past is this, "Is there a signature item that you are most proud of, maybe one that you really like the most?"

NATHANIEL: Yeah, we have about one hundred-twenty products that we make here every day, which is crazy, and during the holiday times it can even go up closer to one hundred-fifty. It's important to know that we have that many varieties of products. We're making them all here, and we're making the base products for them.

NATHANIEL: Like, we have a Camille cake. It's yellow. It's a lemon cream mousse cake. It's lemon mousse and it's almond cake. So, part of the recipe to make almond cake is to have almond paste. So, we make our own almond paste. We cook almonds with sugar syrup and grind it together to make the base that everybody else would buy ready-made.

NATHANIEL: We make that, and then we take that as an ingredient in the next step of making the almond cake layer that's in the cake and flavoring it with natural flavoring without almond extract or any of that stuff. Then, the cake is baked, and then that goes into this lemon mousse cake. So, that's a good example of how this place works.

NATHANIEL: [And then, in an almost accidental, but profound mantra, Nathaniel gives the most concise definition of "made from scratch and on-site," as he says], "*You know, we make the stuff, and we make the stuff that makes the stuff!*"

RICH: And then, I respond, "*I have to write that down!*"

Author's Note: As I am transcribing this interview it occurs to me that this would be a perfect slogan for his bakery's signage and anything else that goes out from his business on printed matter! "*We make the stuff, and we make the stuff that makes the stuff!*"

NATHANIEL: So, it's interesting. That's why we've been able to have people in the kitchen from Connecticut, South Africa, Japan, Nashville, and New York. And, that's just right now. In the past we've had two people from Seattle. It's interesting that people are coming from all of these various places. They realize what's special and what's unique about this place, and they're coming here to be a part of something like this. *And, coming to St. Louis!*

NATHANIEL: *You know, I take a lot of pride in the Midwest! But, I think a lot of people from here "don't," and it drives me crazy. They don't realize what they've got. It really is*

one of my large frustrations. I'd tell everybody I just moved here from Florida, and I used to live in California. Some people would say, "Why did you move here?!" And then, I'd say to myself, "I don't think you must have loved here. You must not have really loved here if you don't know how special this place is!" Like, you don't know what you've got until it's gone. I LOVE IT HERE!

NATHANIEL: So, we've got all of these people who have moved from all of these big markets because they realize what we're doing here and what's special here.

NATHANIEL: So, it's hard to pick a favorite signature item, sort of like how you would pick a favorite from sixteen kids probably, right?! [I figure that Nathaniel is making a reference here to some earlier information about the sixteen children in Connie Wolf's family]. [As Nathaniel is pointing to one of his best creations, he says], "My favorite is pretty simple. It's this actually, and I'm going to send one of these home with you. This is my favorite thing that we make, and it's not the most glitzy or glamorous thing by any means. It's a milk chocolate, hazelnut pound cake."

RICH: O.K., Wow! Thank you very much. That's so nice of you.

NATHANIEL: You're welcome! So, the pound cake inside is a hazelnut pound cake with fresh lemon and orange rind inside. So, we bake that all off. And, when that has been baked off, we dip it in the milk chocolate with caramelized hazelnuts on the outside. So, you have this wonderfully moist hazelnut with a little bit of light citrus acidity to the pound cake. And then, the outside is covered with milk chocolate. What gets better?! It doesn't get better than that! You take that with the coffee in the morning or just at night, you know. But, to me it's one of those things you can eat all day! And, I really like hazelnut milk chocolate. It's so flavorful.

RICH: Well, I think I got that right, chocolate hazelnut pound cake, right. Well, thank you very much. We'll share this. My wife's birthday is next Monday.

NATHANIEL: [As an example of Nathaniel's commitment to quality he emphatically urges me to eat the pound cake sooner than my wife's birthday!] "Well, eat it before then. It should be eaten in the next three days." So, let me know what you think of it. That's my favorite thing. The other is probably the chocolate chip, pecan cookie. That's probably what I eat the most of, either that or the brownie.

NATHANIEL: The pecans, they're from a farm in St. Charles. They asked me when I talked to them, they said, "Well, what size do you want?" And I said, "I don't care about the size. Which one tastes the best?" And, they ended up sending me this little one. I've never seen them like this before. There almost round, the shape of the pecan. They're just gorgeous. They're all named with some kind of native American name. I forgot which varietal it is. They're unbelievable. They taste like butter and pecans.

RICH: This is an embarrassing admission, but I never knew that there were varieties of pecans.

NATHANIEL: I didn't know there were as many as I found out there are, I can tell you that. But, they usually want to grow those big, fat, long ones like this. You know, this is an example of how we think and how I run this place, because everybody wants the big, nice-looking ones. Who cares if it's big?! Tell me which one tastes the best?!

It turns out that they're the little bitty, short dumpy ones that nobody else wants. I'll take 'em all, you know! [And, at this point Nathaniel somewhat grins in a triumphant sort of way.] And, they sent them to me, and they were absolutely right. They're the best pecans I've ever had in my life! They were so good.

RICH: Let me make sure I get something else here. The first item you mentioned was the cake with the almonds. What was the official name of that?

NATHANIEL: Oh yeah, I was just telling you how we make the almond paste. The name of it is the Camille. And, it's a lemon, almond, and raspberry cake. And, the lemon curd that we make for it. It's made from fresh lemons that we juice here. We don't buy a bottle of lemon juice or anything like that. We juice our own lemons, we zest our own lemons all fresh, make the lemon cream like a lemon curd, and from that we lighten it with whipped cream. So, you go home at night, and you smell like all lemons because you just juiced two cases of lemons! [Then, Nathaniel laughs.] But, that's the difference, right?! You know, it's easy to buy a jar, you know how lemon juice is after it's sat for a day or two, it's like iron or something. It doesn't taste like that bright, fresh taste. So, we juice it, the next day or on the day we're making the curd. And, it's done, that's it. We don't keep it.

RICH: I thought of another question for you. The people you have working here must be really bright people, to be able to learn and digest so much information, and to make it happen, to put it into action.

NATHANIEL: Mmm-m, yeah, I think so.

RICH: I can't imagine. You'd have to have really good apprentices.

NATHANIEL: Well, yeah, we're lucky. I really try to hire good, quality people, and then I train them in their assets.

NATHANIEL: *For me it's about the person, high integrity people who have a passion for service whether they're in the kitchen or they're out in the front because customer service is number one. And, they have to have a good spirit of working, you know, a good work ethic.* The high integrity is very important. You know, you want to work with people that you want to be around, right. So, we hire a certain thing about this work culture. It's about *being here.*

NATHANIEL: Hiring people that are good people, good-natured people, respect people. And then, we train the talent, I mean the talent of the hand skills. We can train somebody in how to make cappuccino. That's my job. We teach them how to make a cappuccino, how to make this cake, how to make this and that. And then, we're lucky that not only do they normally have that part of the puzzle, most of them have a fair amount of a good skill set too that goes with it. But, the first part is more important than the second part. I can't change the first part, I can only change the second part.

RICH: That's right! That goes so much with something that I have always said to the administrators that I have worked for in schools, that when you're hiring, hire nice people, people who can work with other people because you can teach them everything else! They need to be capable of course, but it's an essential starting point, and if they don't have that, then it kind of ruins everything else.

NATHANIEL: Yeah, you can't undo forty years of how a person thinks, I agree, or how their parents or how society raised them.

RICH: There were three things you said were important — high integrity, service-oriented, and I'm not sure?

NATHANIEL: A good *work ethic.* As many bakers have already told you, it's a hard job, and it doesn't change. No matter how many machines they invent or how many holidays you don't work, it's a hard job. There's no way around it. It's a trade. You know, it's just like being a carpenter or being another craftsman, it's a trade.

RICH: Yeah, it's astounding. So, there's just beautiful people out there who are the bakers. That's a consistent thread, you know, and I think it goes with the job. You can't do the job if you don't care about people.

NATHANIEL: You actually can, but you're just not going to be able to stay in business for thirty years to be interviewed by a man like you. You know, you're not interviewing the people that had a bakery besides me that were open for three years. That's just because we're still in business. You know what I mean. *People lasted because they had a foundation of what they believed in. They appreciated their customers, and they obviously did something right with how they baked.*

NATHANIEL: Just like you've seen here, you have people coming in with their kids, who are pressing their faces up against the macaroons on the glass. It's such a riot. *The reward is going to be twenty years, twenty-five years, thirty years from now when that kid comes in with their kid.* That's the reward, and that's the reward I'm invested in. You know, it's not just seeing this kid grow up before our eyes, but it's that long-term thing of her coming in someday and telling her kids that this is where she used to come in with grandpa or somebody like that! And, that's special. [At this time Nathaniel seemed to get pretty emotional about this vision of the future that he was describing!]

RICH: That's exactly the reward, right!

NATHANIEL: That's special! Yeah, that's the kind of environment that we want to harbor, that makes those things possible.

RICH: One of the first interviews I had was with the Smith family from way south at the Carondelet Bakery. I taught all of their daughters. I've taught several baker's daughters at Notre Dame High School, an all-girls high school. It's really funny. Sometimes it's one of the best ways to get an interview. [And, we laugh together.] "I taught your daughter, can I interview you?!" The Smith family from the Carondelet Bakery are wonderful people, and they're on record to have been the oldest continuous running bakery in St. Louis.

NATHANIEL: They had a movie made about them, right? A short movie?

RICH: *Yes, "Bob the Baker." It's on YouTube.* It started out as Doering's Bakery and then became Carondelet Bakery. But, Bob passed away. Before he passed, they made that video of him. He was an endearing man. Is that what you were thinking of?

NATHANIEL: Yes. I think they won some awards for that short film. Yeah, it shows him in the morning getting ready for the day. I'm pretty sure it's the same thing.

RICH: You know, I came across a bakery on-line that I didn't even know existed! Finally, I remembered the name from my youth. It was called Teutenberg's, and I think they were in or around the Union Market, right in the middle of downtown. They had six generations of Fred Teutenbergs. They would also be tough competition for the distinction of being the oldest bakery in St. Louis. They claimed to be there for hundreds of years.

RICH: Well, you have been wonderful to talk to. I'll leave these questions here, and if you think of something else, you can let me know. I've sometimes referred to [what it's like to be working on this bakery book project] that it's like "riding an octopus!" [And, we both laugh!] But you know, I came across a really nice guy at a Schnuck's grocery store. He was an on-site baker, and he was a really neat guy. And, I thought that maybe I should get the other side of the story from somebody like that because they're just trying to make a living too.

RICH: Have you ever heard of Jaudes Bakers Supply? They were in business for eighty-seven years. He had so much information, and he knew all of that because he, his dad, and his grandpa sold supplies to all of the bakers during the heyday of the independent bakeries in St. Louis. They knew everybody. So, it was really interesting.

NATHANIEL: *Well, I can't wait to read it myself, to see everything that you put together.*

RICH: I think it will come together. The problem is that I'm enjoying these interviews so much that I don't want to stop. [And then, we laugh together again.]

NATHANIEL: That's why you'll have to do different volumes, or maybe go to a different city! Maybe Chicago! [And again, we laugh together.]

RICH: Oh no, no! There's so much to do in St. Louis, you know!

NATHANIEL: Thank you for telling me these stories too! I'm interested in hearing about all of these things that I don't know about! But, thanks also for sharing *our* bakery stories with your book!

RICH: Yeah, I loved talking with you. And now, you should go home to that new little boy, [meaning the little boy that was just born to Nathaniel and his wife].

NATHANIEL: Oh, I'm gonna' be here for a little while longer. But, if something else comes up you have my e-mail. Do you like figs by the way?

RICH: Yeah, I do!

NATHANIEL: O.K., I have a fig jam I'm going to give to you! We make all of our jams here.

RICH: Oh, thank you! That's awesome! [At this time Nathaniel walked over to his display case and gathered not only a jar of his bakery's fig jam, but he also asks me if I saw anything in their display cases that I would like, and I had a very ready answer.] I told him that I love Palmiers! He then gets a big bakery box and fills it with not only the fig jam and two Palmiers, but also a loaf of his favorite chocolate almond hazelnut cake, plus a lemon raspberry pastry!

Author's Note: I was blown away by Nathaniel Reid's generosity and his gracious manner, both by his freely giving his time and candid conversation and in the kind gift of his own bakery items! I was very thankful.

Pfeifer Bakery
Interview With Rosemary Myers Pfeifer

I wanted to ask you about some kind of sponge cake that was your specialty at
Pfeiffer's Bakery.
Oh, it was called the
Black Forest Cake
...It was made with a yellow
sponge cake, and we didn't use cherries.
We used strawberries instead because grandma and grandpa
had been to Germany.
Grandpa had become familiar with the Schwartwalder Torte,
the Black Forest Cake. So, that's how we changed the Black Forest Cake.
— Rosemary Myers Pfeifer

ROSEMARY: There was a baker over in East St. Louis named Deck, but he couldn't speak the language. He couldn't make himself understood. So, he came over to North Kingshighway and opened a bakery there. Carl Pfeifer and another man worked for him. Later, Carl, my father-in-law, bought him out. Basically, the store was right across the street from the old Blessed Sacrament church on North Kingshighway, north of the old McBride High School. They lived upstairs. And grandpa said to his wife, "If we're gonna' make this go, you're going to have to come and help me." He knew that he couldn't take care of the customers and still work in the back doing the baking.

RICH: Mary Anne Horst, who is a good friend of mine, said that you and she are good friends and cousins. She said that your first bakery on North Kingshighway was known for making soda bread.

ROSEMARY: Yes, yes, Irish Soda Bread. People would come in every St. Patrick's Day, and the Irish who would come in said that we had one of the best Irish soda breads. [Rosemary laughs at this time.] They would always say that the Germans made the best Irish soda bread! Funny, I just saw that recipe somewhere. So, they were there on North Kingshighway for close to twenty years.

RICH: Yes, so Blessed Sacrament was an Irish parish, right?

ROSEMARY: Yes, definitely. There were Irish all around there. So, grandpa Carl had some problems with bursitis, because he did a lot of things with whipping cream and had to whip things by hand. And then, he closed the business for awhile. And then, they moved up on Riverview, grandpa and grandma and my husband, Richard. When grandpa was retired he would go up to St. Stanislas, the Jesuit seminary, and he would teach some of the brothers how to do some baking. There was a Brother Eiffinger out there. He had a lot to do with the grapes, because you know they made their own wine. Well, grandpa taught him how to do some of the baking, and sometimes they would even take stuff that was left-over from the store out to St. Stanislas for the seminarians.

ROSEMARY: So, then they moved and opened the bakery out on Clayton Road in 1949. They opened it when my husband was graduating from high school. Before he moved the bakery, grandpa asked my husband, would he come out with him and work in the bakery. Well, my husband wasn't really a student per se. So, my husband kind of hemmed and hawed and eventually said he would.

RICH: Do you think he had any idea about what he was getting into? [Laughter.]

ROSEMARY: [Laughing, but rather emphatically she says,] No, no, he had no idea. But he still said, "Yeah, yeah, sure I'll come and work for you." And then, he ended up working there for 40 years! Yeah, so they were in business altogether around 60 years.

RICH: So, he was on Clayton Road for how long?

ROSEMARY: From 1949 to 1989, for 40 years. Grandpa bought the building on Clayton Road, and after the first year he bought part of the storefront on the side of him and expanded the bakery.

RICH: I wonder if those buildings are still there? I wish I had known about Pfeifer's Bakery, and I wish I had gone there.

ROSEMARY: Well no, you lived south, and you had all of those good bakeries down south. Oh yeah, Kitchen Conservatory is in the building now. The bakery was right across the street from the Tropicana Bowling Alley.

RICH: Rosemary, you can help me out here. I'm trying to picture where all of the Clayton Road bakeries were. I know Armin's was on the corner of DeMun and Clayton, but I can't figure out where the other ones were. I know there was Armin's, and then Lake Forest, Pfeifer's, and Andres.

ROSEMARY: Well, Lake Forest was just down the hill from Hanley on Clayton Road, and then we were next down the hill before Brentwood. And, Andres was actually on Brentwood south of Clayton Road on the east side of the street. It was kind of funny that we were so close together with Lake Forest because people would get us mixed up. They'd come to us for things that they wanted to get from Lake Forest, and they'd go to Lake Forest for things that they thought they could get there that were really from us. So, we just had to tell them, "No, that's not us. You have to go up the road to get that." There was a family who originally opened Lake Forest. What was their name? Oh yes, Shatkin.

RICH: Yes, Mr. Schmeimier told me that was the name.

ROSEMARY: And then, a man named Walter Bender took it over.

RICH: Now, I wanted to tell you something important while I think of it. I was very sick for about a year and in the hospital for a pretty long time. But, what I wanted to tell you was how important it was for me to have people come in and bring me communion. And, I know that you do that!

Author's Note: In her retirement Rosemary brings communion to homebound people or to people in hospitals.

ROSEMARY: Yes, I do visits and I bring the Eucharist to people. Yes, I enjoy it. It's very rewarding to me. As I go I say, "Come on, Jesus — here we go!" [At this point Rosemary smiles with a little twinkle in her eye!] And then, sometimes I bring the pix with me and I forget to take it back. So, then I say to him, "Oh, I forgot. So, you're coming home with me!" [Another twinkle in her eye.] Yes, I go to St. Mary's Hospital. It's nice to know that it meant so much to you.

[At this time, Rosemary got out an album of black and white photos of some of the people who worked in Pfeifer's Bakery. And then, she offered it to me to borrow and to take with me. It was so generous.]

ROSEMARY: You know, years ago they'd try to promote the bakeries in any way they could. So, there was a group called the "Baker's Dozen." Heimburgers were in it. McArthurs were in it. Pfeifers were in it. We'd get together periodically. It was more of a social thing. So, one of the things they decided to do was to have a "Miss

HOW OUR HEARTS WERE STÖLLEN

Cheesecake contest." Well, the young lady who represented us won, and her name was Cindy Marklin. She was a senior at Villa Duchesne. We also had a ball dance. [At this time Rosemary showed me some of the pictures that she was going to loan to me.]

ROSEMARY: Grandpa Carl became very friendly with the Jesuit priests. Carl Pfeifer, Jr. was in the Jesuits for awhile, but later came out. And, you can see in these pictures all of the fancy cookies that we'd make at Christmas. And, who would come and pack these cookies with us? The Jesuits, because grandma and grandpa would always take bakery goods down to West Pine, at St. Louis University. See here were some of the stöllens we would make, Rich. And, here were some of the people who worked in the store. This lady stayed with us almost until we closed.

ROSEMARY: [We continue looking at pictures.] I don't know who all of these people are, but we would have it all organized for them to pack Christmas cookies. Each person would have a certain kind of cookie to put several in the box, and then they would pass it on to the next person. Then, we would wrap them in Christmas paper, one and two-pound boxes. [Rosemary continued to show me people in the pictures that were friends of theirs. She didn't remember some of the names of the people, but she <u>did</u> know how many years and length of time they had been part of the bakery!]

RICH: You know, Roy Schmeimier was telling me that they were very loyal to their employees, and their employees were very loyal to them. It seems like local businesses had more of these kinds of relationships than the big corporations did. You just don't seem to see that loyalty anymore.

ROSEMARY: Yes, this one woman was with us all the way to the time we closed, and she was with us shortly after we opened. You know, at one point my husband decided that we were going to sell wine. And, this was what he drew up for a store display wine rack. And you know what, it's on the wall in our dining room. And, when the store closed it came home to our house, and I did not want it. I hated, hated, hated it! So, then it came to this house, and now that my husband passed away I can't get rid of it. Yeah, at that time we had wine and cheese and gift baskets.

RICH: And now, I want to share something with you. When I talked to Roy Schmeimier, he showed me and loaned to me a cookbook called, The Route 66 St. Louis Cookbook. It's a fantastic book that highlights about ten of the major bakeries in St. Louis, and you know what, Pfeifer's Bakery was one of them!

ROSEMARY: Oh yeah, here's something else that mentions Andres Pattiserie and Tea Room. And then, there was Grau's near Hampton. And then, there was Missouri Baking, and Cravings was in Webster on Lockwood. Then, there was Lafitte's, but they're gone. Well, were you familiar with Blatt's, Elmer Blatt's. That was on Hampton as well.

RICH: No, I don't think so. What is that publication that you're reading from, Rosemary?

ROSEMARY: It's St. Louis Dining, Issue Number 6. Oh yeah, here is a picture of that lady who was with us for so many years, even on the last day we were open. And here is Anthony Bommarito. He would come in.

RICH: Anthony Bommarito from Tony's, the high-end restaurant?

ROSEMARY: Yeah, Anthony Bommarito. He was a good friend. And, of course we had the wines for sale. Yes, before he did anything else, you know, he added in teas, and he started with Constant Comment, even before it became so popular. Then, he got candles. And then, we got paper goods. He was trying to make it so that when people came in they could get everything at one place if they were entertaining.

ROSEMARY: And then after that when people weren't coming to the bakeries as much as they used to, that's when he came up with the idea of adding wine and cheese. Then, he added gift baskets because you could have the wine and cheese and bread for the gift baskets.

RICH: You know, so many of the bakeries developed these side items, especially the ones with the delis that they added to their stores. Lubeley's did it, Schmiemeir's did it, and Chris Helfer did it on the north side. You know, he's still in business, and he is such a nice man. All of these people are so nice and they're always willing to talk about their stores!

ROSEMARY: Yes, because they're <u>proud</u> of what they've done. You know, my husband always used to say, "We're not only a business, but we are a manufacturer. We have to make our products before we can even sell our products." And, like I've said, it was really hard. What's interesting is that everybody had their own little niche. You know, when we were on North Kingshighway we did a lot of work with caterers and cateresses who had their businesses out this way in West County. So, that was one of the reasons why we came out west on Clayton Road. Another reason that we moved was because of Byron Cade, a florist and gift shop, that was near us a couple of blocks away. Well, they moved out first to a location on Clayton Road at DeMun. Grandma knew Mrs. Cade very well. So, I guess Mrs. Cade probably talked to grandma and told her that they should come out on Clayton Road.

RICH: You have done a great job already of telling me about the family business. But, one of the things that I feel is an important part of the big bakery story is the downfall or demise of the independent bakeries. And, I think everybody knows that it was at least partly the development of the supermarkets that became competition for the bakeries.

ROSEMARY: Oh absolutely, absolutely. Without a doubt they cut in. Yes, and I think another thing was that a lot of women started working. You know, when they were at home, the housewives could go to the bakery every day. But, the woman who is working outside the home doesn't have time to be going every day. So, she would go to the grocery store, and she was gonna' pick-up what she needed from their bakery.

RICH: Sure, one stop shopping.

ROSEMARY: So, that hindered the small independent bakery. But, then you have the week-end come, and you've got everybody coming in on the week-end to pick-up the items that they wanted. So, during the week, business was dead. Nobody was coming in. Of course, when the holidays came, you really couldn't handle it. And then, you have Sam's and Costco, and what do they have? They have a lot of the frozen things and things that are pre-cut. Well, if I'm a housewife in those times that's what I'm looking for. No, they didn't have to make it. They bought it! It's pre-made. Another important thing was the mixes. With these you can make it yourself. You know, you can buy the pie crusts. You can buy the filling.

RICH: Yeah, and the cheaper choice was homemade box cakes, right?

ROSEMARY: Yes, and I didn't have to go anywhere. And then, the icings started to come in, the ones in the cans, and so on! Well, like anything else, life changes. Just like when they came out here from North Kingshighway. Life changes. And, that's something that my husband said, "Maybe we should have changed. Maybe we should have opened earlier. We didn't open until 10:00 o'clock in the morning. If we had changed to open earlier maybe we could have gotten some of the people on their way to work. Maybe we should have eliminated some of the items we'd sell. These are things you think about — 'maybe, maybe.' And, we were closed on Sunday and Monday. Maybe we shouldn't have been closed on Sunday." Most people were home. They were off of work.

RICH: Those were all big decisions, weren't they.

ROSEMARY: You know, they are all decisions, but you do your best. You just don't know, you just don't know at the time. And, even though the business was ours, his dad worked for him. His dad and mom both worked for him. They were there, and of course it was <u>their</u> business. They built it up. It was their baby. Well, you know, after we got married and after we had our first child they asked me to come and help at the store. And you know, grandma was really the face of the store. So, grandma gave me a desk behind hers in the back of the store, and I got to lick the envelopes! She would hand-write the bills, all of the personal charges, and I got to lick the envelopes. So, I said, "You know, I can lick the envelopes at home." So, I didn't go back to the bakery for awhile.

ROSEMARY: Well, look at Panera. When they started they just did sourdough bread. And, my husband said, "They're not gonna' make it just on bread." And, look at them now. They are thriving, and it's just a very well-run organization. It's a national business, and they started in St. Louis.

RICH: Yes. You know, my dad was in the restaurant business, and he always said, "It always depends on whether you've got the right formula." And, Panera's definitely has the right formula!

ROSEMARY: Absolutely, absolutely. You know, the man who started it knew nothing about baking.

RICH: Well, Roy Schmeimier thought that the man who started it was a lingerie salesman.

ROSEMARY: Yes, they were in retail, something in retail. And you know, one of the man's brothers, or somebody in the family, was a pilot, and I heard that he was in San Franciso and brought back the starter dough for the sour dough bread. And, a big part of it is in packaging for them. People want to come in, and they

want to pick it up because they don't want to wait! [Rosemary laughs.] And so, it's a different life. You know, the bakeries today, when they say "bakery," they mean something different from what we think of as a bakery, an old-time bakery. They're specialty stores. And, you know I appreciate what they do. I always want to be respectful of that. You know, it's a craft, and it takes time. People today don't know that, and they don't appreciate that. Don't get me wrong, some people do appreciate it. Yes, it takes money.

RICH: I was just amazed when I talked to Roy Schmeimier. He said that he provided half of the Baskin-Robbins places in St. Louis with the things they needed from a bakery.

ROSEMARY: Yes, well we served Busch's Grove. Every day they got fresh rolls from us and fresh pies. Every day. And, that was for a long time that we serviced them. We also served a lot of your catering companies and a lot of your nice restaurants. You know, they have a great program for cooking at Forest Park community college, great culinary as well as pastries. It's a junior college certificate program, but they do a very good job.

RICH: Now you know, O'Fallon Tech high school had a very good apprenticeship program in baking. And then, the top national school seemed to be the one up north called The Dunwoody School.

HOW OUR HEARTS WERE STÖLLEN

ROSEMARY: Well, my husband didn't go to a baking school, but his father sent him to a program in Naperville, Illinois. I think it was run by the Wilton Company, and that's where he went to learn decorating. In fact, we sent our son there too. My husband had a real talent for decorating. He had a nice handwriting that would flow.

RICH: *I also wanted to ask you about some kind of sponge cake that was your specialty at Pfeiffer's Bakery. What was it called?*

ROSEMARY: *It was called the Black Forest Cake, and that was one of our signature items. It was different in as much as we did not use the chocolate cake. It was made with yellow sponge cake, and we did not use cherries. We used strawberries because grandma and grandpa had been to Germany. Grandpa had become familiar with the Schwartwalder Torte, the Black Forest Cake. So, that's how we changed the Black Forest Cake. That was all done by grandpa who changed it and adapted it to the American tastes. Carl Sr. changed it.*

RICH: Rosemary, what did you find yourself doing after you got out of "licking the envelopes?!"

ROSEMARY: You mean, after I got promoted?! [We laugh together!] Well, I started by filling the orders. And then, I did the packaging for the special orders, like for Busch's Grove and other places. And then, talking to the customers.

RICH: How much wholesale business did you do?

ROSEMARY: We did quite a bit. Of course, we sold wholesale to the caterers and the restaurants. And, we did do the St. Louis Symphony's New Year's Eve party. And then, we did "The Wednesday Club," down on Lindell. I think it was a group of women. We'd do sheet cakes for them. And, we'd do country clubs.

RICH: Now, I wanted to ask you, "Who created the gooey butter cake?

ROSEMARY: I don't know. All I know is that it was an accident. And, I know Heimburger would say that he did it. But, that was his *schtick*. I do know that we made a good gooey butter cake, and Lake Forest made a good deep butter. So, everybody had their own thing.

ROSEMARY: When grandpa moved to Clayton Road they started doing a lot of the fancier things, and "small" things. We would make tiny danish as well as your bigger danish. So, if people were entertaining, they would want something they could pick-up, you know bite-size.

ROSEMARY: Later when my husband was older my one daughter came over and asked him about the cabinet that had the French pastries in our walk-in, and she asked him if he could remember what they were. Well, not only could he name them, but he could remember which ones were on each shelf from the top to the bottom. Of course, he did, because he was the one who put them in there. We also had macaroons, the fancy kind. We had so much. We had all the fancy things, but we also had all the everyday things. We had donuts, we had danish, we had coffee cakes, we had fancy cakes.

RICH: Yes, Roy Schmiemeir had a name for that. He said that now we don't have very many *full-line bakeries*.

ROSEMARY: No, we don't have many at all. Very few.

RICH: Yes, I would say that McArthurs is close, or actually, is a *full-line bakery*!

ROSEMARY: Yes, they were well-known, I would say, for their decorated cakes and their decorated wedding cakes. They had some excellent decorators, and they would do some things that we didn't do, like putting pictures on their cakes, and so on. But, my husband would say, "We're not doing that." He'd kind of go on and on about it. He'd say, "This is what we do!" [And we both laugh together.] But, McArthur's is very good at wedding cakes!

ROSEMARY: Well, then there's another McArthur's in Kirkwood. [They were closed for awhile.] The other place that was good was Party Pastry out in Ballwin. We would have some trouble with that name because people would be calling Party Pastries, and we were called Pfeiffer's Party Pastries. Later, they moved to Woods Mill and Clayton Roads.

RICH: I have to tell you that all of the stories that I hear are just so good. And, the "big story" about the dedication of the bakers and their kindness to one another is beautiful to me. You know, Roy Schmiemeir told me about a week ago that he managed to get his children out of the bakery business. So, somehow all three of his sons are now working for Mid-Continent Paper.

ROSEMARY: Another name you might want to know about was Jaudes Bakers Supply. We were personal friends with Leo Jaudes and his family.

RICH: Yeah, Jaudes is still in business, and Ron is still in the business. [Jaudes Bakers Supply has since the time of this interview closed.] Roy Schmiemeir said, "If you want to know anything about the bakeries in St. Louis, talk to Ron Jaudes." [I found this to be very true!]

ROSEMARY: We have two sons who worked with us. Our oldest and another son who later became a chef. They knew that they didn't want to work as hard as their father. They saw that he was always on his feet, and he would say to them, "Use your head and not your feet." So, they did.

RICH: Now, were you involved in the St. Louis Bakers Association?

ROSEMARY: Yes, we were. We were also involved with the St. Louis Baker's Co-Op, and we were a union shop. The baker's union was not all that powerful, but they did have a union.

RICH: Yeah, the Baker's Co-Op was an interesting thing, and there weren't very many of those around, right? The idea of the Co-Op was that they could buy things in larger quantities at a lower price, right? So, they could give a discount on things. And then, they would also give a dividend at the end of the year.

ROSEMARY: You know, they didn't carry everything that we needed, but we bought some things through them.

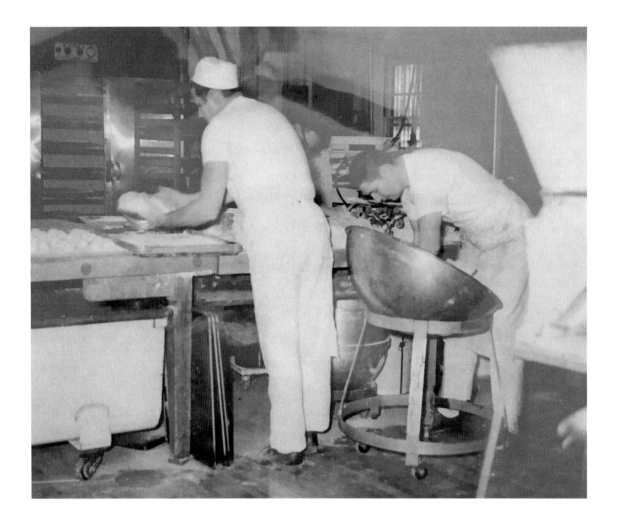

HOW OUR HEARTS WERE STÖLLEN

ROSEMARY: I don't know about that, but we were a union shop. Still, grandpa would tell us, "You can't pay minimum wage. You have to pay <u>more</u> than minimum wage." And then, he'd say, "You have to pay your people a decent salary because they have to be able to support their families!"

Author's Note: I felt that this quote by "grandpa" was another important example of the support and fairness the owners gave to their bakery employees!

Schmiemeir Bakery
Interview With Roy Schmiemeir

From my experience during the interviews
bakers had been really nice people, and they were very proud of what they have
done, which they should be! Here was Roy Schmiemeir's response to my comments:
"It's a nice field because it's creative, and
when people come into your
bakery they are always <u>happy</u>!
Nobody is mad when they get dessert!"
— Roy Schmiemei

Author's Note: This was an exceptional interview with a tremendous amount of information shared by Roy Schmiemeir both about his bakery and about many other bakeries in the St. Louis area.

RICH: Well, I wanted to show you that I'm legitimate. I wanted to show you an interview that I've done with Carondelet Bakery and the Smith Family.

ROY: Oh yeah, Bob Smith — I worked for Bob in that bakery before I went into the business.

RICH: I wanted to show you the McArthur Bakery interview. I feel like I know David and Myndi McArthur pretty well now too, and I've met Randy.

ROY: I don't know if you know it or not, but three of my children work for Mid-Continent Paper Company, and they know a lot of the bakeries. Bob and Kathy Grommet are the owners.

ROY: My son, Darren, is the vice-president of operations, Jeff is the vice-president of sales, and my son, Kevin, is their warehouse manager. So basically, they will know every bakery in St. Louis, Kansas City, and in a multi-state area. They're big time. They have 70 employees, and they operate in about fifteen states, all the way over to West Virginia.

RICH: You know, this "Bakery Book Project" has been a delightful thing to do. I grew up with a love for bakers and bakeries from my grandfather who took me almost every morning to the St. Louis Pastry Shop on Meramec and Virginia avenues. So, this is kinda' like a detective story with the interlacing of all of these bakers and bakery families.

ROY: Yes, and the inter-marrying of so many bakery families. Some of those were the Wolfs and the Millers. You know there used to be a group called the "Bakers Dozen," and they were mostly the retail bakers of South St. Louis County. Two of them, I think, were Bob Lubeley and the Federhofer brothers. The Federhofers had Carondelet Bakery before Bob Smith owned it.

ROY: Lubeley originally had his bakery in Webster Groves, and then that was taken over by Shatkin, and then after Shatkin left, it became Cravings. I believe all of them were in the same location. Yeah, Lubeley's was a family operation, and Bob Lubeley's father began on the corner of Yorkshire Plaza. Then, he and his son moved to the new location just east of Yorkshire on Watson. You know, they closed about a year and a half ago. I think they just decided it was time to get out. It seemed like once the father and then Helen were gone, they just lost their pizzazz to really keep going.

ROY: You know, I managed to get all of my children out of the food business. I told them to find something that's more lucrative and with a little easier hours.

RICH: *Good for you! I know it's a lot of hard work. In my experience with all of the interviews there are two consistent things. Bakers are really nice people, and they are very proud of what they've done, which they should be!*

ROY: *It's a nice field because it's creative, and when people come into your bakery they are always happy! Nobody is mad when they get dessert!* And, customers come to you — you never had to "sell" your product.

ROY: For awhile I did a lot of wholesale stuff, and then I dropped out of that. I used to do, gee, half the Baskin-Robbins stores in town. I did all of their cakes and icings. And then, I did all of the Houlihan's Restaurants in town too. I did the breakfast products for Friendship Village, and then also for Enterprise Leasing. I guess I liked it because of the cash flow. And, you know, your employees always had work.

ROY: The "Bakers Dozen," was like a club. Fred Heimburger was in it, and I think I have some flyers about it somewhere in the house. George Loux had a bakery, but now it's a cupcake business at Delmar and 170. I was open seven days a week, mostly because of the wholesale business. It was at 11744 Manchester Road in Des Peres. We had about eighteen hundred square feet with twenty-two employees.

RICH: You really <u>were</u> in production, weren't you!

ROY: Yeah, we had a lot of people to pay. You may also have heard of a place called Fav-Rite Bakery on Cherokee Street. I was working at Lutheran Hospital, and I went to Fav-Rite to interview for a job. The guy there said, "No, you'll never be a baker!" [At this we both laughed.] So then, I went to work for the St. Louis Bakers Co-Op, which was a supply business. I worked for a guy there named Harold Candy, and we made icings and toppings. At the time I was going to school at O'Fallon Tech, taking decorating and baking. The class was taught by a guy named Jacolleta who was the head baker for Famous and Barr, which later became the Macy's department store. Later, he was running the bakeries in the Venture stores.

ROY: Harold Candy was one of the owners of Busy Bee Candy Company. When I was working for him the guy at the Baker's Co-Op was Armin Schwarz. Eventually he opened his own place called Armin's Pastries across from St. Mary's Hospital at

Clayton Road and DeMun. He used to make a lot of stuff for Cyrano's Restaurant, which was located nearby.

RICH: Armin's was kind of high-end, wasn't it?

ROY: Yeah, well they were serving in the Clayton area. Armin's dad owned the Town Hall Restaurant down the street, and his dad also owned the Three Flags Restaurant in St. Charles. So, he had some ready outlets for his product. Armin also supplied a lot of the fraternity houses nearby at Washington University.

RICH: So, you worked for Armin, right?

ROY: Yes, I worked for him in '63 and '64. I got married in '65 and then I quit and went back to work for Heimburger. *Fred Heimburger was the nicest guy I ever worked for.*

ROY: Fred got his start working at Carondelet Bakery, and at that time it was owned by Herman Doering. Herman Doering and the Federhofers were partners in that business. Then, Bill Federhofer moved into Al Miller's place in Affton. Ed Federhofer then took over the bakery business for Bettendorf-Rapp.

RICH: You know, a question I always have to ask is, "Who invented the gooey butter cake?" A memorable answer I got to that question was, "Fred Heimburger," and an additional part of that answer was, "but he claimed a lot of stuff." [We both laugh.]

ROY: Actually, Fred was a very good promoter, a very good cake decorator, and a very good businessman. I basically worked for Fred for nine years, from '65 to '72. You know, a lot of the bakers were older. Many of them were German. Many of them were Catholic and had larger families. You could list about four families who owned most of the bakeries in St. Louis. Two of them were the Wolfs and the Millers. Al Miller, if he didn't run it, he owned it and rented it to other bakers.

RICH: You mean the smaller ones?

ROY: Yeah, he probably owned half of them.

RICH: But, he was a baker, right?

ROY: Yeah, but he developed the real estate end of it. Have you talked to Ron Jaudes? He comes from a lot of generations of owning Jaudes Bakers Supply. Ron is a really nice guy. You know, there's a pretty big bakery up by Wood River Illinois called Wood's Bakery. Oh yeah, I worked for awhile at Missouri Baking Company making bread sticks.

RICH: You know, one of the questions that's on the interview sheet that I gave you was, "Can you think of any *signature* items that your bakery was known for, any that you were especially proud of?"

ROY: "Hah!" [Roy's wife Judith shouted from another room, and then they both said it at the same time, "German Chocolate Cake!"] We made a lot of German Chocolate Cake! In the old days it was made with melted down dark chocolate. Now they just mix chocolate cake and white cake together and put the stuff on. We used to cook all of the toppings in a steam kettle, melt the chocolate, and fold in all of the egg whites. Those cakes were a lot of work. And, we would make quite a few carrot cakes. You know the reason they're doing it that way now is for consistency, so that it all turns out exactly the same. [And, from the other room Roy's wife, Judith, shouts out], "Don't forget, we sold a lot of decorated cookies!"

ROY: One day a lady came in and said that we ought to make some decorated cookies. After that, and for the next ten years, the business just exploded. We ended up making cookies for places like Enterprise Leasing and the St. Louis Zoo Association, cookies with their insignias on them and stuff. It was nothing to make hundreds of dozens of cookies in a single day. You know, bakers would also buy a lot of cookies to mix in with their own from a place called Cookie King. They would buy ones that were harder to make and more time-consuming like the German made Springerles and Annise Cookies. Just a lot of steps. The German cookies are just a pain, whereas the Italian cookies are mostly made from the same dough. You know, it's very traditional for Italian people to buy big trays of cookies at Christmas time.

RICH: Yes, I've seen that. Our family still makes a lot of cookies at Christmas time.

ROY: I still make seventy-five to a hundred pounds of cookies at Christmas time and give them to neighbors and stuff. I also donate some of them to cookie sales at different churches.

ROY: When I sold my business I told them you can have everything — I'm just taking my sign off the wall!

RICH: I congratulate you for having the good sense to step away from it.

ROY: Well, you can congratulate the one in the other room because I had no intention of quitting. She gave me an ultimatum. I was only fifty-seven, and that's pretty young to retire. After that I went to work with my kids for seven years, part time in a warehouse.

RICH: For Mid-Continent Paper Company, right?

ROY: Yes, at that time they were trying to sell two million a year, and now they sell seventy-five million a year. That's a lot of boxes and paper bags! [At this time Roy went "on a roll" with a whole lot of information.] The girl who was the decorator at my old business on Manchester Road [which is now Bello's Bakery] is Carol Zimmermann. She used to own Sweet Encores. Her dad used to own Brick Oven Bakery in Warson Woods. Before Grau had it he was on Chippewa across from Ted Drewes Frozen Custard. And then, Brick Oven moved out to Fenton, and that guy bought Party Cake Pastries at Clayton and Kehrs Mill Road.

RICH: You know, Roy, I keep telling you that you ought to be writing this book. I'm serious.

ROY: Well, I know a lot of people. [And then, we both laughed together.]

RICH: No, what I meant to say was that you have a "picture" of it.

ROY: It's kind of like Wolf's Bakery on Kingshighway. I grew up there at Kingshighway and Gravois. I knew everybody at Our Lady of Sorrows church. All of us kids played together. In fact, my dad was a doctor and had an office nearby. He used to take care of all of the sisters at Seven Holy Founders even though he wasn't Catholic. Somewhere we've got a couple of framed letters from the Vatican thanking him for all of his free service to the sisters.

RICH: Wow, that's very neat.

ROY: I used to ask him, "How come you never turned Catholic, Dad?" And then, he'd always say, "Naw, it takes too much trouble." He had six kids.

RICH: He could have qualified to be Catholic!

ROY: Yeah, he probably could have! Let's see, I <u>didn't</u> come from a long line of bakers in my family. On your list of questions it asks, "How hard was it to keep the doors open?" Well, I started in '72, and in '73 is when sugar went up to seventy plus cents a pound. The cost of supplies sky-rocketed, and that was a tough couple of years. I can remember a salesman came by and told Fred Heimburger about the price increase coming for sugar. Fred immediately went out and bought 200 bags of sugar.

ROY: So, we had it stacked up everywhere just to save 60 cents a bag! Nowadays, if somebody heard that sugar was going to go up that much, they wouldn't think anything of it! You probably remember when the big supermarkets came in and Warner-Knoll was in the Liberty Market over on Chippewa at River Des Peres. Now there's a Dierbergs there. Well, Warner-Knoll had one of their plants there. They had another plant at Gravois and Kingshighway where the Kingsland Theater used to be. It was also a Cook's Market, and they converted that market into a plant. Most of their cake-making happened at Bettendorf-Rapp in Hampton Village before it became Bettendorf-Rapp.

ROY: Warner Knoll was a big baker, bigger than Lake Forest. Then, there was a major fire in the Cook's Market location, and after that they couldn't survive. At one time Warner-Knoll bought out the Ellerbrock Bakeries. Yeah, at one time they had thirty bakeries and two production plants! That was a big deal when they went out of business. It kinda' shocked me because they were so well-known. They were closing some of their bakeries because they weren't taking in over five hundred dollars a week. Heck, I had to sell three thousand dollars a day just to make my overhead. You know, you could go down Meramec Street and run into another bakery every two blocks!

RICH: Yes when I was growing up, in South St. Louis it seemed like there were four things on every corner — a filling station, a confectionary, a tavern, and a bakery.

[We laugh together.]

ROY: I see on your question sheet, "What about the big superstores getting into the bakery business?" Well, at one time they all got into it. They all thought that was the best way to make money — sell bakery goods. Now, it's groceries, but I don't really see that.

RICH: Yeah, we've sorta' scaled ourselves back in our shopping, and we're especially campaigning against people buying so much of their stuff on-line. There seem to be fewer and fewer of the small local stores, and even some of the big department stores are closing because of people buying so much on-line. And, that's a shame.

ROY: Yes! The different bakers I worked for <u>did</u> seem to care. You know, I worked for Don McArthur, the dad of David and Randy when he was in the city on McRee. When I worked for him he hired a man who was deaf and who couldn't speak. You know, people like that really find it difficult to get a job. And, this man was so good. He could knock stuff out twice as fast as anybody else.

ROY: People need jobs! And, the small local business owners do seem to care more about their employees

RICH: Yes, my dad once told me about a man who worked in the kitchen at St. Mary's Hospital. He was very disfigured from birth, so they felt like they couldn't have him serving out front, but my dad said he was a really good cook.

ROY: Yeah, you and I both know that the religiously affiliated hospitals would hire people like that in housekeeping and other areas. And, parents who had children with learning disabilities could pretty much call "Fr. So and So" and say my kid needs a job. And now, if you have a child like that there's nobody even in your family that has a small business for them to work in.

RICH: I have noticed that Schnuck's and Home Depot are pretty good about hiring people with disabilities.

ROY: Yes, and Dierberg's is pretty good too, if you're sixty-five or older! [We laugh together]. Oh yeah, St. Louis Bread Company is pretty good about that too. You know, the guy who created St. Louis Bread Company, someone told me, was originally a lingerie salesman. In about five years they say it had grown to 20 stores before Panera bought it.

ROY: Somebody else told me that when he sold St. Louis Bread Company to Panera he made about 23 million dollars. Part of the story that didn't get told as well was that he had 22 million dollars of debt. I don't think they ever made a lot of money. I think it was more for good fun until Panera got into it. Now they're big, really big.

ROY: And, Starbucks too. Now, my grandkids tell me at Christmas, "Don't give us anything. Just give us Starbucks gift cards." When I had my bakery, I had a soda machine in the deli. When you bought a canister of soda it cost 32 dollars, but you got 1600 ten-ounce cups out of it. You made the cost of the soda with about 30 drinks, and the rest was profit.

ROY: In the old days bakers would share their left-over products sometimes with employees. In fact, when I was working for Armin's Pastries in Clayton they'd cook a hot breakfast for you every morning. So, it was different then.

RICH: Yes, it seemed so much more personal. I would think you'd feel appreciated.

ROY: Yeah! You always felt like you were kind of attached to the place! So, if my boss said, "Do you think you could stay a couple of hours?" I didn't care. People would come in the back of my store and see me washing dishes, and they would say,

"Aren't you the owner, and you're washing dishes?" And I'd tell them, "That's the nice thing about being the boss. You can do any job you want. I don't mind washing dishes." I used to tell Fred Heimburger that, "I get paid by the hour. I don't care if I'm washing dishes, or sweeping floors, or making cookies. It's all work!" And you know what, Fred never laid you off. I'd clean off all of the canned goods and clean the walls if there wasn't any other bakery work to be done.

ROY: You know, every so often the health department inspector would come by, and I'd say to them, "Aren't you guys gonna' look around?" And he'd say, "No problem, I just came from such and such grade school. It wouldn't be fair. If a school can't be clean, there's something wrong." And then he'd say, "I don't know how you do it, but your place is cleaner than any school that I've seen, and I wish you'd train a few other people in this town."

RICH: Well Roy, how long did you have the deli?

ROY: I'd say about 20 years, and I had ice cream before that. But, you had to be open until 9:00 or 10:00 at night. That didn't go too well, because the kids who worked didn't keep very good track of what they sold. At that time my wife and I made a deal that if the deli did well and made money in the first year, I'd close on Sundays. So, it did make money. We opened up in March and by December we already made 103,000 dollars in profit just on the deli. And, I said to myself, "Where has that been all of my life!" [We laughed together.]

ROY: When you think about it, it was really dumb. We made the bread. We made the dressings. Why not put meat on it? And, all of the other bakeries were doing it, like Lubeley's and The Daily Bread which was right across from my bakery. He had two or three stores, and when he moved in everybody said, "Oh, that's really gonna' hurt your business." It <u>didn't</u>. If anything, it helped our business. We sold more.

ROY: Bakers were <u>not</u> really that competitive. Like with the Kirkwood Bakery with Tony and Mary Baloto, we were both selling to the Kirkwood area. If you needed a bucket of apples or ten pounds of yeast at 3:00 in the morning, you weren't gonna' drive into the city.

RICH: I tried to trace Fred Heimburger through his kids but unsuccessfully.

ROY: You know, his bakery was at South Lindbergh and Baptist Church Road, and he had his house behind it. He used to rent it from one of his relatives. And, his mother used to live where the bank is now, on another corner. And, his uncle owned another corner. So that was a family-owned corner. At one time there were three bakeries in Concord Plaza.

ROY: One guy that I really remember worked for Grau's Bakery for a long time. And God, I admired that man. He was so good. There was nothing that guy couldn't make. His name was Joe Poneth. There were two Joe's that worked there. [At this point Roy called to his wife again in another room saying, "Judith, who was the Joe who worked with Joe Poneth?"] And she responded, "Joe Merton. He had the bakery by the Cinderella Theater." Yeah, I worked with those two old guys, and they were characters.

RICH: Tell me about Joe Poneth. Why was he so important to you?

ROY: There wasn't anything about a bakery that he didn't know. Before he worked in a small bakery he worked for Freund. He knew how to make rye bread. Any product that Freund made he knew how to make it. He was really good. It was all in his head.

RICH: And, what was his story?

ROY: He worked for Heimburger all the time. I would say 90% of all that I learned about bakeries I learned from him.

ROY: He'd always ask me, "What are you getting paid?" I'd tell him, "I'm happy here. I'm making ninety-two dollars a week." You know it was in the 60's. And then, he said, "I'll tell Fred to give you a raise." The next week Joe says, "Did you get a raise?" And I said, "Well, it depends on how you look at it. He didn't raise my check, but there was a twenty-dollar bill in my envelope." That went on for about a year or so.

[Editor's Note: I feel this small episode in Roy Schmeimier's story shows how the bakers loved what they did. I think it also showed the personal quality of their ability to be satisfied with their life and their financial means.]

ROY: And then, one day Fred asked me, "Are you and your wife interested in delivering wedding cakes?" So, I asked him, "How much?" And he said, "Ten dollars a cake, and you can use my car." That was big time money for a part-time job. We'd go to the Biltmore Country Club, or we'd go here and there.

RICH: Yeah, it was a night out, right?

ROY: Yeah, we'd deliver two or three cakes on a week-end. So, we were making thirty to fifty dollars over a week-end above my check!

RICH: That's interesting stuff. You know, some of the stories I love in the Bakers Bulletins are the ones where they talk about taking the wedding cakes to the wedding receptions before they had air-conditioning. And then, in the heat the cakes would all slide and have to be redone at the reception.

ROY: Yes, and couples would want 'em filled with jelly. They'd want raspberry or lemon filling. Oh, and I did even better than that! I can remember taking a cake downtown that was filled with Baskin-Robbins ice cream on the 4th of July! We had to take it in boxes filled with dry ice to a wedding on one of the riverboats!

ROY: I remember this big shot from west county telling us that he wanted a wedding cake, but he wanted something different. So, I said, "What's different?" Holy cow! So, we get downtown, and I tell the caterer, "I've got a wedding cake filled with ice cream, but it's packed in dry ice." With that the caterer says to me, "Well, that's good because we have no electricity!" I said, "What? No refrigeration?!" So, I thought, "How is this gonna' be possible? But, the dry ice held and saved it, and the cake made it through the reception. But I thought, "An ice cream cake on the 4th of July?"

RICH: Yeah, exactly! [And then, we laughed together.]

ROY: You know, I used to take wedding cakes down to hotels in the city and to the Botanical Garden. And, one time one of the caterers asked me, "What do you get paid for a cake like that?" And, I'd say, "About 175 dollars for a 3 or 4-tiered cake." And the caterer just laughed and said, "Do you know that the florist is getting 190 dollars just to put the flowers out?"

ROY: And then, we would go to the hotels, and the waiters would ask us, "How much does your cake cost?" And, I would say maybe 350 dollars." And then, they would say, "You bakers will never learn. We get 7.50 a plate just to slice it and serve it. So, think about it. We're gonna' make 2,000 dollars for serving a cake you only got 300 dollars for making it?!" I thought, "Something's wrong with this picture." But, I was glad to make the 300 dollars. [Author's Note: Another example of bakers living a satisfied life.]

ROY: So then, I talked with my sister-in-law and asked her if she wanted to work on week-ends. I thought I could just rent her out to the wedding receptions. So, I asked her, "Barb, do you want to make an extra fifty bucks by going to the Biltmore Country Club or wherever and you cut the cake for them?"

ROY: You know, there were the Schmidt brothers who had a bakery in Grasso Plaza, and then Wolf took it over. Also, I would encourage you to look up this guy, Ron Jaudes. The Schmidts were somehow related to him.

RICH: Yes, his name has come up again and again in the Bakery Bulletins.

ROY: Oh yeah, oh yeah. It was pretty much known that if you wanted to hire an employee you could tell Ron that you were looking for a baker, and he would know some country club or some place where someone wasn't happy and was good at what they did.

RICH: Yeah, I've got it in my notes that I should talk to Ron Jaudes at Jaudes Bakers Supply Co. [Later I did interview him, and he was amazing.]

RICH: You know, there is so much information here that it kind of blurs together. I lose track.

RON: That's O.K. You can come back and talk to me some other time.

RICH: Do you mean that?!

ROY: Sure, any time that you've got questions about people.

RICH: I'd love to talk to you more. In my mind I get confused if bakeries were in the same area or what, like Lake Forest and Armin's. Were they near one another?

ROY: Yes, Armin's was on Clayton Road at DeMun, and Lake Forest was at Clayton and Hanley. And then after you went out a little farther you got to Pfeifer's and then Andres. Pfeifer's was on Clayton Road almost at Brentwood.

RICH: O.K., let's get this straight. Who was involved in the Lake Forest Bakery?

ROY: That would have been Walter Bender and Walter Schukardt. They were partners. The bakery finally closed, but there's still Lake Forest Pastries. Actually, they used to buy all of those from Clayton's Bakery.

ROY: At one time though Lake Forest was a bakery to envy. Lake Forest, "Boy!" I'd get five bags of sugar, and they'd get thirty bags, and hundreds of bags of flour every week.! They could really sell some stuff. At one time they had twenty-five bakers!

ROY: Yeah, they were down the hill a little bit west from Hanley and Clayton. And then, when you got down to the bottom of the hill you had Pfeifer's Bakery, which was also known kind of like Andre's, the one on Clayton Road across from Galleria. But Pfeifer's Bakery was really known for gourmet stuff!

ROY: Pfeifer's son moved to California and opened up a hamburger bun production plant. He supplied McDonald's in California, millions of 'em. They were kind of like Haas, but way bigger than Haas which was here. So, there were three bakeries on Clayton Road within a distance of a mile, and they all did well! The oldest one was Armin's across from St. Mary's Hospital because they still used a brick oven in the back. It used to be wood-fired. When I worked there it was oil-fired, and before that it had a stoker. If you want to see a brick oven go down to Carondelet Bakery. They've got three of them, and they're all underground. Yeah, Bob Smith was the nicest guy in the world. He used to serve Royal Orleans and Genesis banquet centers.

RICH: Yes, his wife, Linda, is such a nice person. You know, there was a video on You Tube called, "Bob the Baker." It's about Bob Smith, and it's really charming!

ROY: You know, I've got a couple of eight-track tapes I think somewhere in the basement that I made for Channel 9, (the PBS channel in St. Louis), on how to make donuts and fry 'em and all of that stuff.

RICH: Wow! And, they're on eight-track tapes? What do you play them on?!

ROY: I've still got an eight-track tape player! [And, we laugh together.]

RICH: You need to get those transferred to another medium!

ROY: I probably should for my grandkids. They were all born after I got out of the business. My oldest grandson is twenty-one, and he was only three at the time. So, I've been out of the business for eighteen years now.

RICH: Chris Helfer said that I should really talk to people at Mid-Continent Paper Company. Do you think I should?

ROY: Yeah, Chris Helfer knows my kids.

RICH: Do you think they'd be willing to talk to me?

ROY: I'm sure Jeff would. He's a talker. He could tell you where every bakery in town was. Also, Ron Jaudes! As the old saying goes, "he would be the guy who knows whose check is good!" Ron knows everybody if they're in the bakery or restaurant business, a very nice guy. Like I said earlier, he was a CBC graduate. He just retired in the last year and a half. I told him one time, "For gosh sakes, Ron, you're seventy-seven years old." And then he said to me, "Well, my dad was still running the office until he was ninety and playing golf every day!"

RICH: Was Jaudes Bakers Supply a pretty successful business?

ROY: Yes. They were on South Broadway, and it was a <u>very</u> successful business. They had it for close to a hundred years. As Ron used to joke, they would load up the truck on Monday morning and head up Meramec Street starting down on Broadway, and by the end of Meramec they would have emptied the whole truck! And, when they'd deliver to me they'd have about ten stops in three blocks. Sometimes I'd have to tell them, "You know, I can't pay you this week, and I'm already about three weeks behind." And then, he'd say, "Quit worrying, about it — grandpa's not worried." And then, I'd say, "Grandpa ought to be worried. I owe everybody in town!"

Author's Note: I felt this was just another example of how the bakers and suppliers lived within a relationship of trust and co-operation.]

RICH: You know, that's what's so encouraging about the bakery story in St. Louis. The bakers really were a community or "extended family!" That's my starting point, and the picture that I've seen all along the way, and the bakery community in St. Louis seems to really live up to that!

ROY: *Yes, there really was no competition.* You know what somebody said to me at one point? They said, "You know, there's going to be a new Schnuck's store moving in up the street, and they're gonna' be tough competition." And I said to them, "You know, they're really not, because they're not going to be able to compete in the quality of the product. It would be different if everybody was selling gooey butter cakes, but they're not. They're all selling something different."

RICH: *Yes, and that came out consistently in the Bakers Bulletins too. It was amazing, the kindness and help that the bakers showed to one another.*

ROY: *Yeah, if one guy had a good recipe that really sold, almond rings or whatever, he'd just pass it on to the other guy and say, "Here, just try this one out."*

RICH: [Laughing.] I just think it's an interesting and inspiring story. Honestly, I have learned so much. You know I interviewed a man who was involved with the Ellerbrock bakeries. He was ninety-two years old, and his wife was ninety-two also. His name was Richard Marklin. They were so sharp and so helpful with information, and so nice.

ROY: There was also a George Eichelmann who had a bakery on South Grand across the street from St. Mary's High School. And then on Gravois and Loughborough you had Klund's Bakery. Elmer Klund had Klund's Bakery.

RICH: I should put together a map that shows where all of these bakeries were, shouldn't I?

ROY: Yes, you should just take a big blow-up of St. Louis and start putting dots on it!

RICH: Yeah, exactly!

ROY: You know, I was told when I got into the business that there were still five hundred bakeries in the city. And now, it's worked its way down to — and I'm talking about full-line bakeries — to about 30. I mean ones that make wedding cakes, cookies, pies, ones that make everything. There's a lot of specialty shops that just make cupcakes and so on, but not many of the others.

RICH: There are some new ones. There are some young kids getting into the bakery business. Not a lot, but there was one called Black Bear Bakery in the city, and then on Cherokee called Whisk. [Black Bear Bakery is now closed.]

Author's Note: This concluded my interview with Roy Schmiemeir, but with the possibility of more to come. This conversation with Roy Schmiemeir was a tremendously pleasant and enormously helpful interview!

The Blue Owl Bakery
Interview With Mary Hostetter and Connie Wolf

*I love the people, and for me that's what it's about…Make them
happy. If they ask for key lime pie, then make sure we have a key
lime pie…Our whole life is full of God-sends. It really is.*
— Mary Hostetter

Author's Note: The Blue Owl Bakery Interview began with Mary Hostetter describing her mother and father's migration to St. Louis because of a hurricane event that hit Galveston and closed the island for three weeks.

MARY: We were born and raised in Galveston. After the hurricane they went to my brother's first. They called me, and they were crying because there was no place to bathe. They had to jump in the swimming pool. Then, they said, "Can we please just come to your house in St. Louis?" Well, I had begged them to come. So, I flew down, and I brought them back. They stayed with me for two weeks, and they finally said, "What can we do to help you. We don't want to just sit here." So, they came and they peeled apples for the apple pies, because we have eighteen apples in all of our pies [While looking at some photos together,] Mary comments, "This is Kim who runs the bakery now. She runs The Blue Owl. She was six when I started making cookies in my home so that I could support them. So, now Kim is forty-two, and she runs the entire bakery operation. She started here when she was nineteen and grew up in the business."

MARY: [While looking at another picture Mary says], "This was my grandfather, Albert Rothfuchs. He was the head pastry chef at the Galvez Hotel in Galveston, a famous historic hotel. He was also at Boening's Bakery in downtown Galveston, and here are some of his recipes. He and my grandmother came over from Germany, but they met here. He passed away when he was only 38 years old. My grandmother's name was Selma Hinkle Rothfuchs.

MARY: I opened a sweet shop next door in 2009, which was originally a part of our dining rooms. My grandmother lived just around the corner from us. So, every day she would make homemade dinner rolls for us. She would also make cinnamon rolls and streusel coffee cakes.

RICH: So, this is the only Blue Owl location, isn't it?

MARY: Well, this is The Blue Owl Restaurant and Bakery, and my daughter has The Blue Owl production facility in House Springs right at the intersection of Highway MM at the Bucheit store. It is also called The Blue Owl Sweet Shop because it is also a donut shop and a bakery.

MARY: One day Oprah called us, and she wanted to feature us as one of her favorite things for the holidays. So, when they did that Kim told me that we were running out of space there. She said, "We need to look for another location."

MARY: And so, she found this donut shop. The owner then vacated, and we signed a new lease with him. There was a tattoo shop next to the store. After a couple of years the tattoo shop moved out! And then, she was able to take over that space! So, they do a lot of our cake decorating there and a lot of weddings out of there. They do all of our shipping from there because we ship all over the United States, and Kim handles all of that. We have our tasting room there. And then, we have the donut shop and the bakery.

RICH: Did you do a feature with Oprah?

MARY: Actually, we were featured in her magazine as one of her favorite things for the holidays in 2011. but it's not until you're actually in the magazine and it's published and on the stands that you know you're in it. So, that can really hurt people because if you aren't prepared with enough staff, it can kill you. When Oprah says, "This is a great product, and you need this for the holidays," you have to be ready.

MARY: And then, three days later a women's magazine contacted us, and they wanted to take our big apple pie to New York to be on the Today Show and feature it as the best gift to ship from the Midwest. So, that on top of Oprah was absolutely insane. My daughter worked around the clock. Eventually, we had to put out the message, "If anybody wants to earn Christmas money or if you know of any college students coming home, let us know." She had a volleyball team and a basketball team available because one of her part-time bakers was a coach. And, she called them, and there they were, all peeling and slicing the apples.

MARY: And, Oprah had interposed us on her show with the pie, and she talked about it. So, the orders just kept rolling in. In 2006 Paula Deen's sons called us, and they wanted us to be on their show on the Food Network, which was called, "Road Tasted." In order to be on their show they wanted us to send several of our things that they thought would be a perfect fit. And, whatever we picked we had to be sure it could be shipped around the United States. So, when I was talking to the people here I said, "Well, make sure that they don't choose the "Levee High Apple Pie!" So, we sent one of the "Levee High Apple Pies," some smaller pies, and a pastry tray.

MARY: Sure enough, they called three weeks later and said, "We're coming. We're going to film you at your restaurant, and we want you to teach us how to make a 'Levee High Apple Pie' with a caramel pecan topping." And, I said, "Well, we can do that." So, we did that on the Food Network with Jamie and Bobbie Deen. That show was very successful, and that was the first time we had ever shipped pies.

MARY: I put my daughter in charge of that project. So, she had to find out if people really ordered the pie, where we would get the coolers and how we could ship it, baked or unbaked. At that point we didn't even have the proper sized box for the pie. So, we had to have a secure box made for the height of the pie. We had to have two thousand coolers shipped to us, and those coolers had to be in a box. After that, we needed all of the bubble wrap and everything for packing. So, all of that had to be coordinated. She was in charge of the whole thing. Besides that, she had to create a "gift shop" on-line.

MARY: So, the night that the story broke the website crashed because of the number of people who wanted to order the pie! At that point the cost of the pie became 125.00 partly because of the overnight shipping. The cost wasn't because of us, because at that time the pie by itself cost 32.95, but the inflated cost was because of the shipping and packaging.

MARY: I told her, "If it costs that much in shipping there's nobody that's going to buy that pie. So, don't even think about signing a contract with UPS or Fed Ex because nobody is going to buy it!" Well, the first night twenty-five people bought it! I can't even tell you how many pies she shipped. After that it was featured in the Wall Street Journal, and recently it's been highlighted in several places on the Food Network.

MARY: And, it seems like they are going to come again. But anyway, I call them sprinkles from heaven, because God sprinkles us with these little sprinkles to keep us going.

CONNIE: Well, I'd say you've had some pretty big sprinkles!

RICH: Now, you talked about the "coolers." What does that mean? How do I picture that physically?

MARY: Well, what we did was we shipped a pie to my mom and dad to try it out. So, we took a pie that was baked, and we shipped it in a cooler with dry ice. So then, my mom took pictures, and because the crust was so tender it fell apart or sometimes the pie fell in. So, then we decided, "O.K. we have to ship it frozen and unbaked in dry ice." And, we did. So, it's like an eighteen-pound package. They can ship it two-day air now because the dry ice will not melt for two days. So, they've got two days to get everywhere.

RICH: Wow! So many variables!

MARY: Yes! Oh, very much so! And then, we ship pecan pies, butterscotch pecan pies, and I think some cheesecakes and other things. You can go to our website, and our website is "theblueowl.com". So, we ship the gooey butter cheesecake, gooey butter cake, and then the big apple pie. People have to bake it, and they get an instruction card on how to bake the pie. Also, if they want the caramel with it, they get a container of that.

RICH: So, how big is your production plant.

MARY: Well, it's not as big as you might think. [At this point, Mary describes the floor plan of the production plant that fits into two storefront lengths.] Years ago Kim did go out and buy a walk-in oven. You can put a whole rack inside of it. For example, you can fit ninety pumpkin pies in it at a time.

MARY: We used to be here all night baking pumpkin pies before Thanksgiving. Kim runs that whole operation, and I'm right here at The Blue Owl because it's a lot for both of us.

CONNIE: Your daughter runs that operation, but who does all of the logistics of getting the orders and so on?

MARY: She does. We do take orders here, but she provides all of our baked goods. So, I place my order with her, and tell her I need this many cherry pies, peach pies, apple pies, and all of that.

CONNIE: How much staff does she have?

MARY: Probably about 15 people. But, she's a smart young lady. She really is, and she's very business-oriented. I always ran my business not so much from the brain, but from the heart and I continue to do that. I love the people, and for me that's what it's about, just please the people. Make them happy. If they ask for key lime pie, then make sure we have a key lime pie. Whereas, for her the cost of production is expensive. And, if you stop production to make a key lime pie for someone, you're never gonna' make up the money — but her brain and my brain are very different.

MARY: She and the younger generation are different. They watch that bottom line. I just always knew in my mind that if I pleased the customer the money would be there for me to be able to do what I needed to do. And so, that's just how I always did it. So, I'll say, "Everybody always wants raspberry cream cheese pie." And then, she'll say, "Mom, we make it, and then they don't buy it." And, I'm like, "Well, if we had it on a regular basis, or we could tell them when it's gonna' be here, then they would buy it. They'd come in that day."

MARY: What we really should do is have a list and call people when you have chicken velvet soup or you could call them when you have creamy Vidalia onion because they want to know! And, you call them when you have banana split pie, or you call them when you have red raspberry cream cheese, and they will come. I guarantee you they will! But, that's a lot of work. [We agree, and then we laugh together!]

MARY: So anyway, I will have people sometimes now who had a certain kind of cake that we made for a long time like Italian cream cake, and we don't make that cake anymore. Italian cream, carrot cake, Irish apple, and red velvet were our four signature cakes.

MARY: But, I have customers who for years have had that Italian cream cake for their child's birthday or their husband's birthday, and they have to have it! And, do you know what, I go right back there, and I make it myself!

CONNIE: You, personally make it?!

MARY: Yes, personally. I do, because I know how much that means to them! Yeah, to me that's how I built this business. And, I've owned this for 34 years. At first I baked out of my home. Now I have a really beautiful husband! He's such a sweetheart.

RICH: Yes, I read that in your story.

MARY: My husband's name is Jerry, and he's a wonderful man. So, when you go through trials, and you ask God, "Why me?" It's because God had another plan. So, I've been very blessed all my life. But, this is a hard business, a hard business. And, I was a single parent. So, I kept my hours from 10:00 until 3:00. I could work while my kids were in school, and then I could be home in the evening to help them with homework and be there for them. And, I've always kept to those hours because I can help other people working for me who have children so that those people can be home with <u>their</u> kids too. My daughter closes on Sundays. She's very involved in her church, and she feels that's the Lord's day. So, about a year ago she started closing on Sunday. I mean, I'm very loyal to God, and I think God understands. It's the busiest day of our week!

[Mary laughs heartily!]

RICH: Well remember, Jesus even rescued a donkey for someone on the Sabbath!

MARY: And, I always feel like this is a vocation. I don't feel like I have a career. It is dedicated to God, I can guarantee you that! He's led these hands every single day. Without God I could never have been at this point really, I mean to be interviewed by somebody! [Laughter.]

RICH: Well, yours is a great story, and that's what this book is intended to be. Really, a love story about bakers and bakeries. I've interviewed twelve major bakers so far.

MARY: Did you get to interview Mrs. Federhofer before she passed away?

RICH: No, but I taught Cheryl Federhofer. I was a teacher at Notre Dame High School.

MARY: Oh, O.K., you were? Did you know Maria Hoft?

RICH: I sure did.

MARY: Yeah, she was one of my bakers in my home!

And then, she baked for me in the very beginning. She did my cheesecakes, baklava, the Italian pizzelles, and all of that! And then, she would come over to my house sometimes when I had thirty-thousand orders for Christmas cookies!

MARY: When I came to St. Louis I was a thousand miles from home, but I prayed to God, and I said, "Dear God, if you're gonna' take us away from family and friends, and our home state, please let this be a great experience." And, look what He's done!

MARY: So, my neighbors would come over after all the kids were in their beds at night at around 10:30, and they would have rolling pins in hand and wearing aprons. And, I just had a regular oven. I would have all of the Hungarian butterhorns and the Russian teacakes, pecan tartlettes, and all of that with the dough ready. And then, they would roll the dough and make the cookies. Then, I would work the ovens and get all of the baking sheets ready again. I didn't even know about parchment paper because my mom never used it. She always used Crisco! [Mary laughs.] So then, we would bake until around 1:00 or 2:00 in the morning. That way they could make some extra money for the holidays.

RICH: Do you know Maria's Hoft's daughters?

MARY: Oh, yes! Well, Jennifer went to school with Kim, my daughter. And then, Andrea was just a couple of years older.

RICH: Andrea is one of my daughter's very best friends!

MARY: Oh, O.K.! She's beautiful! Isn't she beautiful! I was at her wedding!

RICH: Yes, she is beautiful, and we were at her wedding too!

MARY: Yeah, so I saw you there! [We laugh together!] Maria Hoft was just in not too long ago. She is so sweet. Beautiful people. She used to have us over for spaghetti and meatballs. We had so much fun together. She's a very dear friend of mine. And, she always calls me on my birthday.

RICH: Now, I have to ask the big St. Louis question, [Wink, wink]. What high school did you go to?

MARY: In Galveston I was at Ursuline in my freshman year. At that time Ursuline Dominican, the other all-girls school, and Kerwin the boys school, combined together, and it became O'Connell in Galveston. I had great high school years, great school years period. You know, having Ursuline sisters in Galveston and then having the Ursuline sisters right down here in Crystal City was so good. Before I knew it, all of my high school teachers would bring all of their friends into the restaurant, my 6th grade teacher, S. Anne Marie, S. Teresita, and S. Jane Marie. She was my principal in grade school.

RICH: It is a small, small world, isn't it. Yeah, my mom went to Ursuline Academy in Arcadia, Missouri, and that building is still there. Do you feel like you inherited your baking "gene?"

MARY: Yeah, from my mom and my grandma. I never knew my grandfather. Yes, my mom and my grandma Selma. There were five children in our family, and every one of them love to cook and bake, and it was because my mom and my grandma both used to say, "Come here and help me cut the onions and the celery for the dressing, and let's cut the potatoes for the potato salad." Yes, definitely. They taught me so much. And then, my mom taught herself cake decorating. We didn't have a lot of money, so she taught herself how to make our birthday cakes and all of that. And then, she taught me. I also took a class here in St. Louis.

RICH: Did you take it at O'Fallon Tech.

MARY: No, it might have been at a Karen Ann's, or it might have been at a Michael's store. Actually, it was at Penney's. They used to do it.

RICH: Which Penney's?

MARY: The one at South County. They used to do it downstairs in their basement.

RICH: You must have quite a few decorators?

MARY: Yeah well, it all happens at the production bakery. I think Kim has three decorators. Have you seen all of the cakes? It's crazy, oh my goodness. They do things that you think, "Oh, really?" They sometimes do fifteen weddings in a week-end. It's amazing what they do.

MARY: And, they have a wonderful wedding coordinator. Her name is Laura Costello. [While looking at an album of wedding cakes Mary goes on to say], "I'd love to show you the cakes that they do, but you can just see." They also just did the Stanley Cup cookies for the Blues, for their going-away party.

CONNIE: And, who did you say is making all of these cakes?

MARY: Well, it's at my daughter's bakery, and it's in House Springs.

CONNIE: Your daughter must be something else. See, just the thought of managing all of that, and these cakes, my goodness!

MARY: She doesn't make these. She has a decorator that makes these, but if she had to go in and fix something for a cake or something, she could do that. They have so many cakes. I mean, there's one cake that's more beautiful than the next. A lot of people don't want icing on the sides of the cake. They want it to be naked. If you could see what she did for my little grandson. She has a four-year-old. And then, she has a twenty-two year-old and a nineteen-year-old. So, they do all of the shower cakes too.

RICH: Is she also the scheduler and takes the orders and everything?

MARY: Right. Well, Laura talks to all of the brides and everything. Laura is from the Mangelsdorf family. Laura was a big event coordinator up in New Jersey with her husband. And then, she wanted to come back home. So then, Kim met her, and they hit it off, and she's been with us ever since. She does a beautiful job.

MARY: We get all kinds of compliments because people come in here to eat, and they'll say, "Oh, you did our wedding for us. Your dessert buffet just blew us away. People at the wedding didn't really want to eat food. They just wanted to eat dessert!" That's true. That happens a lot! [And, we all laugh!]

MARY: So, my niece got married, and she wanted us to bring a cake to California. I told her that there's just no way that I could carry a wedding cake to California. I just wouldn't do it. I carried one to Texas, but I was driving to Texas. And so, she went to a bakery in California and got a wedding cake. It was awful. Nobody even ate it, it was so bad. And, I felt so terrible because I thought that was my fault.

MARY: So, it's interesting that they never have anything left over when they serve our cakes. And, I always say, "Well, that's because our key ingredient is _love_!" It really makes a difference. If you love what you do, you do what you love.

MARY: [And once again referring to the wedding cake album of photos, Mary says,] "See, there are some of those dessert buffet items. With that they may just do a small wedding cake. Or, they may just do an apple pie with a sparkler in it for their wedding cake!"

CONNIE: Well, it looks like they custom make each cake for each person!

MARY: Oh, for sure! Definitely so. There just is no ordinary cake that we do.

RICH: No standard models, right?

MARY: No standard models.

RICH: You know, with something this broad and big, you must have a finance person or business person. Kim doesn't do that besides, does she?

MARY: We have an accountant, but Kim handles all of her own books and everything. I don't do that. I have a secretary, and she handles all of the books and all of that stuff for me. And then, we turn that over to an accountant. I just did some of that yesterday.

MARY: I'm going to be meeting right after this with the Kimmswick merchants and with Channel 2. I'm going to be on television at 9:00 o'clock tomorrow morning.

RICH: Are you going to be on "live T.V.?"

MARY: Yes, they have the morning show on at 9 o'clock. On that show we'll talk about Kimmswick being open, that we are open! Because of the flooding this spring and summer we weren't open. Highway K was closed for 9 weeks. It was unbelievable. Everybody had to come in the back way. I mean, our business was so far off it felt like winter. It felt like it should be snowing outside. I took a few days off here and there because I couldn't stand it. We're used to the lines by the doors being continuously filled with people. But, when they saw that Highway K was closed, they just thought that we were under water too. So, people would just turn around and leave.

CONNIE: Because they wouldn't know how to get here, right?

MARY: Well, we had detour signs hung up all along the way. We hung up fifteen detour signs. But then, somebody takes this one down, and somebody steals that one. And then, when they took the closure down on Sunday a week ago, they opened it because the water was far enough off the road that they could come in on Highway K. On that day we had three hundred people. This time of year we should have between 400 and 500 people on a Saturday and a Sunday for sure. But I mean, we're way off as far as numbers go.

CONNIE: Do you ever take a day off? Do you ever go on a vacation?

MARY: No, not really, but once in awhile we do. Yet, my whole heart is into this, because when people walk in the door you just want to be there.

CONNIE: But, you must have people that you can trust.

MARY: [An interesting story!] I can remember the day I got married to Jerry. It was March 11th of 2000. And, I can remember two weeks later somebody came in and they said, "We came in on Saturday, and you weren't here! And, we brought people who were from England. And you were supposed to be here so you could meet them. I promised them that you'd be here." And I said, "When was that?" They sometimes do fifteen weddings in a week-end. It's amazing what they do. And, they have a wonderful wedding coordinator. Her name is Laura Costello.

MARY: We did a post last week on Facebook for Highway K being open so people would know it, and it actually reached 7,250 people. Yes, that many people read it on Facebook. So, hopefully, tomorrow morning we will have even more people looking at Channel 2 showing that Highway K is open!

MARY: [Meanwhile, a pause while Mary looks through the Interview Questions.] So, the bakery that my grandfather, my grandmother, my mom, and aunt worked at was called Boening's Bakery in downtown Galveston. My grandfather was the one who was actually the pastry chef. He came over from Germany, met my grandmother who became a nanny, and then they got married. He continued to be a pastry chef for the rest of his life. My grandmother would cook for all of the wealthy people in Galveston, people like the Moodys and the Feallies.

RICH: What was your grandfather's first name?

MARY: Albrecht, Albrecht Rodfuchs.

RICH: You talked about your signature items.

MARY: [The following are reflections on the flood of '93.] "The Levee High Apple Pie" is the one that has been all around the world, and it continues to be. Actually, the story behind that pie happened because of the flood of '93.

MARY: Instead of building the levee around the back of the places here, they decided to build it down the street high enough to withstand a fifty-foot crest. The water continued to rise. So, we completely moved out for two months. We sand-bagged the house directly across the street trying to save it, but the water got three-fourths of the way up their picture window. So, everything was under water on the other side of the levee.

MARY: When I got up the next morning the levee in Valmeyer had been breached, and that town is right across the river from Kimmswick. So, with that being breached Valmeyer was destroyed, but Kimmswick was saved. The whole town of Kimmswick could have been destroyed. The whole town of Valmeyer was later moved to a spot up above its original location on a hill.

MARY: When we came back we wanted something positive to remember the flood of '93. We were one of the only towns along the Mississippi that was saved. So, we decided to build a pie that resembled the levee that saved the town of Kimmswick.

MARY: [Mary then gave a description of how to make a Levee High Apple Pie.] Well, we took a lettuce keeper bowl from Tupperware, we sliced the apples, and then we put them on top of each other layering it like a beehive. Then, when we came to the top of it we rounded it off. After that we took the 9" pie crust and put apples on it so that there wouldn't be any air or gap between the apples. You know, I taught the Deen brothers how to do this on their T.V. show. Finally, you take that bowl, and you have to flip it in mid-air. And the lip of the bowl has to go right inside that pie crust. You set it down on the counter, and you tap the bowl. And then, you have this gorgeous mound of apples right there. So, it's very beautiful.

MARY: So, when I did it for the Deen brothers, I had to have three pies ready in case something went wrong. You can see it on You Tube. The show wasn't live, but in the middle of the show I said to Jamie and Bobbie, "Do you all want to flip the pie?" I was never expecting them to say yes, but they said, "Sure, we'll do it, we'll try it!" And

I thought, "Oh my gosh, if they miss we're gonna' have to start over." But, they did it. When you have the apples in place all of that juice rolls down and into the pie.

MARY: This whole thing is on You Tube, probably under "The Blue Owl and Levee High Apple Pie." For our 30th anniversary of the restaurant my daughter and our staff gave me a television set, and she had videos of some of our shows that we had been on, like teaching Kent Ehrhardt and stuff like that. So, here I am with the "Road Tasted" crew and the Deen brothers from the Food Network show. Some people tried to play off of our instructions for making the pie. Somebody tried to make what we were making, and it was nothing like it.

MARY: The Deen brothers were darling. They were like down-home, like my little brothers. They were walking down the street, and one of them said, "Hey brother, doesn't this remind you of beautiful downtown Mayberry (the fictional town from the Andy Griffith T.V. Show)?" It was really cute. So, we had a good time. They were here for five hours filming. They even put the caramel pecan topping on the pie. And then, they had ice cream with it.

HOW OUR HEARTS WERE STÖLLEN

RICH: Is the caramel pecan topping sort of the glue that keeps the apples in place?

MARY: No, the crust goes on top of the pie. Do you want to see one? You've got to see it so that you know. [Meanwhile, Mary goes out of the room to get one of the Levee High Apple Pies, and she carries it in to show us.] Do you want to feel it?

RICH: Sure! [And, as I take it nervously from Mary's hands], I say, "Oh, my, it's really heavy!"

CONNIE: That's amazing, really amazing. I wish I could show my dad. Maybe he's looking down from heaven.

MARY: He sees it, believe you me!

RICH: That's right, that's right.

CONNIE: How much does it weigh?

MARY: It weighs about 10 pounds, 18 pounds when they ship it in the cooler and in the box, and in the outer box.

MARY: The apples are all there in the Tupperware bowl. You then flip it over onto the bottom circle crust. All of the apples are there in a big mound. Then, you have your pie crust, and you roll it into a bigger circle, and you drape that over the top part of the pie, and then you go through and flute it and all of that.

RICH: How do you eat it? What's the best way to eat it?

MARY: Oh, you slice it with a serrated edged knife, and we get eight slices out of there.

CONNIE: So, how long did it take you to create that, to figure out how to do it?

MARY: Well, we just had to figure out how many apples to put into it to make it really tight. And then, once we figured that out, it was just a matter of making sure the crust was firm on the apples and that the apples were tight. They're not going to go anywhere, but you have to make sure that it's not slanting. The hardest part for me is the crust on the top and the fluting.

MARY: My grandma would make homemade lemon meringue pies and stuff like that, but my granny on my dad's side would go out and pick the blackberries and the dewberries out of her backyard. Then, she would come in and make a fresh blackberry cobbler. I could taste it right now and have the ice cream with it!

MARY: I mean, we were a food family! We did not have much money. We were probably considered to be poor, but we had a lot of love in our family. Without a doubt we had our faith. We had a great family, a great mom and dad, and food was our one big thing. Their priorities were our faith and our food. Well, faith, family, food, and education. That's how it went. My mom would cook a home-cooked meal for us every night, every single night.

CONNIE: Your family was so much like mine, it blows me away! Those were the priorities, and we had a big meal every night.

MARY: Every night, around the table. We wouldn't think of not sitting at the table! It's the best thing in the whole wide world! Now, when my siblings come to visit, what do we do?! We cook! We cook all the time, and it's like one person after another. We just have fun together.

CONNIE: And, my mom said, "I was the favorite!"

MARY: Me too! They all say that, "Well, Mary was the favorite!" I'll be right back. [Mary laughs loudly, and then walks to another part of the restaurant to take care of something.]

RICH: The favorite, that's a good place to be.

MARY: Faith, family, food, and education, and that was Catholic education! And, my mom didn't even have a high school education. But do you know she was the assistant librarian for Ursuline Academy.

RICH: By the way, Connie was the librarian at the Missouri Botanical Garden.

MARY: Really?! The Botanical Garden? We do their event every year, the "Best of Missouri!" We work hard on that week-end. I'm not kidding you. That's like a sixty hour week-end for us because we go back and forth. Later we have to come back and wash all of the dishes, get everything ready for the next morning, and be back there at 5:00 a.m. We have to be back there because then we do biscuits and gravy in the morning for people. We start that at 7:00 a.m. And, it's crazy.

MARY: And then, my daughter has a second booth. She has one under the big tent right there. She has a big bakery booth. We sell her bakery goods too because then people don't have to go back and forth. But, she has a huge booth there with cakes, cheese cakes, cookies, pies, little mini-pies.

RICH: Did you know that Connie is from the Wolf bakery family and is the youngest of 16 children.

MARY: Oh, my goodness! Wow!

RICH: And, they lived above the bakery!

CONNIE: We did live above the bakery. I will say that we had a very good upbringing, but we were crowded! I have a brother who was a priest and two sisters, and they left the house even before I was born or shortly thereafter. Actually, twelve was the most we ever had at home.

MARY: My mom looked and looked for a house, but couldn't find one to rent. No one wanted to rent to children. And then, the man across the street passed away, and his sister came to my mom and dad and asked if they were interested in buying the house, a house built in 1906, and they sold it to them for 6,000 dollars.

RICH: Talk about a God-send, huh?!

MARY: Our whole life is full of God-sends. It really is. You know, people look back at their childhood and they look back at their teen-age years, and I look back on all of those times, and I was so happy.

CONNIE: You seem like you had the personality of the youngest in your family. You seem like an exceptionally happy person. Were all the people in your family so happy?

MARY: Uhh-h, not everybody. I was just a happy child. I just feel like God was always such a part of my life. I feel very blessed. But you know, God had a plan, a bigger plan, and it really worked out beautifully. God just blesses us, and I'm very fortunate that my family are all here together.

RICH: You know, Connie and I agree with you. I taught in the religion program at Notre Dame High School, for almost 40 years. So, spirituality is very important to me.

MARY: I know my husband Jerry, when I was in the business years ago, and somebody would quit or get mad at me or didn't get the right day off, I would be so devastated. And, I would go, "I don't know what to do." And then, Jerry would go, "Mary, have you asked God for help?" And I would go, "No, I think I might do that!" And then I'd say, "O.K., thank you for the reminder!"

CONNIE: Did you always get the help?

MARY: Oh, in one way or another, and even putting the right people there like Maria Hoft to be somebody who understood me. [At this time Mary gets a phone call from her grandson about cutting her grass.]

RICH: You know, there is an important question on the Interview Questions sheet at the very end. And, I don't have any expectations of anything, but do you know of any other St. Louis bakers? This is a project that has really picked-up momentum. But, I just try to "follow my nose" to the next story.

MARY: Now, this is really funny — when she was sixteen my daughter, the one that owns the bakery, she didn't want to work for me. So, she worked for the Haas Bakery. She didn't drive. So, I had to drive to Gravois to pick her up. And, I remember on Thanksgiving she had to be there at five o'clock in the morning. But she worked for them, and now he works for her! He closed his bakery, and now works for us.

CONNIE: Yeah, my brother Sam did the same thing when he closed his bakery. But you know, it was in his blood. So then, he worked for another baker. I'm pretty sure my brother Jim worked for Haas Bakery. Jim was a baker, and my other brother Sam owned Wolf's Bakery.

MARY: And then, there's Randy McArthur — do you have the McArthur Bakery?

RICH: I started out with Randy. They were my first interview, and I have a story to tell you, but tell me about Randy.

MARY: I just know him from being in the restaurant business and being at all of the food shows.

RICH: Now, I was just at McArthur's Bakery yesterday, and they're doing very well. Their wedding business is really good, and they're still putting out a full line. They have cut-back on their in-store café. They only do breakfasts, and they've cut out their other sandwiches, but they do serve breakfast all day. [Since the time of this interview the McArthur bakery has cut back more, but not on their wedding cake business.]

RICH: One day when I was interviewing David McArthur and his wife Myndi, David says to me, "I've got something in the trunk of my car. I've got something to give you." Then, he showed me three full-size paper ream boxes filled with fifty years of the St. Louis Baker's Association bulletins. You know, that organization dissolved sometime around 2007, and Randy was the last president. So, I edited those and tried to take two years from each decade. I tried to simplify them and take some of the best stories out of them. They were amazing.

MARY: That's all awesome. Well, did David McArthur then go to work for Bono-Burns? He was my rep from Bono-Burns for a little while, and I think he was Kim's rep too.

RICH: David was really good to me. He got me started on the Bakery Book Project and was really encouraging to me.

MARY: See, I was president of the Restaurant Association of St. Louis, I think in 2009. And, I was on the board forever and ever. But then, it got to the point where not many restauranteurs were participating, and it was all just suppliers.

Author's Note: This interview with Mary Hostetter was one of the most inspiring of all of the interviews! Her faith and trust in God's guidance through all of her life was refreshing and beautiful! As of July of 2021 The Blue Owl and Mary Hostetter have started offering yet another bakery item called a "Piecaken," a bakery treat created by Zac Young, a world famous pastry chef who is often featured on the Food Channel. There are several videos on YouTube that focus on Zac Young. A "Piecaken" is a unique combination of cheesecake, pie, and cake all iced together!

"The Sweet Divine Bakery"
Interview With Jenna and Jason Siebert

...we have a great picture of Jason's grandfather in our bakery
where he's working in his bakery...it's a pretty good-sized
picture that we have hanging up in the bake station.
So, grandpa is always keeping an eye on us, you know,
making sure everything turns out good!
– Jenna and Jason Siebert

Author's Note: This interview with Jenna and Jason Siebert was done by phone for reasons of safety during the virus.

RICH: Well, let me ask you a question. How is your farmhouse rehab going?

JENNA: It's going well.

RICH: I think I mentioned in my e-mail that I think your website is really outstanding.

JENNA: Well, thank you. I was the one who created it.

RICH: Did you! That's cool! I think art really changes our lives. And, you even made it happen with your creating of your bakery! I loved what you said on your website that the bakery was just another media for your creativity. So, you designed your bakery website?!

JENNA: Yeah. It took me a couple of days to get it up and going. You know it's funny, when we started the actual bakery, we were like, "We need to do this quick!" because we were asked to be in a cake contest, and we had to be an official bakery. We weren't at that time, but we created an LLC superfast, and I designed the first website, like that night.

RICH: So, it was an all-nighter?

JENNA: It was an all-nighter, for sure! Yeah, we had lots of those in the beginning!

JASON: Lots of those in the beginning, for sure!

RICH: I'm really glad that I got ahold of you to be in the book. It's been a ten-year project so far.

JENNA: Wow! A labor of love, right!

RICH: Yes, it is! It is exactly that! There's going to be two main parts to it. I did editorial "samplings," from an archive. I was given a gift on-loan of fifty years of bulletins from the St. Louis Bakers Association. That was an organization that was very important to bakers in those times. The bulletins from the Bakers Association ran from about 1950 to the year 2,000. It's just an amazing story. You would be very proud of the bakers. They were a community. They were almost an extended family. They were so involved with one another. They socialized with one another, shared baking supplies when another baker needed something, all kinds of things like that!

JENNA: That's so cool. You know, we're not a part of that, but we should look into that.

RICH: Well, just for information, the Bakers Association was pretty much dissolved around 2007.

JENNA: We didn't even know about that.

RICH: Well, I see you as the pioneers of a new time. There's an estimate that during the 1950's there were about five hundred independent bakeries!

JENNA AND JASON: My gosh, that's a lot!

RICH: Now, there's maybe 20, but I think that number may be growing.

JENNA: Yeah, it's so different, so strange.

RICH: So, there's a story there too. I had to ask the bakers from the historic bakeries, "What caused the decline of the independent bakeries?" The answer was pretty much that the supermarkets took over the bakery business.

JENNA: Yeah, that's where I would see it for sure. You know, with us it's such a specialty thing that we do, that I feel like the supermarkets really can't compete with what we do.

RICH: Yeah, that's how you had to find a "niche" to be able to do that. I looked at your menu, and I looked at your "Special Events." I really liked what I saw on your website. It's great!

JENNA: Thanks, yeah!

RICH: I did try to understand the economics of the whole thing. There are some of these independent bakeries on Cherokee Street, I think you probably know about some of them.

JENNA: Yeah, "Whisk."

RICH: Yes, "Whisk," I just interviewed her. But, places like "Diana's Mexican Bakery" and other small bakeries who sustain themselves with ongoing accounts and regular orders that go out. That's how they seem to make it through lean times. So, I was just curious if you have any of those.

JENNA: We have a couple wholesale accounts that we do, but we rely on our weddings as our biggest thing. There are weddings and the whole "food truck" scene. Also, our location is such a fun destination spot. So, we get a lot of tourist business really. We're right across from the trolleys.

JENNA: People come to our place before they go to the Cardinal baseball games or concerts. Overall, it's really the traffic and weddings, and food truck events that keep us going. Growing our wholesale accounts is actually one thing that I'd like to see us move forward a little.

JASON: We had a couple good ones before the virus hit, but then it slowed down with the virus. We were wholesaling places like the St. Louis Symphony. You know, with niche markets like that we had some pretty good accounts. When the virus hit and when everybody had to shut down, we've kinda' put all of that on hold.

RICH: Well, Jason, I saw in your website bio that you started making breads and pastries and your favorite, which is cookies.

JASON: Yep, I'm a sucker for the cookie, that's for sure. [Jenna is laughing in the background!]

RICH: You are not alone! [My laughter.] I could <u>be</u> the Cookie Monster, really!

[Again, Jenna laughs in the background!]

JASON: I would always just kinda' dabble with baking around our house. And, when Jenna started getting busier with making cakes, I would jump in and help her bake stuff from scratch. You know, it started off as just generally a hobby. At first she would go to Schnuck's and buy the one dollar cake mix and just add an egg and some oil, and she'd decorate it really cute for friends and family. She just wanted to decorate!

JENNA: [Here Jenna laughs gleefully!] Yeah, I <u>did</u> just want to decorate!

JASON: So, when that started to get busier, I was like, "You know, if we're going to do this let's make this stuff for real!" So, that's when I started jumping in to help! So, if Jenna said, "Hey, make me a chocolate cake!" I'd say,"Alright!" So, that's kinda' how it all got started!

RICH: Nice! You know, one of the things I was really taken by was how much the two of you sound really together as a team!

JENNA: YES!!

JASON: The whole experience from start to finish has been a collaboration of both of our efforts. The idea and the vision was <u>all</u> Jenna. And then, it took a little convincing for me to get on-board, especially when I saw the demand once we started making stuff. Then, it was a pretty crazy ride. Like I said, it started in the kitchen of our home, which turned into a full-scale commercial kitchen in our basement.

JASON: That turned into a conversation late one night around the fireplace where we said, "We either need to make this a hobby again, or let's go for it!" And, we decided to go for it!

RICH: That's very neat! You know, I think I sent a list of Interview Questions?

JENNA: We got it. I have it open.

RICH: Oh, you do? Good! They're not essential, but they're just kind of jumping-off points. One of the other things I saw about you in the bio, Jason, was that your grandfather was a baker. Is that right?

JASON: He was! He was a baker his whole life. His name was Art Siebert, and he worked at Klund's Bakery until it closed, I think in the late 80's.

RICH: Do you know where Klund's Bakery was?

JASON: Yes, it was right on the corner of Gravois and Loughborough. It's a plumbing supply place now.

RICH: O.K., that's good to know. I have heard the name. But, I don't really know anybody who's still around, who can tell me about Klund's Bakery.

JASON: Yeah, I wouldn't even know where to begin to find that kind of stuff either, other than my grandma! You know, I can probably set you up with her if you want to talk to her! She's still around.

RICH: I might in the future.

JASON: Yeah, just let me know. She'd probably get a kick out of that. She's ninety-six years old now and still as sharp as a tack. She still tells some good stories and could probably tell you all about that place.

RICH: That is really neat. You know it's a bit of an exaggeration, but it's been said that South St. Louis had a bakery on every corner.

JENNA: Yep! That's all you need! [And, we all laugh!]

JASON: Yes, sir!

JENNA: Yeah, we have a great picture of Jason's grandfather in *our* bakery where he's working in his bakery! [Jenna laughs!]

JASON: Yeah, I have a really cool picture. It's a picture of him just cutting some dough, you know, with his head down working. My brother actually had it printed for me. So it's a pretty good-sized picture that we have hanging up in the bake station. So grandpa is always keeping an eye on us, you know, making sure everything turns out good!

RICH: Yeah, that's really beautiful! I'm anxious to get to see your bakery. We pretty much don't go anywhere because of the virus. We're very careful.

JENNA: No, I understand. It's weird.

JASON: Yeah, it's a strange time, that's for sure.

RICH: So, as soon as I can I'll come in to see you. I would love to meet you!

JENNA: For sure! Yes.

RICH: So, I looked really carefully at your bio on your website. I wrote down some things that were highlights and that I want to learn about. When it says that you sculpt and carve cakes, Jason, what does that mean?

JASON: Well, ultimately what it means is that Jenna and I can take a cake and pretty much make it look like whatever you want! We've done some of my favorite ones, like we've actually taken a cake and made an exact replica of a man's motorcycle.

JASON: People come at us with ideas saying, "Hey, do you think you could make this into a cake?" And, we are always willing to give it a try. One part about that is that I have a construction background. So, sometimes it takes some engineering to actually get out in the workshop and build a structure that's going to hold this cake. But yeah, between the two of us we can pretty much sculpt a cake into just about anything.

RICH: That's very neat.

JASON: You know, it was a skill we kind of developed during the whole time of our growing the bakery. Throughout high school I never took an art class. It wasn't anything that I really pursued, nothing that I could ever see myself doing until we started doing it. And, I actually learned all of it from Jenna, all of the decorating. When I saw what she could do, I eventually became more interested in doing it myself. Sometimes people didn't know it was a cake. We've even done Thanksgiving Day turkeys for people for their tables to kind of fool their guests!

RICH: That sounds like fun! As I think of stuff I just want to throw some information your way too. But, some of the bakers in the past had those rotating ovens. When Thanksgiving rolled around they converted their ovens to cooking turkeys. They made turkeys for people.

JENNA and JASON: Sure! That's a great idea. You know, they were adapting and "doing the pivot" even back then, weren't they!

RICH: Yeah, exactly!

JASON: I know that at my grandpa's bakery, Klund's, they would actually do some catering. They would cater whole wedding events where they would make big casseroles or roast beef, and stuff like that. I remember as a kid those big rotating ovens.

RICH: Well, you've got some other highlights in your bio. There's some nice positive highlights that I want to talk about, but let's get the negative one about the "fire" out of the way. Oh my gosh, I cannot imagine.

JENNA: Yeah, it was intense.

JASON: You know, interestingly enough, the fire happened on a Monday morning while we were closed. So, that was kind of a blessing. Nobody was there, so nobody got hurt. And, the fire department saved the building. You know, the building was minutes away from "going up." We could have lost the entire building. Our outcome probably would have been a little different, but we didn't lose the building.

JASON: We sustained a lot of damage. We had to gut the entire bakery and the two floors upstairs. So, when the proverbial "smoke cleared" and we got our heads straight, we said, "Well, we gotta' rebuild this." It gave us an opportunity to not necessarily rebrand the bakery, but just restyle the bakery and make it into what it is today.

JENNA: Yeah, stronger, you know.

RICH: It looks like you really did come out of it stronger.

JENNA: Yeah, that was our mission. We were like, [Jenna pauses here and exhales a powerful sigh.], "O.K., if we're gonna' do this, let's dive in 100 percent!"

JASON: *I'll tell you the one thing that was really cool for Jenna and myself. We had the fire on a Monday, and this just shows you how friendly things are in the baking world. By Wednesday we were meeting with the owners of McArthur's Bakery.*

JASON: *They had heard what happened, and Scott, the current owner of McArthur's, reached out to us and said, "Hey, here is an oven that I'm not using. Here are some freezers and refrigerators that I'm not using. Here's a work space that I'm not using. Whatever you need, I'll put it on the first truck tomorrow morning. It'll be there at 5:00 a.m. Make sure your people are there to go to work. By Thursday we had our bakers and our office managers and our truck driver back to work!*

JASON: *And, it was because of Scott at McArthur's. He was amazing. He sat us down and said, "Listen, this is not the end for you guys. You guys have a unique thing that St. Louis needs." He was like, "I want to do whatever I can to help and make sure you guys make it out of this." He was just amazing!*

RICH: *That's fantastic! Yeah, I have a very close history and friendship with the McArthurs of the McArthur Bakery.*

JASON: Oh really!

RICH: *Yeah, I have three ten-ream paper boxes in my living room, and right now they are filled with these bulletins from the St. Louis Bakers Association. They were given to me by the McArthurs.*

JASON: Oh, that's awesome!

RICH: Randy was the former owner, and his brother David was so nice to me. They are the sons of the McArthurs who started the bakery. They're very good guys, very nice people.

JENNA: We haven't had the pleasure of meeting them, but we've heard a lot of great things about them. They've been around for a long time, right.

RICH: They <u>have</u> been around for a long time. They originally were down in the city, I think on McRee, which I think is near the underpass of Vandeventer and Highway 40, somewhere around there. Then they moved to South County.

JENNA: Yeah, most bakeries have experienced a move or two.

RICH: It sounds like you have a great location where you are.

JENNA: We do! You know, when we looked at this building it was like, "Yep, this is it!" You just know. The location is absolutely awesome, right on the corner in Soulard. And, you know it's funny, I have family from Soulard from a long time ago. So yeah, it felt like home from the minute we were in that building! So, I love it.

RICH: This is not really all that important, but I'm curious, where did the two of you grow up?

JENNA: I was from the Jefferson County area. Well, we both were.

JASON: I grew up in Imperial and went to school in Festus. I went to high school at St. Pius X in Festus. I spent a brief semester at Mizzou. Then I came back and I've lived in the St. Louis area my entire life.

RICH: Do you know of Nathaniel Reid's bakery out on Manchester?

JENNA and JASON: Yes!

RICH: He's from Farmington, and he went to Mizzou. He's one of the nicest people I've ever met!

JENNA and JASON: Really! Yeah, we haven't met him yet.

RICH: Please go in and meet him, and tell him I sent you. He's just a nice man, and his resume is crazy! Well, when I interviewed him, I asked him the obvious question and said, "And, why are you in St. Louis?! [I'm laughing a little as I'm saying this.] You could work anywhere in the world!" And he said, "I love St. Louis! I love the Midwest. I chose to be here, and I wouldn't want to be anywhere else!" I thought that was really inspiring!

RICH: So, Jenna, you grew up in Jefferson County too?

JENNA: Yes, my parents built a couple different houses. We lived in Hillsboro, Festus, and DeSoto. DeSoto was the last place I lived with them. So, I went to DeSoto High School down south.

RICH: I know the area. I want to say that the pictures on your website of the bakery interior are so impressive. The whole website is really pretty!

JENNA: Thank you! Thanks very much!

RICH: That's why I want to get down there and see it! What do you call the bakery truck? Is it "Georgie?"

JENNA: Yeah, "Georgie," our cupcake truck! So, I have a funny story about how we started that. This is from when we were living in Barnhart. And, we thought, "What are we doing?!" We like to renovate things, you know, and create things. So, we had our bakery, that's where it started, like the hobby in the kitchen, and then we moved down to the basement. So, we had a legitimate commercial style bakery in our basement. And yet, I knew the next step that I really wanted was a commercial space, you know, with a cute little storefront. It was one of my dreams!

JENNA: We lived so far south, but because of Georgie we had a following that was getting bigger in the St. Louis area. So anyway, after really thinking about it and talking it through we decided it would be best if we could grow our clientele a little bit more before we opened up that storefront, because we paid for our whole business out of our own pockets, no loans or anything. So, I had this wild idea that I really wanted to do a cupcake truck. At that point food trucks were new to St. Louis. There were only four or five other trucks before we launched ours. So, I surprised Jason. He came home from work one day, and I said, "Babe, I'm gettin' ready to go to Georgia to pick-up a truck!"

JASON: That's not exactly how it went. So, I got home from work one day, and she wasn't home. So, I called her and said, "Hey, where <u>are</u> you?" And she said, "Well, I'm with my mom. We're on our way to Georgia to buy a cupcake truck! [At this we laugh together!]

JENNA: "Surprise!" [We all laugh again.]

JASON: "Well, O.K. then!" That's the truer side of the story. I knew that she had been talking about getting a cupcake truck, and that it was something that she wanted to do, but I did not have a clue that was going to be the day.

RICH: Yeah, a little spontaneous there, right!

JENNA and then JASON: Oh yeah! Exactly, exactly!

RICH: That's great!

JASON: And, that turned out to be a great move for us!

JENNA: That's what really grew our clientele for us from the get-go. As soon as we launched that truck, we had a strong following. Then, after our following grew it was time for our storefront.

JASON: With the truck we could reach so many different people. We could take it to downtown, we could take it to St. Charles, we could take it all over and reach so many different areas and clientele. So, it was a really great first step for us.

JENNA: Yeah, it was a storefront on wheels that grew us to a brick and mortar store!

RICH: That's fantastic. That never would have occurred to me! Actually, what you just said is true, because it was basically a billboard on wheels. It was better than a billboard on wheels, right!

JENNA: Exactly, a great advertisement!

RICH: And, is "Georgie," your Food Truck, still doing well?

JENNA: She is, but she's a little slower because of the virus right now. We <u>have</u> noticed an improvement lately. So, we try to make it happen as often as we can get her out there!

RICH: That's neat. We've gone to a lot of the Food Truck meet-ups, or whatever you call them, at Tower Grove Park on I think the first Friday of the month.

JENNA: They're amazing especially like the first several years that they began.

JASON: Yeah, the newness kind of wore off for the past couple years. The first four or five years they were insane! I mean, all we could do for four hours was hand-out cupcakes.

JASON: There were days when we would do that event, and we would sell 2400 cupcakes in four hours. I think the best event we ever did was when we sold out, and we had started with 2700 cupcakes!

RICH: My gosh, that's a great take for one day, isn't it! I think it will soon get better because people will be so starved for those kinds of events! They will just be exploding, I think. [These comments were referring to the "opening up of events" after the virus winds down.]

JENNA: So, hopefully it will be like that when things start up again!

RICH: O.K., there were some other things. I know you were on the Food Network T.V. channel several times.

JENNA: "Yes, we were on four different times, weren't we?" [Jenna asks Jason.] You know what, we were not on the same show each time. We were on Cupcake Wars twice, Cake Wars once, and then Food Truck Nation.

RICH: Wow! That's really cool!

JENNA: Those were so much fun!

JASON: Yeah, the Food Network has been great to us. Ever since that first Cupcake Wars competition it seemed like they were reaching out to us on a pretty regular basis. So, they've been great about keeping us on their rotation.

RICH: Great!

JENNA: We've been asked a couple times to come back and do like Hallowe'en Wars and Holiday Wars, but we've turned them down. We were like, "No, no, it's too much." Like when you're filming, it's so much. You have to be there, be away from work and be away from our kid, you know. So, we've turned those down. But, there have been some times when I've thought, "Oh man, doing those shows is just great publicity! It's fun, and it's a cool experience."

RICH: I'm sure it was exciting.

JENNA: Yeah, it's _really_ exciting! So yeah, that's a lot to ask because you're away from work, so you're not creating revenue, right. You can't take orders. So, you have to take that into consideration when you do these shows. You're out there for almost a week, for that one-hour show. You know, it's goofy.

JENNA: But, what they did for us was, they paid for our transportation, they flew us out, they had somebody pick us up, run our errands, and get us back to the hotel. And so, they're called "wranglers." So, financially they do cover the hotel, the flights, and then you get a per diem for food. They also have food catered for lunch while you're filming. So overall, it didn't really cost us anything to go. It was just the loss of orders for that week, especially when it was just Jason and I running the shop.

RICH: So, your staff people filled-in for you, right? That must mean that you have people that you can really trust.

JENNA: Yes, 100 percent! They are amazing! You know, it takes awhile to find a good team, to find the right fit. We have a good group. Yep, we love 'em. They've been with us for awhile. And I mean, it takes a team to run a business, it really does. Jason and I were trying to do everything ourselves, everything — dish-washing, driving the truck, making the stuff, decorating the stuff, shopping, everything! So, it came to a point where we said, "What are we doing?!" And so, when we had that talk it was like, "We have to down-size or go-for-it!"

RICH: Yeah, that's a consistent theme for all bakers. I mean, you have to take care of yourselves or else *the bakery owns you*, right?

JENNA and JASON: [And, together they respond,] "Right, exactly! Oh, my gosh!"

RICH: Well, I'm glad to hear that you've learned that. Yeah, my dad was in the restaurant business. He was a cook and a bartender. When I was growing up he warned me often when he said, *"You never want to own a restaurant because you never will own a restaurant, it will always own you!"*

JENNA: Oh gosh, there's so much truth in that. Yeah, we had to step away, really.

RICH: Good for you! Can you tell me anything else about your team?

JENNA: Yeah, we can. So, we have our baker and pastry chef, Tim. He's still with us,

JASON: Six years now, I think. We have an interesting story about him. Our bakery is located right down the street from a pizza joint called Epic Pizza. We would go in there for lunch all the time. So, we kinda' knew Tim because he was a cook there. Our pastry chef who was working for us had put in his two week notice and wanted to move on. Tim caught wind of that pretty quickly as the rumor mills flew around Soulard.

JASON: We were in there getting lunch one day, and he approached Jenna and me and said, "Hey, I have experience in pastry. That is really my passion. I'm making pizzas just to make ends meet, but I would really love an opportunity to come and bake for you guys." So honestly, I didn't take him very seriously at first. If you ever met Tim, he was one of these guys who was a heavy metal guy with super long hair, and with tattoos all over the place.

JASON: You wouldn't picture him as a guy who would make a macaroon or a dainty little petit four, or cupcakes, or what-have-you. When he came in I said, "Oh, if you want to give it a shot, show-up at 6:00 o'clock tomorrow morning." And, he was there at 5:45! Then, he just knocked it out of the park, and a couple hours later Jenna and I were both like, "You're hired!" He's been with us ever since, and he does a great job!

JENNA: Yeah, he's great. He's fantastic!

JASON: We have Mike, and he's kind of in the management role, but he also runs the truck. He managed the wholesale accounts that we did have. He also decorates cakes. He has no formal training at all, but he is very artistic and very well thought-out in his designs. He can do almost anything that Jenna and I can do when it comes to cakes, as far as sculpting and carving. Like I said, he manages the truck, so he's very personable. He's also been with us for close to six years.

JASON: Well, the two of them have been working together for so long they understand each other. So, that helps. They do butt heads a little at times. You know, they are both bull-headed thirty-year-olds. [We all laugh together!]

JENNA: They're like brothers!

JASON: Exactly! They're more like brothers than employees. And then, our most recent hire is a young girl. Her name is Susie.

JASON: She manages our weddings and our storefront. She does all of the wedding consultations and coordinates all of that. She decorates most of those cakes and pretty much sees all that stuff through, from start to finish.

JENNA: She's awesome!

JASON: She is awesome! She also does the training for the storefront girls and makes sure the storefront has what it needs. She makes sure that Tim is making the menu, and does a lot of our day-to-day frosting and decorating. She's also the peace-keeper between Mike and Tim! [I laugh at this point!]

JASON: You know, the ladies and guys we've got working in the bakery are all really young, which is encouraging for the industry. She's twenty-four, very well-rounded, and very passionate about the baking and the industry. And, very creative as well!

JENNA: Yes! Very creative!

JASON: She's an excellent cake decorator, working in bakeries her entire adult life since she was sixteen. She was actually working for Nathaniel Reid when she came in to speak with us about a possible position at our bakery.

JASON: So, those three are our core. Tim produces everything. He makes absolutely everything that comes out of the bakery. Every now and then Susie will hop in with a ganache or a filling here or there.

JASON: Anyway, between those three they pretty much take care of everything! And then, the storefront people who can make coffees and put cupcakes in a box and do dishes and stuff like that, those come and go quite a bit. But yeah, those three people are our team!

RICH: That's really neat. That comes across very clearly on your website too.

JENNA: Oh, good! Thank you. Yeah, they're important to us! Yep!

JASON: Yes, we try to take good care of them. They know how much we appreciate them, and we know that they're the reason that everything clicks the way it does!

JENNA: And, they give Jason and I that freedom where the bakery isn't owning us right now!

JASON: It gives us the opportunity to take a look and maybe explore different things.

JENNA: Yeah, doing different designs and pursuing different opportunities. But, the bakery is our baby and always will be, like we were there for the past two days, just poppin'-in and hangin'-out with the team, checking out what's going on, and sneaking a cupcake here and there! [Here, we all laugh!] You know, it's "quality control!"

JASON: Yeah we <u>call</u> it "quality control!"

JENNA: You know, it's crazy, like from the beginning when we started everything and how Jason and I did absolutely everything. You know, when you do so many years of that, [Here Jenna sort of gasps!], it's like, "O.K., we just have to step away for a minute!" It feels nice to have that break. But yeah, we love it, it's our creation!

RICH: Yes!

JENNA: It's such a cool thing to see that not only were we creating delicious desserts, but we were creating a bakery, from scratch, you know. That was so much fun! Yeah, and there's so much to say too about our real estate interest. We play a little part in that too. Real estate is another one of our passions, just doing rehabs and homes. Yeah, it's so fun, and I'm so into the art of that too!

RICH: Well, I don't want to forget to ask, "If you were going to come into your store, what would you buy, what would be your highest choices, your favorite flavors?!" And, a separate but related question probably is, "What are your signature items, what is your store known for, what sells the best?"

JENNA: So, I have to tell you, one of my most favorite things that we have in the bakery is our "Banana Whoopie Pie!" That's true for both of us. That's like our go-to! [I laugh loudly, just at the name.]

JASON: I would say the "Banana Whoopie Pie" or the Chocolate Chip Cookie, one of those two!

JENNA: Yeah, I think we have several different varieties and offerings, like our French Macaroons. They are, "Oh, my gosh, so amazing!" And, they're so pretty. So, I'm gonna' say that I would definitely recommend those, and that's what I would get, if I were to walk into the bakery and see those. But, we are really well-known for our cupcakes because of the "Cupcake Wars" T.V. show and from our Food Truck cupcake business. We do have a lot of people who come in for the cupcakes.

JASON: Yeah, people come in for the cupcakes. That's what they're here for. We keep a couple of flavors. You know we have a flavor called "The Drunken Pig," and that's in the display case every day.

RICH: O.K. can you describe the "Banana Whoopie Pie?"

JASON: Well, it's like a banana cake cookie. So, it's made with real crushed bananas and sour cream. And we just make a loose batter that we scoop onto a sheet pan, and bake it off like a cookie. So, it's a soft cookie, and then we fill it with vanilla butter cream. It's just dynamite!

JENNA: And then, there's the Chocolate Chip Cookie Sandwich, and it has a big spoon of butter cream, I'm good with that too! We do love our butter cream!
[At this point, we all laugh!]

Author's Note: You can tell why they are bakers. They love their sweets and their own bakery goods!

RICH: I'm with you on that! [We're still laughing!] You know, just between us, I'm giving you my preference. I get so disappointed when a cake has a whipped cream icing instead of butter cream. My heart just drops! [And then, we laugh together again.]

JENNA: [Jenna responds right away!] I'm right there with you! It's gotta' be butter cream!

JASON: I know it, right! [Here Jason is talking about the butter cream icing!]

RICH: *Oh, my gosh, yeah. Well, these are great stories. I love everything you've been describing. I especially love the fact of how close you are as a team, the two of you together!*

JENNA: *Yeah, thank you!*

RICH: *Really — that's a gift, and it's beautiful, isn't it!*

JENNA and JASON TOGETHER: *It is!*

JASON: *We've learned how to do pretty much everything together! I mean, not only live together, and be husband and wife and have a daughter and a family, but to work together, and be creative together. It really has been a gift. It's been a blessing for sure!*

JENNA: *Yeah, it's been fun!*

RICH: That's very neat, very beautiful! I don't mean this as too personal of a question, but are your families pretty supportive? Do they endorse what you're doing?

JASON: Oh, absolutely! I'd say both of our parents, Jenna's mom and dad, and my mom and dad have been huge supporters, always around in the beginning, "What can we do to help?" type of stuff from the very beginning. And, you know, with my grandpa being a baker for so long a lot of my aunts took an interest right away because they all grew up working in *his* bakery. So, they're around a lot. Yes, huge family support from both sides!

JENNA: Yes, one hundred percent!

RICH: That's really great! That's very encouraging, isn't it!

JASON: It is!

RICH: I haven't really pursued this with many others, but with your Cupcake Wars and Cake Wars T.V. shows and awards, do you have any news stories that you could tell me about?

JENNA: I'm sure we do. Actually, we made the cover of "WHERE" magazine right after the "Cupcake Wars." They had our cupcakes on the cover, and they were talking about us winning on the Cupcake Wars.

Author's Note: I was so impressed with Jason and Jenna, especially because of how close they were as a team, as husband and wife, who built their dream together, and how they are continuing to dream and create their life.

Wedding Wonderland Bakery
Interview with Mike Temm

*...my story actually starts at the age of six...When I
was six-years-old Santa Claus brought
me an "Easy-Bake Oven!" I'm the youngest
of six boys. While they were all out playing football I was inside making a cake for
half-time. In later years my mother said to me, "You know, your dad felt that boys
shouldn't do that kind of thing." Back in the day he was highly against Santa
Claus bringing me that "Easy-Bake Oven." But, my mother made it happen!*
— Mike Temm

RICH: I've done quite a few bakery interviews already, ones like with Rosemary Pfeifer who had a pretty high-end bakery on Clayton Road by Galleria, and about fourteen others at this time.

MIKE: You've been all over town.

RICH: Yeah, it's been really inspiring, to talk to all of these people. And then, I did a lot of archive work with some materials that I received from Randy and David McArthur. They gave me fifty years of monthly bulletins from the St. Louis Bakers Association. I've spent a lot of time just getting highlights from those. I've got so much material that I'm not sure what to do with all of it.

MIKE: Right, right! It's a little overwhelming, right. So, do you want me to answer these questions [from the Interview Questions sheet]? How would you like to work?

RICH: So, let me start with this, because I don't always remember to ask this question. Your location is at 449 Dunn Road, right? And, do you have a length of time that you've been at this location?

MIKE: Yes, the doors opened in 1986. It was a 900 square foot unit back then.

RICH: So, then you bought the building next door?

MIKE: Right. So, the middle section is the original "Wedding Wonderland." The 449 address used to be a florist. They moved out, and I made this my showroom. And, Trotter Photo used to be on the other side, and I made that my 2,000 square foot kitchen.

RICH: Wow! You expanded. Do you know when you expanded?

MIKE: Yes, in 2001 I bought the florist. In 2005 I took over Trotter's Photo.

RICH: [Mike's phone begins to ring, and I tell him to do whatever he needs to do.]

MIKE: Yeah, the health inspector is here. So, she'll be interrupting us.

RICH: So, I'm not sure, but do you only do weddings exclusively?

MIKE: Yeah, yeah, "Wedding Wonderland" has always been the name. And, I've worked here since the beginning, but I didn't own it until 1995.

RICH: Who was the owner before that?

MIKE: Jeannie and Joe Katroba. They started "Wedding Wonderland" cake shop. They were absolute perfectionists. Wonderful people. They're no longer with us.

MIKE: They retired and moved to Boca Raton, Florida, and I think it was three years, and they passed, too young. This was their passion, and I took it over.

RICH: Maybe they missed the work. That's really an interesting phenomenon. I was very touched by Cynthia Knodel. You know she and her husband have a very disabled daughter. They introduced me to her, and I took the risk of asking them, "How is that going?" And, they answered me with, "She's the best thing that ever happened to us." I was very touched by them.

MIKE: Yeah, they have quite a story. It's a shame that their bakery didn't last.

RICH: Yeah, that's one thing I wanted to tell you too is that I never put anything in that's negative. I'm really careful about what I put into my notes. It's all positive is what I'm saying.

MIKE: Well, it is what it is. It's a unique struggle, especially for me to be able to survive. I'm proud of the fact that my reputation has been strong enough to survive. So many businesses have failed. Whatever the reasons were, they did fail. Things were nerve-racking at times, but I kept my faith, and I never went negative. I just stayed here, and nothing ever happened here, and we made it. It just so happened that we were on The Learning Channel Cake Boss show, "The Next Great Baker." And, we were having watch parties. The last watch party we had was with 800 people here at Yacovelli's. And, I really attribute and thank the good Lord above that for some reason somehow that happened. The Learning Channel called us and wanted us to compete nationally. So, that was going on, and that was crazy. The year 2014 was a crazy year, with ups and downs.

RICH: Now, was Al Watson the one that was on that show?

MIKE: Yes, he's the one, and he was with Leah Weber. So, TLC called and e-mailed me. And, I was not eligible to go on the show because I owned the shop. It had to be workers. And so, I chose two workers. We trained them, and we sponsored them. We did all that. They went, and we won the whole thing! Yeah, it was pretty cool!

RICH: That's fantastic. Cynthia Knodel told me about that. She told me about Al Watson. She even gave me his phone number, and I've tried to call him two or three times, but I think he's really happy being an electrician!

MIKE: Oh, I wouldn't put it past him to respond because he loves to talk. He is busy, but yeah, he would be a good one to talk to.

RICH: Now, did you work anywhere before Wedding Wonderland?

MIKE: I did, at Wetterau Bakery. I don't know if you remember that name. Right across the street there is the factory, and it became Pillsbury. Huge. It was a flash frozen bakery. We supplied all kinds of grocery stores throughout the nation like Publix and Kroger. And, we did all of the work right there, froze it quickly and sent it out. Big old building right across the street. Now it's Arcobasso's bakery. Wait a minute. They just changed names again. Now it's called Nature's Bakery.

Author's Note: After pursuing the name Nature's Bakery, I found an article from 2014 by Lisa Brown of the St. Louis Post-Dispatch that said it was a large producer of a specialized kind of fig bar. It has also made a 4.1 million dollar bid to acquire Theodoro Baking Co. in Hazelwood which filed for bankruptcy in August of 2014. However, the Theodoro Baking Company had a licensing agreement with Apted-Hulling Incorporated to produce the Miss Hullings famous cakes to local retailers including Straub's Markets. Apted-Hulling's attorney said, "We are of the belief that Miss Hulling's recipes are revered in the St. Louis community."

MIKE: Yeah, so I graduated from high school, and I was so burned out on book work that I told myself that I would go to work for a year and then go back to college. But, I got so interested in the bakery business that I didn't go back.

RICH: I guess it's all about passion. I'm very thankful that you have been willing to talk with me. It's just, umm, [and a pause here] — inspiring — because people are dedicated to this. They wouldn't do it if they didn't love it!

RICH: So, the stories I've heard are very interesting. I mean all the way back to a guy named Roy Schmiemeir who owned Schmiemeir's Bakery on Manchester, just east of West County Shopping Center. He talked about taking a cake for a wedding downtown on the 4th of July for an outdoor wedding in 95 degrees! They had to pack the cake in dry ice! [At this, we both laughed together!]

MIKE: Yeah!

RICH: There are stories from some people whose families were in business for a hundred years or more. They would have to go with the cake to the wedding so that they could repair it because of the humidity and heat.

MIKE: And, all of that is still a factor today, but now we have air-conditioning in vans. It is a different ballgame today.

RICH: Yeah, and part of the story for me is that it is hard to give up doing these interviews. I don't want to stop these interviews because I love doing them!

MIKE: Yeah, that's cool!

RICH: Yeah, you know, some of the stories out of the "St. Louis Bakers Association" bulletins tell a story that they were a community! At that time, around the 1950's, was the heyday of the independent bakeries. I mean some people estimate that there were around 500 of them. They really took care of one another. They were really kind to one another. They were not competitive with one another, and they even socialized together. It was like an extended family! It's hard to find the words to describe it.

MIKE: It was definitely a tight-knit community! Also, if you just started talking bad about each other, that would have been the death of your business.

RICH: Yeah, it really is out of the way in terms of why would you do that, right? Yeah, so it's great to talk to you. So, you started at the Wetterau bakery?

MIKE: Correct. I worked the night shift, the graveyard shift. I swept floors, whatever I could do until I got on the decorating line. And then, it was a year later until I was promoted to the lead man on that line. And so, I was in charge of 40 men and women decorating on an assembly line. That's where I learned my speed because in this business it's all about labor. And, the faster you are the more money you make!

MIKE: *However, my story actually starts at the age of six. It's a unique story, and I never used to tell it, but now I'm an older man, and I'm proud of it. When I was six years old my mother and Santa Claus brought me an "Easy-Bake Oven!"*

MIKE: *I was the youngest of six boys, and while they were all outside playing football and all of that, I was inside making a cake for half-time!* And, I never stopped. I didn't go to the sports. I didn't follow in my brothers' footsteps.

MIKE: I never stopped baking cakes out of that "Easy-Bake Oven!" I didn't go to school for this. I didn't go to class. No formal training. I did take art classes at school. I did do that. So, I could draw quickly on a cake and duplicate something that somebody wanted. *Well, yeah, it all started with an "Easy-Bake Oven," and the original that I got for Christmas is right around the corner, [as Mike points to a spot in his showroom]. You passed it when we were coming in here to my office.*

RICH: Oh, so you mean that it's in the store?! Wow, I didn't see that! That's great. OK, that's cool! Now, that was a unique toy, wasn't it.

MIKE: Yes, very unique. Light bulb and everything. Everything was burnt to a crisp, and dry as heck. [We both laugh loudly here!] But, I was proud!

RICH: That was great! No kidding. Well, just a personal side note, our grandson is four years old, and his daddy is an outstanding chef, a personal chef for a Hollywood screen writer. So, do you know what he was on Halloween? He was a chef, with the whole chef's outfit on, you know, with the hat and all?

MIKE: [Mike laughs at the thought of Max in his chef costume.] That's awesome. You got a kick out of that, didn't you!

RICH: Yeah, it was great. *But yeah, it starts young, you know, the importance of pretend play!*

MIKE: *It does. Yeah, it really does. And you know, in later years my mother said to me, "Well you know, your dad is very manly, and felt that boys shouldn't do that kind of thing. Back in the day he was highly against Santa Claus bringing me that "Easy-Bake Oven." But, my mother made it happen!* [At this point Mike had to stop the interview in order to take time out to meet with the health inspector in the showroom.]

MIKE: So, we've been here 14 and 19 years, 33 years all together. Same spot.

RICH: So, I want to pick-up on that story about Al Watson and the Cake Boss show.

MIKE: Yeah, it was called the "Next Great Baker." It was a Learning Channel, show, and the "Cake Boss" was a judge.

RICH: So, Al Watson was picked as "America's Next Great Baker," right?

MIKE: It was a team. It was Lea Weber and Al Watson. The hoops and hurdles to get them on that show were just insane, and the expense for me to sponsor them was crazy. Basically, what I've learned in a nutshell, as far as Hollywood goes, is that they get us the common folk to give them hired movie stars, for lack of a better term. They had to work hard. Sometimes they would have eighty plus hours of footage for a 40 minute show until they got the show the way they wanted it.

MIKE: It was amazing. The marketing expense was incredible, but yet it has done wonders for my business.

RICH: That's cool. Now, when you talk about the marketing, do you mean the expense of having them prepared?

MIKE: Everything they needed, videography, everything of the interview process so that they could get the right people on their show. It was all at my expense. It's genius! And, people love it! The average person loves it, and they think it's "real," what they're seeing.

RICH: I know. And, it's not even close, right! [And then, we laugh together.]

MIKE: Not even close. And you know, I get into that discussion with some people, and they don't want to hear it because they don't want their world busted. It was very interesting, what we learned from that show. *And yes, it has done great things for my business.*

RICH: Yeah, what kind of time are we talking about?

MIKE: They were in New York for seven weeks I believe. And, once they got to that point, the final episode, the show did pay for the hotel and stuff. I didn't have to pay for that, but all of the other marketing expenses were on me.

RICH: I've heard other kinds of stories like this.

MIKE: I'm telling you the truth. For example, little things, like when you see some-one drop a cake. They were told to drop that cake to create drama! None of my employees have ever dropped a cake! [Mike laughs.]

MIKE: [While looking at some pictures of Mike's cakes, he says,] These are just basic ones. These are the cakes that people see right off the bat. They're beautiful, and they're less expensive. But, we do have some fantastic cakes!

MIKE: And yet, they're not out there because if people would see a price tag for six thousand dollars for a cake, they're gonna' be out of here, and they're gonna' think, "Oh, it's so expensive." Like, just recently I did a cake for Miss U.S.A. about two weeks

ago, and it was ten feet tall! It was very expensive, and it lit up and everything, everything but "fly"! So yeah, we can do anything.

RICH: That's exciting. It's the artistry that's so exciting. I think I saw a picture of it out in your showroom. What a great way to display your cakes on that slide show! I took several pictures off of that. I think it was something like five layers, with pillars holding up the layers, and with you standing next to it.

MIKE: Yeah, that was me. That was earlier this year, and that wasn't even finished.

RICH: Off the record, can you tell me how much that cake cost for Miss U.S.A.?

MIKE: Uhh-h, very expensive. But, I didn't even know how much to charge. You know, I sat down with her mother, a wonderful person. She wanted this unbelievable cake, and I didn't even know how to price it, because I had never made a cake like that.

MIKE: I mean, my quality speaks for itself. We are not the cheapest, but we're not the most expensive either. I can't charge high prices, because of my location. I can't be the most expensive. So, I blurted out a ridiculous price, and she immediately says, "Done!" Man, I should have said ten thousand dollars!

MIKE: Everything I do is a specialty item. So, every cake is priced differently. It's very challenging in my world, because it depends on how long the decorator has to labor. Everything out there is about labor. Cake costs nothing. Cake is pennies. It's all about the labor, the delivery, and the sales. [And then, Mike laughs.]

RICH: Yeah, when I talk about "the business of baking" in the book, it's an important part of the story. I mean, customers come in and they see that the cakes are beautiful, and they don't mind paying. But, there's a lot behind it.

MIKE: And, like I've said before and continue to say, I'm not a full-line bakery. I chose to go with the high profit item in the bakery, the decorated cake and focus on that.

RICH: Yeah, things have changed haven't they?

MIKE: Dramatically! I have a large place here for a small bakery. There's 8,000 square feet here. My showroom is the largest in the midwest. The overhead is incredible. So, I really have to stay in that 10% range of "Best Cakes, Best Quality, and Best Service" in order to survive.

RICH: Yeah, I'm sure. Wow! Like you say, location is a factor.

MIKE: *You know, I live here, and I love North County. It's a beautiful place to live! I raised all five of my kids here. It's beautiful!*

RICH: I have to tell you about someone who is similar to you in age. Have you ever heard of Nathaniel Reid? He has a three-year-old bakery at Geyer and Manchester.

MIKE: I don't think so.

RICH: He's very young. He's probably in his mid-thirties, a very nice man. He said the same things about St. Louis. He's from Farmington Missouri and went to school at Mizzou. He discovered that he loved baking, went to Le Cordon Bleu in Paris, got trained there, and then worked for award winning pastry chefs in Los Angeles, Las Vegas, and Florida.

RICH: I would encourage you to just walk in there and meet him sometime. He makes pretty high-end stuff. But, I said to him, "It really matters that you're in this location, doesn't it?" And he said, "Yeah, it does." And, I said, "The people here, as I see it, they want quality, I mean high quality, and they're willing to pay for it, right?" It's part of the reality, and he said the same thing.

RICH: *He loves what he's doing, and this is his dream to do this. He could literally work anywhere in the world. But, he said, "This is what I want to do, this is my love." You*

HOW OUR HEARTS WERE STÖLLEN

know, I just feel in the bakery world there is so much variety! Everyone has their own admirable story. So, I hope that's what the book is going to be about.

MIKE: *Right. It will be interesting to read from everyone's different perspective. I WOULD LOVE TO READ IT.*

MIKE: How often have I thought about a satellite location in Ladue for instance, what's the word I'm looking for, for the prestige, the visibility, you know. But then, I go back to, "How good my cake must be for me to be able to survive in this hidden little gem in Florissant." And, I'm proud of that. I don't mean that in a pompous way. But, it's true.

RICH: Right, right. And you know, my dad was in the restaurant business, and later he ended up being a grocer, but early in his days, he'd say, "You know, the biggest failing of a restaurant and any kind of food business is that they expand too fast. They overspend. And, people who take their time and grow slowly, those are the people who last."

MIKE: Hence, the thirty-four years here so far!

RICH: Yeah, yeah. Amen!

MIKE: Yeah, and I mean, this place has given me a great life, I guess having all of my kids happy, and they all went to college. Yeah, I can't ask for anything more. Hard work kinda' paid off here!

RICH: Exactly! Now, was your father a part of the business too? Or, anybody else in the family? You didn't inherit the bakery from somebody? You started it from scratch, right?

MIKE: No, nobody. Actually, my wife and I bought "Wedding Wonderland" for fifteen thousand dollars. We didn't have money back then. I worked at a factory, and she was a teller. And, what hit me was what my father said, God rest his soul because he never saw this place. He told me, "For you to pursue your passion, think of it this way, it's the price of a car. You might lose a car for the chance of a lifetime."

And, that's what made me buy it! I didn't have fifteen thousand dollars. And, he put it into a perspective, "All you're going to lose is a car if it doesn't work out." The next day I bought it!

RICH: *Yeah! Very cool! I would call that a great blessing! He gave you his blessing!*

MIKE: *Yeah, I know. I think I'm gonna' cry!*

RICH: *Yeah, me too! But, it's too good of a thing to cry about, right?*

RICH: I did interview Chris Helfer, I don't know if you know Chris.

MIKE: *Oh God, awesome! There is a _fine_ example of how we work together, especially on inventory. Whatever I have is hers, [meaning Kathy Helfer, Chris's wife], and whatever she has is mine. If I need something, it's a phone call away! She has even dropped things off here that I needed, I've dropped things off there. I mean, we just work together. You know, we're in the same community. We're doing the same exact thing. And, I couldn't be happier with our relationship.*

RICH: You're probably referring to Chris's wife, Kathy, right? I was so impressed with them. They're just such pleasant and gracious people.

MIKE: Yes! And, they work their bottoms off. Holy Cow! They are there 24/7. I mean, we all work hard, but they have worked so hard for what they have!

RICH: Yes, I really enjoyed that interview. They are such nice people!

MIKE: I don't know him as well at all, but Kathy, we're back and forth all the time.

RICH: They're not that far from here, are they?

MIKE: Oh gosh, no. Less than a mile. They're just right there, [as Mike points out the window and down the road].

RICH: Is that right? I guess because I'm from South County, I don't really know where things are in North County. [I laugh at my lack of orientation to North County.] For me this is like going to Minnesota! [More laughter.]

RICH: The Helfers were great. So, I'm telling you about the Northside bakeries that I've been able to contact, because I wanted it to be an area-wide kind of thing, you know. I got to know a lady named Rita Andres, who is an Ellerbrock. I don't know if you have ever heard that name. I interviewed her and her cousin. They were delightful too. And, I interviewed a relative of theirs who was 92. His wife was 92 also. Their names were Richard and Marie Marklin. Well, Ellerbrocks had nine or more bakeries on the Northside. They had one at the Jamestown Mall.

MIKE: Jamestown and Northland Shopping Center are huge. Or rather, we should say, they _were_ huge.

RICH: Finally, I said to them, "Can you send me the locations [of all of your family's bakeries]? I'm making this map." In reality, they sent me nine actual addresses of Ellerbrock bakeries.

MIKE: Huh, I wonder why I have never heard of that?

RICH: Well, they were before your time. At one point a company, named Warner-Noll, bought them out. They were kind of a chain, like Haas. But, there are so many stories within this story! _I have asked most of the bakers I have interviewed, "What do you think was the downfall of the independent bakeries that went from five hundred or more in the 1950's to maybe thirty or so at this time?" Most of the bakers agreed that the biggest reason was that supermarkets all started to have their own bakeries._

MIKE: Also, the Wal-Marts and Sams of the world. You just can't compete. I mean, unless someone wants quality and service that I can provide, I mean they don't carry your cake out to the car, little touches like that. In ordering the cake, you can have an on-line order kind of thing, but you can't compete with the price! These days people are struggling, and why not go somewhere else and spend twenty-five cents on a cupcake versus a dollar here? So, in the future, I believe, it's gonna' be one big Amazon world.

RICH: No, no! We're campaigning against that.

MIKE: It's interesting, that whole big business thing.

RICH: They've sort of driven local businesses out, haven't they!

MIKE: Brick and mortar ones. My wife and I have talked about this. What's stopping me from buying a house right here, buying two or three houses and making my quarter of a million dollars out of these houses with no overhead? What's stopping me? It would be a better investment to do that.

RICH: And, a lot less work, right! [We laugh together.] And, you know it's a tribute to you all! That's what the book is intended to be, you know, that you care enough to survive. It's not just quality either, I mean it is quality, but it's a connection to personal relationships, you know, with customers.

MIKE: Yes, exactly! And, people still appreciate that! I mean, that's why I'm still in business, because some customers really do want that.

MIKE: I have some customers who have been with me since the beginning, and they just beg me not to go!

RICH: Yeah, I would add to that. I would beg you not to go. I really do!

MIKE: Well, I don't plan on going anywhere, so long as I can keep up. I'm praying that my son, Tyler, takes over the business!

RICH: I was able to talk to him a little bit, and it looks like that's in the future in his mind too!

MIKE: Right! One out of five kids — I was hoping that one of them would want it! The other ones and my wife, they stay away. They're thinking, "I don't want anything to do with all of that. It's too much work!" [Mike and I laugh together again.] There were sacrifices. I mean, gosh, when I first took over I didn't have much, if any, family time. As a matter of fact, when Tyler was born during the first two years of his life, I wasn't around. My wife raised him just to try to make this happen.

RICH: Yeah, there was probably a lot of time needed just getting it off the ground.

MIKE: Yeah, because I was working full-time over at the Wetterau plant and more than full time here for a year and a half to make sure this was going to work.

RICH: I normally ask a question here, and it's probably pretty easy for you to answer. The question would be, "What do you think is your signature item?" "Oh, I guess that might be wedding cakes, right!" [Laughter.]

MIKE: Yeah, a very focused item here. I have thirteen different flavors here. My white with the raspberry filling is very popular. Seventy percent of all of my cakes are still the white with the almond flavoring in it. I created that back in the beginning in 1995, and I have not changed the recipe since because I can't even beat it. I have a banana cake that's amazing, I have a strawberry cake, and the white cake is still number one. People drive for miles. Everyone is moving out to Wentzville and St. Charles, and I can't tell you how many customers I have who drive all of the way back to me because of that white cake!

RICH: That's really neat! Well, I would say that you can't go wrong with that raspberry filling!

MIKE: Actually, the raspberry is not part of it, but the white cake, yeah. And, the fact that to this day I still don't have a freezer. [I marveled at the fact that Mike doesn't have a freezer!] Everything is made fresh. And, that's unheard of in the bakery world. Go to a supermarket and go to a lot of bakeries, your cake could be six months old, and, it's made with mold inhibitors and all of those preservatives. Everything is fresh here, guaranteed, even when we end up with seventy-five weddings on a Saturday. Seventy-five weddings! That's our record so far!

RICH: Oh my gosh. Wow!

MIKE: We do over 2,000 weddings a year, but that week in October we had seventy-five weddings on one Saturday, and perfect — not one complaint — and, every one of those cakes was baked that week! Yeah, I'm very proud of that.

RICH: My gosh! Did you have to bring in extra people?

MIKE: No — it was just the family atmosphere. The people that I have are dedicated, and they just worked their tails off!

RICH: Did you say 2,000 a year?

MIKE: Over 2,000 a year is my average for wedding cakes. And, we average forty to eighty birthday cakes a week. For some bakeries that might not seem like a lot, but for a small bakery and the profit margin that I have, it keeps the doors open!

RICH: Sure! Those are amazing numbers, Mike. I was gonna' ask you that very last question on the interview sheet. "Are there any St. Louis bakeries that you know of personally that you could introduce me to, so that I could share their story as part of the 'Bakery Book Project'?"

MIKE: Yeah, Al Watson, who was the person who won the title "America's Next Great Baker," even though he's not a baker anymore. He's got a heck of a story! He came from Knodel's, and he came to me because of my reputation. He learned even more from "Wedding Wonderland." He was blown away by the quality here!

RICH: You know, everything here is positive to me. And, the whole story is a beautiful story. So, can you think of any other North Side bakeries that were historic or anything. I mean, Ellerbrocks were here, and Helfers has been here too.

MIKE: You hit the ones that I really know. I did not grow up in north county. I moved here in 1986. So, I'm not familiar with any past bakeries other than Helfers, and of course, Knodels. [And then addressing one of his decorators in another room Mike says], "Ken, what other North County bakeries are there, are there any?" [And, Ken replies from the other room], "Oh gosh, I'm from the Affton area."

RICH: Ah, the Affton area. That's really interesting because I taught Cheryl Federhofer at Notre Dame High School.

MIKE: Oh, Ken used to work for Federhofers.

RICH: Is that right?

KEN: No, I lived down the street from them. I worked for McArthurs since '94, and I worked for Lubeley's off and on. I mean, Randy McArthur is an awesome guy. He trained me in a lot of stuff. But, I've learned more in the past few years from Michael, [referring to Mike Temm], than I've learned from anybody. I've always known Bob Lubeley, and he's always been a great guy.

RICH: There are some great stories! There was a bakery called Teutenberg's that was in downtown St. Louis. They started there, and then they had several other locations. The bakery went through something like five generations of Fred Teutenbergs. They were around for a long time.

MIKE: Well, this has been a pleasure. I wish I had more time, and if you need more just let me know, maybe down the road.

RICH: I'll come back. I should do this, you know, and maybe it's a sub-conscious reason that I want to come back and see you again for any photos that you could share. I'm not sure how to do that, but I'm sure it's easy. I'll take pictures of your photos or something. And, I'll bring a release for you to sign so that I can use the content. And I'll use it very carefully.

MIKE: Sure! Of course! And, you can take the photos right from the website! I've got a picture on my website with my Easy-Bake Oven too! [And, we laugh together!] The whole story is on there.

RICH: That's neat, that's very neat! Well listen, this has been great, Mike.

MIKE: Well, thank you. Thanks for stopping by. I appreciate it. It's fun talking about my own business, of course!

Whisk: A Sustainable Bakeshop
Interview With Kaylen Wissinger

There's another thing that makes me so excited.
[Kaylen makes a small pause here and says,]
I am just so excited to read about the traditions and the history of
baking in St. Louis, because it's like Nathaniel Reid said,
I love St. Louis!... "I am so excited to read your book!
I am really excited to just learn from these people, the interviewed
bakers and the others mentioned in the book, who have been bakers
or whose families have been bakers for generations. It's special!
— Kaylen Wissinger

RICH: First of all, I'm interested in how your mom and dad are doing.

Author's Note: Kaylen's mother was a colleague to my wife and I at St. Margaret of Scotland School.

KAYLEN: They're good. Yeah, they bought a building and have been working on it. It's about two blocks from their house in the Soulard neighborhood. They've spent the last two years rehabbing it, and they just finished. They're doing good. Thanks for asking.

RICH: Yeah, we worked with your mom at St. Margaret of Scotland school. We really enjoyed knowing your mom and dad. We were at their house one day when we had a little get-together for the St. Margaret faculty. Their house is very pretty.

KAYLEN: Yes, I have a little dream that one day they might give that house to me. I have a secret fantasy that they'll retire and move to a smaller place and leave the house for me. It's a nice thing to think about, I guess.

RICH: [My laughter!] Yeah, you must like that house!

RICH: Well, it would be good if you knew just the basics of this project that I've been working on. It's about ten years in the making now, and I'm happy to say that I'm reaching a milestone with your interview. You will be my 20th interview. So, I'm very excited.

KAYLEN: That's awesome. I'm honored.

RICH: I'm shooting for twenty-five, and I think I'm going to stop there, but it has been so enjoyable. I've really been touched by the stories and everything about the bakers who I've talked to. So, I hope that will all come out in the book. I've also edited a lot of selections from an archive of the St. Louis Bakers Association, which is a beautiful story about the independent bakers who were pretty much thriving during the 1950's and 60's. It has been tremendously enlightening and inspiring for me to know that they were such a great community together. The story is really beautiful in the sense of how good they were to one another. That will be told in the book too. It's been wonderful to learn about them.

RICH: Please talk as much as you want, because this is about you and your story. So, the first thing that comes to mind is "How did you get onto this idea?" When did you want to become a baker?

KAYLEN: Yeah, that's a good question. You know, I didn't really grow up baking a lot. My mom baked for birthdays and special occasions, and she would occasionally make a batch of cookies. She always made everything from scratch. She never used any mixes or anything. But, I wasn't really a "Mom, let me help you out in the kitchen kind of gal." I tended to read a lot of books and watch movies and stuff and was kind of a bookish child. I didn't really get into baking until college. One day I saw a recipe on-line for some kind of cupcake, but it was about a year before cupcakes became the in-vogue thing in the world.

KAYLEN: I was like, "Oh, yeah, I want to make cupcakes." But, I was in college in a dorm room, and I didn't have a kitchen. So, my boyfriend at the time, who is now my husband, his dorm room had a kitchen. So, I made banana butterscotch cupcakes, and they were delicious. That was the first thing that I made as an adult. And, I just kind of fell in love with the process of baking.

KAYLEN: So, I was in college and didn't really have a lot of disposable income, or any disposable income. So, I would just get tons of baking cookbooks out of the library and would pore through them. I would take notes on the how's and the why's of baking and why things happen the way that they happen. The older I got I just did more and more baking and filled the greater space that I had. That was my freshman year of college. My junior year of college I had my own kitchen in my dorm room. So, I got to do a lot of baking then, and from there it just kind of continued.

KAYLEN: I graduated in 2010. I had gone to St. Louis University and had gone to school to get an English and Education degree. I thought I wanted to be a high school English teacher and realized a little too late that wasn't at all what I wanted to do. But I didn't want to start over because I just didn't care I guess.

RICH: Sure, I understand.

KAYLEN: Yeah, I went to Rosati Kain all-girls Catholic High School, and I recognize now that this comes from an immense place of privilege, but it wasn't a question of, "Are you going to college, but 'where' are you going to college?" So, I think it's just a huge amount of pressure to put on an eighteen-year-old to decide like, "Hey, take out 120,000 dollars in loans and figure out what you want to do for the rest of your life." Anyway, that would be a whole different conversation!

RICH: [My sympathetic laughter.] Yes, I'm sure!

KAYLEN: Yeah, I enjoyed a whole lot of people I met in college, but I'm not a teacher, so that didn't work out! But yeah, after graduating I actually got a job in the advancement office at Rosati-Kain High School. I was there for nine months, and I hated it. I mostly just sat in front of a computer and did spreadsheets and wrote parent newsletters. And I didn't get to stretch my creative talents at all. It was really tough. And, the one thing that kept me solid was baking at home. I gained a lot of weight because I was like, "Ooh, scones! Ooh, cookies! Ooh, cupcakes! Let's make 'em all! It's gonna' be great! It's gonna be so good! You know, I wasn't happy about that.

KAYLEN: Enough friends and family tried the stuff I was making, and you know, I feel there was kind of a turning point with being a cottage baker or a hobby baker. And if enough people say to you, "Oh you should sell this stuff." So, it finally hit me like, "Oh, I should sell this stuff." And, if I'm gonna' do it, now would be the time when I'm young and have the energy and don't have a mortgage payment or a car payment or children. Like, if I'm gonna' get into this, I should do it while I'm dumb enough to get into it!"

RICH: Right.

KAYLEN: And so, that was in 2011. I was twenty-three, and I found a kitchen space available that I could rent by the hour downtown, and that was when I opened a business called "Farm Fresh Cupcakes". We sold cupcakes using local and seasonal ingredients. We sold them at craft fairs, music festivals, and farmers markets. You know, I kind of had a dream of being able to have my own space, but I didn't have a bunch of money just sitting around. I had gotten out of college, and I had worked about eight and a half months, at a "big kid job." So, I didn't have all this money set aside to play with. Anyway, it was a good first year.

KAYLEN: In the winter I got a job baking at Local Harvest Café, which doesn't exist anymore, but one of the market organizers at the Tower Grove Farmers Market was one of the owners of Local Harvest. At the end of the Farmers Market season he asked me, "What are you going to do over the winter?" because most of the events that we sold at were outdoors. So, I was like, "I don't know, I've gotta' figure that out. Something to be worried about, I guess." So, he was like, "Well, we need a baker at Local Harvest. Do you want the job?" which was serendipitous and wonderful!

KAYLEN: I had worked at a number of restaurants and food service places but always in the-front-of-the-house," never in "the-back-of-the-house." So, Local Harvest was a great way to get my feet wet and to experiment with recipes and ingredients that weren't "on-my-dime." Also, Local Harvest's morals really coincided with mine in that they utilized a lot of local, seasonal produce and worked with a lot of area farmers and producers. That was the most important thing to them. And you know, they passed that cost on to the customer, but people appreciated and enjoyed that because they knew that they were supporting as many local people as they could.

KAYLEN: So all in all, it was super inspiring and really important for me to be in that environment every day. Like I said, I'd never been in the "back-of-the-house." I was always a server or a busser or a hostess. So, it was kind of interesting to see how that whole background worked. And, I worked there for not even a whole year before we found the storefront on Cherokee Street. So, I signed the lease in April of 2012, and we opened in November of 2012.

RICH: Wow! That's quite a story!

KAYLEN: Yeah, it was very long — I'm sorry.

RICH: Oh, no, that's great. How long did you work at Local Harvest?

KAYLEN: I was at Local Harvest from maybe November of 2011 till July of 2012.

RICH: I can't imagine what I'll do with all of the knowledge and information that I have from these interviews! [My laughter.]

KAYLEN: [Kaylen's laughter!] I think you could become a Master Baker at the end of this! After interviewing over twenty different people I'm sure you're learning all kinds of fun stuff!

RICH: Oh, I'll tell you, it's been amazing! It's been spectacular. I've loved doing it. You know, there are some bakers that I wish could meet one another. There are people I think of, and I think, "Oh my gosh, you would love to meet this person." But, these would be old-timers. And you know, they have a different story, but they have really interesting stories.

RICH: I interviewed one supplier I have to tell you about named Ron Jaudes. He and his dad and grandpa had Jaudes Bakers Supply. He was unbelievable in terms of the knowledge he had because he delivered to all of the bakers. I was just blown away by the breadth of his knowledge

KAYLEN: Yeah, I love that.

RICH: So, that was a lot about your motivations and the start-up of your bakery. How did you come up with money to finally get a place of your own?

KAYLEN: Well at that point, my costs were really low. I was working out of a shared kitchen, so the overhead was minimal, and I didn't have any employees. It was just myself and my husband, who would occasionally help me in the kitchen. But mostly, I was the one working during the week. He was going to school for an education degree and is now actually using it!

KAYLEN: He helped me over the week-ends and over the summer, but other than that it was just me. So, between working at Local Harvest, and being in business with Farm Fresh Cupcakes I had a little bit of money saved, but not enough to open a business. Unfortunately, my grandmother passed away, but she left money to her children. And then, my dad very generously decided to split what he received from his mother between myself and my younger sister. That was I think fifteen thousand dollars. Of course, it was bitter-sweet because Nonni was gone, but it meant that I could now do my dream. So, that was kind of cool.

KAYLEN: So, we had money from that. I also launched a kick-starter campaign in 2012 that was very successful. We went over our goal with a little over fifteen thousand dollars as well. At that time the building that Whisk is in now was not in good shape. It was a big mess.

KAYLEN: One of the reasons I wanted to work in this building was because the apartment above it was available, and I loved the idea of living above a bakery that I owned. Previously, before Whisk there was a restaurant there called Shangri-la Diner. Pete and I loved it. We actually had our wedding rehearsal dinner there when we got married. So, it's always felt really special to me, but I had never seen the kitchen! Let's just say that seeing the kitchen was not a good thing! So, I learned a lot about that.

KAYLEN: I signed the lease in April, and we didn't open until November. It was seven months of dirty, grueling, exhausting work. We had to replace the whole plumbing system. So, we scrapped and recycled and donated and sold, and tried to clean and re-use what we could.

RICH: I'm curious, did you have to rehab the apartment above the bakery too?

KAYLEN: [Kaylen laughs!] We should have, but every penny that we had available we used for Whisk. We lived above Whisk for about three and a half years with unfinished sheet rock for walls and various mismatched wooden flooring. But, I was hardly ever there. For the first three years I never hired an employee. So, if we were open, I was working, and we were open five days a week. So, neither of us were home very much. It would have been good if we had taken the time to make it nicer, but we just didn't have the energy, the time, or the resources.

RICH: Sure. So, you moved away from there, right?

KAYLEN: We did. So, in the lease that we signed I put in an option to buy the building in the lease. And, I was like, "Hmm-mm, it would be really cool to buy this building because I live and work here." After being there for over a year I realized how much work, love, attention, and money the building needed, and I was like, "I'm twenty-three years old, and I don't have the money, time, or know-how. I wouldn't know what I was doing."

KAYLEN: But, my dad at the time was going through a bit of a mid-life crisis, and he was like, "I'll buy the building, I'll rehab it, I'll make it better."

RICH: [As a dad myself, I knowingly laughed, on the inside!]

KAYLEN: So, he and my mom did that, which selfishly was really great for me. Nothing was ever urgent to him. So, if there were any problems I would call my dad and say, "Dad, please help!" And, he did. But, they bought the building and basically evicted Pete and I from the upstairs apartment because they knew it was in bad shape and needed to be rehabbed. We ended up buying a house instead, and we live over in Tower Grove South right now.

RICH: Oh, good! That's where our son lived originally. So, we know that area.

KAYLEN: Yeah, a good spot.

RICH: Our son is an artist and publisher, and he's rehabbed a beautiful single family house on Illinois, about two blocks east of your store. He's devoted to Cherokee Street. So, it's good to have a place of your own, isn't it.

KAYLEN: Yes, initially I was very anxious about moving away and the separation was kind of a hard transition, but eventually it did wonders for my mental health, to have both actual and mental space between my work and my home.

RICH: Sure. Well, that brings up a question. I'm curious. Do you have to do the baker's early morning shift, rising early, the way a lot of bakers do?

KAYLEN: You know, we wake up early, but we don't have to do any breads. Actually, in February of 2020 we shut down to remodel Whisk because we needed more kitchen space. We actually got rid of all of the seating and moved our counter up 30 feet. So, now it's just a walk-in place, and that was the plan long before the virus hit.

KAYLEN: Yeah, at the beginning of the year my first chopper would get there between 4:30 and 5:00 in the morning to get the ovens on and to get stuff going.

KAYLEN: Also, before the virus hit we had about fifteen wholesale accounts that we worked with, and we had multiple deliveries each week for each place. So, we'd get the first round of baking done and dancing out the door early. And then, the second group would bake just for the shop's retail sales. So, we don't do croissants or breads or anything like that. We make cookie doughs or scone doughs or muffin doughs. We freeze them and then just bake however many we need each day.

KAYLEN: That definitely makes things a little more efficient and gets things done a little faster, which is helpful.

RICH: Yes! You said you had around fifteen wholesale accounts. Did that suffer, I imagine, with the virus?

KAYLEN: Yeah. Every account halted their orders because for a long time everyone was completely shut down. I agreed with that. If we hadn't been shut down already to remodel we certainly would have shut down. So, a good thing was that we didn't have to have bakery people around construction dust during that time.

KAYLEN: It was nice to not have to worry about structuring our contractors. And we did most of the work ourselves because, look at my parents, that's just how I was raised. So, that's just what I do. Yes, every one of our accounts shut down, some are still shut down, and a couple have closed for good. Some are back open and are ordering again but much less than they had been doing. Wholesale probably makes up about 40% of our sales for the year. Only two are ordering from us right now. It's been a big hit on us for sure.

RICH: Wow! Yes. Sadly, it is a very common story.

KAYLEN: I totally get it. If I had to think about how I could cut costs to save money and if I ordered ready-made products to have at Whisk to make sure that my staff could stay on, I might have done that. But when I could, that would be the first thing that I would get rid of. So, I harbor no hard feelings, I totally understand why people were doing it. Financially, we're actually doing great right now. It's kind of incredible. So, it's not something that really bothers me too much.

KAYLEN: It is kind of sad if I think about it too much, but I am happy to not have to deal with that. And, I don't have to wake up super early anymore, which is great! I get to wake up at 6:00 and take my dog for a walk, instead of rolling out of bed half asleep, and then drive to get there at 4:30 in the morning. So, I'm good.

KAYLEN: Also, apologies in advance for the many words you'll have to sift through to get information, because I tend to talk a lot!

RICH: No, not at all. It's great!

KAYLEN: Yeah, I've always loved eating sweets. I love the sugar! And, I'm also a do-it-yourself kind of gal. It's like, "Well, if I need to make a dessert for my friend whose birthday it is, I would much rather learn how to make that myself than go buy it from somewhere else. Come on, even if it costs more to buy all the supplies and the ingredients and everything to make it, I would still do it. I like learning how to do stuff. And, I'm just kind of a curious person by nature, so I think that definitely plays into it.

RICH: That's interesting. You probably know a lot of the independent bakeries were two, three, or more generations of family members who continued the business. Those are interesting stories!

KAYLEN: Yeah, absolutely!

RICH: I actually interviewed Helen Lubeley, and she was so kind. She said that they just couldn't do it anymore. They just ran out of gas, you know.

KAYLEN: You know, anytime that I hear of places like that closing, it's sad. But having been in those shoes a fraction of the time that some of these places have been operating, it's like, "Oh, I get it. It's exhausting. It's hard, and there's no break."

KAYLEN: I was telling a friend of mine last week that our sales are double of what they were at this time last year, and I feel very lucky about that! It's wonderful, but you know, I could work twenty hours a day and not have done everything I need to do for that day, and that's hard. That's a difficult mental thing to live with. I just feel like, even though I'm working my hardest every day, it's not good enough. It's not enough to get everything done.

KAYLEN: I certainly don't fault people for needing to step away from places because you only live once. And if you're not totally in love with what you're doing, it's not worth it.

RICH: Yeah, I was wondering if you have other employees besides yourself now?

KAYLEN: I do! I have five employees now!

RICH: Good! How has their work experience been? Do they come to you and learn on the job?

KAYLEN: Yeah, I was just thinking about that the other day. We'll have been open for eight years in November, and in those eight years I think I've had fifteen to twenty employees. I've only had to fire three of them. So, a pretty good track record.

KAYLEN: The team I have with me right now, all of them have been working at Whisk for at least a year. So, it's really important for me to foster an environment where everyone feels happy and comfortable and taken care of, where their ideas are being heard because you know, I had a job where that wasn't happening, and I was miserable.

KAYLEN: I feel like as a boss it's my responsibility to make sure that not only are things getting done that need to get done, but that people feel happy, good, and fulfilled in what they're doing. And, I probably put too much emphasis on that.

KAYLEN: So, two of the employees I have right now, they are both classically trained. They've been to culinary school. They've worked and "staged" at lots of pretty impressive places. When both of them sent me their resumes, I was like, "Why do they want to work here?!" [My laughter here.] They were people who have even worked at Tartine in San Francisco. I have not been there, but I follow them on-line, and I have their cookbook. It just looks phenomenal and beautiful. It was like, "You worked at Tartine?" The other three employees are all people who have enjoyed baking and had been baking at home. All three of them grew up baking with their families more than I did. Yeah, lots of on-the-job training!

RICH: Yeah, I'm going to throw-in a question here. Have you ever been to Nathaniel Reid's bakery?

KAYLEN: Yes! I love Nathaniel. He is so nice. Everything he makes is so good! It's similar because it's just like, "Dude, why are you here?! You were classically trained in Paris, and you're in Kirkwood!" He is so nice too! I have kind of a chip on my shoulder about working for people in food service that *weren't* nice, and not just male but also female chefs, who are just rude and somewhat abusive in the kitchen, and aren't patient. And, I hate that. I know a lot of people like that in the culinary scene in St. Louis even today.

KAYLEN: And, I kind of assumed just because of his pedigree that he could fall into that category. I know people who have worked for him, and having met him myself, he just seems like such a sweet and caring person and so connected to his business. I love and appreciate and respect that about business owners because I feel like it's kind of easy to just pass stuff off to people and put it on "Auto." But, that's not what I want to do. So, I like other people to <u>not</u> do that too.

RICH: I'm proud of you for that! But, I want to tell you what he said to me! I did ask him an obvious question. I asked him, "Why are you here?!" And, he said, "I love St. Louis, and I love what I've decided to do." He then said, "I searched myself, and I said to myself, "You know what I want to do? I want to do exactly this. I'm as happy as can be, because I'm doing exactly what I want." It was really inspiring.

KAYLEN: Yeah, that is something like what *I* would say, "Whew!" Even on the really hard days, like the eighteen-hour workdays where our refrigerator breaks down and multiple things go wrong. You know what though, I'm not super happy today in general, but *I am so incredibly lucky that I created a job for myself and that it's working and that people like this place. How insanely great is this, that this is what I get to do every day! It is certainly not something that I take for granted.*

RICH: Yep! I understand and agree completely! I'm very glad for you! So yeah, I interviewed Anna from Diana's Bakery (on Cherokee Street) and Fred Domke from Bridge Bread (also on Cherokee Street).

KAYLEN: Oh, wonderful! They're great!

RICH: Fred Domke told me that there were seven bakeries on Cherokee Street. I was talking to a good friend this morning, and he said, "Well, I wonder why there are so many bakeries on Cherokee Street?" And, I said, "Well, it's a renewed area! I mean, it's a renaissance there, and I think people really think about eating when they go to Cherokee Street!"

KAYLEN: Absolutely! And, it's so fun to kind of hop around and just hit up all of the spots! It was like that before we even opened here. I really enjoyed just hopping around to all of the different places, especially all of the Mexican bakeries because it was not something I was really exposed to as a kid.

RICH: O.K. — Kaylen, I've got a favorite question for you now. What do you think are your signature items? What are you most proud of — though I'm sure you're proud of all of it.

KAYLEN: [Kaylen laughs a little.] So, in terms of bakery items we are probably best known for our cookies, but we make homemade pop tarts as well. You know, we call them Pop Tartlettes, because Pop Tarts is trademarked. Yeah, we have a lot of fun with both of those things. I don't like making things that you can get anywhere. So, I want the majority of the stuff that we have to be special, fun, and unique, just kinda' wacky and out there. So, we have a lot of fun just making a crazy assortment.

KAYLEN: The thing I love about every member of my staff right now is that all of us bake at home too. They come in and bake at work, but then they still take time to do it at home on their free time. I feel that is just awesome because it means that they love it! And, I love that they love it! "Yikes!" [Kaylen seemed a little emotional at this point.]

KAYLEN: So, we came out of quarantine with three new cookies that I love! It might be because I'm still in the honeymoon phase with them, and I'm not sick of them yet, but also I just think that they're really good! The most special and unique one is our butterscotch-curry cookie. I don't know anyone else who is doing anything like that.

KAYLEN: One of my staffers came up with it. He lives a block away from me, so we had a lot of porch meetings during the quarantine. So, he was like, "What do you think? Here it is. O.K. let's try this again. Let's do it in this way and add this ingredient." So, that one is great! It's just a fun and different flavor!

RICH: That sounds really good!

KAYLEN: We also came out with a salty caramel, oatmeal pecan cookie. It's a really good combination of a good chewy texture, and little bits of caramel flavored explosions in your mouth. I mean, I love toasted pecans, and they kind of round it out really well. So, I think people who are our regular customers joke about coming in to Whisk and having to say a long name for a cookie. [I laugh at Kaylen's description of her interactions with her customers!]

RICH: Yeah, that's great! I love that! And, was there a third new flavor cookie?

KAYLEN: Yes, the third one is our "Cinnamon Toast Crunch, Marshmallow Cookie." And, that is totally nostalgic for me, because Cinnamon Toast Crunch was my favorite cereal growing up. So, it's like a snickerdoodle but totally pumped up because there's extensive caramelized cereal in there. And, marshmallows make everything better in my opinion!

RICH: That's great! Alright, any other signature items? If you came into your store, what would you buy?

KAYLEN: Umm-mm, cookies for sure, and the house-made pop-tarts are great. We tend to do a lot of seasonal fillings with those. So, they're made with a nice, heavier-duty, and thicker pie crust. We fill them with compotes or house-made jams or jellies. We do like lemon-curd sometimes. So, I recommend those things.

KAYLEN: We've made homemade Twinkies, homemade Ho-Ho's, Ding Dongs, Donut Sticks and Oatmeal Cream Pies. It's nostalgic and fun, but the flavors are elevated because they're not made by machines.

RICH: That's neat. It sounds like you really like your own baking! [My laughter.]

KAYLEN: I do! Maybe too much! Yeah, we're so small that there's just a lot of heart in everything still.

RICH: You know, if you're surviving and more, I'd say you're doing great. Yeah, I had a favorite saying that I used to say to my students, "Don't underestimate survival! Just surviving means a lot!"

KAYLEN: That's kind of how I feel too. Just like, "Alright, let's get through this year, and we'll see about 2021."

RICH: Isn't that the case! Yes, I agree. You know, I would love to hear you describe your feelings about being "sustainable" and what that means to you?

KAYLEN: Yeah, I would love to. *It was really important for me to include "Sustainable" in the name of the bakery.* Between working at Local Harvest for nine months and prior to that at farmers' markets I just got to know a lot of farmers and even did farm visits. I got to see the places where they raised their hens, where they grew their produce, where they processed their meats, and where they made their cream.

KAYLEN: So, between that and being in college having the time and the space to think a little more critically about where our food comes from, it just all kind of met at this point. It made me realize, "O.K., it's really important to utilize the local food sources that are here and to support those people because it's way better to buy heavy cream from a local dairy farmer. I'm now sending that local dairy farmer's kids to school or paying for dance lessons or helping them make their rent. It's important to me to be supportive to like-minded people in our community who are also following their dreams.

KAYLEN: So, the sustainability aspect is that we just try to utilize as many local ingredients and products as we can, everything from where we get our business cards printed locally to local seasonal produce. For example, we have a lot of blueberry stuff in the case these days, because it's definitely blueberry season. And, all of our "to-go" packaging materials are compostable. We also compost all of our food waste in-house. We work with St. Louis Composting, so they just come and pick it up. Actually, most restaurants utilize their services. So, that's diverting hundreds of thousands of tons of waste which is amazing.

KAYLEN: So, those are some of the important things to keep our dollars as local as possible and work with our neighbors and friends who are doing the right things in my opinion. So, you can order compost or mulch or soil from St. Louis Composting, and they'll deliver it to your house, which is just so cool! I love it!

KAYLEN: Yeah, it's awesome. It's just like a great loop. Back in March and April, before we could reopen for orders, I started a huge veggie garden in my backyard. So, now more than ever I've grown my own stuff and bought my own compost and mulch. And, I'm just learning about all of that.

RICH: Well, kudos to your dad and your mom for their "sweat-equity" in your business, right! [My admiring laughter!]

KAYLEN: Oh, yes! One hundred percent. Even just yesterday my dad helped Pete and myself move a new freezer into the shop. I guess you know as a dad that helping your kids never really ends! Yes, they've been wonderfully supportive and helpful.

KAYLEN: There's another thing that makes me so excited. [Kaylen makes a small pause here and says,] *"I am so excited to read your book, the "Bakery Book" because I don't really have a lot of history with baking."* [I express grateful laughter here!] I wish baking <u>was</u> in my bones, and I wish that I had that kind of a romantic story like, watching my grandmother bake or like doing my homework next to my mom when she would make a cake or whatever. I just don't.

RICH: Sure, sure!

KAYLEN: *But, I am just so excited to read about the traditions and the history of baking in St. Louis, because it's like Nathaniel Reid said, I love St. Louis!* I could have left for college, and I didn't. I could have moved away after college. *But, I am so happy to be here and to be part of the food scene here. And, I love history. So, I'm really excited to just learn from these people, the interviewed bakers and the others mentioned in the "Bakery Book," who have been bakers or whose families have been bakers for generations. It's special.*

!RICH: *[My thankful laughter.]* Well, if you pray, pray that I get this to press sometime. [And, we both laugh heartily!]

KAYLEN: Well, I'm excited, and I can't imagine the amount of work and research that you've put into it. So, kudos to you for making it happen.

RICH: Yeah, thank you. I really appreciate that. It's been a total joy, and as one of my friends always reminds me, "The joy is in the doing!" So, I really hope that you remember us to your mom and dad. Sue is my wife, and she and Linda worked together. We knew your mom really well, and we love her. Please remember us to both of your parents. We really enjoyed them. Kaylen, I wish you nothing but the best, and you have been a great interview. And, I'm proud of you for doing all of this because it welled-up in you!

KAYLEN: Well thank you. It definitely did! I love that. That's very astute!

RICH: I will definitely come back sometime, and I just pray that I can get this to press. Pulling it all together is really a daunting process. So, I am right now praying and asking other people to pray for me to go in the right direction for finding the publisher and printer that will help me put it all together.

KAYLEN: Yeah, absolutely. Well, that's what they're there for. That's their job. It's just a matter of finding the right fit, for sure.

RICH: Well, thank you so much. I appreciate it!

KAYLEN: Thank you! You guys, stay safe and be well, and thank you so much for thinking of me, for giving me a little spot during the day to reflect, something I don't do often enough. I appreciate it.

RICH: Well, you have a lot to be proud of!

KAYLEN: Thank you.

RICH: I will talk to you again, I'm sure.

KAYLEN: That sounds great. I will tell my parents, "Hi."

RICH: Please. That would be great.

Wolf Bakery
Interview With Connie Wolf

*Everyone who knew my father,
Simon Wolf, knew he was an amazing, wonderful man. Everybody liked daddy.
He had a wonderful sense of humor, he was intelligent,
and he was a hands-on kind of person.*
— Connie Wolf

CONNIE: You know, Mr. Lubeley had a son that they had a little later in life, like my parents had me a little later in life.

RICH: O.K., so you're talking about Bob, the son of the original owner. Yes, I know Bob a little bit. I used to shop there once a week for about ten years.

CONNIE: Wonderful, wonderful. Well, I went to talk to him one time about my father and his father knowing each other and being good friends.

RICH: That's great. Now, your father was Simon Wolf, right?

CONNIE: I have a whole family tree if you want it, and we have a website called "The Wolf Family." It has information, and it has pictures because I know you want pictures. I've also thought that I would like to write a memoir, partly because I'm sure there are some nieces and nephews that didn't even know we had a bakery. In fact, I talked to one of my great nieces, and she didn't know. So, I want to pass it down to them. You know, it's going to help me a lot to talk to you, because it will bring out things that I want to remember.

RICH: Yes, isn't that true! Yes, when we talk to people about things it sort of jogs our memories and cross-germinates things, doesn't it!

CONNIE: Oh yes, I'm so excited to talk about the Wolf family bakeries. And, I'm willing to do other things that you might need, like go places together and talk to other people from other bakeries. I'd be able to take you to the Carondelet Bakery and talk to the Smith family. I know they wanted to retire.

Grandpa Ulrich
1871–1944

RICH: Well, you know, I taught all of their daughters at Notre Dame High School. And, I don't know if you knew that Bob Smith, "Bob the Baker," passed away a year or so ago.

CONNIE: No, I did not know. But grandpa was part of Carondelet Bakery and helped them to get started in 1875. I'm not sure about all of this, but I'm pretty sure it originally was Ulrich's Bakery. Those are my maternal grandparents.

RICH: You know, Carondelet Bakery was the oldest continuing functioning bakery in St. Louis.

CONNIE: Yes, and they still used my grandparents' recipes. A couple of years ago a group of us went down to the bakery after we first went to a restaurant across the street. Anyway, we talked to Linda for awhile, and she was so nice. They were the nicest couple.

RICH: You might want to write this down. On You Tube, and I hope it's still there, there was a video with Mr. Smith in it called, "Bob, the Baker." Did you know Roy Schmiemeir? He's another wonderful person.

CONNIE: *Well, of course, _all_ bakery people are wonderful people. [Connie says this with a twinkle in her eye!]*

RICH: Yes, they are. I'm so glad that you have this strong English and editing background, because I'm sure you will notice that there are threads and themes that are very consistent among all of the bakers. One of those consistent themes is that they are so proud of their bakeries. As a result, they are always willing and enthused in talking about their bakeries!

CONNIE: It was so amazing growing up in a bakery. I thought I was the luckiest kid in the world!

RICH: You know, we have become very involved in St. Margaret of Scotland parish, due to our working in the school there.

CONNIE: Is that right?! Well, that's really interesting because so many of my brothers and sisters went to school there. You know, there was a bakery right across the street from the church. [There now is a specialty bakery in that location named Sweet Art.]

CONNIE: And then, Ehnes Bakery was further north, but they went out of business because highway 44 came through there and cut the neighborhood in half.

Author's Note: In a later interview with Mr. Ehnes, he said that highway 44 construction was <u>not</u> a factor in their closing.

CONNIE: You know, our bakery was on Thurman between Botanical and Shenandoah. Also, Clever's Bakery was two blocks from us. So, there were so many bakeries at that time. Our bakery was on 39th and Shenandoah.

RICH: You know, one of my best friends was Vic Clever.

CONNIE: Was he related to the bakery family of the Clevers.

RICH: I don't know. I kinda' doubt it, but I can check. Now, don't let me slow you down. You've been on a roll of giving me so much information already.

CONNIE: When there were twelve children still at home, my father started looking for a bakery. And, he found out that the man who owned the Thurman Bakery was looking to sell it, but the brother of this man wanted it. However, the owner of the bakery felt my father should have it.

CONNIE: *Everyone who knew my father knew he was an amazing, wonderful man. Everybody liked daddy. He had a wonderful sense of humor. He was intelligent.* He had gone to McBride high school, but as a sophomore he said, "Well, this is stupid," because *he was a hands-on kind of person.* But, he *was* smart because he knew how to do the business end of it. And, I think that's much harder than being a baker. He didn't finish at McBride because he was a "worker." My parents worked seven days a week, taking care of the family and taking care of the bakery. Of course, we lived there, and they were never gone, until I was in about 5th grade. And then, they started to travel. We would close the bakery every summer for 2 weeks.

RICH: So, which location came first?

CONNIE: Well, first they were at Kingshighway and Milentz. And then, the man who owned that building wanted the building back. That's when daddy and mama moved to Thurman.

RICH: Do you have the address on Thurman?

CONNIE: Yes, it was 2309 Thurman. The zip code was 63110. And, I even remember the phone number!

RICH: You remember so much, and there is so much to remember! Connie, do you know that you get a special tone in your voice when you talk about your dad?

CONNIE: Oh, yes. You know when he passed away, I was nineteen years old and a freshman at Webster College. When he passed away the funeral was so big at Kriegshauser's they had to move it to the chapel. And, the funeral parade, you could not see beyond it. He was a beloved person. You know, he went to Mass even on Saturdays, and that's before you could go to Mass on Saturday for Sunday. He'd go twice on the week-end. One time I was talking to my brother Jim about what I remembered, and I told him, "Jim, tell me about what you remember." So, he did, and it was exactly the same as what I remembered.

RICH: And, do you have the years of the bakery when they were on Thurman?

CONNIE: Yes, my father was the head of the bakery until 1962, and he passed away in 1962. He worked until the day he passed away. He passed when he was 67, and he was an old man. He had gotten old. He didn't seem to have much purpose, and he didn't take very good care of himself. He used to make fun of health nuts, of which I am one. He would say, "Maybe the health nuts are living longer, but they aren't having as much fun!" Then, Sam ran the bakery from '62 until '67. At that time my mother moved to "the flat." That's this place where I live now, the four-family flat.

RICH: Do you remember an approximate time when the bakery closed on Thurman?

CONNIE: Yes, that would be either in '68 or '69. I can ask Jim. Then, Sam moved and opened a new bakery in Grasso Plaza. Sam did exceptionally well.

RICH: What was the bakery at Grasso Plaza called?

CONNIE: It was called "Wolf's Bakery!" [And, we both laugh!] We actually have a picture of my daddy holding the Christmas stöllen that we took to the nuns for 100 years! My grandpa, daddy, and Sam made some huge Christmas stöllens. My father was always giving to the nuns.

RICH: That's very cool. It's so consistent with how generous so many of the bakers were! You know who I'd like you to meet is Rosemary Pfeiffer. She's wonderful. She was the wife of the man who owned Pfeiffer's Bakery on Clayton Road.

CONNIE: I'd love to meet her. If you can give her my number that would be great. I love to talk about personal history. I love to talk to people like her. I'm sure she would remember us.

RICH: Why don't I give you her contact information right now! I think the two of you would be fast friends! Rosemary is the wife of the original baker. I think his nickname was "Dutch" or Richard. She is 83 years old.

CONNIE: You know, Sam went to work for a bakery on Clayton Road, and I think it was Lake Forest. He always said they only used the best ingredients. Well, that's one of the things that my father and Sam disagreed about. My father wanted to keep using the best ingredients, like real pecans, and Sam wanted to use a mix of pecans with soy. Sam was always interested in money. My mother and father were the kind who always trusted that "the money would come." And, they were right.

CONNIE: That's another thing that my mother talked about. When they moved from Kingshighway, and they did really well there, my mother was so disappointed because she loved living close to Our Lady of Sorrows Church. I remember they would walk to church holding hands. The bakery was one block south of Our Lady of Sorrows, and our flat was one block north of Our Lady of Sorrows. The difference between the two locations was that on Kingshighway before they moved, it was a cake trade. And, after we moved to Thurman it was a donut trade.

CONNIE: My father was 67 and my mother was about 63, and you know, they never talked about saving money for retirement. When I wanted to go to Webster College, they immediately agreed to help me. They didn't check their finances or anything. They just said, "Do it." They were thrilled that I wanted to go to college. They were even going to let me go away if I wanted.

CONNIE: And again, they made more money on Thurman. I was the youngest of the sixteen kids. So, they didn't have to worry about the other children. They did send some of the other ones to college. The idea back then was to be a secretary, get married, and have kids. I couldn't be a secretary. I couldn't type or take shorthand, and S. Isabel always said sort of a funny thing. She'd say, "If you can't type or take shorthand, you're gonna' end up working in a dime store." But, my mother and father said "Yes" immediately to my going to college.

CONNIE: My mother had three children after the age of forty, and I was the youngest of all of the children. But, my mother was worried about my being O.K. as an infant without birth defects. So, she was extra thrilled when I decided to go to college. Well, back to this feminist thing. You know, my grandmother was the brains behind the Ulrich bakery. So, the women in this bakery family were very essential to the success of the businesses.

CONNIE: I want to show you this one family picture. You can see that everyone is dressed to the "T's. So, my point is that my father worked very hard, but my mother worked very hard too.

RICH: I'll say! I can't imagine how she did it with all of those children.

CONNIE: Well, she did have some help with a laundry woman and a cleaning lady. And you know, they never asked me to do much work, except maybe putting the cherries on the cookies and things like that. But, they never asked me to do housework. So, I was spoiled in a way. My mother was very particular about not over-burdening the children. She was also very conscious about not handing down clothes. For me, she would take me downtown and buy me new things.

CONNIE: They had plenty of money. So, she felt like they could spend some. And, here's the picture of all sixteen of us, the same picture that was in "Our Lady of Sorrows" church picture. You know, I was a librarian, but I often feel like I'm not very organized. Like, I want to give you some copies of pictures, but I'm not sure where I put them.

RICH: I understand. This morning I was looking at our house, and I'm thinking where can we go with all of this stuff? But, my wife and I are so busy and involved with so many things we accumulate a lot of things.

CONNIE: You know, that's a good thing because it's very helpful and important to keep active and keep your mind active.

RICH: Yes, I agree, and it's very satisfying to have all of these experiences with all of these bakery people! I can't tell you how comforting and encouraging it is to meet people like you, Mrs. Pfeifer, Mr. Schmiemeir, Chris Helfer, and the Smiths. I feel like meeting people through this bakery book project has brought me into contact with a whole world of goodness!

RICH: Well Connie, I'm interested in knowing what you think about the idea of having a coffee table book instead of an academic book. I really value your opinion.

CONNIE: I love your idea of having all of the in-depth information on-line. Also, make sure you have lots of good pictures! I hope I can find all of those pictures that I want to share with you. I have a picture of my grandfather and grandmother and my dad. People say that I looked more like my dad.

RICH: Your dad definitely had a very charming face.

CONNIE: Yes well, he smiled a lot. So, I think that a book that is interesting is one that has really nice pictures and doesn't have really small print, and one that has plenty of references. And then, have it on-line, and your son will be able to figure that out.

RICH: You know, I have another really interesting book for you. I found it by way of Derrick Goold. He's possibly the best sportswriter in the country who works for the St. Louis Post-Dispatch. He's from St. Margaret of Scotland too.

RICH: Anyway, I asked him, "Derrick, where can I go to find out who are the local interest publishers for St. Louis books?" And, he said, "Why don't you just go to the Missouri History Museum gift shop and browse their local interest books."

RICH: So, I did, and I found this one book that Roy Schmiemeir recommended to me called the Route 66 Cookbook. It is beautifully layed-out and so interesting with great information about all of the restaurants and bakeries from the St. Louis Route 66 locations. There is also a beautiful new book that was put together by a man named Cameron Collins. He put together a large book called Lost Treasures of St. Louis. Oh my gosh, I just realized that's what I want for Christmas! [We laugh!]

CONNIE: That's interesting. I have a niece that works at the History Museum.

RICH: Wow, with the size of your family you probably have a niece that works everywhere! [And again, we laugh together!]

CONNIE: Yes, you wouldn't believe it. I have nephews and nieces who span a tremendous number of years. I'm seventy-five, and I have a nephew who is seventy-two, and all of the way down to in-utero!

CONNIE: So, we have five generations going on! It's interesting, but my nieces and nephews are now the older generation. And, I call myself "the leading generation." I think that four generations have actually lived in this flat that my dad built for our family.

RICH: Well you know, I volunteer two full days a week at St. Margaret of Scotland School, and they are pretty demanding academically. Their student population is almost 500, and they just built a new building for a middle school. It's beautiful, and you should come and see it, especially since the Wolf Bakery was in that area for awhile. Well, it has an incredible spiritual and academic leader in the principal. Her name is Julie Hesed.

CONNIE: You know, I just met her. She came to one of our luncheons a few weeks ago. I was in the class of 1957. From our class there were about twelve of us, and I still see these people. So, Ms. Hesed is a nice lady

RICH: Well you know, we always celebrate the feast of St. Margaret of Scotland, and the parish is devoted to her as our patron saint. The kids learn all about St. Margaret, and Ms. Hesed is responsible for that. Also, Ms. Hesed's husband is Peter Hesed, and he is the music director there. He is a wonderful person and an amazing musician.

Author's Note: This was one of the first in-person interviews that I had, and from the very beginning Connie Wolf was very enthusiastic about the Bakery Book project!

Wolf Bakeries
Interview With Ron and Noel Ladd

Ron and Noel felt the reasons for the demise of the independent bakeries were boxed cake mixes, pre-packaged sliced bread, and brown 'n serve pre-packaged rolls. Most of all, they felt that the grocery superstores were a major reason because they began to have their own bakeries inside of their stores.
— Ron and Noel Ladd

Helen Wolf was Ron Ladd's mother. Simon Wolf Sr. owned the first Wolf bakery located at 3120 South 7th Street. Later that bakery moved to South Kingshighway close to Our Lady of Sorrows Catholic church. The Wolf family lived above the bakery at the store when it was at Kingshighway and Milentz.

Noel Ladd would walk home from school with her friend, Mary Lou Wolf Ottenlips, and they would stop for bakery goods on the way at the 39th Street location. Mary Lou Wolf was Noel's friend, and the Ladds thought she would be a great source of additional information.

Charlie Ladd was Ron Ladd's brother, and he worked as an apprentice for a baker named Bishop at Bishop's Bakery. Ron felt that he would also be a great source of information. Ron said that he would take his father around to deliver bakery goods to the convents at St. Margaret of Scotland School and at St. Elizabeth's High School.

When I asked if Wolf's bakery had any signature items, Ron said that they had two special breads, and those were Butter-Topped Bread and Cream Bread.

When I asked what they thought were reasons for the demise of the independent bakeries, *they both said boxed cake mixes, pre-packaged sliced bread, and brown 'n serve pre-packaged rolls. Most of all, they felt that the grocery superstores were a major reason because they began to have their own bakeries inside of their stores.*

They also felt that the entrance of the Haas and Entenmann bakery goods into the grocery stores were an additional drain on the business of the independent bakeries. So, all of these things cut down on the number of "stops" customers would have to make for their food shopping!

Charlie Ladd had a store for awhile at Bates and Virginia Avenues, but he could hardly make it there. So, he moved that bakery to Concord Plaza on South Lindbergh. Ron Ladd's grandfather on his mother's side was Simon Wolf, Jr. Simon Wolf, Jr.'s daughter was Mary Lou Wolf Ottenlips.

Sam and June Wolf opened a bakery in Grasso Plaza. One of the Schmidt bakery owners then bought the Wolf bakery in Grasso Plaza. For the Schmidt family the Grand Avenue bakery came first. Finally, Rozanek Bakery bought the Grand Avenue bakery from the Schmidts.

Conclusion to the In-Person Interviews

I hope you have enjoyed these interviews as much as I enjoyed doing them. It is my hope that this nostalgic cartoon will communicate the simplicity and life-giving qualities that this mythical bakery is about to give to these shoppers. In a way, this bakery might be seen as a life-giving church up on a hill on a Christmas morning.

"CHRISTMAS AT THE BAKE SHOP"

From the Bakers Bulletins

From January of 1982

APPENDIX

"The Icing On the Cake"

- BAKERY MAP LOCATIONS FOR THE IN-PERSON INTERVIEWED BAKERIES

- DETAILED LIST OF ADDRESSES AND SOME HISTORIC LOCATIONS

- SIGNATURE BAKERY ITEMS FROM THE INTERVIEWED BAKERS

- WHO REALLY CREATED THE ST. LOUIS GOOEY BUTTER CAKE? A "POSSIBLE" ANSWER AND EXPLANATION

- BAKERY STATISTICS FOR THE UNITED STATES FROM 1849-1946, NUMBERS OF BAKERIES, TOTAL BAKERY WAGE-EARNERS IN THE COUNTRY, AVERAGE NUMBER OF WAGE-EARNERS PER BAKERY, TOTAL VALUE OF PRODUCTS IN THE COUNTRY, ALL BY INDIVIDUAL YEAR FROM THE BAKERS BULLETIN OF JANUARY, 1959

ST. LOUIS MAP LOCATIONS
FOR

BAKERIES FROM
THE IN-PERSON INTER-
VIEWS

1. BRIDGE BREAD BAKERY
2. CARONDELET BAKERY
3. DIANA'S MEXICAN BAKERY
4. EHNES BAKERY
5. ELLERBROCK BAKERIES
6. FEDERHOFER'S BAKERY
7. HANK'S CHEESE CAKES
8. HAUSEL'S BAKERY
9. HAUSER BAKERY
10. HELFER'S PASTRIES AND DELI
11. JAUDES BAKER'S SUPPLY
12. KNODEL'S BAKERY
13. KRUTA'S BAKERY (COLLINSVILLE)

14. LAUGHING BEAR BAKERY
15. LUBELEY'S BAKERY
16. MARKLIN'S BAKERY
17. MC ARTHUR'S BAKERY
18. NATHANIEL REID BAKERY
19. PFEIFEER'S PARTY PASTRIES
20. SCHMIEMEIER'S BAKERY
21. THE BLUE OWL BAKERY
22. THE SWEET DIVINE
23. WEDDING WONDERLAND
24. WHISK BAKESHOP
25. WOLF'S BAKERY

Historic Bakery Locations

Bridge Bread Bakery 2639 Cherokee St. St. Louis, MO 63118 Still Open in 2022	Ehnes Pastry Shop 1807 South 39th Street Closed
Carondelet Bakery Oldest Continuously Operating Bakery in St Louis Previously Ulrich's Bakery 7726 Virgina Avenue Closed	Federhofer's Bakery 9005 Gravois Road St. Louis, MO 63123 Still Open in 2022
Diana's Mexican Bakery 2843 Cherokee Street Still Open in 2022	Hank's Cheesecakes 1063 S. Big Bend Blvd Still Open in 2022
Hausel Bakery Hampton at Itsaka Closed	Hauser Bakery At Alabama and Holly Hills 1936 -1978 Closed

Ellerbrock Bakery Locations All in the City of St. Louis Main Location First started in 1889 1444 North 13th Street Closed	Heimburger's Bakery At the Northeast Corner of Baptist Church Rd and South Lindbergh Closed
Ellerbrock Bakery 1610 Olive Street Relocated to Larger Space	Helfer's Pastries and Deli Café 380 Sr. Ferdinand Street Florissant, MO Still Open in 2022
Ellerbrock Bakery 2585 West Hebert Street Closed	Jaudes Bakers Supply 422 S Sixth Street 1st Location
Ellerbrock Bakery 5407 Riverview Blvd Closed	Jaudes Bakers Supply 1440 South Broadway 2nd Location Closed
Ellerbrock Bakery 6105 Theodosia Ave. Closed	

Ellerbrock Bakery 2906 Union Blvd Closed	Knodel's Bakery 1st Location 6715 West Florissant Closed
Ellerbrock Bakery 412 Washington Ave. Closed	2nd Location 6621 West Florissant 1901 – 2018 Closed
Ellerbrock Bakery 715 North 6th Street Closed	Kruta's Bakery 800 St. Louis Road (100th Anniversary in 2019) Collinsville, Illinois Still Open in 2022
Ellerbrock Bakery 4001 Utah Street Closed	Laughing Bear Bakery 1st Location Centenary United Methodist Church 1610 Olive Street St Louis, MO 63103
Ellerbrock Bakery 7024 West Florissant Ave Closed	2nd Location Still Open in 2022

Ellerbrock Bakery Northland Shopping Center Closed	Lubeley's Earliest Location Near Christy and Kingshighway Then later in Maplewood
Ellerbrock Bakery Gustine and Gravois Closed	Lubeley's Later Location at 8149 Big Bend Blvd Webster, MO This Location Became Shatkin's Then Cravings Cravings Still Open In 2022
Warner-Noll Bakeries Bought Out Ellerbrock Bakeries in 1966	Lubeley's Several Different Locations At Yorkshire Shopping Center 8021 Watson Road Later and Permanent Location 7815 Watson Road Closed
Warner-Noll Bake Shop 4415 South Kingshighway Closed	
Warner-Noll Bake Shop 2810 Sutton Ave.	
Warner-Noll Bake Shop Hampton Village Market Closed	

Wedding Wonderland 449 Dunn Road Florissant MO 63031 Still Open in 2022	McArthur's Bakery 1st Location Tower Grove Ave. & Arco Closed
Whisk: A Sustainable Bakeshop 2201 Cherokee Street St. Louis, MO 63118 Still Open in 2022	McArthur's Bakery 2nd and Permanent Location 3055 Lemay Ferry Road Still Open in 2022
Wolf's Bakery 1st Location South Kingshighway at Milentz Ave	Nathaniel Reid Bakery 11243 Manchester Road Kirkwood, MO 63122 Still Open in 2022
2nd Location 2309 Thurman Ave. Both Locations Closed	Pfeifer's Frozen Pastries Began in the late 1930's 2612 North Kingshighway 1st Location Closed
	8021 Clayon Road 2nd Location Closed

Schmidt Brother's Bakery
125 Years at Corner
of Walsh and South Grand
Closed

Schmiemeir's, Bakery
Then Clayton's
And then Bello's Bakery
11744 Manchester Road
St. Louis, MO 63131
Bello's Bakery Still Open in 2022

The Blue Owl
Restaurant and Bakery
6116 2nd Street
Kimmswick, MO 63053
Still Open in 2022

The Sweet Divine
1801 S. 9th Street
St. Louis, MO 63104
Still Open in 2022

Signature Items For Each Bakery From The In-Person Interviews

BRIDGE BREAD BAKERY — CINNAMON ROLLS and SOURDOUGH BREAD

CARONDELET BAKERY — COFFEE CAKES and ORIGINAL RECIPE GOOEY BUTTER CAKES

DIANA'S MEXICAN BAKERY — TRES LECHE CAKE and CHURROS

EHNES BAKERY — DECORATED CAKES and DANISH PASTRIES

ELLERBROCK BAKERIES — CARAMEL STÖLLENS WITH NUTS, WEDDING CAKES, & FRENCH DONUTS

FEDERHOFER'S BAKERY — GRANDMA'S CUSTARD PIE and DOERRING'S BAKERY SPRINGALIES

HANK'S CHEESE CAKES — TIRAMISU CHEESECAKE and KEY-LIME CHEESECAKE

HAUSEL'S BAKERY — SMALL DESSERT PASTRIES for CATERERS

HAUSER BAKERY — RYE BREAD, BREAD-ENDS, and FRUIT PIZZA

HELFER'S PASTRIES AND DELI CAFÉ — STRAWBERRY and REAL WHIPPED CREAM CAKES and PASTRIES

JAUDES BAKER'S SUPPLY — "OUR JOB was TO SELL OURSELVES!" and OUR BAKERY SUPPLIES.

KNODEL'S BAKERY — DECORATED CAKES and A SPECIALTY DREAMSICLE CAKE

KRUTA'S BAKERY	"FUDGIES" and GLAZED DONUTS
LAUGHING BEAR BAKERY	DREAMSICLE CHEESECAKE and "BEAR CANDY"
LUBELEY'S BAKERY	"DOBOS TORTE" and DANISH PASTRIES
MARKLIN'S BAKERY	"LAMB" CAKES and ASSORTED GERMAN PASTRIES
MCARTHUR'S BAKERY	WEDDING CAKES and FINE DANISH PASTRIES
NATHANIEL REID BAKERY	CHOCOLATE HAZELNUT POUND CAKE and CHOCOLATE PECAN COOKIES
PFEIFER'S BAKERY	IRISH SODA BREAD and BLACK FOREST CAKE (ADAPTED FROM THE SCHWARTWALDER TORTE)
SCHMIEMEIR'S BAKERY	GERMAN CHOCOLATE CAKES and CARROT CAKES
THE BLUE OWL BAKERY	LEVEE-HIGH APPLE PIES and FINE DANISH
THE SWEET DIVINE	BANANA "WHOOPIE PIES" and MACAROONS
WEDDING WONDERLAND	"WEDDING CAKES," BIRTHDAY, and FAMILY EVENT CAKES
WHISK BAKERY	POP-TARTLETTES and INVENTIVE FLAVORED COOKIES
WOLF'S BAKERY	WEDDING CAKES and CHRISTMAS STÖLLENS

Who Really Created the St. Louis Gooey Butter Cake?

The story of St. Louis bakeries and bakery goods would not be complete without an exploration of the question: WHO REALLY CREATED THE ST. LOUIS GOOEY BUTTER CAKE?! If one wants to pursue this question there seems to be no shortage of conjecture about this mystery. I was able to find multiple sources on the internet, but the following website seemed to be the most convincing.

Gooey Butter Cake Recipes And History, What's Cooking America

https://whatscookingamerica.net/History/Cakes/GooeyButterCake.html

According to this website, "The Gooey Butter Cake originated in the 1930s, and according to legend, a German baker added the wrong proportions of ingredients in the coffee cake batter he was making. It turned into a gooey, pudding-like filling.

Check out the two different family stories on the creation of the Gooey Butter Cake.

The first story is from Richard Danzer (from November 22, 2006).

"In late 1942 or early 1943, Johnny Hoffman of the St. Louis Pastries Bakery... made what eventually turned out to be the Gooey Butter Cake. You're right, it was a mistake! He subsequently called my dad, Herman Danzer, and told him he thought he may have something and asked him to come to my dad's shop on Spring and Gravois to see if they could duplicate it. When my mom came into the shop from the store and when she tried it, she said, "This sure is gooey," subsequently the name.

Author's Note: This description goes on for several more lines and another paragraph, but this was the essential story.

The second story and information is from Marilyn Koppe Galati, Westchester OH

(from October 30, 2008). "Our following family history will add to the confusion of who invented or first made the Gooey Butter Cake in the early 1940s. My father...owned and operated Koppe Bakery...at California and Arsenal Streets in South St. Louis. The Gooey Butter Cake was a smash hit with customers...it was very gooey, rich, and exceptionally delicious...You could eat it with a spoon! The top was sprinkled with powdered sugar, and the edge was slightly crisp to hold it together — almost like a pudding. It was baked in a square shape and of course, was light colored, like butter.

...dad sold his business and went to work for the St. Louis Pastry Shop on Meramec and Virginia Streets for Marge Langer. It was there that he gave them the recipe, and it too sold like hotcakes. I also worked there as a clerk in the storefront.

As far as I know, my father 'created' the gooey butter cake. There is no proof that I know of about the creator of the recipe...My father was friends with a lot of the other Master Bakers in the city, so I imagine they shared recipes and tips...It's all just childhood memories. I was just a child then, but I remember how the store would be packed with customers, and the popularity of the GOOEY BUTTER CAKE."

From the Bakers Bulletin of January, 1959

Number of Bakeries For the Past 100 Years
and Other Verified Statistics for the United States

YEAR	NUMBER OF BAKERIES	WAGE EARNERS	AVERAGE WAGE EARNERS PER BAKERY	VALUE OF PRODUCTS
1849	2,027	6,727	3	$13,290,000
1859	1,930	6,514	3	16,980,000
1869	3,550	14,126	4	29,530,000
1879	6,396	22,488	4	65,820,000
1889	10,484	38,841	4	128,420,000
1899	14,836	60,192	4	175,369,000
1904	18,226	81,278	4	269,583,000
1909	23,926	100,216	4	296,865,000
1914	25,963	124,052	5	491,893,000
1919	25,095	141,592	6	1,151,896,000
1921	20,173	148,500	7	1,089,972,000
1923	18,739	162,163	9	1,122,906,000
1925	17,684	160,411	9	1,268,195,000
1927	18,129	171,995	9	1,394,700,000
1929	20,785	200,841	10	1,526,111,000
1931	17,718	183,161	10	1,190,048,000
1933	14,830	182,161	12	919,778,000
1935	19,068	218,423	11	1,235,073,000
1937	17,193	239,388	14	1,426,162,859
1939	18,399	230,706	12	1,411,816,633
1946	23,000	241,400	10	2,500,000,000

Data for 1849 from Kyrk & Davis, the American Baking Industry, Appendix Table VI, p. 82. Data for subsequent years from U.S. Census of Manufacturers. Data for 1946 is estimated.